CUSTOM MAID
For New World Disorder

Political Dust Storms, Corrosive Money and Slick Oil

A contemporary post 9/11 geopolitical "Manifisto" for constructive change. How Americans can re-orient and clean up their act to survive, thrive and continue to guide in the 21st century

Peter G. de Krassel

CAL Books
Hong Kong

Copyright©2004 by Peter G. de Krassel
All rights reserved
Published in Hong Kong by CAL Books
Library of Congress Cataloguing-in-Publication Data is available
ISBN 988-97666-1-2

THIS BOOK IS DEDICATED TO OUR CHILDREN WHO ARE OUR FUTURE. "RESPICE FINEM-E PLURIBUS UNUM" – AN EYE TO THE END-FROM THE MANY, ONE

The New World Disorder

The Future Will Be Better Tomorrow - Governor George W. Bush, Jr.

"The Paradox of our time in history is that we have taller buildings, but shorter tempers; wider freeways, but narrower viewpoints; we spend more, but have less; we buy more, but enjoy it less.

"We have bigger houses and smaller families; more conveniences, but less time; we have more degrees, but less sense; more knowledge, but less judgment; more experts, but more problems; more medicine, but less wellness.

"We drink too much, smoke too much, spend too recklessly, laugh too little, drive too fast, get angry too quickly, stay up too late, get up too tired, read too seldom, watch TV too much, and pray too seldom.

"We have multiplied our possessions, but reduced our values. We talk too much, love too seldom, and hate too often. We've learned how to make a living, but not a life; We've added years to life, not life to years.

"We've been all the way to the moon and back, but have trouble crossing the street to meet the new neighbor. We've conquered outer space, but not inner space; we've done larger things, but not better things.

"We've cleaned the air, but polluted the soul; we've split the atom, but not our prejudices; we write more, but learn less; we plan more, but accomplish less.

"We've learned to rush, but not to wait; we have higher incomes, but lower morals; we have more food, but less appetite; we build more computers to hold more information to produce more copies than ever, but less communication; we've become long on quantity, but short on quality.

"These are the times of fast foods, and slow digestion; tall men, and short character; steep profits, and shallow relationships. These are the times of world peace, but domestic warfare; more leisure, but less fun; more kinds of food, but less nutrition.

"These are days of two incomes, but more divorce; of fancier houses, but broken homes. These are days of quick trips, disposable diapers, throw away morality, one-night stands, overweight bodies, and pills that do everything from cheer to quiet, to kill.

"It is a time when there is much in the show window and nothing in the stockroom; a time when technology can bring this book to you, and a time when you can choose either to make a difference, or to just hit Esc or Delete..."

The Internet – Author unknown

Don't Stop Thinking About Tomorrow

-Fleetwood Mac-

A Better Tomorrow

-Leslie Cheung-

Contents

Sources and Acknowledgments
Like a Rolling Stone - Bob Dylan

I have had an exciting and interesting life. I have not cruised in dull waters. I'm a modern day hobo who's been a witness on the periphery of history in the making. A universal nomad. A global pilgrim. A space gypsy. A lost cowboy. I feel like the perennial fly, make that flying raconteur, on the wall. I want to thank all the bar flies and the numerous intoxicated fellow "glassmates", philosophers of life with whom I have been cruisin' and boozin' and had effervescent conversations the last several decades on several continents. You fueled me through a personal multi-civilizational journey of conscience. We argued, fought and exchanged ideas that are now crystallized into this trilogy.

I am eternally grateful to my mother Riva, whose words of wisdom and advice still ring true and periodically echo in my mind.

Dr Pauline Taylor deserves special mention. We met in 1999 when she literally picked me up from my favorite bar stool and encouraged and enabled me to finish writing. Without her emotional support this trilogy would not have been completed.

I want to also thank my ex's Gail and Julia, my children Alexandra, Jonas, Austen and Michael, very good friends, friends, clients, and business associates. I want to extend special thanks to Jake and Kristin Berman, their children Alex and Lielle, Michael and Michal Yudin, Bob and Lu Alter, Robert "Bob" Schwartz, the Barnard clan, Ralph Herman, Joshua and Barbara Simons, Jorunn "JoJo" Recalt, Bruce Baron, Dr Feng Chi Shun, Isa del Rosario, Mio Hani, Joe and Carol Hempfling, Mary Catherine Harold, Ami and Perla Karney, Chuck and Lydia Levy, Terry and Ruth Elkes, Rica

Thio, Kevin McBride, Earl Klein, Catherine Newman, Jun Valenton, Tony Manton, Jamie McGuire, Zev and Barbara Yaroslavsky, Mark & Ana Sharp, Peter Makant, Phil Curlewis, Rudy and Tzmadar Cohen, Joshua Michaely, Nelson Wong, T. C. Wu, and Grover McKean who patiently and understandingly listened and challenged my ideas and thoughts over the years. They helped me develop my ideas. I want to especially thank Mark Tigan and Arthur Hacker who assisted me with the research.

To the researchers who worked with Mark, I also want to extend a special thank you: Carolyn Bray, Kelly A. Buckley, Eric Ethier, Susan Lynch, Monica Maurer, Eric Sherman, and W. Bruce Wright. You did a great job. Thanks! Their extensive chapter notes and bibliography are available for free at custommaid.net

I want to acknowledge fifteen writers and their painstakingly researched books that helped me verbalize my personal experiences, thoughts, impressions and beliefs of the people and places from different cultures and civilizations I experienced. They also helped me focus and crystallize my thoughts as to how our New World technologically advanced tribes and civilizations can grow and interact constructively, peacefully and hopefully without any more internecine terrorist clashes in the new millennium.

James Carroll's *Constantine's Sword The Church and The Jews: A History*, Samuel Huntington's *The Clash of Civilizations and the Remaking of World Order,* E.J. Dionne, Jr's *Why Americans Hate Politics,* Ziauddin Sardar and Merryl Wyn Davies' *Why Do People Hate America?* Harry S. Ashmore's *Civil Rights and Wrongs,* David S. Landes' *The Wealth and Poverty Of Nations,* Daniel Yergin's *The Prize,* Michael Lind's *The Next American Nation: The New Nationalism and the Fourth American Revolution,* William McNeill's *The Rise of the West: A History of the Human Condition,* Gary Zukav's *The Seat of The Soul and the cluetrain manifesto* by Rick Levine, Christopher Locke, Doc Searles and David Weinberger. They are books I highly recommend to those who want to better understand our human heritage and its future.

Three additional books, and their authors, that deserve special mention for their political philosophy and statistical facts and figures on America's growing political and economic decay are *Democracy and Disagreement* by Amy Gutmann and Dennis Thompson, Donald Bartlett and James Steele's *America: What Went Wrong?* and Mark Zepezauer and Arthur Naiman's *Take The Rich Off Welfare.* Great airplane reading, especially when flying across America. Bartlett and Steele's other books, which address political reality and statistical facts on America, are also insightful. George Will's *Restoration,* Richard Nixon's *Beyond Peace,* John Naisbitt's *Megatrends Asia,* Linda Grant's *Sexing The Millennium,* and David Halberstam's *Century* not only helped me formalize some of my thoughts, but are also great reading anywhere, anytime.

The career politicians who voted the Patriot Act into law deserve special mention. Their unpatriotic act of depriving Americans of our basic civil liberties infuriated me so much that I was invigorated to finish what I started in 1968.

Gene H. Winick who graciously introduced me to Jim O'Shea and Hillel Black deserves a special acknowledgment. Jim and Hillel gave me priceless editorial guidance after they read the manuscript. Jim suggested I restructure the text to give the Hong Kong Foreign Correspondents' Club a more prominent role throughout the trilogy. Hillel got me to focus on what America can learn from Hong Kong rather than China and the rest of Asia. Their editorial wisdom and guidance enabled me to fine-tune the trilogy to a managable and, hopefully, enjoyable read.

Hank Scott, Peter Miller, Steve Chicorel and Jay Johnson gave me a crash course on publishing. Russ Barnard and Jamie MacGuire reviewed my first draft and made constructive suggestions that got me on the right track. Stuart Wolfendale's editorial wit helped me slog on and eliminate unnecessary pages. Luke Hunt's insights on Afghanistan, Kashmir, Iraq and the American Empire rounded out some of the rough geopolitical edges. Mark Caparosa designed the captivating covers and layout, and Jonathan Sharp, the technical editor-proof reader, is both sharp and to the point.

There is one individual who deserves special recognition for her editorial advice, patience, and guidance – Diane Stormont, who helped me focus and fine-tune my verbose thoughts and guided me into giving the critical editorial enema that cleaned out excessive verbiage and retained what you are about to read.

The things that weigh heavily upon my mind are these: failure to improve in the virtues, failure in discussion of what is learnt, inability to walk according to knowledge received as to what is right and just, inability also to reform what has been amiss.

The philosopher K'ung Fu-Tze (Confucius) 600 B.C.

We will never have true civilization until we have learned to recognize the rights of others.

Cowboy philosopher Will Rogers; November 18, 1923

**American Axis
Hypocrisy, Knowledge Less
& Apathy
A Post 9/11 Trilogy**

*Where Were You When
The World Stopped Turning?* - Alan Jackson

New World Disorder

      I was burned by legal proceedings and geopolitical conflicts that reflected the American sunset of the 20th century. The sunburn left a permanent scar. When the U.S. spy plane landed on Hainan Island on April 1, 2001, after clashing with a Chinese jet, I was in the midst of an acrimonious divorce with my mainland Chinese wife who was holding our son and business hostage in Shanghai. The tension and rhetoric between my wife in Shanghai and me in Hong Kong escalated against a backdrop of Sino-U.S. saber-rattling framed by the detention of the 24 American servicemen and women and their high tech spy plane.

On September 11, 2001, a Hong Kong judge enjoined my wife from proceeding with her second divorce and custody proceeding in Shanghai. Later that day, terrorist kamikaze bombers tried to torpedo the freedoms of America and the Free World to the cheers and toasts of many mainland Chinese. They were happy even though Chinese nationals also died in the attack.

My wife's appeal against the September 11 ruling, like the Taleban's, Al Qaeda' and Saddam Hussein's appeals to the Islamic world to rise up, was only a limited success.

The acrid personal and geopolitical parallels contain many lessons. I hope this trilogy can derail the tortured relationship and contribute to the demise of the cultural and political misunderstandings the two major Pacific powers have of each other as we embark on the 21st century. I'm talking of both people and governments. Good relations between America and China are indispensable for all humanity if terrorism is to be defeated. America and China both have a common enemy against whom they should join forces to fight together in the new millennium.

When I went to Ground Zero to see firsthand the jagged remains of the humbled smoldering Twin Towers, I felt I was witness to a temporarily crippled self-impaled America. The spiritual idea of the Founding Fathers is in agonizing pain. People grieved not just for the dead, injured and their families but for America.

Like the public-address system in the World Trade Center that announced it was safe for people to return to their offices, the public pronouncements of career politicians are nothing but hypocritical misleading lies that we have been conditioned to believe and accept.

Government intelligence agencies failed to "protect" America and its citizens. Government commissions, committees and knowledge-able experts repeatedly warned the U.S. government of the imminent terrorist threats, corporate implosions, and the dangers they pose to America and its citizens. How much more do taxpayers have to pay for these commissions and committees whose recommen-dations are swept aside?

The government deliberately chose to ignore the warnings while America's career politicians coddled and sun-bathed with their corrupt corporate campaign donors and the petro-dictators and monarchs who financed terror. The career politicians decided to create an artificial, easily identifiable enemy. Not a mysterious enemy hiding in the shadows among us. China fitted the bill perfectly.

China is the career politicians' ideal enemy of the 21st century. A communist dictatorship that is easily identifiable. An illusory enemy with drastic fatal consequences to America. Corporate America's domination of government and suicidal terrorists and the dictators and monarchies that oppress and suppress their families while financing their terror are the real threat to the New World Disorder.

Osama bin-Laden, al-Qaeda, Saddam Hussein and Iraq were around doing their mischievous thing before September 11. They were brought into sharp focus by the events of the day and took central geopolitical stage in the post-September 11 divisive vocal and violent new world disorder in Babylon. The cameramen focusing the political lenses are our religious career politicians, their moneyed interests and collective spin-doctors.

The world as we knew it ended on September 11. The bombing of the World Trade Center not only changed the landscape of New York City, but the corporate and geopolitical landscape of America and the New World Disorder it leads. September 11 is a fulcrum from which we will examine our political, corporate and cultural heritage and challenge the future. Emotionally, physically, politically, economically, locally, regionally and globally. The age of innocence and ignorance is over. The attack on the World Trade Center was not just an attack on America. It was not the "American Trade Center" that got destroyed. The target represented everything that is the insensitive, ignorant modern Western World that America leads.

Goal

I have been planning on writing a book since I graduated from college in 1968. During my travels the last thirty-five plus years I clipped interesting articles, copied e-mails and data off the Internet and made voluminous notes and outlines on various topics, political, cultural, social, moral, sexual, religious. Periodically, I'd update my notes and trash dated ideas. What started out as a book became a trilogy.

Over the years I had several false starts. My goal was to write a book that is a relevant civics and history discourse. A condensed fusion of history and contemporary events that converged yet again as the new century dawned. A bloody history because of our continued collective voluntary disengagement from an abandoned political process, leading to the dire consequences confronting America today. It would be a contemporary snapshot, a slice of apathetic and parochial life in America today. Both timely and timeless. Honest, substantive observations. A social commentary on the perversion of the political process and system in America by career politicians. An easy one-stop read in our wired world. An accessible reference guide that has the potential to shatter illusory beliefs and practices. Shakespeare reminds us that the past is prologue. Sir Isaac Newton and Albert Einstein paraphrased the Bard. The difficulty is that we have to know what to look for to better understand each other's nuances and textures. Knowledge brings tolerance and understanding.

We have to look way out and way back, so that we are better equipped to look way in, at our country and ourselves. The present is the product of the past. The future will be the product of the present that we create.

During my search, I came across the cowboy philosopher Will Rogers. I decided to fuse a few of his observations, which became the premise and foundation of this book. "Humanity is not yet ready for either real truth, or real harmony," he said at the beginning of the last century. Will Rogers also believed that Confucius "perspired out more knowledge than the U.S. Senate has vocalized out in the last fifty years." My goal is to get *We the Apathetic People* to accept these truths in the 21st century. I also believe that the cowboy philosopher's observation that "The last man that knew China was Confucius, and he died feeling that he was becoming a little confused about 'em'" is a timeless comment that also applies to Rogers' fellow Americans today. My hope is this trilogy can contribute to the education needed to dispose of the negative image ingrained in Americans' psyche of the Chinese and Asians.

The Trilogy

Religion, politics and sex are three subjects we are constantly admonished not to discuss because of the emotions and passion they each evoke. Why? Is it possible our religious leaders, career politicians and their enforcers have subconsciously conditioned us not to look closer at their malfeasance? I believe religion, politics and sex are at the root and core of today's dysfunctional world disorder and this trilogy examines the reasons in depth. Human beings are the most self-abused and dysfunctional animals on earth. We are fundamentally flawed and a determined source of our own destruction. We are the victims of a conscious and deliberate multi-generational psychological political conditioning campaign to become absolutely submissive and politely accept and subject ourselves to the whims of religious and political leaders. If we don't address our shortcomings and continue to blindly follow career politicians down the self-destructive speedway they've put us on, future species will study us the way we do dinosaurs. Our tendency of ignoring bad experiences has been seized upon by the houses of worship and political halls of power.

It is my hope that this trilogy will correct the misconceptions Americans have of themselves and Sino-Latino civilizations and enable Americans to acknowledge their double standards and shortcomings. By doing so, they will become patriotic citizens of the global village, capable of understanding their fellow villagers as they try to bridge their disagreements and misunderstandings. From that understanding the trilogy explores the benefits of a synergy between free-wheeling Anglo-American capitalist and Chinese-Latino authority-conscious societies. A synergy that has been tested and proven to work in Hong Kong. That cross-pollination will enable us to create a roadmap for society to follow, arriving at a New World Order: *a civilizational blending of religious, political, cultural, moral, ethical and economic harmony.*

I hope this trilogy will be thought-provoking. Its primary purpose is to stimulate personal multi-generational dialogue and debate between grandparents, parents and children be they dropouts, nerds, social rejects, loners, gifted, generation-Xers, professionals with degrees or just plain ordinary folks. Hopefully, the discussions that start at home will provoke each family and community to decide how it should live and interact with others and bring an end to the current deaf dialogue of the apathetic.

The trilogy proposes a homeopathic cure, drawing on existing human ready-*maid* remedies for the New World Order. The prescriptions are *made* to last in the hope they can contribute in some small way to our survival and growth in the new millennium. In fact they've been with us the last millennium but were legally swept under the competing religious and political rugs by career politicians with their selfish agendas, an abuse we have unwittingly facilitated at the expense of *We the Apathetic People,* a collective which Americans should constantly apply to what is being done around them in their name.

In examining the current human condition, Volume I of the trilogy focuses on political and religious hypocrisies and why they are the main causes of today's modern ills. Volume II is a concise history of modern imperial conflicts and their geopolitical legacy and impact on U.S. domestic and foreign policies that have to be studied and corrected in the Sino-American 21st century. The third volume expands upon the models proposed for a viable future in the first two volumes. It is a roadmap on how Americans can get politically active to get rid of the current personal, political and geopolitical pain being experienced. Volume III spells out the resulting personal, national and geopolitical rewards to be reaped by current and future generations once we become engaged and active in cleaning up the political mess we are mired in.

To achieve this, the opening three chapters of Volume I identify the hypocritical and defective religiously-driven domestic and international policy agendas and policies of America and their expensive long-lasting cost to taxpayers. Volume I then goes on to explore the cultural and historical backgrounds that led to the current condition, and compares Anglo-American societies with their Sino-Latino counterparts in the areas of religion, politics, sexual practices, economics, philosophy, family and life. Basic human, individual and institutional flaws are identified and explored. Fundamental failures are examined and challenged in the literary version of fast-paced music videos. Volume II points out why institutions have taken over the rights and lives of *We the Apathetic People* because we have been duped into allowing them to clean up while they hijack us at our own expense.

Ideas, themes and possible solutions evolve and are further developed in subsequent chapters of each volume. An evolutionary discussion.

Volume III incorporates conclusions from Volumes I and II and proposes alternative working models. It points out why we should re-capture these institutions and fuse a synthesis of the best each culture has to offer. Why career politicians and their special interests have no role to play in a functional New World Order. It is time to replace political retreads. America needs new political engines, wheels and drivers if the country is going to have a smooth productive political ride in the 21st century. Especially if Americans want to continue winning the global political race.

Debate and deliberation are encouraged. If they fail, political activism on all levels is proposed as a viable alternative. Reconvened constitutional congresses, conventions, local, regional and national forums and referendums are also under-utilized tools. All violent means, confrontations, riots, terrorism and wars are not acceptable solutions in the New World Order.

People, not their churches or career political leaders or bureaucrats, should decide issues of the day in the New World Order. People have to recapture their God-given rights and liberties from the gods of politics and the gods of religious denominations. Church and State have to be separated as the Founding Fathers, the Last Prophets, intended.

Volume III concludes by proposing the vehicles to be used and pathways to be followed by America and the forward-thinking world to create a workable blend of Eastern and Western thought that will re-emphasize the basic human goals, beliefs, convictions, and desires that allow humankind to move forward in a cohesive functional manner to a New World Order worthy of its name.

Custom Maid
The "American Century" and its "New World Order" ended with the passing of the 1990s. The American Dream, however, is for many just that. They keep waking up. For others it has become a nightmare that has to be confronted at the dawn of the new millennium. Those who think America is a sweet dream should stop reading now. Otherwise they will also start waking up in a nightmarish cold sweat, or worse – not. Chaos is no longer just a theory. "Everything under heaven is chaos and the situation is excellent" is a timely ancient Chinese proverb. The identity of the 43rd president was left dangling in a constitutional, legal and political twilight zone in Florida in 2000. A political never-never land. A prelude to the dangling steel girders of the World Trade Center and Pentagon. Both were the result of duopolistic bipartisan anarchy that includes the nation's Supreme Court and nepotistic American political dy

nasties duking it out in Florida and Washington's legal and political swamps. Security disparity between career politicians and working people is as wide as the income disparity. The widest it's been since the crash of 1929, and it continues to grow. The ranks of the insecure and poor are growing. Fear and unemployment are on the rise. The poor feel more threatened and get poorer while the rich get safer and richer. The total net worth of the top one percent of Americans is now equal to the total net worth of the bottom ninety percent of the population. The sweeping language of the Patriot Act that became law in the wake of 9/11 swept away many hard fought-for civil liberties. A good reason to wake up and protect what is left. The New World Order America advocates and leads is a disorderly mess – thanks to career politicians. We have to clean it up. The United States of Apathy desperately needs a maid. One that is custom made.

Globalization to many is the equivalent to Americanization. Whatever happens in America today has geopolitical ramifications. The diversity of the American mosaic society, thanks to the endless waves of immigrants that flood America, is making the country a congested two-way super highway with a wide off ramp for those kicked out – and a narrow on ramp for those let in.

Americans
America is a borderless and seamless ideal created by the Founding Fathers. Many throughout the world dream and aspire to become "Americans". The term American in the book therefore refers to all Americans. Citizens, residents, dreamers and wannabees. The true believers, Atheists, Buddhists, Christians, Hindus, Jews and Muslims that worship the Ideal that is America.

Made-in-the-U.S.A. babies are a booming global tourist sector. Babies born in America and its territories are entitled to U.S. citizenship which exempts them from compulsory military service in their parents' countries and entitles them to all the rights and freedoms so many in America take for granted.

Throughout history, immigrants have brought new ideas, ambition and mere labor to America – and to all countries that let them in. Always have. Always will. They are all Americans in the good old American cowboy tradition. In the words of the playwright

Mark Harelik who wrote The Immigrant, "We as a nation are experiencing massive alternative waves of fear and loathing of the stranger and pride in diversity."

The outpouring of sorrow, sympathy, flowers and tears at American embassies and consulates around the world after September 11th magnified the number of global Americans. People who believe in individual liberty, religious freedom, free trade and democracy. The empathy, pain and global suffering were universal. Americans all over the world mourned with America. Most are not citizens. They merely believe in the Spirit of America and the ideals for which it stands – and stand up for. America is their "beacon of hope". They are fellow family members of all cultures and religions. In Hong Kong, a large floral American flag representing freethinking Hong Kongers was left outside the consulate on behalf of kindred spirits.

Cherry Garcia White Patched Butterfly

Immigration, the Information Age and netizens have magnified America's institutional shortcomings and multi-ethnic makeup. They cross-pollinated with the cultural misperceptions that have become ingrained in America's everlasting New World Order. Conceptualized by the Pilgrims, memorialized by the Founding Fathers, America since has failed to come to terms with its continuously changing cultural, economic and religious fabric. Mythology replaced reality. Spirituality has failed to keep up with technology. Debt has consumed equity. America has undergone a tremendous transformation since the Pilgrims landed. America has changed from vanilla WASP to Cherry Garcia white patched butterfly, with butterfly ballots. Or is it a multicultural scoop of Ooey Gooey cake? Apple pie America is a racial blender of caramelized apple. Rich, heavy and lite.

At the dawn of the third millennium, America with only four percent of the world's population produced more than twenty-seven percent of global output. Its stock market capitalization accounted for more than fifty-three percent of global stock market capitalization. A country where trillions of dollars of equity were wiped out the last year of the millennium. One where $4.6 trillion were lost in one week of the opening year of the 21st century. The equivalent of wiping out the U.S. auto, steel, electrical machinery and oil industries within a week. More than the federal debt! It then got worse in 2002. The second year of the new millennium kept the momentum going when $2.4 trillion were erased in the first six months. More than Germany's gross national product. The U.S. consumes over half of all goods and services of the world; its citizens and residents spend over $10 billion annually on pet food alone – $4 billion more than the estimated total need to provide basic health and nutrition for everyone in the world; their expenditure on cosmetics – $8 billion – is $2 billion more than the annual total needed to provide basic education worldwide; a place where the three richest people have assets that exceed the combined gross domestic product of the 48 least developed countries. To make matters worse, the U.S. government announced a budget deficit of over $156 billion after it gave a tax rebate to the rich of the long overdue existing surplus. A recipe and ingredients that can ignite the largest global financial crisis yet. A crisis that U.S. capitalism may not survive.

Home Grown and Imperial Dramas

As a kind of real-time Hollywood, America has directed and produced some of the most dramatic events. These events have fast-forwarded Americans' misperception of themselves and other countries, peoples and cultures, especially China, Muslims and the East. Without these cataclysmic events I would not be able to rationalize my thoughts as easily or logically. The attacks on the Twin Towers and the Pentagon; Iraq War; mothers killing their children; the Internet; Ruby Ridge; the senseless killing of our children in schools; the largest accounting fraud in history and corporate skulduggery represented by WorldCom and Enron; Waco; impeachment of a sitting president; Kent State; trash can babies; the Oklahoma City bombing; political sex scandals at the highest levels of government – highlighted by Monicagate; the liberation of over one hundred million people in Eastern and Central Europe from Soviet communism in 1989; the slow formation of an international military force to reverse Iraqi aggression in the Persian Gulf war in 1991 and Osama bin-Laden, the Taleban, and al-Qaeda in 2001; the collapse of communism in Russia in 1991; the re-unification of Germany; the end of Apartheid in South Africa; the acknowledged failure of communism and the mass movement toward capitalism in China.

These dramas cry out for the dated cold war international relics – the United Nations and International Monetary Fund – to be replaced by new global organizations that are relevant for the changed realities of the 21st century.

The closing year of the old millennium in America ended with an illuminating political, military and media circus in Florida. One that exposed American doubts about the political system it proselytizes to the world and the American family. A presidential "electoral joke" – and the Elian Gonzalez family reunion. The new millennium then witnessed, for the first time in history, a change in the party controlling the U.S. Senate without an election. That, along with the change of the New York skyline after the Twin Towers imploded, forever changed a people's misperception of themselves. Fear and the quest for knowledge and understanding became very personal.

Americans conveniently overlook the facts that America's "Twin Towers", its "secure free democratic model" and "transparent corporate governance" have become global jokes. America is the world's largest arms dealer, has the largest nuclear arsenal and is home to the largest corporate frauds and bankruptcies. The U.S. threatens the security of anyone who is a threat to its corporate or geopolitical agenda. Yet America always gets a favorable deal from the United Nations, even when it is delinquent for several years in paying its dues. It is crowned the world's sole superpower and has all the makings of becoming the global bully of the 21st century. Some would say it already has. The successor to England and Spain, America imposes its will on the United Nations and other international organizations such as NATO, the International Monetary Fund, the World Bank and the World Trade Organization. They then pass it on to taxpayers and to Asia like shopkeepers passing a price increase on to the consumer.

America's evolving New World Order is dominated by tense dysfunctional communities that share two sharply defined conditions:
-Expensive political, corporate and religious hypocrisy and
-Social and economic models that are being warped in a vain attempt to emulate the glorified ideal of the "American model" with its crony capitalists sitting becalmed in an intellectual Dead Sea surrounded by Reaganesque lifeguards.

The miles of manicured dysfunctional palatial estates and political monuments off the gridlocked Washington Beltway, built by slaves, camouflage the crying terrified families and croaking political institutions and corporate malfeasance that are America. Americans ducking into cars, homes and schools to avoid a sniper's bullet. A Pentagon aflame merely reconfirmed how dysfunctional and insecure America is today. Enron, WorldCom and Global Crossing are examples of what a bankrupt fraud America has become. America is offline.

Magnified Anglo-American and Sino-Latino Differences

Historically, the differences – rather than the similarities – in Anglo-American and Sino-Latino societies have been emphasized, leading to the belief in America that Chinese and Latinos are not just different, but in many ways inferior. The jokes that the reason the Florida recount was taking so long was because it was Manuel are a glaring recent example. This image has been magnified in recent years by self-serving zealots. Some argue that if Nazi Germany and the former Soviet Union were the monsters of the 20th century, Chinese societies have all the makings of becoming the monsters of the 21st century. A "21st-century version of the Soviet bear," America's top military official pronounces. The Chinese government buys American politicians with illegal contributions, steals nuclear technology from the U.S., illicitly sells arms and technology to other countries, violates human rights with impunity, amasses nuclear weapons, continues to occupy Tibet and threatens Taiwan's safety and security. Yet it always gets a sweetheart deal from the U.S. and is crowned a most favored trading nation.

China, unlike illusive, faceless, shadowy corporate and foreign terrorists, is an easily identifiable target for America's career politicians with all their shortcomings and frustrations. Conservative Republicans add China to the list of countries that harbor terrorists and should be bombed. China is mentioned in the same breath as Afghanistan, Iraq and Libya! Not being included in the "Axis of Evil" was a progressive millennium step. My hope is this trilogy can contribute to the education needed to dispose of the negative image of Chinese ingrained in America's national psyche.

American career politicians who are loyal party cadres, in both parties, perpetuate the differences by fear-mongering. The Republican Party millennium platform regards China as "America's key challenge in Asia". The start of the 2004 presidential election saw China again made a political scapegoat. Faced with a sputtering economy and increasingly unpopular war in Iraq, China again became the whipping boy. It was blamed for the failed 2003 WTO meeting in Cancun and accused of keeping the value of the yuan artificially low to maintain a trade advantage over U.S.-based manufacturers. Economists who warned the Bush administration of the potential of a trade war that will destabilize China's economy and set off a global financial crisis were shunted aside in favor of the political spinmeisters who wanted to appease the voters in the critical rust-belt states of Michigan, Ohio and Pennsylvania. To listen to some of the politicians on the right, you'd think the old Japanese internment camps were being dusted down for new occupants. Chinese are about the same color and size. They'll do. Oops, actually South Asians and Arab Muslims will do for now.

However, American and Sino-Latino civilizations have much in common, as well as much that is different, that can be used by America to learn, understand and grow. A "marriage of East and West" similar to what Alexander the Great did when he officiated at a mass wedding of 9,000 of his soldiers to Asian women, a conscious act of state. Even President Bush acknowledged this is needed to President Jiang Zemin at his ranch in Crawford, Texas, in 2002.

Made in Hong Kong
Since Hong Kong's reversion to Chinese rule on July 1, 1997, it has developed the potential to become a model society for America to emulate. It blends the best of Anglo-American and Sino-Latino cultures which already are the cornerstones and foundations of today's Eastern and Western civilizations.

America and Hong Kong have a common heritage. America, like Hong Kong, was fertilized and created by the same colonial parent. Both are capitalist democracies with a solid foundation rooted in the Anglo-Saxon rule of law and religious freedom.

America and Hong Kong are vacuum cleaners that keep hoovering in adventurous people. Both have been largely built by people who moved from elsewhere – the British, the refugees and immigrants from all over the world. Both America and Hong Kong were molded by Scottish entrepreneurs, Chinese workers, Latino merchants and Irish politicians.

The Hong Kong Foreign Correspondents' Club (FCC) is the laboratory which embodies these diverse fused functional cultures. The Athenian democracy practiced around the Main Bar objectively addresses and questions the American ideal. The divergent views on Yankee dysfunctionality from families to political institutions and foreign policy flaws are passionately debated with dispassionate interludes of deliberate discussions.

Most remarkably, in the tradition of the "Lion and the Mouse": The United States and Hong Kong have a parallel multi-ethnicity and culture which are complementary and not at all alien to each other. We in America have to sweep in the merits and benefits of the Hong Kong solutions for constructive change to begin in the 21st century. America should, once again, be "doing a Nixon on China". That phrase is standard political lingo that refers to dramatic change. Political and corporate.

It is time America sobers up from its moral and political hangover. By doing so it will be able to identify and deal with the real enemy. *We the Apathetic People.* The American Constitution and Declaration of Independence have to be revisited so that We the...can clean up our act so we can better understand our diversity and distinctions as a common humanity. It's up to us to write the obituary for politics as usual. If we don't, terrorists will. Radical times require radical changes.

Going By The Book

- Johny Cash -

HYPOCRISY
Political Dust Storms, Corrosive Money, and Slick Oil
The Wall - Pink Floyd

The walls of denial surrounding America have to be shattered and our individual and collective flaws honestly addressed if America is to survive, thrive and continue to guide in the 21st century. Volume I of the trilogy surveys the geopolitical historical facts underlying the dysfunctional racist, sexual, moral, religious and political hypocrisy and myths perpetuated by the media, church, career politicians and their lobbyists, lawyers and spin doctors in America today.

Chapter One

The Hypocrisy of Fake Morality With Real Orgasms

The way to get rid of temptation is to yield to it -
Oscar Wild

A Refreshing Oasis

The Hong Kong Foreign Correspondents' Club (FCC), established in 1943 in Chungking (now Chongqing), China, by a colorful group of pioneering newsmen, is now home to some of the world's best traveled and most experienced "journos". Located in a historical, low-rise former ice house – or refrigeration plant – at the top of Ice House Street in the Central business district, it has a brick colonial certainty.

The FCC Main Bar is amongst the most active and dynamic smoked-filled meeting places in East Asia for correspondents, photographers, visiting journalists and a host of local bankers, lawyers, accountants, madams, hookers and world class regional cocksmen and their red lipped ladies. Immortalized by John le Carre in *The Honourable Schoolboy,* the Club, which fled to the former British colony from Mao's Communist troops, survived the doomsayers and survived the 1997 return of Hong Kong with aplomb. On Friday nights it is impossible to get to the bar. It is packed several people deep. During the handover period it was home to the several thousand reporters who converged on Hong Kong and one had a hard time even getting into the place as the crowd spilled onto the street.

During the week it is a little more genteel although the language used on occasion is somewhat barbaric "Anglo-Saxon". Nevertheless, the conversation is always stimulating. Discussions can be heard in numerous English and Chinese dialects, occasionally pierced by guttural Dutch, German or sing-song Hindi or French. Chess, bridge and quiz competitions take place between the more intellectually minded members. Its distinguished list of Guest Speakers has included Zhu Rongji, Muhammed Ali, Mahathir Mohammed, James Clavell, Robin Cook, Alain Delon, Steve Forbes, Clark Gable, Katherine Graham, President Suleiman Demirel of Turkey, Lee Kuan Yew, Gough Whitlam, William Holden, Jose Ramos Horta, John le Carre, Roger Moore, Richard Nixon, George Soros, Gary Trudeau, Liv Ullman, Sir Peter Ustinov and PJ O'Rourke.

Most of its members are not in fact journalists, photographers or correspondents. Lawyers, judges, doctors, bankers, advertising executives, diplomats, writers, private investigators, civil servants, accountants, traders, saloon keepers, and their wives, mistresses, girlfriends or boyfriends will exchange views and debate the issue of the moment and usually undress it to its naked core for what it is in any culture or civilization. Much like the *Barbershop* scenes in South Side Chicago, the FCC is a *de facto* social club and debating society where people from all social classes spend their evenings talking about politics, religion and their favorite subject – hypocrisy in high places. The hypocrites are of all colors, religious beliefs and race. No one is spared.

On occasion they even get down on each other as well. There are numerous jokes on the unusual moments at the FCC. My favorite one is: Two Hong Kong journalists are talking after crawling out of their beds at lunchtime after a typical night at the FCC. "Was it crowded at the FCC last night?" the first reporter asks. "Not under my table," responds the second.

Clubs in Hong Kong have strict dress codes. The FCC's code is relaxed and the resulting mix is of people in suits, tuxedos, jeans and shorts, arguing, smoking and periodically screaming and yelling or falling off bar stools, usually on their own, on occasion with a strong nudge or fist from angry colleagues. Dubbed the "Foreign Fisticuffs Club" and "Fight Club" by the local press makes it the unique place it is. A place where *FABDAWGs* abound. That is the acronym for Fantastic Asian Babe Dating Average White Guy.

The FCC is the kind of place the late Kay Graham, former publisher of the *Washington Post* and owner of *Newsweek* magazine, could comfortably repose and casually discuss with her editor Ben Bradlee whether to go ahead and publish the Pentagon Papers – the leaked Defense Department study that revealed government deceptions about the Vietnam war, and the merits of breaking the Watergate story no matter what pressure she was subjected to by any political administration. She could compare her experience of covering the notoriously rough San Francisco dock labor union days with Clare Hollingworth, the doyenne of Hong Kong correspondents and a permanent fixture at the FCC. Clare is quite possibly the most famous female correspondent of the 20th century. She is best known for breaking the story that World War II had commenced when she saw German tanks crossing into Poland on Friday, September 1, 1939. She also won acclaim for her coverage of the Algerian and Vietnam wars and for her 1963 scoop on the defection to Moscow of spy Kim Philby.

Leonardo DiCaprio, the actor and presidential interviewer, would be welcome to share his opinion on why journalists are upset at him for interviewing President Clinton in an Earth Day special and the horse manure he throws at photographers. The FCC Asia brothel connoisseurs would be happy to forgive his journalistic indiscretions in exchange for the real story of the Paris call-girls he invited to his room after the Paris premiere of *Gangs of New York*.

It is a place where Joseph Farah, an Arab American journalist of *WorldNetDaily,* would feel comfortable correcting American journalists about their misperception and lack of knowledge about the significance of Jerusalem to Muslims and the Palestinians. A bar where Larry Flynt, the outspoken publisher of *Hustler,* would feel right at home discussing hypocrisy with fellow journo bar flies.

Naked Beauties
A picture of Arthur Hacker in the full, if fake, regalia of British Governors of Hong Kong on the cover of a local magazine used to greet patrons entering the Main Bar before it was refurbished the summer of 2002. It was quite a contrast to the bare-breasted New Caledonia beauties adorning the front of a fashion magazine

and the bare butt of a Scottish Black Watch squaddy exposed by a breeze lifting his kilt, which hung on either side of Arthur's picture. Posing in profile, he stared at the bust of the doyen of Asian journalism, the late Richard "Dick" Hughes CBE, and a recently-discovered black and white photograph of Mao Tse-dong and Chiang Kai-shek reluctantly toasting each other at the original FCC in Chongqing. The undemocratic decision to remodel the Main Bar, driven by the Club's Board, presided over by an American, created its own political controversy and resentment by the club's international membership similar to the resentment President Dubya generated globally with his unilateralism.

Arthur is the local talking Encyclopedia Britannica who was usually found seated on a bar stool facing himself. A proud, self-professed WANK (a "White Anglo Norman 'Celt'") and an avid fan of the British satirical magazine *Private Eye,* he repeatedly reminds new correspondents posted to Asia of the importance of satirical journalism in a democracy. "The 18th-century journals exposed vice, folly and humbug, and we're in that tradition, to tell the truth smilingly, to question the official view. It's fantastically useful in democracies to have someone saying 'No'," Arthur reminds his listeners quoting *Private Eye's* editor, Ian Hislop. "Why regret going after the truth and the big guys at the same time?" Arthur is the quintessential eccentric English bachelor. Formerly a civil servant and government propaganda spinner, he is an artist, cartoonist and local historian. Dressed as though permanently prepared to go fly fishing, he sports a thickness of beard that gives him the face of a graying yeti. His voice is deep, raspy, lolling public school with a languorously confident delivery at a volume that can be heard two blocks away.

Most people entering the bar feast their eyes on the naked beauties and converse with Arthur. During one such conversation, I shared with Arthur a story about how the Turkish soldiers during the World War I battle of Gallipoli had difficulty shooting at the Maoris of the ANZAC troops because the Maoris didn't wear shirts. A Muslim man cannot look at naked bodies that aren't family. As a result no Maoris were killed at Gallipoli. Whenever a Turkish soldier saw a naked Maori he'd look sideways, fire and miss. "Hell, all the British troops should have done is have all their soldiers take off their clothes and charge," was Arthur's contribution to the failed British strategy.

When President Bush announced he would remain in hot pursuit of the terrorists who attacked America on September 11th I shared with Arthur some of the humorous e-mails about America's war against terrorism. Arthur's favorite that brought about his renowned guffawing laugh was: "The President has asked that we unite for a common cause: Since the hard line Islamic people can not stand nudity, and consider it a sin to see a naked woman that is not their wife... tonight at 7:00, all women should run out of their house naked to help weed out the terrorists. The United States appreciates your efforts, and applauds you. God bless America."

The "No War" "No Bush" anti-war slogans modeled by thousands of naked women in America and Australia for aerial photographs didn't garner even a chuckle.

Politics

The politics of the club and alleged indiscretions of its presidents and board members, like the politics of Hong Kong and America, are openly discussed in local gossip columns.

The annual election of the FCC Board and its politics are representative of the democratic process in America and Hong Kong. The turnout reflects the apathy of voters in both places. The Club's board gets returned by less than 20 percent of the membership. Correspondents, journalists and their non-journalist associate members prefer to complain about elected officials and their policies and politics rather than bothering to vote. Listening to opinionated writers, editors and newscasters, who constantly lecture the public on how to change the world, drown their opinions of the changes needed in the FCC in a bottle rather than a ballot, is a daily reminder of how apathetic *We the Maids* have been conditioned to behave.

American hacks seeking elected office to the FCC Board campaign as hard as their presidential and congressional counterparts in America. Very aggressively for 30 to 45 days before the election. But, like the real world, once elected, most of the American Board members are never seen mingling with their constituents at the Main Bar. The campaigns of the non-American hacks are usually

more low-key. The exceptions, of course, being the lawyers trying
to get, and stay, on Board. The 2002-03 FCC President, an American,
like his counterpart back home, spent the people's surplus funds
on taxing and rebuilding the Main Bar and building already inflated
Board egos instead of listening and doing what is in the best interest
of their constituents.

Correspondent members, even though they comprise the minority
of the membership, each have 25 votes per person to everyone
else's single. These, obviously, are highly prized voters that are
aggressively sought out by the numerous candidates and can drink
their way to election day without spending a dime. Their livers
quiver at each Ganbei (bottoms up or down the hatch) as they
toast the buying candidate's victory. Watching some members accept
drinks from opposing candidates for president while toasting them
all is a quaint liquid reminder of how voters will take what they
need in exchange for their promised vote. Watching critics of the
election process in Hong Kong practice what they criticize makes
the drinks they buy that much more enjoyable. Listening to the
criticism of and cynicism about the Hong Kong and U.S. political
process while watching it replay itself annually at the Main Bar
by vocal critics seeking office is a refreshing reminder of the hypocrisy
of the media and its representatives when they seek office. The
lobbyists for each candidate work just as hard as any political
machine in Washington DC.

Athenian Democracy

The regulars at the Main Bar have been searching for and sharing
the bare truth their entire career. People like Charlie Smith. Charlie
first went to Japan after World War II, then on to Korea and Vietnam
before landing in Hong Kong as the bureau chief for UPI. He
accompanied Nixon on his first trip to China. He knew one phrase
in every local language: "My friend will pay!" We used to laugh
at how visiting dignitaries would be impressed with his knowledge
of the local lingo. Charlie, however, was generous to a fault when
he was in the club entertaining friends or having a drink. He always
bought everyone he liked several rounds. Those he didn't like knew
it. "You are full of shit and don't know what you are talking
about," he said as he turned around to dress down Ted McFarland,

the regional president for Hughes Electronics. Ted was trying to explain the meaning of "Bubba" to an "Aussie". "It's guys like you who perpetuate ignorance, hypocrisy and prejudice."Charlie happened to be a good ol' boy from Alabama.

Charlie would periodically argue with journalists steeped in religion on the subject of God and politics. Europeans liked to remind him that the particular debate was no different than those between pagans and religious zealots at Thingvellir, northeast of Reykjavik in Iceland, where the world's first parliamentary republic established itself against the rule of gods in 930 A.D. Swordplay often resolved legislative debates. Just like the cutting verbal duels at the Main Bar. The fact that Reagan and Gorbachev held a summit at Reykjavik to bring an end to the Cold War was not lost on certain veterans.

Charlie had a heart attack and died in the FCC. A brass plaque, the only one at the old Main Bar, was, to the regret of many, unceremoniously removed and placed on the bar column closest to his favorite stool when the bar was redesigned. This action reminds us all of the importance of integrity and truth that Charlie so stubbornly upheld. "Muslims only drink when training in America" is something Charlie would say about the strip joints and bars the kamikaze pilots frequented while preparing for their deadly missions. One of the perrenial questions Charlie asked at the Main Bar is: "if Muslims don't drink how come they make and consume so much arak?" "The Arabs discovered how to distill alcohol and the word alcohol derives from the Arabic alkohl. Arak was the first distilled spirit and the Arabs have never stopped making arak to this very day. Every Arab country, including Saudi Arabia, has illegal stills making arak" I responded the first time he posed the question to me. "I'm impressed smart ass," Charlie responded, "but I like to challenge these ignorant asses around the bar, so pretend you don't know," he kindly requested.

The truth in a democracy can be collectively determined only after a rational and continued discussion by its citizens. Athenian democracy involved each tribe sending fifty of its representatives to its council of five hundred. Not to vote, but to discuss issues and policies. Western European democracy evolved from coffee houses and pubs where citizens discussed how they should be governed. The town hall meetings of seventeenth century America were really the foundations of its democracy.

The media were an essential part of democracy then, even though the earliest newspapers were really extended manifestos. Today the news media, like politics and democracy, have also been "commoditized" to the most cost-effective common denominator, and have become little more than entertainment outlets. The fate of Winona Ryder for shoplifting received more exposure than the mid-term elections and Iraq. Winona appealed to the shoplifters in most members of the public and all public servants. Paula Jones boxing Tonya Harding. Sexy zipper sound tracks, eye tucks, and re-colored hairdos in the style wars for ratings are the most depressing media news. The Tonight Show's Jay Leno officially merged politics and entertainment with his highly visible role in Arnold Schwarzenegger's gubernatorial campaign. Recent surveys show that nearly half of those under 30 use the late-night shows as sources of news about politics. Late-night shows have more impact than news programs. The death of Katherine Graham in the opening year of the new millennium in many ways is symbolic of the death of traditional fact-finding media.

One of the major changes after the handover in Hong Kong is the self-restraint or "self-censorship" imposed by the media on themselves. China and its leadership are still criticized. Especially when they try to muzzle the press. The press is still quick to criticize government policies, Chinese officials and the Hong Kong Chief Executive and his bureaucrats. The difference is it is much more deliberate and thoughtful. Careful self-regulation. Something the media in America should try to emulate.

World Trade Center
The diversity of Americans in Hong Kong was mirrored in the twin towers of New York's World Trade Center that were reduced to rubble on the day of the city's mayoral primary election. Americans from over eighty countries in Africa, Arabia, Asia, Australasia, Europe, Greater China, the Indian Subcontinent, Indo-China, Latin America and the Middle East died as one. They were global capitalists interacting harmoniously in the heart of New York. People working to finance and feed their families and the world. Citizens from

countries on all continents of the globe representing different cultures, religions and ethnic origin working together.

Globalization is not just a one-way street from America. Globalization brings many civilizations, cultures and people to America's shores. The suicide bombers of America's global capitalist symbol were a grim reminder of the ugly underbelly of polarized angry people that also take the 21st century super highway to democratic America to vent their unspeakable hatred. A highway taken by many natives, including the Unabomber and Timothy McVeigh.

The fear, concern and frustration that gripped America after the deadliest day in modern U.S. history echoed around the world. The first foreign attack on America's continental soil that killed thousands in a matter of hours was felt globally. The worst terrorist act in history struck not only at the capitalist heart of America but Hong Kong, the capitalist heart of China.

It was 8:48 pm Tuesday night in Hong Kong when One World Trade Center was struck by a Boeing 767 and 9:06 pm when Two World Trade Center was hit by the second terrorist bomber. I was at my girlfriend Pauline Taylor's apartment at the time. A friend called me on my mobile phone to tell me the World Trade Center had been hit by a plane. I ran to Pauline's window from where the Hong Kong World Trade Centre building is clearly visible as part of the neon-lit skyline. "Are you sure?" I asked. "I'm looking at it as we speak and it looks fine." "The World Trade Center in New York not Hong Kong!" was his exasperated response. "Turn off your dick and turn on the TV," was all Earl could say as we hung up.

Watching the replays of the planes crashing into the twin towers, followed by the fireballs that seemed to instantly implode the two structures while desperate people jumped into pillars of ashen smoke below was heart-wrenching. The phone was constantly ringing to convey repeated emotional outbursts in search of comfort and understanding. I could only shake my head in disbelief and share the occasional tears.

Everyone seemed to be heading to the FCC to watch the different news channels simultaneously on the big TV screens and numerous computer screens at the entrance to the Main Bar. Others sought out correspondents to find out if they had been in touch with their New York bureaus and had any unreported updates. By 11 p.m. the Main Bar was a sardine-packed mass of silent humanity with eyes glued to screens while drowning away their pain, anguish and frustration. The only piercing sound repeatedly interrupting the silence was mobile phones that are usually prohibited in the club. They were allowed for the first time to ring and bring angry desperate people together.

The bartenders refilled everyone's glasses as they left after 3:00 am. Teary-eyed Americans lingered on. Overwhelmed, shell-shocked and numbed. Mourning Americans refused to go to bed. To the admiration of the local Chinese, they debated the American ideal and spirit and questioned its meaning in a fanatical world of heartless extremists oblivious to the American resolve and how it will never be cowed. On the contrary, it unites and energizes America and the democratic free world. Walter Kent, a perennial late night FCC fixture and New York City native, wanted to go back home "to at least donate blood." Other Hong Kong natives and Americans wanted to join him. To donate blood, volunteer to remove debris and look for survivors. People never felt more American and proud of it. Everyone was an American emotionally. Everyone felt helpless but wanted to do something. Anything to contribute to the clean-up of the mess and unfolding tragedy in America.

The natural law of the universe allows Americans to see the light move into darkness. They saw it after the attack on Pearl Harbor. Hong Kong was also attacked by Japan, which invaded on December 8, 1941. The comparison with September 11, 2001, America's darkest moment, and how the pall of America's dark smoke and moment of darkness will again settle over Hong Kong in the 21st century was unavoidable. Not only because Hong Kongers also perished in New York's Twin Towers, but because the world's first aircraft hijacking that took place on July 16, 1948, involved a Hong Kong's Cathay Pacific Catalina flying boat on a flight from Macau to Hong Kong. Hong Kong is also home to the largest number of expatriate nonmilitary Americans outside North America. It has around 80,000 Muslims, is home to more U.S. and Western mul tinational regional headquarters than any other country in the region, U.S. and Western military personnel on R&R frequent its Fenwick Pier and Wanchai bars. It is part of China, a country fighting Muslim extremists in Xinjiang province. An Asian beach-head of British and American imperialism with Chinese characteristics.

Ramsey Yosef, the Osama bin-Laden follower convicted of the 1993 bombing of the World Trade Center, traveled to Hong Kong to plan his hijacking of eleven planes over the Pacific, at least two of which were to originate from Hong Kong. Many flights to Hong Kong originate in countries in the region with known al-Qaeda cells and sympathizers. The Philippines, Indonesia, Malaysia, Thailand, Pakistan and Iran, countries that are a few hours away and where airport security is lax. Such planes could be flown into any one of the high-rise towers in Hong Kong.

The spread of Muslim extremism as the U.S., Hong Kong and regional economies encounter economic hardship and unemployment is a 21st century reality that leaves everyone feeling vulnerable. Hong Kong came to terms with the reality of terrorism when the bombing of a Bali nightclub killed Hong Kong rugby players, some of whom were familiar faces at the FCC. The 2003 suicide bombing of the HSBC bank headquarters in Istanbul confirmed Hong Kong's vulnerability to terrorism.

The question of whether anti-China Muslim terrorists will also strike Hong Kong, now that China has joined the World Trade Organization and also joined America in the war on terrorism, is inevitable. In fact a Hong Kong couple dubbed "Hong Kong's bin-Ladens" were arrested after they threatened to poison drinks in supermarkets if senior government officials didn't resign.

Hong Kong police and intelligence agencies gladly exchange intelligence with their U.S., European, and Mainland counterparts. The resulting high- profile arrests of terrorists sought by America that had Hong Kong contacts are sprinkled throughout the world media. The information received and acted on by Hong Kong authorities has managed to preserve the city's unique skyline.

Missed 9/11 Opportunity
September 11 galvanized the world behind America. NATO declared

the attack to be an act of aggression against the entire alliance. The Muslim world, including Iran and Pakistan, condemned the attacks and joined the U.S. in the fight against terrorism. China and Russia, traditional U.S. antagonists, chose to join America in the war against terror because of their own Muslim separatist concerns. September 11 presented America a rare geopolitical opportunity to unite the world and lead it to a prosperous and healthier 21st century. An opportunity America consciously and deliberately chose to ignore and go it alone. "At some point, we may be the only ones left. That's OK with me. We are America," President George Dubya declared. Is it? Who pays the piper and who benefits from the oil-carrying pipes?

A Pew Global Attitudes Project which surveyed 16,000 people in 20 countries and the Palestinian territories in May 2003 found that those who have a favorable opinion of America declined dramatically. Not just in Muslim countries, but Europe, Latin America and Asia. In fact, most fear America and its foreign policies more than they do terrorists. Some even classify America and its war on terror in Afghanistan and Iraq as acts of terror. America clearly lost world support on the neocon military highway somewhere between Kabul and Baghdad.

The boisterous arguments around the Main Bar between Americans and their allies, versus the rest of the world, on the merits of the War on Terror grew as the war moved from Afghanistan to Iraq. The sad part was listening and watching America's early allies switch sides and launch heart-wrenching verbal assaults that could not be deflected or countered. There were times when even objective American citizens, including former members of the U.S. armed forces and diplomatic corps, reluctantly joined the anti-American chorus and agreed America had missed the geopolitical opportunity it had been handed on a golden platter by 9/11.

Patriotic Media Charge
Media talking heads beating competing war drums to lead the charge on Muslim countries to convert them to Christianity mesmerized America and created an illusory sense of national unity in the aftermath of the attack. Patriotic flag-wearing and waving choreographers of the United States of Apathy, a country that has been "dumbed

down" by local news devoid of global content. A 21st century "Crusade" of "Infinite Justice". "Cowboy-in-the saloon rhetoric... wanted dead or alive." No different than the pronouncements of the deaths of Princess Di, John John and the impeachment of Clinton that was supposed to kill him politically – more media hype. The media-led hype of the Bush war chants that continued for weeks after September 11 should have been substituted with the necessary analysis, criticism and reporting the facts about Osama bin-Laden and the Taleban. The fact that they, like the Ayatollahs in Iran, Saddam Hussein in Iraq, and the Royals in Saudi Arabia are the creations and results of America's dysfunctional foreign policy. Failed U.S. foreign policy strategies. Just like the failed domestic security policies and procedures of the FBI and all counter-terrorist organizations and programs were a colossal annual $30 billion failed taxpayer blunder. A taxpayer rip-off.

The non-representation of facts only makes matters worse. Whether a replay of the presidential election flip flops, impeachment or war. People who tried to question or debate the media's patriotic fervor on any front were fired or accused of being unpatriotic. Dr Samuel Johnson noted in 1775, on the eve of the American Revolution, that patriotism is the last refuge of the scoundrel. The American heretic Ambrose Bierce begged to differ – it is, he said, the first. The Iraq War only made matters worse. Occasional drop by bar fly Pulitzer Prize-winner Peter Arnett became a bar buzz when he got fired for saying in Baghdad what the media were spinning. "The first war plan has failed because of Iraqi resistance. Now they are trying to write another war plan.

"Clearly, the war planners misjudged the determination of the Iraqi forces. In my TV commentary, I tell the Americans about the Iraqi forces and their willingness to fight." He also shared with an Iraqi TV interviewer that "the anti-war movement was growing". Arnett won his Pulitzer for his coverage of the Vietnam War, was the first Western journalist to interview Osama bin-Laden and was fired by CNN in 1999 for his story that America used sarin to kill U.S. defectors during the Vietnam War.

The media also downplayed the government's lack of preparedness for a terrorist attack. The U.S. Commission on National Security, headed by former Senators Gary Hart and Warren Rudman, warned of the dangers of a terrorist attack and the lack of homeland security, yet it was grossly under-reported by the media. After the September 11 bombings, former Senator Hart observed that the bombings "ought to call into question what is important in our society and how the media cover it....There seems to be no self-reflection, no understanding by the media that they have a job under the direction of the Constitution to inform, not just entertain, the American people." When the Hart-Rudman report came out, the media were too busy ferreting the latest dirt on the supposed defacing of the White House by Gore loyalists and the Gary Condit sex-murder scandal, overage Little Leaguers and shark attacks. The media also exaggerated the threat to Air Force One and the President after the bombings of the Twin Towers and the Pentagon. Any wonder that as the days, weeks and months ticked away Americans started raising doubts and losing faith about any of the patriotic missions President George Dubya launched to fight terrorism, to the media's hype and encouragement?

The public displays of patriotism by the media go against traditional U.S. journalistic standards of maintaining a visible neutrality or objectivity. How can one report the facts objectively when clearly obsessed by the patriotic fervor of the hour? Alex Jones, director of the Shorenstein Center on the Press, Politics and Public Policy, correctly stated this idea that American news "cooks the books". Journalism "is supposed to be as close a rendering of the complete story as you can offer, not preaching a declared slanted perspective." One can be a patriot and a journalist but practicing "patriotic journalism" sounds suspiciously like propaganda. "Bin-Laden the Dirtbag" falls a wee bit short of a useful profile of the enemy. Ellen Goodman of the *Boston Globe* described it best. "Maybe the phrase that works the best is the one offered by *The Tampa Tribune's* Gil Thelen, who describes the role as one of 'committed observers'. American journalists have – or should have – a strong commitment to the community, a stake in their country, a stake in creating a more secure world. And a role as independent observers."

Why weren't the horrors of terrorism embraced and more widely discussed and disseminated by the media to the public in America before 9/11? The decades of IRA bombings in the United Kingdom. The massacre of Israeli athletes during the 1972 Munich Olympics. The terrorist bombings in China, Sri Lanka, Israel, Kashmir and Indonesia. Why is terrorism only acknowledged as a universal threat after America experiences the pain?

Who are the real victims of the Patriot Act enacted on behalf of Americans' "war on terror"? The words of Taleban leader Mullah Mohammad Omar in his address to the American people on September 25, 2001, unfortunately ring true. "You accept everything your government says whether it is true or false. ...Don't you have your own thinking? ... So it will be better for you to use your sense and understanding."

In an interview with the BBC's Newsnight, Dan Rather disclosed that he and his colleagues no longer asked career politicians tough questions. He said the climate of patriotism that had enveloped America after September 11 had made journalists hesitant about offending politicians. "Rather's revelation might come as news to the American public, but it is something foreign correspondents in the U.S. have felt since September 11," said Thomas Abraham, then editor of Hong Kong's *South China Morning Post*. This was brought home a month after the war in Afghanistan started when Walter Isaacson, president of CNN, issued an edict to his journalists in the field asking them not to waste too much time reporting the Taleban's point of view, or to dwell too long on the damage produced by U.S. bombers. Instead, he urged journalists to "talk about how the Taleban has harbored the terrorists responsible for killing close to five thousand innocent people." Real patriotism compels journalists to ask career politicians tough questions. Both Abraham Lincoln and Thomas Jefferson defended the right of the press to be free, to lash out at the government and its leadership, even if the criticism should be harsh and excessive. "In a country where values are collapsing, patriotism becomes the hand maiden of totalitarianism," Norman Mailer reminds us.

Instant replays of patriotic media hype flooded the airwaves to justify war and regime change in Iraq. "[They have] wrapped themselves in the American flag and swapped impartiality for patriotism," BBC director-general Greg Dyke lamented, criticizing American television and radio networks for their "shocking" and "gung-ho" coverage of the war in Iraq. To its credit, the BBC, a government-funded broadcaster, openly challenged and questioned Prime Minister Tony Blair and his government about their justification for going to war in Iraq because of "sexed up" evidence of Iraq's weapons of mass destruction.

The media spin and hype in America that followed immediately after 9/11 got "America united" but was short-lived and illusory. It was a passionate, sincere but anemic attempt to believe that *We the Apathetic Maids* re-United the States by waving flags and seeking vengeance and mis-reporting the facts. "The truth is often simpler and yet more horrible than people imagine," Russian investigative reporter Andrei Konstantinov reminds us. "But people prefer to believe the illusions, to see a heroic fairy tale where there is none." Any wonder that as the weeks and months ticked away Americans started raising doubts and losing faith about the patriotic mission statements President Bush aired to fight terrorism with the all-consuming media hype and encouragement? The same happened with the Iraq War. Only the instant gratification fuse got shorter. George Dubya promised that the Iraqi regime would crumble like a "house of cards", and Iraqi soldiers would lay down their weapons when confronted by their "liberators". Didn't quite work out that way. Even America's initial gung-ho RA-RA media at the start of the war down-shifted and looked for driveways to do U-turns.

Why is it necessary for a national crisis or tragedy to bring out America's national character? Why can't *We the People* be just as passionate about our government all the time so that career politicians and their career bureaucrats don't make multi-billion dollar blunders that lead to preventable tragedies that re-Unite the States against a common enemy who capitalized on the blunders at our expense? The career politicians and their bureaucratic security failures are something *We the Apathetic Maids* have to clean up and remove from our political door steps in Washington and State capitols.

Fighting Media

When the Hong Kong Government drafted the equivalent of a Patriot Act, an anti-subversion security law commonly referred to as Article 23, the Hong Kong media, unlike their U.S. counterparts, objected vociferously. The FCC passed a resolution against the proposed law and led the charge to have it scrapped – or at least defanged. Editorials and articles openly criticized the law continuously as a guise and excuse to trample on people's individual rights that will compromise Hong Kong's competitive advantage and reputation as a free and open society. Hong Kong Government officials were accused of kowtowing to Beijing. Members of the Hong Kong Bar Association, the Bars of England and Wales, the New York Bar, bankers and business leaders, usually quiet on such political matters, joined the media chorus. Retired government officials soon followed suit. The media urged the public to join the public demonstrations to express their outrage. Over 500,000 joined the march on July 1, 2003, with banners to express their concerns. Close to 10 percent of the population responded to the media's call for action. Isn't this what the U.S. media should have done when Congress considered the Patriot Act?

"As a journalist, it is not always easy to maintain the fine line between observation and participation. Thus, when I finished work early last Tuesday and set out to join the massive demonstration against Article 23, I wanted to be counted among the 500,000," said Edith Terry, editor of the opinion pages of the *South China Morning Post.* The Hong Kong protest, like Martin Luther King Jr.'s Civil Rights movement, was an updated version of Mahatma Gandhi's Satyagraha movement, his non-violent resistance movement of the 1920s that threw India's British rulers a curve ball. Anger and violence were absent during the demonstrations. The public's peaceful expression of free speech got the government to back down on the legislation, delay its implementation, water it down and forced the Security Secretary who was its foremost proponent to resign. Why didn't U.S. citizens do the same? Ordinary citizens can and always have made a difference.

Compromised Coverage For Oil

Terrorists have been killing innocent victims for decades in the

New World Disorder. In Algeria, China, Egypt, Indonesia, Ireland, Israel, Kashmir, Philippines, Russia, Spain, Sri Lanka and most countries in Africa and South and Central America. Media coverage was limited to periodically reporting terrorist attacks and the number of victims. No explanation. No in-depth analysis. No continuity of coverage. The fact that Saudi businessmen supported terrorist charities – in the same way Irish-American businessmen supported IRA terrorist charities – warranted no media coverage. Why not? Aren't they great stories?

Things changed very quickly after September 11. In-depth investigative news coverage of terrorism and the politics of the Middle East and oil came back in vogue several weeks later after the patriotic drumbeaters got weary of waving the flag and cheer leading the patriots. However, this time round, the "hands off" approach to the U.S.-Saudi sixty year alliance, U.S. military protection of the Saudi Royal family in exchange for oil, was shattered, and became prime time news.

Stories of Saudi funding of terrorist charities that previously were routinely run through the Islamic Affairs Department of the Saudi Embassy, a fact known for years to U.S. Security agencies and the media, finally made the headlines.

Before September 11 anyone warning America of the dangers of terrorism was soundly rebuked by the media. When Reagan's Secretary of State, George Shultz, identified terrorism as a threat to all democracies and called for stronger action to deter terrorist acts on October 25, 1984, he was scorned and dismissed by the media. *The Washington Post* described the speech as "harshly worded" and mocked the Secretary in an editorial as one preoccupied by international terrorism. Mr. Shultz "has gone too far," the Post said.

The New York Times condescendingly opined that "Mr. Shultz is right to express his frustration" but warned against any measures stronger than international sanctions. "Nor should terrorism loom up large only when Americans are the victims," The Times piously intoned. Columnists were even more critical.

No one undermined the message more than Shultz's own superiors,

President Ronald Reagan and Vice President George H.W. Bush. Bush said: "I don't agree with that."

Secretary Shultz was speaking shortly after Irish terrorists had nearly blown up Prime Minister Margaret Thatcher and Arab terrorists had attacked the U.S. Embassy annex and Marine Corps barracks in Beirut.

What the Reagan administration and the media took offense to was the truth. Shultz accurately described terrorists and how they must be treated. "They are depraved opponents of civilization itself, aided by the technology of modern weaponry." In a fundamental sense, he said, terrorism would always be aimed at democracy – "against our most basic values and often our fundamental strategic interests."

"If the modern world cannot face up to the challenge," he warned, "then terrorism and the lawlessness and inhumanity that come with it will gradually undermine all the modern world has achieved." He called for better intelligence and co-operation with allies. He warned that America must offer "firm resistance", must "consider means of active prevention and retaliation" and must" be willing to use military force". In the speech's most quoted passage, Shultz concluded: "We cannot allow ourselves to become the Hamlet of nations, worrying endlessly over whether and how to respond...Fighting terrorism will not be a clean or pleasant contest, but we have no choice."

Why has the press not been as critical of the government today as it was of Secretary Shultz? The U.S. government has failed to heed its own numerous commission warnings of imminent terrorist threats to America or apologize for its failure to do so.

A commission on national security headed by former Senators Hart and Rudman warned the U.S. Congress as recently as February 2001 that America was not prepared to fight terrorism at home. It called for a cabinet-level agency combining customs, law enforcement, the Coast Guard and other non military federal agencies to co-ordinate homeland defense. The Hart-Rudman report received little attention in the media, the White House or Congress. This was not the first time the government had been warned. Only the most recent. In a 2000 report, Congress's General Accounting Office concluded that "the threat of terrorism against the United States is an ever-present danger."

Five years ago, James Woolsey, former director of the CIA, and Joseph S. Nye, dean of the Kennedy School of Government at Harvard, headed a government study that also found a lack of preparation by the U.S. to face catastrophic terrorism. All such warnings were unheeded by the media or government until after September 11.

Two of the main kamikaze bombing suspects entered the U.S. using their real names, even though those names were on a security watch list circulated to other countries. Mohammed Atta told immigration authorities he was coming to the U.S. "on a march to spread the word of God". Continuing to use their own names, they bought tickets on U.S. airlines and boarded them without being stopped. They trained how to maneuver jumbo jets at U.S. flight schools without attracting the notice of the intelligence services. To make matters worse, six months to the day after Atta and Marwan al-Shehhi blew the World Trade Center – and themselves – to smithereens, the Immigration and Naturalization Service sent them their student visa approvals which were post marked March 5, 2002!

How about letting Osama bin-Laden, who the U.S. military acknowledges was present during the battle for Tora Bora, slip away? The mission of U.S. troops was to hunt him down. Yet they let him slip away because the U.S. military relied on Afghan allies notorious for accepting bribes to let people pass through Afghanistan's porous borders.

These slips were perpetuated by government agencies funded by taxpayers to analyze and anticipate terrorist threats and moves. The evidence was out there in plain view but was not properly analyzed and acted upon by either the intelligence agencies or the media. The U.S. jet fighters that scrambled after the Federal Aviation Administration belatedly notified the air force of the hijackings were also late! Why have the media played this down?

The media played many more important stories down. Mohammed Atta blew up a bus in Israel in 1986. He was captured, tried and imprisoned. As part of the Oslo agreement Israel had to agree to release all so-called "political prisoners". They refused, however, to release any terrorists with "blood on their hands". A well-meaning Ronald Reagan and George Shultz "insisted" that all prisoners be released. Atta was freed and showed his gratitude to America by flying an airplane into Tower One of the World Trade Center. This was briefly reported by many of the networks while America was suffering Post Traumatic Shock Syndrome but was then censored from future reports. Why?

In 1996 Sudan offered to arrest Osama bin-Laden and turn him over to the U.S. The Saudis and U.S. balked at the proposed plan. The media and government did not bring this to public attention at the time and only reluctantly disclosed it after September 11. Why? The media also failed to bring out, until after the war on terrorism started, the fact that as early as 1997, the U.S. formed a covert CIA tracking team to capture or kill bin-Laden and destroy his al-Qaeda network. Their mission failed – in part because the team of about fifteen operatives was paid less than $1,000 a month. Considering the devastation, waste and financial havoc September 11 brought to America and the world, wouldn't it have been worth paying them more to get the job done? After all, you get what you pay for in such situations!

Why were these developments overlooked? Probably for the same reason President George W. Bush had the FBI and other security agencies stop investigating prominent Saudi Arabians with connections to bin-Laden. Oil! America with just four percent of the world's population consumes one-quarter of the world's energy.

Saudi Arabia has the world's biggest oil reserve. It accounts for a quarter of the world reserves. President Bush and his father, the former president, had a number of prominent connections to the Saudi royals and bin-Laden family. The BBC's Newsnight brought this to public attention a couple of months after September 11. Why didn't any U.S. media organization report it?

The program said it had obtained evidence that the FBI was on the trail of bin-Laden family members living in the U.S. before, as well as after, the terrorist strikes but were told to back off. Why?

Newsnight pointed out that President George Dubya made his first million some 20 years ago with an oil firm partly funded by the chief U.S. representative of Salem bin-Laden, a company run by bin-Laden's brother. Dubya failed to file the proper forms as a board member and member of the audit committee when he sold his stock before the company financials were made public. The accountancy firm involved? Arthur Andersen.

The President and his father the former president also received fees from the Carlyle Corporation, a small firm which has become one of America's biggest defense contractors. A firm in which the bin-Ladens had a significant stake until they sold it after September 11.

Newsnight said it had been told by a highly placed source in a U.S. intelligence agency that there had always been "constraints" on investigating Saudis, but under President Bush they had become much worse. After Bush's election, the intelligence agencies were told to "back off" from investigating the bin-Laden family. That policy was reversed after September 11 after the bin-Ladens had been escorted out of America courtesy of the U.S. and Saudi governments.

The head of the American visa bureau in Jeddah from 1987 to 1989, Michael Springmann, told *Newsnight:* "In Saudi Arabia I was repeatedly ordered by high-level State Department officials to issue visas to unqualified applicants, people who had no ties either to Saudi Arabia or to their own country. I complained there. I complained here in Washington... to the inspector-general and Diplomatic Security and I was ignored." He added: "What I was doing was giving visas to terrorists."

"The Saudis are active at every level of the terror chain, from planners to financiers, from cadre to foot soldier, from ideologist to cheerleader," the Rand Corporation concluded in a Pentagon briefing to the Defense Policy Board.

The Bushes, Saudi royals and bin-Ladens have unwittingly done Osama's work by estranging America from Saudi Arabia. The irony of Bush-Saudi greed generates endless guffaws in the wee hours at the FCC Main Bar. Isn't it time the U.S. – Saudi marriage of convenience got annulled? Isn't it time that *We the Maids* sweep in a new pre-nuptial agreement if this marriage of convenience is to continue in the 21st century?

U.S.-Saudi Roilmance
America and Saudi Arabia have embraced each other since the days of Franklin Roosevelt. The relationships between the House of Saud and the United States, and with President Bush and his father, have been downright convivial and mutually profitable at the expense of American taxpayers and the Saudi Bedouins. Saudi Aramco, owned by the Saudi government, was created by nationalizing the interests of Exxon, Chevron, Mobil and Texaco in the 1970s. The high cost of gasoline is a recurrent complaint at the FCC because Hong Kong gas prices are among the world's highest. Club members repeatedly bemoan the fact they have to sacrifice gassing themselves up with "one for the road" thanks to Aramco and Exxon.

The oil windfall to the House of Saud has been a monumental misfortune for the peoples of Saudi Arabia and America. "It has intoxicated rulers, henchmen, and purveyors, who have slept on piles of money, wasted it largely on worthless projects, and managed to exceed their figuratively (but not literally) limitless resources. Even Saudi Arabia cannot balance its books. In the process these spoilers have infuriated the Muslim poor, who in turn have sought an outlet for rage and outrage in fundamentalist doctrine," David S. Landes, author of *The Wealth And Poverty of Nations,* pointed out in 1998.

The best comparison is with 16th and 17th century Spain. Saudi royals, like their Roman Catholic predecessors, are cursed by easy riches and led down the path of self-indulgence and laziness. *Wasta fogul kanoon,* or "influence is stronger than the law," allows the five thousand members of the Saud family to do as they please with a total disregard for the law. That includes importing and selling liquor, women and slaves.

Perhaps to atone for its shameless behavior at home, the Saudi ruling family finances terrorism and Islamic centers around the world that propagate its creed, Wahhabism, the most rigid form of Sunni Islam, which rejects tolerance of other religions. Edward

N. Luttwak, a senior fellow at the Center for Strategic and International Studies, reminds us that "the United States has long lived with this paradox, but in the wake of the September 11 attacks, whose perpetrators included Saudi citizens, it would be imprudent to overlook this connection any longer. It would be futile to hunt down one Osama bin-Laden while America's ally is nurturing many more." Let's not forget that 15 of the 19 terrorist hijackers on September 11 were Saudi citizens.

The media did not expose this cozy cold-blooded oil-for-profit diplomacy that compromises and perverts America's constitutional ideals because as long as the oil flowed from the Kingdom's deserts into American cars, U.S. career politicians didn't feel it necessary to do anything about the extreme Muslim fanatics being bred and funded by the kingdom. Any wonder the White House refused to declassify 28 pages of the Congressional intelligence report on 9/11 that discuss the links between individuals in the Saudi government and some of the 9/11 hijackers?

Oil executives and the U.S. government have been preoccupied the last several decades at maintaining the House of Saud in power at any cost so that oil can flow without interruption to America. The Saudi royal family has, in effect, been paying protection money to the Muslim extremists at home to focus their hatred on America. The attack on an American bus in Jeddah in 1995, the major attack on Khobar in June 1996 in which 19 U.S. servicemen died, followed by the bombings of U.S. Embassies in Africa and the attack on the USS Cole were all downplayed by the government and media because of the direct links such attacks had to the House of Saud. That started to come to light after September 11.

Good diplomacy mandates that U.S. ambassadors speak the language of the country they are posted to. This is fundamental diplomacy. However, when the U.S. sends Arabic-speaking diplomats to Saudi Arabia the House of Saud demands their removal and replacement with oil-loving presidential cronies who do not speak Arabic, are clueless on how to penetrate Saudi Arabia but can get their voices heard in the White House. Thomas Friedman cites the case of Ambassador Hume Horan, a fluent Arabic speaker with the ability to understand Saudi society, as evidence of this sad historical relationship. "As long as the Saudis kept the oil flowing, what they taught in their schools and mosques was not its business. What it didn't know wouldn't hurt it. Well, on September 11 we Americans learned just how wrong that view was."

"We just can't go on looking at the Arab world as a giant gas station, indifferent to what happens inside. Because the gas is now leaking and all around people are throwing matches," Middle East analyst Stephen Cohen reminds us.

The same holds true for the demonic rule of the despots of the oil-rich Stans. Kazakhstan, Uzbekistan, Kyrgyzstan and Turkmenistan. Kazakhstan's Nursultan Nazarbayev makes the House of Saud and Saddam Hussein look like democratic zealots. Yet America embraces him because of his country's proximity to Afghanistan and his vast oil reserves. A convenient military ally. Just as Saudi Arabia and Iraq used to be.

The House of Saud's "Visa Express" at the U.S. Embassy in Riyadh, which facilitates the easy access of Saudi royals and terrorists to America, the land of religious freedom, is particularly ironic when one considers that the American forces keeping the royals in power are not even allowed to pray on Saudi soil. When the first President George Bush visited the troops in Saudi Arabia during the Gulf War, he was forced to retreat offshore to a ship to pray!

In the late 1980s, Michael Springmann was a consular officer in Saudi Arabia. In 1988, two Pakistanis applied for visas to attend a trade show in the United States. But when they were unable to name the show or the city in which it was taking place, Springmann refused the visa requests. He was overruled by the chief of the consular section. On another occasion, an unemployed refugee from Sudan applied for a visa to the U.S., which Springmann turned down. Again he was overruled by his boss. In total, about one hundred applicants – Pakistanis, Syrians, Lebanese, Palestinians – all of whom he felt were unqualified, were approved for visas over his objections.

Springmann later found out that the U.S. Embassy in Saudi Arabia was being used to funnel Islamic militants to the United States for training before heading for the battlefield in Afghanistan to fight the Russians. In other words, the consular section was run by the CIA. An operation the CIA and State Department have forgotten to close down. Any wonder that 15 of the 19 hijackers on September 11 were from Saudi Arabia?

As long as Americans want their gas guzzlers, career politicians take the easy road dictated by the oil industry and their lobbyists. "Either we get rid of our mini-vans or Saudi Arabia gets rid of its textbooks," says Michael Mandelbaum, a John Hopkins foreign policy specialist. "It's dangerous to go on assuming that the two can co-exist." He pointedly adds: "Ideally, we get rid of both."

Yet there is an alternative that is politically safe. One that Hong Kong taxis must use by law. Liquefied Natural Gas (LNG). Gigantic LNG fields have been discovered in the Netherlands, Russia, the North Sea and Australia, all in the control of democratic non-Muslim countries, as well as in Muslim Nigeria, Algeria, Oman and Malaysia. LNG could easily replace oil now.

America went to war in the Arab world for the second time in ten years because the career politicians that *We the Apathetic Maids* let run our government are in denial of reality in the Middle East. These politicians have become the puppets of America's oil barons. Building an American empire wherever oil gushers sprout. Anyone who questions or doubts this conclusion must ask themselves what was the only security concern America had when it went to war in Iraq? The oil facilities! Refineries, pipelines and pumping stations. Not hospitals, schools, museums, or anything else for that matter. Looting and destruction were widespread – except at oil facilities. "An imperial, colonial power occupying impoverished Islamic lands and appropriating their oil riches in collusion with corrupt monarchies and dictators," Jann Wenner, the editor of *Rolling Stone,* concludes.

Cuban Smoke Screen
Trade embargos imposed and used as the economic nuclear weapon in America's arsenal to fight its enemies in the new global war have proven ineffective. The world's longest-running economic trade embargo was imposed by America against North Korea in 1950. It has failed to remove the country's leader Kim Jong-il, just as it failed to remove his father Kim Il-sung, the nation's founder. The trade embargos against Castro's Cuba and Saddam's Iraq have

also been failures. Trade embargos have a 2,500 year history of failure. The first recorded trade embargo dates back to 432 BC when officials from Athens barred traders from the Greek state of Megara from the city's harbor and market. The effort failed, sparking the Peloponnesian War, which ended Greece's democracy.

The visit to Cuba by former President Jimmy Carter blew away the hypocrisy of the U.S. trade embargo of the island like the clouds of Cuban cigar smoke that engulf the FCC Main Bar. Every U.S. global brand name company's presence in Cuba was on full display during the Carter visit. Banks, credit cards, soft drinks, cigarettes, hotels, cars and dollars.

The Cuban smoke screen put up by career politicians and the Cuban exiles in Florida was highlighted by the election crisis created in that state during the last presidential election of the 20th century. Florida has 25 pivotal electoral votes and the 883,000 active Cuban exiles who hate Castro can swing the electoral votes to any presidential candidate who perpetuates their communist Cuban smoke screen.

Listening to President Bush declare to the Cuban exiles that he will recognize Cuba and lift the embargo when free elections are held, while his brother Governor Jeb stood by his side in his re-election campaign, hammered home the point that in America today politics is about family business over the country's interests.

The U.S. support of more oppressive dictators and regimes such as Saudi Arabia, Uzbekistan and anywhere else with oil and the lack of a significant vocal body politic or voters' constituency, was mocked to no end in the FCC Main Bar during Carter's Cuba visit. A U.S. White House oiligarchy putting its interests and those of its extended family members again over country. Is this what America is really all about? Is this what the Founding Fathers had in mind?

"Blowback" Flawed Foreign Policy
America under President Dubya was reluctant to get involved in the Middle East peace process even though all parties concerned pleaded and begged. When it finally did so, it mishandled its role as impartial arbiter because it was pre-occupied with trying to rally support on behalf of its war against Iraq. What happened to the

notion that "Every nation in every region now has a decision to make. Either you are with us, or you are with the terrorists?"

President Bush and Vice President Cheney thought that their representation of the buyers of the Arab oil would get them the political and military support of the dictators they finance. A Middle East Enron-style approach. Just because petro-dollars buy politicians in the U.S. and finance one Bush after another under the great constitutional foundation stone laid by America's "Magnificent Seven" Founding Fathers, doesn't mean they work with the Magnificent Seven Oil Sheikdoms.

Isolationist America was a reluctant participant in both world wars, and a late bloomer in coming to terms with its power and the reality of contemporary international relations. It was an inexperienced, arrogant teenager when compared to other civilizations, history, and its understanding of honoring long term commitments to its allies – member states and countries whose memories of slights and history are multi-generational rather than limited to the span of the latest hot music or fashion statement.

After oil was discovered in Saudi Arabia in 1938, and before it entered World War II, America became a careful planner with the British on how it could assist the allied war effort with "Lend Lease" schemes and other political strategies. However, it required collateral from the British in the form of their vast Middle East oil reserves. The arrangement was sealed when President Franklin D. Roosevelt met Saudi King Abdul Aziz in 1945 in Egypt on a U.S. aircraft carrier decked with Bedouin favored carpets. President Harry Truman later confirmed the arrangement in 1950.

Americans don't know history as well as they should. Others do. Even Osama bin-Laden. America brought the House of Pahlavi to power in Iran for the same reasons. Oil. In 1953 America toppled the popular democratic government of Mohammed Mossadeq, a Western-educated, charismatic leader poised to lead Iran to become the first truly Muslim democracy under the country's 1906 constitution. He was ousted by a CIA-run coup because he nationalized the country's oil industry, then controlled by American and British companies, and replaced by Shah Mohammed Reza Pahlavi, long perceived as a puppet of the West. America continued to support the Shah, even though he failed to gain the support of his people. Had democracy been allowed to flourish in Iran without the intervention of petro-politics, little known clerics such the Ayatollah Khomeini would have remained little known. It was only a matter of time before a new generation oppressed by the Shah's repressive regime would rise up in rebellion and adopt radical fundamentalist Islam as an alternative. The motive is no different for the oppressed younger generations in Saudi Arabia, Egypt, Algeria, Indonesia and other countries where petro-politics fuels U.S. foreign policy.

The unintended consequences of America's half-baked ill-reasoned foreign policy in Iran was an undesirable "blowback", a term coined by the CIA to refer to the unintended consequences of covert operations that come back to haunt America.

The Ayatollah's coup in 1979 encouraged Iraq's Saddam Hussein to invade Iran. Why? Because when the Shah was ousted, Washington policy wonks were stunned. The Iranians weren't and hence their resentment of America. What did America do? It supported Saddam Hussein in his war against Iran and gave him many of the weapons it later wanted to destroy. Much like what happened in Afghanistan where the U.S. supplied the "Osama bin-Ladens of the 1970s" with Stinger missiles and other advanced weapons to attack the Russians. When a U.S.- emboldened Saddam attacked Kuwait, also for oil, the U.S. came to the support of Saudi Arabia to liberate Kuwait in exchange for more oil and the assurance of stable oil supply and prices.

The Iraqi Kurds want to support America but cannot forget the Henry Kissinger double-cross of so-called support for the 1974 Kurdish rebellion. Nor can they forget that of the first President Bush after the Gulf War. The Kurds revolted to help overthrow Saddam in accordance with exhortations of then President George Bush to the Iraqi people to "get rid of Saddam". But no help from America arrived. The result was that two million Kurds became refugees in Turkey and Iran after Iraqi troops expelled them from Iraq and destroyed their villages. The Kurdish city of Kirkuk holds 60 percent of Iraq's oil. Any wonder the Iraqi Kurds were suspicious and reluctant to support America in its renewed effort to topple Saddam? The same happened in Shiite Basra and Marshlands of

Mesopotamia. They also listened to America. Like their Kurdish brothers-of-armed resistance they were let down by America and paid a high price.

One misstep led to the next, and the next and still continues on the slick stairway to oil heaven. Even in Afghanistan, a point overlooked by the mainstream media because of their focus on the war on terror and capturing bin-Laden. Afghan leaders have tried to create a close diplomatic relationship with America since independence from Britain in 1919. The U.S. repeatedly declined because it could not see a "sufficient geo-strategic interest or economic opportunity in Afghanistan," Amin Saikal, who directs the Center for Arab and Islamic Studies at the Australian National University, reminds us.

Mohammad Daoud, who overthrew the monarchy of his cousin, King Zahir Shah, and declared Afghanistan a republic in 1973, warned in 1976 that Afghanistan faced a serious Soviet-backed Communist threat. Washington played the problem down and directed the Afghans to seek help from the collapsing regime of the Shah of Iran. Had the U.S. shown more foresight, the Communist takeover in Kabul in April 1978 and the Soviet invasion of Afghanistan the next year might have been avoided. So, too, the expensive U.S. campaign of assistance to Afghan and other freedom fighters that eventually forced the Soviets out and prepared the groundwork for Osama bin-Laden, his terrorist organization and the Taleban to take root. This mistake was again repeated by America after the Soviet defeat in 1992 when the moderate Islamic government of Burhanuddin Rabbani sought closer ties to the U.S. but was politely rebuffed and nudged to Pakistan which created the Taleban and sent them to take over.

The Caspian Basin is the focus of the world's latest oil rush. Osama bin-Laden and the Taleban offered U.S. oilmen George Bush and Dick Cheney a golden geopolitical opportunity to lead the charge to find the best way to get the oil to their constituents, because he who controls the flow of oil controls global politics. Halford Mackinder identified central Asia as the key to control Eurasia (and thus the world) a century before the U.S. oilmen-politicians found themselves still trying to ensure access to the vast oil reserves located near Mackinder's "geographical pivot of history".

The world has sufficient oil today to meet its current demands. However, according to CIA estimates, when China and India reach South Korea's current level of per capita energy use – within 30 years – their combined oil demand will be 120 million barrels daily. Today total global consumption is 60 to 70 million barrels daily. In other words, the major powers will be locked in fierce competition for scarce oil, with the Gulf and Central Asia the focus of this race. Central Asia's oil and gas producers are landlocked. Their oil therefore has to be exported through pipelines.

Russia, the world's second-largest oil exporter, wants Central Asian resources to be transported across its territory. Iran, also an oil producer, wants the energy pipelines to end at its ports, the shortest route. On the other hand, Pakistan and the U.S. have long tried to build pipelines running due south from Termez, Uzbekistan, to Kabul, Afghanistan, then down to Pakistan's Arabian Sea ports, Karachi and Gwadar. This route, however, will require a stable, pro-Western Afghanistan.

Since 1989, Iran has worked hard to keep Afghanistan in disorder, thus preventing Pakistan from building the Pakistani-American pipeline. When Pakistan stopped supporting its ally, the Taleban, after September 11 to side with Washington in the war on terrorism, Pakistan thought it could seal the pipeline deal. However, while America's oilmen were busy bombing Afghanistan to pieces in an effort to find Osama bin-Laden, they failed to notice that the Russians had taken over half the country.

The Russians achieved this victory through their proxy: the Northern Alliance. Moscow, which has sustained the alliance since 1990, rearmed it after September 11 with new tanks, armored vehicles, artillery, helicopters and trucks. To the horror of Washington's oilmen, the Russians rushed the Northern Alliance into Kabul, in direct contravention of Bush's orders. Eric Margolis, a foreign affairs columnist for Canadian and Pakistani newspapers and author of *War at the Top of the World – The Struggle for Afghanistan, Kashmir and Tibet,* correctly points out: "By charging like an enraged bull into the South Asian china shop, the U.S. handed a stunning geopolitical victory to the Russians and severely damaged its own great power ambitions. Moscow is now free to continue plans to dominate South and Central Asia in concert with its strategic allies India and Iran. The Bush administration does not appear to understand its enormous blunder and keeps insisting that 'the Russians are now our friends.' The President should understand that where geopolitics and oil are concerned, there are no friends, only competitors and enemies."

The end result is that Russia today is in control of the oil flowing out of Central Asia. Azerbaijan and Kazakhstan will be capable of producing roughly three million barrels a day by 2010. Russian companies will also be the dominant players in Iran because of flawed U.S. policies there. This gives them control of an additional six million barrels a day. Add to that Russia's own production, which totals more than seven million barrels a day and it is clear it controls double the current production of Saudi Arabia.

Misconceived U.S. foreign policy is not only perpetuated in Muslim countries, but in China, Vietnam and next door in Catholic Cuba.

In China, Mao Tse-dong fought alongside the U.S. forces there against Japan and then wanted President Franklin Roosevelt and the American government to establish diplomatic relations with his new government. His communications to the State Department were conveniently misplaced as the pro-Taiwan China lobby in the department decided unilaterally to continue supporting Chiang Kai-shek. Unfortunately for Mao and America, the anti-communist lobby and pro-Taiwan lobby prevailed and have dominated America's foreign policy towards China since the inception of the People's Republic.

Ho Chi Minh, like Mao, wanted to ally himself with the U.S. to fight the Japanese occupation during World War II and did. Like Mao, however, he was also abandoned and betrayed by the U.S. after Japan surrendered. Had the U.S. supported Uncle Ho as Roosevelt advocated, the Vietnam War could have been avoided.

Roosevelt had no liking for European colonialism and was seeking to find the means of restoring to the colonies of Hong Kong and Southeast Asia their independence after the end of the war. Roosevelt clearly had a particular animus against the French role in Indochina, and was quoted on one occasion as having remarked: "France has milked it for 100 years. The people of Indochina are entitled to something better than that." Although Ho was well aware that the U.S. was a capitalist society, he had always expressed admiration for its commitment to democratic principles. Ho and his Vietminh met with U.S. representatives of the Office of Strategic Services, the predecessor to the CIA, in Kunming, China, and later in Chungking, birthplace of the FCC, to help the U.S. in its war effort against Japan. They delivered Lieutenant Rudolph Shaw, a U.S. reconnaissance pilot rescued from the Japanese, to the Americans in China and had a meeting with General Claire Chennault in Kunming to volunteer their services to the Americans. Ho received weapons and communications equipment, the code name "Lucius", and went back to Vietnam where he worked for the OSS.

After the defeat of Japan, Uncle Ho and the Vietminh, like Mao and his communists, were rebuffed by the U.S.

Now that Russia has closed its spy center in Cuba and removed its last soldiers from the country, the island's 11 million people want more than just food and dollars from relatives in America. They, like Castro, Mao, Ho and Chinese and Vietnamese of earlier decades, want normal relations with a country that has an irrelevant and irrational fixation with Castro and his brand of politics. He may not have oil, but he has cigars and rum that Americans love. The Cold War is over and both can go a long way to warm Americans hearts for their neighbors. The alternative? Another generation of haters of America because of its irrational foreign policy. U.S. foreign policy that rejects political leaders because they are "commies" and its unwavering support of repressive regimes because of their oil, religion, or blind support of America has done more real harm in the long run to its foreign policy than any short-term illusory gains.

Pakistan and the India-China-Pakistan relationship were as stable as they have been for years before America launched its war on terrorism in Afghanistan. Pakistan sided with America and hedged its bets with the radical extremists operating out of Pakistan who attacked the Indian Parliament on December 13. This helped bring the two nuclear powers to a war footing which further destabilized the region. The U.S. established the new 21st century precedent that a country is either with the terrorists or against them. India echoed the sentiment and demanded Pakistan crack down on the Lashkar-e-Taiba and Jaish-e-Mohammed fundamentalist Kashmiri militants operating in Pakistan.

While America was waging the Afghan war and trying to calm the tension between India and Pakistan, another U.S. foreign policy failure came home to roost on its back porch. A democratic repressive coup in a Venezuela modeled after America that violently slowed the steady flow of oil to American gas guzzlers and Argentina. Evita's Argentina, more than any other developing country, bought into the promises of U.S. – promoted "neo-liberalism". Tariffs were slashed, state enterprises were privatized, multinational corporations were welcomed, and the peso was pegged to the dollar. Now Argentina is in utter chaos. "Some observers are even likening it to the Weimar Republic. And Latin Americans do not regard the United States as an innocent bystander," Paul Krugman correctly points out. Moreover, when the economy went sour, the International Monetary Fund – which much of the world, with considerable justification, views as a branch of the U.S. Treasury Department – was hopeless. IMF staffers knew for years that the peso-equal-dollar policy could not be sustained. The IMF could have offered Argentina guidance on how to escape its monetary trap, as well as political cover for Argentinan leaders. Instead, "IMF officials – like medieval doctors who insisted on bleeding their patients, and repeated the procedure when the bleeding made them sicker – prescribed austerity and still more austerity, right to the end," Krugman said.

"As the U.S. has supported brutal dictatorships in Chile, Indonesia, Cambodia and many other places, including until quite recently Iraq, the idea that the U.S. represents the democratic ideal through its foreign policy is laughable. It is hypocrisy and self-righteousness..." Kester Bramley told the editor of the *South China Morning Post*. "To most countries it is unsettling to see the U.S. and Britain wield so much power," Kester started hesitatingly, "but once this insecurity is dealt with and the end result is seen, history will mark this time in our world's history as the beginning of an important time, a time when finally the unjust were taken to task – one by one – and were held accountable. The war in Iraq should scare the hell out of those countries with issues to be dealt with," Kester concluded to a round of applause from the regular bar flies at the Main Bar.

U.S. defective foreign policies have to be swept out by *We the Maids* in the 21st century if we want to eliminate others' growing hatred of our children.

Policy Flip-Flops

America's inconsistent and contradictory pancake domestic and foreign policies are constantly being questioned and debated at the FCC. By speakers, bar flies and policy wonks. "Yes, people know Mr. Hussein gassed his own population, but the U.S. voiced no outrage at the time. Indeed, it continued to back Iraq as a bulwark against Iran. Will America flip-flop again in the future, leaving its allies in the lurch?" asked Clyde Prestowitz, president of the Economic Institute in Washington.

The release to the media of pictures of Saddam's dead sons Uday and Qusay after the U.S. protested when Arab television broadcast pictures of Americans killed in Iraq resulted in a free-for-all. "That's about as hypocritically double-faced America can get," Bob Davis, a photographer and FCC regular, pronounced. Philip Bowring, a columnist and past president of the club, went further. "On the international political front, the biggest change by far has been in U.S. policy towards the rest of the world and its own citizens. September 11 has given free rein to Bush administration instincts that can only be described – and I do not use this word lightly – as fascist. These include the large-scale, often race-or religion-based detentions without trial, the Guantanamo concentration camp, the use of the Patriot Act to justify all manner of illiberal acts such as reporting on neighbors – a favorite of the former East Germans. The cabinet prayer meetings and strong identification with Christianity fudge the church-state divide central to the U.S. constitution.

"The right-wing, but libertarian, Cato Institute now regards the neo-conservative right of U.S. Defence Secretary Donald Rumsfeld, Attorney-General John Ashcroft and company as more dangerous to U.S. liberties than discredited socialist doctrines. The U.S. was the standard-bearer of liberal democracy, but is it now? Hong Kong's secretary for security is a model of tolerance compared with Mr Ashcroft. America was the great growth market, but its debts will now hobble it for a generation. Hong Kong needs to take that on board." Don't we all?

The repeated sighs of dismay every time America does a domestic or foreign policy U-turn are audible across the Main Bar. America's rejection of international treaties such as the Kyoto agreement on global warming, the international agreement to ban chemical and biological weapons, the treaty limiting exports of small arms, the agreement banning the use of land mines, and the International Criminal Court, all of which Washington played a large role initiating, is held to be totally incomprehensible.

Honest Political Dialogue
The stupidity of oil politics, terrorism, U.S foreign policy, the security breaches that led to September 11 and the impeachment of Bill Clinton paled in comparison to the ridicule the American political system was subjected to in the Main Bar after Election 2000. Paul Belden, a Floridian and staff writer for a Hong Kong magazine, said: "I suspect that had Bush been a Palm Beach voter, he would have wound up voting for Mr. Gore, possibly costing himself the election."

Charlotte Parsons, a Hong Kong columnist at the time, did a wicked impersonation of a drooling idiot-Bush. Quoting him. "I mean in this century's history. But we all lived in this century. I didn't live in this century...People that are really weird can get into sensitive positions and have tremendous impact on history....." Bush is supposed to bring respect back to the White House. The humor, suspicions and ridicule America endured are pathetic.

With amused amazement, stories of broken voting machines, ballot shortages, missing names on registration lists, missing ballot boxes and African-Americans being denied their right to vote, nepotistic political dynasties, and electing a dead man were shared, and brought up repeated comparisons to the Philippines, Indonesia and banana republics. Does Lady Liberty deserve this ridicule? That elections in America, as in the Philippines and other developing democracies, are determined by "guns, goons and gold", was a common theme. Now it is "guns, goons and Black Gold". The Florida election showcased all three. Does the beacon of democracy have to show the world that its battery-operated and that the batteries have run out? With its democratic ideals depleted, and exposed for the outdated political process it lives with, what right does America have to criticize other countries for doing the same?

Sandy Cate, an anthropologist from San Francisco, echoes many of the comments expressed by the denizens of the FCC. "It's pretty interesting that the future leader of the world's last superpower is going to be determined in a state known for its vote fraud, blotted voting rolls and corruption...There is a certain irony to the idea that while the U.S. harps at Eastern Europe, Africa, Asia et al about democracy and fair elections, its own has come down to Florida, Miami-Dade and the rest of South Florida."

Miami political vice at its finest. The legitimacy of the process is suspect. But then again, what can we expect of an America where President Bill Clinton was caught between two Bushes? A prickly mush of exaggerated democratic orgasmic claims, with lots of Cuban cigars.

When *The New York Times,* after a six-month investigation, released its conclusions on what happened in Florida, it confirmed the fears of the regular FCC bar flies. Florida officials accepted hundreds of overseas absentee ballots that did not comply with Florida election laws. The flawed votes included ballots without postmarks, ballots postmarked after the election, ballots without witness signatures, ballots mailed from towns and counties within the United States and even ballots from voters who voted twice. All would have been disqualified had the state's election laws been enforced.

In a "war room" within Florida Secretary of State Katherine Harris' office in the state capitol of Tallahassee, veteran Republican political consultants helped shape post-election instructions to county canvassing boards. They frequently questioned civilian ballots, for example, while defending military ballots with the same legal defects. They ridiculed Gore lawyers for raising concerns about fraud, while making eloquent speeches about the voting rights of men and women who were defending the nation's interests in remote and dangerous places.

The unequal treatment is at odds with statements by Bush campaign leaders and the Florida Secretary of State, that rules should be applied uniformly and certainly not changed in the middle of a contested election. It also conflicts with the equal protection guarantee that the U.S. Supreme Court invoked in December 2000 when it halted a statewide manual recount and effectively handed Florida to Dubya. The Republican political operatives outsmarted their Democratic counterparts. They got the public to rally behind their drive to count the overseas absentee ballots of military personnel.

Any wonder the call for international observers at future American elections was repeated for years at the Main Bar, every time the question of Democracy in America was brought up? In fact the jokes of Bosnia sending peacekeeping troops were the most popular. Yugoslav President Kostunica was quoted as saying: "We must do all we can to support free elections in America and allow democracy to gain a foothold there." He added: "The U.S. is a major player in the Western Hemisphere and its continued stability is vital to Serbian interests in the region." Few in Yugoslavia or elsewhere see the U.S. as a model. "It is obvious that the U.S. system is obsolete. It's not logical," says Nebojsa Bakarec, a close associate of the Yugoslav president.

The Palm Beach and Florida debacles magnified similar problems in New York, Detroit and all across America. The country doesn't even have a uniform voting system. It's left up to each county and state. As a result, voting machines first introduced in 1892, vote punches, pens and pencils are used as well as touch screens. *The Wall Street Journal* estimated that the Shoup lever machines – infamous for malfunction and unreliability – were used by one in five of the 100 million Americans who voted.

Italian columnist Bepe Severgnini summed up the confusion best. "The other night when I went into a restaurant in Santa Monica, there was one President – Clinton. When I ordered a pizza there was another one – Gore. When I paid the bill there was a third president – Bush. When I walked out on to Ocean Boulevard there was no president, because Bill is now the husband of a senator from New York." Any wonder the Clinton presidency will be remembered as sex between the Bushes? That type of political humor ended on September 11 when Muslim extremists torpedoed our politically apathetic lives.

The political humor returned to Florida with gale force after the state spent $30 million to upgrade its voting system for the 2002 elections – which echoed the botched 2000 presidential election, only louder. Malfunctioning new touch-screen machines, election volunteers not knowing how to operate the machines, uncounted votes, closed or late opening polling stations only added to the chaos that is America on election day.

Oral Bites

"Oral sex is not an affair? Are you Yanks joking? Who cares? What is the big deal?" Brian Jeffries asked me. Brian had been with AP in Iran in 1979 when the Ayatollah came back and was there during the American hostage crisis. "Don't you Americans have issues of more substance to discuss? Is America that shallow?"

Americans are shallow. Most issues of substance are watered down to snappy sound bites. "Just Say No!" "Talk to your kids." Talk about what? The very essence of sex, morality, religion and politics has been swept deep into our subconscious or out of our very tiny minds. The media exploit this by sensationalizing what appeals to our voyeurism. Minnesota Governor Jessie Ventura, himself a victim of gross misreporting, says: "The media's fixation on fights and scandals is a gross misrepresentation of what they are supposed to be doing...So much of the media's current disrepute is a result of taking honorable journalistic principles to stupid extremes."

It takes correspondents, photographers, editors and publishers like those at the FCC and Larry Flynt to flush out hypocrisy. After all, "in the land of the pious hypocrites, the honest pornographer is king."

In a country where everyone assumes that all politicians lie, politicians themselves regard a certain kind of lying as a special kind of sin. Interesting juxtaposition? Used to be Larry Flynt was the sinner! Now he has come to the defense of the President of the United States.

Photographers and correspondents periodically get killed trying to bring us the truth. They risk their lives to expose the truth.

The political turmoil in Iran where journalist Zahra Kazemi, a Canadian of Iranian descent, died of a brain hemorrhage after being detained by the police, and the wars in Chechnya, Afghanistan, Iraq and Northern Ireland were stark millennium reminders. Irish crime journalist Veronica Guerin was assassinated in 1996 for her exposes of Dublin's drug barons. "I vow that the eyes of justice, the eyes of this journalist will not be shut again," Guerin declared after a previous attempt to silence her. Russia is the most dangerous place for reporters in Europe because of the prominent role organized crime plays in protecting the business oligarchs, 17 of whom are billionaires, in a country where over 40 million people live below the poverty line. Yet once revealed we still choose to continue pursuing living and repeating lies, be they old avoidances or catchy sound bites.

In the first year of the new millennium, 2001, 37 journalists were killed doing their job, according to the Committee to Protect Journalists. An increase of 13 from 2000.

The kidnap and brutal murder of *The Wall Street Journal* reporter Daniel Pearl during America's post September 11 War on Terrorism was a 21st century reminder of the risks correspondents take in pursuit of the truth. Pearl was the ninth Western journalist killed in the war since the war in Afghanistan started.

The fact that Pearl's throat was slit because he was a Jew after he was forced to say "My mother is a Jew, I am a Jew" was also a reminder of the anti-Semitism still lingering in the world today from the ongoing Crusades.

The Iraq War was considered a Crusade by many Arab journalists covering the conflict for Arab satellite news networks. When their blood was spilt by coalition attacks, many were convinced that the attacks were deliberate to silence the Arab point of view. The fact is war correspondents do sacrifice their lives to bring us the facts and die with their fellow journalistic brothers and sisters of all religions and nationalities who come in harm's way. The Iraq War took the lives of journalists from Australia, Britain, Iran, Iraq, Germany, Spain, Ukraine and the U.S.

America's Sexkateers

At the time of the Clinton impeachment, there was a real hysterical run of confessions from politicians about their sexcapades. They'd do it on camera, forcing you to look at them and making you wince. Affairs are not confined to American presidents. Democrat Wilbur Mills, the powerful Chairman of the Ways and Means Committee, made a public spectacle of himself. Republican Congressman Dan Burton acknowledged he sired an illegitimate son, Congressman Henry Hyde admitted to an adulterous affair as did Republican Congresswoman Helen Chenoweth. The ultimate hypocrisies were House Speaker-designate Bob Livingstone's admission of infidelity on more than one occasion, and House Speaker Newt Gingrich's affair with a congressional aide while persuading his hypocritical fellow congressmen to impeach the president for having an affair with an intern.

American sexual hypocrisy was showcased on America's center stage during the Clinton impeachment. A president lying about his sexual relations with an intern. A speaker of the house leading the impeachment charge expressing moral indignation while having an illicit affair with a congressional aide, and a married preacher, father of five consoling the president while impregnating one of his staffers. Bill, Newt, and Jesse are America's poster boys for sexual hypocrisy. The three sexkateers. They each represent different hypocritical American constituencies.

That's why you have to love Larry Flynt, who took out a full page ad in the Washington Post offering up to one million dollars to anyone who could prove an adulterous affair with a Congressman, Senator or other prominent official and tell the story exclusively to *Hustler.* He managed to flush out Bob Livingstone's hypocrisy – bearing in mind the slight inconsistency with his "belief" that everyone has a right to privacy.

Congressman Gary Condit's new millennium admission of adulterous affairs with an intern and flight attendant only re-confirmed what America and the world already know and practice. What we are talking about is hypocrisy in its highest form. People always lie about sex – to get sex, during sex, after sex, about sex. Why perpetuate the PC myth and veneer in a politically incorrect hypocritical world?

Sexual Parallels

Hong Kong in the mid to late 1800s was just like the frontier towns of America's Wild West. Men far outnumbered women. Consequently, licensed brothels, venereal disease and mistresses became a way of life. In 1872, the year of the first reliable census in Hong Kong, there were 3,264 European men, and only 669 European women living in the Colony together with 78,484 Chinese men and 22,837 Chinese women. With such a small female population it is not surprising that there was a large number of brothels. From 1857-1889, in order to prevent the spread of venereal disease, brothels were licensed and all prostitutes were required to have a weekly inspection at Lock Hospital. However, the licensing of brothels was considered immoral in Victorian England and the Secretary of State demanded that this practice should cease. The Governor, Sir William Des Voeux (1887-1891), supported by the military and naval authorities and the Executive and Legislative Councils, tried to resist the instruction. He failed. Consequently by 1897, half the soldiers in the British garrison were being treated for venereal disease. With no brothels the European male population simply acquired Chinese mistresses. They were known as "Downhomers" by the British troops. During the siege of Hong Kong in 1941, these girls helped their men on the battlefield by carrying ammunition and later, after the Japanese victory, at great risk to themselves, they stood outside the prisoner of war camps and threw food over the wire to the British prisoners. The grateful troops called them the "Angels of Wanchai".

There was a post-World War II super-active Suzie Wong era in Wanchai, when commercial sex was rife. It declined after the Vietnam War. Chinese bar girls were replaced by Filipina and Thai girls. They are not cheerful hookers. Many look like they swallowed a lemon. Today Wanchai's discos are crowded with Filipina amahs (domestic servants) looking for husbands, and husbands looking for Filipina amahs. Permanent relationships have largely replaced casual commercial sex. These amateur mistresses are a far greater threat to marriages than the odd late night drunken sexual encounter with a prostitute. Sound familiar?

Abusive Hypocrisy

We must always keep in mind that character assassination of public figures for sexual infidelity gets the assassin media exposure, sells newspapers and gets TV ratings, regardless of the consequences to the assassinated or country.

Anthony Lewis wrote a timely editorial in *The New York Times* on Clinton's impeachment hearing. "Most of the Western world sees what is happening in America these days as a kind of madness". House Republicans would not have started the impeachment process, the *Financial Times* of London said, if they "had the health of their government and the international community at heart."

Governor Ventura reminds us that: "We're supposed to critique our government; the Founding Fathers designed it that way. We're supposed to be skeptical of our elected officials, and we're supposed to keep a close eye on them. That's healthy and necessary for a democratic society. But there's a huge difference between skepticism and cynicism. We cross the line when we relentlessly tear our leaders down, when we literally go hunting for stories to ruin them. That kind of behavior doesn't serve anybody...Whenever the public isn't involved with its government, it creates a climate where abuse of power can flourish." How much more abuse do We need?

Supreme Court Justice Louis Brandeis wrote in 1928: "The greatest dangers to liberty lurk in insidious encroachment by men of zeal, well-meaning but without understanding."

On a flight from Beijing to Hong Kong during the Clinton impeachment debate, I struck up a conversation with my seatmate, Michael Hennig, the managing director of Barmag, a German textile machinery manufacturer. Michael could not believe how obsessive Americans are about sex. "My mother is 65 and highly moral," he volunteered. "She is very conservative and a typical German woman of her generation. Even she says, enough. Who cares how he held the cigar? People are losing respect. There are more important issues."

"Read these letters to the editor," Michael continued as he handed me *Newsweek*. "Look, letters from Greece, France, Denmark, Germany, Indonesia, Bangladesh, Czech Republic, Norway, England and California, all expressing their disgust and disbelief at America and what it was putting itself through." A typical letter from Jeremy Saxon in Prague read: "My American friends here in Europe are doing something now that I have not heard of since the Vietnam era. They are pretending to be Canadian. It is not that we are ashamed of our president. What they and I are ashamed of are the venality of the Republican Party, the spinelessness of our Congress and the shameless idiocy of Kenneth Starr's entire campaign. Is the president the only member of the government still concerned with running the country?"

Katherine Stanitsa wrote from Athens: "Now that Americans have purified their society by leading the sacrificial sheep to the altar of their supreme hypocrisy, they can lead the rest of the world back to the future." The Americans and the British get the Greeks very hot under the panty-elastic.

Adultery is still a crime, albeit the law against it is rarely enforced, in 27 states. If infidelity does not break as many marriages as it used to, does it make sense to still treat adulterers as criminals? Never mind throwing presidents out of office. New jails would have to be built in every township across America. The largest would probably wind up in Washington, DC. So why perpetuate the hypocrisy? Why legislate fake morality and then gasp at people having real orgasms?

Continued Media Shortcomings
Why does the press in the States repeatedly proclaim the brutal military suppression of the Falun Gong and other religious practices and play up the lack of human rights and religious freedom in China, while deliberately ignoring human rights, shareholder rights, taxpayer rights violations by the U.S. government and religious intolerance at home in America? What about the religious violence in India and Indonesia that was ignored until after thousands of innocents were slaughtered and the stories could no longer be suppressed?

The financial engineering of the Enron Board and management brought to light how meaningless audited financial statements can be. This was no different from the savings and loan scandals of the 1980s. Well-connected political companies that donate millions of their shareholders' dollars to political campaigns and loan their company jets to presidential candidates who win and then dictate America's energy or financial policies that are well-crafted by spin doctors and lobbyists are rarely challenged by the press. In fact the media were preoccupied making CEOs celebrity superstars. Celebrities that they later had to shoot down when the truth could no longer be overlooked.

Jack Welch is the epitome. A superstar of the media's post 9/11 schizoid U-turn. Most of the press was preoccupied with the Bill Clinton and Gary Condit sex scandals because they were a lot more interesting than audited financial statements that failed to fully disclose the truth. Bethany McLean, a *Fortune* magazine reporter, was the only reporter who had the tenacity and perseverance to question and challenge Enron's financials. "The company remains largely impenetrable to outsiders," she wrote in the March 5, 2001, issue of the magazine. McLean took the time to check Enron's Form 10-K required annual filing with the Securities and Exchange Commission. There were "strange transactions", "erratic cash flow" and huge debt. "It made you wonder, if their business was so phenomenally profitable, why they had to be adding debt at such a rapid rate," she asked. Why did all the rest of the main street media overlook these basic reporting fundamentals? Why wasn't any business publication or electronic media outlet really tracking long term the company, stock and debt that so many company employees and U.S. taxpayers were invested in?

The U.S. media which are quick to criticize China and other countries for their human rights abuses were unusually silent about the way Taleban and al-Qaeda prisoners were held and treated in their Guantanamo prison cells.

For the U.S. government and media to argue that the war against terrorism is a fight for justice and then deny justice to the vanquished is unpalatable and unacceptable in the 21st century. "This will strengthen those who believe the U.S. uses human rights as a political tool against those who oppose it, but is willing to flout those rights when its own national interest is involved," Thomas Abraham of the *South China Morning Post* proclaimed after the pictures of the chained, kneeling, manacled, blindfolded prisoners flashed on the TV monitors in the FCC.

"As we strive to create a world order based on the rule of law rather than the law of the jungle, the U.S. bears a particular responsibility in demonstrating that it too is bound by these laws, otherwise it risks losing the moral high ground it has occupied since September 11," Abraham continued. Otherwise, the law of the jungle prevails. The FCC cynics, including Abraham, argue that the world's only superpower can do and say pretty much what it wants.

The American press also overlooked Indonesia, the most populous Muslim country in the world, where there was truly a brutal military dictatorship that slaughtered Catholics in East Timor and Muslim fundamentalists in Aceh and allowed ethnic Chinese to be brutalized for Indonesia's failures until after President Suharto stepped down. Christians are still massacred as the Christmas bombings during Christmas prayers in the closing year of the 20th century reminded us. The fact that they had Muslim ornaments on their Christmas trees didn't help. Massacres the military intelligence knew about but decided not to stop. The continued annual massacres in the 21st century are a constant reminder of the long road we have to journey to find global religious tolerance.

The mismanaged perception in America was that Indonesia was a stable economic country that was good for American business. Time has again proven that slickly managed misperception can only do so much for a finite amount of time if the fundamentals being portrayed are not real. Indonesia could not sustain its corrupt, nepotistic dictatorial leadership. Those Americans at home, un-familiar with Asia, who had Indonesia painted as a hard-working ally realized they were lied to – officially, again. This point was really brought home after September 11 when Indonesia's President Megawati Sukarnoputri, the first foreign head of state to visit Washington after the terrorist attack and sympathize with America, went on to denounce America's war on the Taleban and Osama bin-Laden and his al-Qaeda network in a well-publicized speech in Indonesia's national mosque. The Bali bombings of October 12, 2002, changed both America's misperception and the Indonesian government's attitude towards terrorism.

The fact is that Indonesia has the potential to become Asia's Yugoslavia.

With its predominantly Muslim population of over 230 million, it will make Yugoslavia with a population of a mere 10 million look like a geopolitical lovefest.

Wimar Witoeler, the spokesperson for Indonesia's democratically elected President Wahid, is a refreshing spin-doctor. "I can say with all the honesty I can convey here that this man is a good guy. I can also say that my man does not have the competence to govern." Shouldn't some American career politicians spokespersons be saying the same? How about some of the Saudi leadership's spokesmen?

Like Indonesia, Saudi Arabia, Algeria, Egypt and many of the Gulf States are portrayed as good for American business. Their brutality and repressive regimes are overlooked because, like Indonesia, they have a lot of oil. In fact their leadership is more systematically cruel than China or Indonesia put together. The Saudi leadership, like those in all oil-rich Gulf states, is above the law.

The Saudi airline hijacked to Baghdad the last year of the 20th century brought the Saudi abuses to the world's attention. The hijackers called for an inquiry into human rights abuses in Riyadh and slammed the regime as being under United States hegemony. Saudi Arabia has not yet been fully exposed to the world for what it is. When it is it will implode. The consequences will be dire because it houses Islam's holiest and most contested shrines.

The rapes in Indonesia are at least the results of religious and political riots. The rapes and abductions that take place in Saudi Arabia and the Gulf States are habitual. Overseas maids and female workers are repeatedly complaining about being subjected to sexual slavery. Beautiful women and girls get abducted off the street by the powerful ruling families and are kept as sexual prisoners at the will of their hosts. Taleban abducted women for sexual slavery for their military leaders in Afghanistan or wealthy Arabs in the Gulf states. These royal families are above the law. Some of the stories I have heard make Monicagate look like amateur hour.

Like Saudi Arabia, Indonesia and the Gulf States, Egypt's autocratic ruler Hosni Mubarak is kept in power by the U.S. government with an annual $2 billion taxpayer aid bill while he encourages his state-controlled clerics and media to promote the anti-American propaganda of the Islamic fundamentalist extremists. Anti-American and anti-Jewish slogans are wrapped in pro-fundamentalist mis-information campaigns by the official newspaper and media outlets controlled by the government. Why doesn't the media point this out to *We the Apathetic People?* Why aren't Americans told more about the repressive totalitarian dictatorship that exists in Egypt? A country with no free elections, no human rights, freedom of expression or religion. Muslim fundamentalists, the true believers, are hunted down.

Granted Egypt has endured Islamic terror attacks – from the 1981 assassination of President Anwar Sadat to the death of 58 tourists in Luxor in 1997. Is that reason enough to hunt down all true believers and suspend basic human rights?

Egypt gave America Mohammed Atta. An educated engineer from a well-to-do family who like many of his fellow university graduates in Saudi Arabia, Egypt and throughout the Arab and Muslim world is frustrated and annoyed at the suppressive, corrupt and weak regimes he lives under because of America's continued financial and military support. Contrary to global patterns in Africa, Asia and Latin America, almost every Arab country today is less free than it was in the 1970s. This fuels the anger and frustration of both the educated and illiterate unemployed masses.

It is just another example of decadent and evil whimsy in Arab autocracy. In fact, though there are variously ruthless regimes in predominantly Muslim countries, there are very few governments which are Islamic – despite the managed misperception of the U.S. government that the whole Muslim world is about to charge with weapons of mass destruction. Iraq's President Saddam Hussein was utterly secular and would kill a Muslim cleric as fast as a Kurd or American. The North African countries, including Egypt, are secular governments – except Libya which is simply unpredictable. Algeria has a military dictatorship in place, with U.S. support to prevent an elected Islamic government from coming in. The Palestinians are highly secular – as is monarchist Jordan and socialist Syria. The only fundamentalist regime is in Iran – and that is under pressure. Iranians and Afghans hate each other. Both however would string up the royal rulers of the Gulf and Saudi Arabia – as well as Jordan.

Nobel laureate V.S. Naipaul, in his book *Beyond Belief,* points out, "Islam, although supposedly a universal religion, is thoroughly imbued with Arab culture, in much the same way that Christianity, and Catholicism in particular, is inextricably linked to Greco-Roman civilization."

Americans want to learn more about their Muslim terrorist enemy. They can only do so if the media devote more time to history, culture and religion. The truth. The facts. Not media bites that come back and bite us where the sun doesn't shine.

Office of Strategic Influence
The announcement that the U.S. Defense Department was going to open a propaganda office of disinformation modelled on the failed Soviet model was regarded as a real hoot by the denizens of the FCC Main Bar. The fact that the colossal U.S. media machine could not counter the propaganda pumped out in Muslim countries that convinced their citizens that the U.S. was to blame for both the terrorist attacks of September 11 and the 21st century crusade against Islam in Afghanistan and Iraq was understandably ironic. The fact that it was being geared up to confront Iraq and Saddam Hussein because of the lack of support of America's repressive oil-supplying dictatorships made the criticism and humor that much more painful. The idea of setting up a disinformation Arab propaganda bureau in the footsteps of the Voice of America Arab broadcasts was so completely trashed one was embarrassed to be an American.

The laughter and ridicule got louder when the story that the U.S. Defense Department was going to give the coveted war access denied to the press to a new reality television show. The tentatively titled "Military Diaries Project" which will put digital cameras in the hands of soldiers to tell it and show it like it is was highly suspect and unanimously accused of being bogus.

No one questions the legitimate military tactic of disinformation to mislead and deceive the enemy as the allied forces did before the invasion of Normandy in World War II or during the Gulf War against Saddam Hussein's Iraq. Entertainment and disinformation propaganda of no military utility, however, almost knocked people off their bar stools.

Freedom of the Press

Americans have a fundamental constitutional right to know what is happening on the war front. A front where their fellow Americans are fighting to uphold the values America stands for. Reading about war correspondent Doug Struck of the *Washington Post* being held at gunpoint by U.S. soldiers for doing his job on the front lines in Afghanistan and being told that "If you go further, you would be shot," and the horror of Daniel Pearl being murdered by Muslim extremists for doing his job, really brought into question how America's freedoms differ from those of its enemies at war in Afghanistan. Wars that are financed by the American taxpayer. Sometimes both sides of the conflict! Since when have the people who put up the finance not had the right to know what is happening with their money? Is this a new 21st century New World Disorder phenomenon? What happened to the "Golden Rule?" He who has the gold rules. Don't the funds in the treasury belong to *We the People?*

Before September 11 news organizations cut staffs and downsized or eliminated foreign bureaus. "At TV networks and local stations and at most of the nation's 1,500 newspapers, foreign coverage was an embarrassing joke. The upshot was that the public was shortchanged and totally unprepared for the war against terrorism. Now, many news organizations must lean heavily on local stringers and green reporters," said Marvin Kalb, a former television news correspondent.

After September 11 the government decided to censor all news about the war. To make matters worse, the press was constrained from questioning or criticizing the government for fear of being labeled unpatriotic. Kalb noted that "It is uncharacteristically muted, cautious, ready (however reluctant) to play ball with the White House for what the Constitution calls the 'common defense'. While understandable at the moment, is such a course of collaboration wise in the long run?"

First the media are barred from covering the war against terrorism in Afghanistan. Then they are urged to "exercise judgment" in publishing or broadcasting possible "coded messages" and propaganda from Osama bin-Laden. Why? Was it really a danger to America and the campaign against terror or was it because the White House was losing the public relations campaign? Osama bin-Laden's guerrilla media warfare was just as effective against the White House media machine as he was against the U.S. security machine and that was embarrassing.

The rationale for the media clampdown is that news coverage is a threat to the security of military operations. The fact is that many military officials blamed the media and what they perceived as negative reporting as a major reason large segments of the public never supported the war in Vietnam. In Vietnam, journalists were largely able to go when and where they wanted, often hitching rides on helicopters to go from unit to unit in any part of the country. And they were able to report what they wanted without submitting anything to censors.

Since then, the military has attempted to limit what information the public gets, much as it did during World War II, when censorship was a way of life for all correspondents. It is easy to blame the media for America's military failure in Vietnam. However, by remaining in denial, Americans only allow the military to get away with their shortcomings and the need to carefully examine the merits of any war.

Joe Galloway, a journalist who received the Bronze Star for rescuing wounded soldiers under fire in the Ia Drang Valley in 1965, and found fame in co-writing *We Were Soldiers Once...and Young* with Lieutenant General Harold G. Moore about the first major battle between U.S. and Viet Cong forces, sums it up best.

"A generation of officers emerged from the searing, bitter, orphaned war looking for someone to blame for the failures manifest in our nation's defeat in Vietnam. Many chose to blame the media...," Galloway, who coincidentally arrived in Vietnam to relieve UPI's Hong Kong Bureau Chief Charlie Smith, said.

The reality is that the experience of war will create bonds between reporters and officers that cannot be broken, as was so vividly portrayed by *We Were Soldiers*. War coverage is real. Politicians and generals may not like it. Nevertheless, that does not mean their financial backers, *We the People,* are not entitled to know about a war, or better yet, do something about the political and military leaders who do their utmost that we don't! Listening to war correspondents talk to military officers they have covered in battle has convinced me that the best friends that combat-tried warriors have are the reporters that covered them. This is something the non-combat experience post-Vietnam officers do not realize because of the "Vietnam syndrome".

During the first Gulf War a press operation was set up in Saudi Arabia, known as the Joint Information Bureau. There pool reporters were forced- fed whatever the military decided was newsworthy. The key players at the time were Secretary of Defense Dick Cheney and the Chairman of the Joint Chiefs of Staff Colin Powell. The public was led to believe America was winning a very smart and efficient air war with the arsenal of smart bombs at its disposal. It wasn't until months after the war that Americans learned the bombs weren't as smart as we were led to believe. In fact many missed their targets.

The grossest mis-reporting to the American public during the Gulf War was the scene repeatedly broadcast of the Highway of Death with its scenes of mile after mile of shattered and burning vehicles and tanks on Highway 8. The film gave the impression that thousands of Iraqi soldiers had been killed along with thousands of innocent civilians. America thought it had been a turkey shoot.

Had reporters or camera crews been allowed to film the area rather than just rebroadcast the military film, the public would have found out that most of the occupants of the vehicles had fled to the desert before the bombing and that in fact what people were seeing on their TV screens was a Highway of dead Toyotas in which no more than 150 to 200 people died, Galloway said. Any wonder Saddam Hussein still has his army?

The same happened in Afghanistan. The Defense Department released a grainy video of American paratroopers and Rangers preparing to attack a Taleban stronghold with all the appropriate adulatory tag lines on how the ground war had started. The truth was the attack "came close to disaster" because of the lack of proper intelligence, which forced the Rangers into rapid retreat to avoid a disaster similar to Somalia. The full details of the disaster of the first Afghan ground mission are still unknown.

What is known is that stray bombs killed innocent civilians, U.S. forces failed to rescue rebel Afghan leader Abdul Haq before he was executed by the Taleban and that Osama bin-Laden and the Taleban are tough opponents. This was brought to our attention by the enemy's media machine and then confirmed by the White House. The fact that Osama and his henchmen got away was reluctantly admitted to months later.

The U.S. repeatedly tried to stop Qatar-based Al-Jazeerah from broadcasting from Afghanistan. When the political pressure on Qatar failed to stop the broadcasts the U.S. just bombed Al-Jazeerah's Kabul office.

Myrna Whitworth, program director of the Voice of America, was criticized by the government for airing an interview with Taleban military leader Mullah Mohammad Omar. State Department spokesman Richard Boucher, a former U.S. Consul-General in Hong Kong, confirmed his agency had attempted to stop the interview from being aired. At a briefing for reporters he said, "We don't think the head of the Taleban belongs on this radio station." Whitworth spoke at the FCC shortly after she was reprimanded. "I think in a democratic society where you have thinking people, you have to have a press that forgives all points of view. Sometimes those views may be opposing the government. But as long as you keep things in context and you are responsible, that's the role of the journalist in a free society," she said.

The U.S. closed down the Palestinian independent weekly *Hebron Times* in 2002 because it was critical of Israel and U.S. policy towards the Palestinians. How is muzzling journalists different than silencing them with a bullet for reporting the truth? When Martin O'Hagan, a Northern Ireland journalist, was assassinated for writing about paramilitaries, gun running and drug gangs, the foreign minister of the Irish Republic said: "It was an attack on a dedicated and hard-working journalist, and it also represented an assault on one of the fundamental principles of any democratic society – an independent and unfettered media."

The Bush administration, like all future American administrations, must recognize that in a democratic society the press is not the enemy. It is *We the People's* valuable and necessary ally, if treated with the trust that its role in a free society warrants.

Before September 11, the President's energy policy task force, presided over by Vice President Dick Cheney, placed a premium on secrecy; it resisted efforts to disclose what its members were talking about, whom they were meeting with and what advice they were receiving on the crucial issue from industry lobbyists.

Michael Getler, in a very astute opinion piece in the *Washington Post* points out that since the September 11 terrorist attacks and the October anthrax outbreaks, the FBI and Immigration and Naturalization Service agents have arrested and detained more than a thousand people, a roundup essentially conducted in total secrecy. The government declines to say, with few exceptions, who the detainees are, how many are considered to be material witnesses, where they are being held, what their nationalities are, why they were picked up, what the status of their cases is and how many have been released. No journalist wants to "jeopardize any lives or blow any covert operation," said Owen Ullman of *U.S.A Today.* "But not to have any reporters anywhere near the action makes it kind of hard to do your job. It leaves us stuck trusting other sources that aren't necessarily reliable."

The media and the military roles converged and compromised in Iraq when embedded reporters gave up independence and objectivity for access. Ted Koppel, who also covered the Vietnam War, said it best. "When I was covering the Vietnam War in 1967, we had a lot of access as well. But this time around, we have the kind of access to leadership that was not possible back then. And we now have an intersection between absolute access and the ability to send messages instantaneously."

Secrecy can cut both ways. Some is essential. Too much can undermine success, especially if things go wrong along the way as they usually do.

Partisan Media
Reports of Palestinians dancing in the streets when they heard

of the bombings of the Twin Towers and the Pentagon were downplayed. The Palestinian Authority claimed the footage was staged and fabricated and scared media outlets from airing them, even after the film's authenticity had been verified by both CNN and Reuters, whose cameramen filmed the scenes in East Jerusalem. The e-mails claiming the footage was bogus are a testament to the power of the Internet. A second tape of celebrations in the West Bank was never broadcast. The Jerusalem bureau chief of The Associated Press was told by Palestinian officials that they could not guarantee the safety of the cameraman if the film was distributed, according to an AP dispatch. A third AP video was confiscated by authorities and returned with portions deleted.

The Reuters cameraman, Eli Berizon, vehemently denied the e-mailed bogus claim. He said that he and two cameramen and a reporter from The Associated Press came upon the Palestinian celebrants on Sultan Suleiman Street in East Jerusalem. "Whatever happened, we shot. We are not involved in making the news, staging the news. I've never done that and I never intend to," Berizon said.

Yet scenes of Israel isolating Arafat in Ramallah and destroying bomb making factories in Jenin were repeatedly aired by many global news-networks. Why is it that the media repeatedly succumb to portraying the plight of the Palestinians as victims and the self-defense role of Israel as aggression? Could it be the petro-dollar advertising budgets or is it leftover anti-Semitism?

The White House has some justification and public support for its censorship policies. In today's America, "the media actually get in the way of efforts to deal with important issues," James Fallows asserts in *Breaking the News*. The media sabotage crucial initiatives such as health care reform and scare people away from public service by focusing on scandals and spectacle and not on critical issues. *Washington Post* media writer Howard Kurtz aims at a much easier target in *Hot Air*: America's new "talkathon culture". He surveys a wide assortment of pundits, commentators, and hucksters, including some who pose in journalistic garb to dress up their sensationalism. The price? "The national conversation has been coarsened, cheapened, reduced to name calling and finger pointing and bumper sticker sloganeering."

Surely it is one of the strangest things our information age has spawned, this cadre of People Who Pronounce. They go on television after any big political event, and on shows scheduled just for them, and deliver judgments – scolding, deploring failures, predicting someone's demise. And then, without apology or even acknowledgement, however howlingly wide of the mark they've been before, they return to do it again – just as pompous, superior and smug. I am convinced that these Broadcast Bombasts are one reason the public dislikes and distrusts the media.

Actor Sean Penn summed up many peoples' feelings when he accused talk-show hosts as being just as despicable as terrorists. "I think that people like the Howard Sterns, the Bill O'Reillys and to a lesser degree the bin-Ladens of the world are making a horrible contribution," Penn said.

Think of some of the pronouncements! Most famously, we have Sam Donaldson's solemn declaration on ABC's *This Week* at the beginning of the Monica Lewinsky scandal that the remainder of Bill Clinton's presidency would be measured "not in weeks, but days". What a feast such airy speculation makes for the talk shows and late-night comics. The armchair generals and military experts pontificating on the progress of the war in Afghanistan and Iraq seemed to get everything wrong. It's a good thing they retired.

"On its face, this has the look of a victory for President Clinton," sniffed *The Wall Street Journal* editorial page the day after the Kosovo peace deal in 1999. The editors were unable to hide their irritation that the U.S. would not be humiliated after all, that NATO would survive, and that America had done good in the world at little cost to itself.

Critics of the Kosovo project – some of whom said we should stay out, some of whom said we should go in with ground troops, many of whom managed to say both these things, and all of whom predicted that the Serbs would never cave in – are bitter. President Slobodan Milosevic betrayed them! Doesn't he watch the Sunday talk shows? Doesn't he know that air power never works? Has he forgotten that he represents a centuries-old tradition of ethnic violence? Where is that quagmire he was supposed to produce? Listening to retired General Wesley Clark, the former NATO commander, about what was really going on in the Pentagon and Washington during the Kosovo air war, makes it a wonder that America didn't get bogged down in another quagmire.

The intense suspicion of President Clinton by the Washington spin-doctors and the punditocracy and the extreme partisanship of the Republican congressional leadership heavily influenced the public dialogue on Kosovo. No one called Vietnam a quagmire for five years. Kosovo was declared a quagmire after about five days. Press suspicion and Republican partisanship are reasonable enough, but there ought to be a sense that criticism of a military operation in progress should meet a higher standard of seriousness because such criticism does aid the enemy, whether it is intended to or not.

It is no longer just the public that is upset with how the media cover events. A survey of 552 journalists and news media executives, conducted by the Pew Research Center, found that 40 percent of journalists working for national news organizations and 55 percent of those working for local outlets said that news reports were increasingly marred by factual errors and sloppy reporting.

The Aspen Daily News refusal to cover the Kobe Bryant story because "It's just gossip" is to be applauded. CBS's Dan Rather has become the media's most vocal confessor. After he and his colleagues declared Al Gore the winner he admitted: "We've lived by the crystal ball and learned to eat so much broken glass tonight that we're in critical condition." His reluctance and refusal to jump on the media bandwagon to cover the disappearance of Chandra Ann Levy after Congressman Gary Condit admitted to their affair is to be also applauded. "Basically, we decided that we needed to show restraint with this story," he said. "What we were seeing, what we were hearing, wasn't always solid. Often it was rumor or gossip. We chose not to report that until we had something that we thought was important to the story." "Without passing judgment on anybody else," he added, "I've tried to stand for what I believe in – decent responsible journalism." Isn't it time that all journalists do so again in the 21st century?

Other criticism cited by the Pew survey was that the media were out of touch with the public (57 percent of national journalists and 51 percent of local ones) and that the media had a growing credibility problem (30 percent of national journalists, 34 percent of local). "People don't trust us the way they used to, and they have good reason not to," a local TV assignment editor said in the survey. "A lot of stuff now is slanted toward sensationalism."

Former Nixon aide Charles Colson, who discovered Jesus in a prison ministry he founded after being convicted for obstructing justice in the Watergate scandal, is a columnist in the evangelical magazine *Christianity Today*. He attracted yet again more attention to his misrepresentations among FCC media watchers in his column "Post-Truth Society', in which he decried the ubiquity of lying in America and "dealing in deceit". The column appeared under his photo and byline. It turned out he never wrote the column. The author was Anne Morse. Colson only reluctantly acknowledged the truth.

Richard Nixon, who himself had been subject to justifiable media criticism, quotes Walter Lippman's classic *The Public Philosophy* to justify his criticism of the press. "The right to utter words whether or not they have meaning and regardless of their truth could not be a vital interest to a great state but for the presumption that they are the chaff with the utterance of true significant words. But when the chaff of silliness and deception is so voluminous that it submerges the kernels of truth, freedom of speech may produce such frivolity that it cannot be preserved against the restoration of order and decency."

Changing Attitudes

Laws in many states define sex between two consenting unmarried adults as a misdemeanor. Not just homosexuals, but heterosexuals as well! When it comes to infidelity, the laws apply to married couples in more states than you can shake a dildo at. With monogamy becoming close to a joke, and marriage, theologically the weakest of the sacraments, in an utter shambles, it might be prudent for the state not to just change laws but simply repeal them and put an end to big government in the bedroom. That is one question of size that you don't want between the sheets. This should have immediate philosophical appeal to the Republicans. On sex laws, an abolitionist Congress would be a great start to the New World Order.

During Monicagate, Britain had its own serial sex scandals in the good ol' English tradition. At first it looked like just another chapter in Britain's sex, power and tabloid drama. A Labor Party minister – married with a daughter – resigned after being robbed near one of London's best known gay-cruising zones. The rituals of political humiliation quickly followed. The tabloids did daily battle in three-inch headlines. There was a resignation letter to Prime Minister Tony Blair, a red-eyed press conference, a career in ruins. Blair's Trade and Industry Secretary was outed on television by a respected political columnist, who is also gay. The following week, Blair's Agriculture Minister announced he was gay after a former lover went to the tabloids to offer his story for a price.

Was Blair's cabinet a shambles? His government at risk? Not exactly. Only ex-prime minister John Major was ashamed of his affair with ministerial colleague Edwina Currie that lasted from 1984-1988. Middle England – that mythical region populated by the middle-aged, the middle-incomed and the middle-brow – didn't seem to care whom its politicians went to bed with. Two days after his announcement, Agriculture Minister Nick Brown was stomping around in gumboots, visiting farmers who told him they didn't mind if he was gay as long as he did something about the sorry state of British agriculture and didn't shag the livestock. Peter Mandelson, the Trade and Industry Secretary, refused to discuss his sexuality – and the papers let him be. In fact, by the end of the week, Rupert Murdoch's *Sun,* London's most over-the-top anti-gay tab, vowed not to out people in its pages, except in cases of "overwhelming public interest". "We recognize," said the editorial, "that public attitudes are changing."

It's up to the media to keep us informed. Not misinformed as Geraldo Rivera did on December 5, 2001, when he reported he had "walked over the spot where the friendly fire took so many of our men and the Mujahedin", when in fact he was hundreds of miles away. Governor Jessie Ventura asks, "If the quality of the information they give us is flawed, how then will we be able to make sound decisions?" This was confirmed by Geraldo himself as an embedded reporter during the Iraq War. He was expelled by the military for not making a sound decision. He disclosed and compromised a secret military operation while over-promoting himself to survive the ratings war.

This mistrust of the media may be a sign not only of America's growing maturity, but also of its loss of faith in heroes of all kinds. The DNA tests showing that Thomas Jefferson had an affair with a slave have not endangered his place in the pantheon of American political leaders. But the news does make him appear more human, and thus more Clintonesque.

As for the decline in the stature of journalists in America, recall the scene that ends the movie *All the President's Men*. Robert Redford and Dustin Hoffman, Hollywood's incarnations of Bob Woodward and Carl Bernstein, are pounding away at their typewriters while on a television screen Richard Nixon's presidency is seen to disintegrate.

Then, the media's power never seemed nobler. Today, its ability to shape events has never seemed more negligible. In Hong Kong, like America, the media and journalism are among the least respected professions. This was before it was discovered that John Ellis, director of the "Decision Desk" at Fox News, was George W's first cousin. Fox was the station that first projected Bush's Florida win. Ellis had spoken to Dubya and Bush's brother Florida Governor Jeb several times on election night. How much lower can the public's opinion of media get? Any wonder NBC's newscaster Tom Brokaw said, "We don't just have egg on our face – we have an omelet all over our suits."

A relief in a way and yet a sadness that in its frantic competition, the media shattered the mantle of the Fourth Estate. There is no political utility in continuing legislation for morality or sexual behavior. There is even less in reporting it incorrectly or negatively.

Sexual Reality
Polls repeatedly showed that as far as Americans are concerned, Clinton's alleged sex romps are irrelevant. Kevin Phillips wrote a great piece in the *Los Angeles Times*. "Who cares about whether

the president lied or the rich are getting too much, when mutual funds keep going up? Who cares about whether some White House aide got groped, when Americans bought or rented 600 million – yes, 600 million – 'adult' videos last year?

"Forget jokes about the first zipper. This guy is what the new America is all about....When the Lewinsky scandal broke and a few crazy Puritans started speculating about impeachment, Americans collectively pushed the 'hold' button. The Ozark Casanova's ratings actually rose 10 points, and so did the number of people who identified America as being on the 'right track'."

America is coming out of its sexual hang-up closet thanks to the web. The web has brought pornography from Times Square and sleazy back alleys to our finger tips at home. Privately. Discreetly. Makers of adult videos are the beneficiaries. How else can one explain why Americans spent almost $5 billion annually on adult videos – more than Hollywood's box office returns or the revenue from the U.S. music business? This is mainstream America buying! The global porn business is a $10 billion industry! The stories generated by Viagra and the rehiring of pink-slipped sexual animal Marvin Albert by Madison Square Garden to provide radio commentary for the New York Knicks basketball games and serve as host of MSG SportsDesk are confirmation of the Phillips story.

"Sexual morality has always been hypocritical. Not only in America but, historically, in Europe," FCC historian Arthur Hacker pronounced as he joined us for a round to enliven the already heated Clinton sexual debate. It is not unusual for FCC members to roam around the bar and converse, listen, or debate with fellow members on the subject at hand. It is an agricultural procedure called "harvesting bullshit". Arthur could win prizes for lecture lengths, without notes.

Creativity
Mark Twain, America's greatest storyteller and a seasoned journalist, said: "Ours is a useful trade, a worthy calling: with all its lightness and frivolity it has one serious purpose, one aim, one specialty, and it is constant to it – the deriding of shams, the exposure of pretentious falsities, the laughing of stupid superstitions out of existence; and that who so is by instinct engaged in this sort of warfare is the natural enemy of royalties, nobilities, privileges and

all kindred swindles, and the natural friend of human rights and human liberties."

To get rid of the hypocrisy in the media, politics and sex in the 21st century, we have to keep in mind Twain's admonition and honestly look at ourselves, our history and come to terms with reality constructively and creatively.

Many definitions limit creativity to an original work. That is part of the hypocritical conditioning we have come to accept. Creativity is an amalgam of skills and longings that are sometimes galvanized in response to dissatisfaction with things as they are, and sometimes out of a desire to celebrate things as they are. It is often a spontaneous, unconscious response – an outgrowth of play or fun, for example – which you recognize as new, and value as such, only later, after reflection.

Anglo-American civilization particularly – unlike the Chinese-Latino – risks slow implosion from self-denial, managed perceptions and social hypocrisies. To flourish rather than decay, peoples and their leaderships have to bring honesty and creativity to social and political issues starting with sane soul-searching and extending that into the home, the community, into education and applying it to the power of the state. We are in danger of losing sight of that brief but explosive sentiment – "The Pursuit of Happiness."

Fran and Louis Cox, in their book *Conscious Life,* capture the meaning of creativity: "Creative energy seems to do its best work at the cutting edge, where things are unknown, fresh, new, different, and often risky. The adult self knows that this is okay and enriching. Adults understand that nothing inside them is really dangerous, even though some things may feel absolutely terrifying and may need to be approached slowly and with respect. In fact, creativity can be used to stifle creativity – used against itself. Grownups have been taught to fear their creative energy, except when it is applied to maintaining the status quo. It is paradoxical to think of creativity used for preventing change, but consider the creativity of grownups in coming up with rationalizations that allow them to maintain their unconsciousness about themselves and their harmful behaviors...

"Like consciousness, creativity is highly adaptable. It can be called upon to assist with anything."

La Rochefoucauld's aphorism is as timely in the 21st century as it was in the 17th: "Hypocrisy is the tribute vice pays to virtue."

Why does the government of *We the People* creatively omit to pursue our principles of democracy, freedom and human rights in the Arab world? Why just exert it on China? What about the freedom of the press at home in America about what taxpayers are paying for and our children dying for?

The creativity of political and religious leaders would better serve us if it was applied in the hot forge of truth and not in the maze of myth. The creative power within us cannot be divorced too long from self-knowledge, which is painful but once across the coals, it leads to a calmer society, at home and globally. A functional New World Order must become creative and leave fake morality and hypocrisy behind. Only then will life's pleasures have the orgasmic shiver they should.

Chapter Two

Living Cultural Contradictions
Brave New World - William Shakespeare

Beachcombers

During Christmas, New Year and Chinese New Year, it is not unusual to find many Hong Kongers, Chinese and expats, sunning in Thailand. "Rock fever" is a Hong Kong virus. Bourgeois residents leave the rock whenever they can. It is not unusual to run into friends and familiar faces in Thai restaurants, shops and beaches. Sometimes I feel like all my "glassmates" from the FCC have converged to cover *The Beach.*

On the Thai island of Koh Pha Ngan, the real *Temptation Island,* young Americans of all colors and religious beliefs gather and join Hong Kongers for the monthly Full Moon Party. Worlds collide and everybody loves everybody else. Or so it seems. But the reality is revealed when the drugs wear off: political anarchy, robbery, terrorism, violence and death. People dying for the good life America promises. No different than Washington DC, New York, Los Angeles, Miami, Anywhere, U.S.A. Worlds colliding and merging.

Murder and death dominate American culture and entertainment. A society gone insane. A society that creates "powder puff" hazing of girls with feces, pig parts and baseball bats while watching *Jackass: The Movie* and reading about Laci Peterson, the Green River serial killer, and exploits of Chante J. Mallard. Mallard was the woman who slammed her car into Gregory Biggs as he walked on a Texas highway. She drove home to her garage with him wedged in the glass. He was left there for three days to bleed to death while Chante sporadically visited him to apologize between her sex romps with her boyfriend who then helped her dispose of the body.

Astronauts' body parts and debris from the space shuttle Columbia rained over Texas, Louisiana and the western United States in early 2003 while America's career politicians and their spin doctors scripted the Iraq War. America was too busy absorbed voting for the "American Idol" to notice.

It is a country where white American supremacists introduced literacy tests, poll taxes, intimidation and lynching to disenfranchise minorities and then collaborated with Muslim extremists on 9/11 because they view the U.S. Government and its support of Israel as a greater threat to their freedom than the one posed by Islamic extremists. Shortly after the 9/11 attacks, Billy Roper, a former member of the neo-Nazi National Alliance, based in West Virginia, posted the following on the Internet: "We may not want them marrying our daughters, just as they would not want us marrying theirs...But anyone who is willing to drive a plane into a building to kill Jews is all right by me. I wish our members had half as much testicular fortitude."

It is a country where Timothy McVeigh's bizarre "state assisted suicide" was aired on closed circuit TV so all his victims' relatives could watch the execution. *Hannibal* and *Kill Bill* were the opening double bill to the grotesque America at the dawn of the 21st century.

Andrea Yates, the mother who drowned her five children, brought to the forefront a disturbing pattern developing in America. American families imploding. The six McGurkin children, one only eight years old, along with the Yates televised trial, expose the poverty and dysfunctionality of the world's wealthiest nation. Children in ragged clothing existing on a soupy diet of lily pads simmered in lake water over a camp fire. Living in a run-down home, deprived of water, electricity, sewer and telephone less than a mile from Garfield Bay, where pines sweep down to a lake dotted with yachts. The kind of neighborhood Luke Helder, the five-state mailbox bomber, grew up in. Americans searching and trying to come to grips with a New World dysfunctional community. A community that was awakened on September 11.

"I said that, on the day of the U.S. elections, I was going to do the same as the majority of the U.S. population: go to the beach," said Fidel Castro as he strolled the beach chatting with Americans. The political system in America is a dirty rocky beach that we don't enjoy, benefit from, participate in, appreciate, or understand. We don't because the lifeguards around us are restrictive career politicians whose only interest is self-serving their "beautiful imperialist" objectives, local, regional and global. They keep *We the Maids* off the beach so they can retain power at any cost. It doesn't matter if they operate in a one-party or a two-party system. Dictators and presidents both dictate and preside. They and their parties are so busy politicking to stay in power that they forgot the real interests and needs of *We the People.*

Walking on the white sands of Karon beach in Phuket with Austen, my one-year-old American-Chinese son, on my shoulders, I thoroughly relished the cool breeze and warm waves breaking on my feet. Deep breaths of fresh air cleared the pollution from my American city lungs. This was reminiscent of times I had with my now grown children, Alexandra and Jonas, when they were young in San Felipe, Mexico.

Looking into a cloudless Thai sky enjoying the sight of bare-breasted American beachcombers strolling or running through the surf, I couldn't help wonder why we can't clean up the political system in America so that it is as pristine as the Founding Fathers intended.

"Sir! Where are these women from?" Jessie, Austen's Filipina nanny, asked interrupting my daydream as she nodded towards a couple of well-endowed bare-breasted women holding hands and laughing as they walked by. "Florida, New Hampshire, Iowa, Washington, Virginia, all over the States," I replied as I picked Austen up off the sand and put him back on my shoulders. It struck me as ironic that here I was walking on a beach in Thailand with a fully clothed Filipina whose bare-breasted ancestors had probably been talked into wearing bras and clothes by the missionary forefathers of these walking American boobs.

I couldn't help laugh to myself at the stories I'd heard in Palau and throughout Micronesia and the Pacific Islands over the years about the early missionaries who were distracted by their bare-breasted congregates. They requested brassieres be sent along with the bibles "for the native women". In Hawaii, the religious Puritans went even further and banned surfing in 1821 because they thought it was an "immoral sport". Bras and bibles were eventually distributed to the island women who were told to wear them to church "out of respect for God". When Sunday arrived, the women were still bare-breasted. They had decided the garments had a better use as coconut carrier bags. I guess the great-granddaughters of those missionaries agree.

Why is it when Americans go on vacation, whether it's the coast of Spain, the Greek isles, Thailand, Mexico or the Caribbean, in addition to getting tanned, they live out their drug and sexual fantasies, screw like wired high bunnies and then go home and act like gabby Madonnas? What suppresses these natural human desires at home and allows them to erupt so naturally when away with strangers? Are they modern day missionaries of American democracy? They most certainly are democratic equal opportunity representatives.

Tools

When Austen, Jessie and I returned from our stroll on the beach, my wife Julia and her sister were trying on their newly acquired bathing attire from their morning shopping expedition. Damn, ladies look good with clothes on when you're boobed out!

We ordered room service and I went out on to the balcony to kick back and absorb some more rays. It was December 22, 1997, the end of a considerable year.

It had started in snow-covered Lake Tahoe in January where I went to spend some time with Jonas, my 22-year old U.S. Forest Service firefighter son. I didn't see much of him the year before because every time I was in the U.S. he was off fighting one of those West Coast fires of 1996. However, with the heavy snowfalls he had plenty of time on his hands so we decided to get together and catch up and watch the Super Bowl.

When Jonas decided to become a fireman he found out that, notwithstanding his scholastic and athletic ability, because he is a white male without a family tradition of firefighters, he could not even qualify to take the test because of affirmative action.

"Dad, how come your generation came up with these laws that really screw up the system? Why should people be judged or qualify for positions solely because of their background, race or ethnic origin rather than their ability?" Now there is an irony and generational U-turn.

What did happen to "meritocracy" in America? Yet when the U.S. Forest Service decided on an "open call" to hire in anticipation of the upcoming fire season, several thousand people showed up from all over the country to take the written and physical exams. He drove overnight to get there, showered and went straight to the exam hall. He not only made it, but made the top ten! When he wasn't fighting fires he was working construction as a finish carpenter in Tahoe.

The day after the Super Bowl he drove me to the airport in Reno to catch my connecting flight to San Francisco where I would catch my flight home to Hong Kong. We didn't talk much; it was 6:30 am and dark. We had had only a couple of hours of shut-eye. After watching the Super Bowl, we had eaten a leisurely dinner and spent the rest of the night talking and playing blackjack. We stopped at Home Depot in Reno where he got some tools and helped me select a BBQ to take back to Hong Kong. "Wish I could be there to help you assemble it," he said. "Me too, Jonas." We hugged, kissed and said our goodbyes. As I watched him drive away in his truck with its large built-in toolbox it dawned on me that we all have numerous political tools at our disposal. We just have to know when and where to use the right one.

Changes and Choices

There I was, on my way from sharing some beers with Jonas to giving a milk bottle to Austen. What different worlds my sons grew up in and inhabit. Raising children today is so much tougher than it used to be. Internet porn sites, hate sites, movies, music have all changed the world we live in.

Sex and violence are glorified. Janet Jackson's "Wardrobe Malfunction" is a millennium reminder. Sex, guns and death images are a way of life. When it comes to youth sports, parental "sideline rage" is part of the new dysfunctional "quality family time" in America. I used to coach Jonas's AYSO soccer teams. Granted

I got into some extended discussions with parents, but never arguments. Watching and listening to some parents when I went to watch Mike, my six-year-old grand nephew, play soccer in Santa Monica in 2001 was a real wake up call. Reading about the violence on America's playing fields today is disheartening. Four and five-year-old children watching a father being beaten to death at a hockey game in Massachusetts. Parents brawling at a T-ball game in Florida and 12 to 14-year-old football players being poisoned in Las Vegas.

Left to their own devices, children can easily live in isolation with their computers and televisions. Worrying and feeling guilty about their parental neglect, getting drowned, shot at school, or sexually abused. A 17-year study by Columbia University and Mount Sinai Medical Center in New York, which started tracking adolescents and their TV habits back in 1983, concluded that there is a definite correlation between hours spent watching TV and violent behavior. The average American child watches 25 hours of television a week, four more than the average Hong Kong child who, according to various youth surveys, watches close to three hours of television a day. Talking, reading and playing games around the family dining table instead of watching TV in the den can only benefit Americans in the 21st century.

One in five children who go online regularly has been approached by strangers for sex at least once! A report by the Crimes Against Children Research Center at the University of New Hampshire states that 19 percent of those surveyed said they had received at least one sexual solicitation in the past year. Only 10 percent of those solicitations were reported to the police. More depressing, a majority of children and parents surveyed said they did not know how to report an incident to authorities. A Pew Internet and American Life Project found that one in four of the young people reported being very upset and afraid because of the experience. Neither the presence of Internet filters nor parental monitoring of children's Internet use decreased the likelihood that a child would be sexually solicited by a stranger online.

Two thirds of American eight to 18-year-olds and one third of two to seven-year-olds have TVs in their bedroom. Yet only 55 percent of American parents have rules about TV viewing, according to the Institute on Media and the Family. The interaction with other children takes place primarily in the wired world, not in neighborhood streets or playgrounds. The knock on the door, the kid on the step asking, "Can Johnnie come out to play, please?" has almost fallen back into social history. To help kids build stronger social skills, parents have to pull the plug on TVs and computers.

One can't help but notice how the number of children interacting with one another has changed and decreased. Many are ignorant of basic social skills. They just don't know how to interact with each other. On the other hand, given a world of crack heads, half-way houses, gang cross-fires and sideline rage and youth sport poisoning, what parent would happily say to a child "All right, dear, out you go and play and be back by dinner."? Children can't even play cops and robbers with paper guns in school without taking a grim trip through the juvenile justice system because of school zero-tolerance policies.

It used to be a parent only had to limit the number of hours a child watched TV. Now it's TV and the computer! It is so easy for children to become computer-literate activists and socially withdrawn zombies. The art of conversation, play, and general community involvement are giving way to computerized body-pierced, dyed-hair robotics.

The same holds true in Hong Kong. Where young people name themselves Doctor, Alien and Chlorophyll. They have tea-colored hair and speak *mouh leih tau* (mad slang). They eat Thousand Island dressing-flavored pizza and collect Cartier watches and Mao badges. "Their top hobbies are praising Communist Party leaders and swapping 18k gold Garfields," the FCC's resident satirist, Nury Vittachi, points out.

Nury's interview with Professor Felice Lieh-Mak, Hong Kong's most famous psychiatrist, is revealing about the similarities between America and Hong Kong. Her response to one of his questions was not only an accurate analysis of Hong Kong but of America. "I think Hong Kong has a self-selecting population. The people who have managed to get here are tough, adventurous, freedom-loving. They stay here because they find it challenging and they like the fast life. People who want a slower pace of life leave

Hong Kong. So you see the system screens out people who are not competent to deal with life here."

Declaration of Independence

Hong Kong was all anyone could talk about in 1997. With the handover coming up at midnight on June 30, the Event of the Century seemed to be in every paper, magazine, news program and political commentary. Everyone seemed to be bitten by the buzz. "Are you going to stay there after the Chinese take over?" I heard the question so many times from American inquisitors that my answer became flippant but designed to elicit peoples' perceptions of Hong Kong. "Of course! Why not?" I would respond in an indignant tone. Their responses generally centered on concerns the Communist Chinese would deprive people of democracy, human rights, and religious freedoms, ruin the economy and the environment, overturn the simple flat tax system, and undermine political freedoms.

The last British Governor, Christopher Patten, or "Fatty Patty", was a master politician and "spinner". He convinced the world that he had brought forth a parliamentary model that the Chinese would screw up. He was toasted for his courage in Washington and all European capitals. Indeed, he had brought up a more representative legislature than had ever been before, even diminishing his own power. However, it was at a speed beyond all the agreements the Chinese had been led to expect would be honored so they did screw it up, like a dirty magazine.

Hong Kong has changed since the handover. But not as Patten or *Fortune* magazine predicted. It has changed for the better. It is redefining itself and the direction and course it should pursue in the New World Order. It has more political parties and organizations than America. Hong Kongers let their government and political leaders know their true feelings by protesting peacefully by the hundreds of thousands and making sure that the polls reflect their true concerns. Hong Kong has limitations on campaign contributions and a functional Electoral College. Shouldn't America likewise be redefining itself in the 21st century?

On the fourteen-hour flights back to Hong Kong I wondered what real freedoms, economic and political, do people in America really have? We live in the most regulated society on earth. Regulations, laws and the career politicians and bureaucrats that enforce them, cover everything from busing, affirmative action, sexual relations, morals, education, what one can breathe, eat, wear... You can't even think about questioning the IRS without being busted. In Hong Kong taxpayers are on the honor system. How good are any of the American tax, welfare, education, social, housing, health care, public transportation systems in comparison to those in Hong Kong? More significantly, which have the best prospects of getting better?

We the People have drifted away from the foundations laid down by our Founding Fathers. "The Magnificent Seven" as Joseph Ellis describes George Washington, John Adams, Thomas Jefferson, James Madison, Alexander Hamilton, Benjamin Franklin and Aaron Burr in his book Founding Brothers. We need a new Genesis. A new Basic Law, just like Hong Kong adopted upon the 1997 handover. Isn't it time America goes back to its own Genesis – the Constitution and Declaration of Independence? Isn't it time to adopt new Basic Laws relevant to the 21st century? Time for a Re-Declaration of Independence. Independence from career politicians. Independence from their lawyers and lobbyists. Independence from special interest groups. Independence from overbearing career bureaucrats.

Why continue to live in apathetic denial? We know career politicians lie and mislead us. They have perverted the language of the Constitution and Declaration of Independence to serve their selfish interests while we go about our daily lives doing nothing about it because we have been conditioned to accept our current state of affairs as the American way. The eighth report on the Hong Kong transition, published in the last year of the millennium, by a taskforce headed by Nebraska Congressman Doug Bereuter, describes the handover as a success. "Perhaps the most telling indication of the success of the transition has been its lack of impact on the way of life of the vast majority of Hong Kong citizens," Bereuter's report concludes. "According to Channel News Asia, some 200,000 people who had emigrated before the handover have returned to live in Hong Kong. These people voted with their feet: a vote of confidence in the territory's future." How are Americans going to express their confidence in the future of America?

Thanksgiving

Before heading back to Hong Kong, I decided to spend Thanksgiving in Los Angeles with my daughter Alexandra, Jonas and their mother Gail. Gail and I remained good friends after we divorced and we got together whenever I was in town. We had been married for 25 years but had grown apart and decided it made sense to have an amicable divorce.

Gail was a second generation Los Angelina. Her grandmother went to Venice High. A rare phenomenon in LA in the sixties. Probably even today. That makes Alexandra and Jonas, both born in Los Angeles, third generation natives.

Driving to dinner from the airport I thought about a joke my partner Bob Alter told me a week earlier at Martha's Vineyard. "A lady moved here when she was six and died in her nineties. At her funeral, a couple of local early childhood friends on the Vineyard remarked: 'Great gal. Pity she wasn't a native!'" The joke holds true in every community. People always question "non-natives".

Alexandra was sitting next to her cousin Noah, who worked as a cook in Colorado. His mom Sharon, Gail's sister, is also a great cook. She had worked with Gail at her restaurant Scratch and helped create some of the signature dishes. Noah had been around good cooking his whole life. "Do you and Noah get into any arguments over recipes?" I asked Sharon. "Some of our biggest arguments are on the phone arguing about what ingredients should go into a pasta," Sharon responded. "We agree on the pasta, tomatoes and basic condiments but then he wants to add all these weird Chinese and oriental herbs and spices." "But that's how cuisines are developed! " Noah interupted. "Yeah, you know you're right!" I answered. "Even Naomi Campbell is an eighth Chinese spice."

America needs to add more Chinese herbs and spices! Starting with Denny's and going on to Congress. America's fast food culture has evolved to instant everything. Americans have lost patience and the essence of life. They have stopped smelling the roses and spices. Stopped smelling the lovely aromas of homemade turkey stuffing.

Thanksgiving is a uniquely American holiday, thanks to the Pilgrims who survived their first harsh winter in Massachusetts and celebrated the first Thanksgiving in 1621. They set aside time to give thanks for their bountiful harvest and to live in peace with their Native–American neighbors in the Land of the Free. A land where they could live and worship freely. In his Thanksgiving Proclamation of 1789 George Washington urged Americans to give thanks "for the peaceable and rational manner in which we have been able to establish constitutions of government for our safety and happiness." He also asked them to beseech the "Lord and Ruler of Nations" to "render our National Government of wise, just and constitutional laws, discreetly and faithfully executed and obeyed..."

Turkey has been a mainstay of Thanksgiving dinners from the very beginning. But the modern bird, like Americans, is much different than its earlier ancestors. Earlier turkeys were naturally smaller and more wiry, and they had less breast meat than today's birds, which have been bred to satisfy American preferences for white meat. Today's male turkeys, like many leading American politicians, are so top-heavy that many can't fly or even walk without toppling over, and most are incapable of mating. Was it not for artificial insemination, the species would be extinct.

That over-sized Americans can enjoy their Thanksgiving turkeys while the issue of plump chads and gun control is debated by career politicians and the "Supremes" is a reminder how far America has drifted from the political foundations laid by the Founding Fathers.

Thanksgiving is similar to the Chinese tradition of celebtrating the Mid-Autumn, or harvest, Festival. Families get together and give thanks and celebrate their "bountiful harvest" and prosperity. Thanksgiving, like the Mid-Autumn Festival, is a time to reflect. Both are openly celebrated in Hong Kong, along with Ramadan which also falls around the same time of year.

Restless Nouvelle-Americans
Jonas and his girlfriend Katie came over to say goodbye. I had met Katie earlier in the year. Katie was a beautiful Latina. Funny, I thought to myself. I was born to Russian parents in England and in every country I lived in while growing up, I was a cultural outcast. A chameleon mut. A "TCK" – Third Culture Kid – a term

being popularized for those children of executives, diplomats, aid workers, journalists and military families who spend a significant portion of their upbringing living outside the country that issues their passport. One U.S. survey indicates that these accidental expatriates change locales an average of nine times before they reach adulthood. There are may be nearly a quarter million American citizens of school age in foreign countries.

There are more people of employable age working outside their home countries than ever before. Sociologists have been studying the phenomenon. Richard Alba, professor of sociology at New York State University in Albany, says the disorientation felt by returnees is very common. "There's a lot of literature on what happens to people when they go back home. It shows that the immigration experience really changes people, and that it makes it difficult for them to go back home. They find that they just don't fit in to their home society," he says.

"The Puerto Ricans, for instance, have a word for those countrymen who return after having lived in New York and have trouble settling back in – they are called 'Nuyoricans'. It's common for people to immigrate and say 'I'm only here temporarily,' then never go home."

U.S.-born Greta Goetz has found re-establishing ties and a settled life in New York difficult after her experience living in Hong Kong. "On arriving in America this past time I was bitterly disappointed and extremely 'Hong Kong sick'," says 24-year-old Goetz. "The people were coarse and gone were fishing villages I would love to go to in the outlying islands of Hong Kong to relax. I also missed the numerous small shrines that can be seen everywhere in Hong Kong.

"America felt so unspiritualized and the culture seemed somewhat contrived – even with its air of 'being developed'."

Goetz had been moved to Hong Kong at the age of three with her family from the U.S. She returned to Hong Kong as a young adult because she missed it too much. She worked as a journalist for a period, then went back to New York to pick up on her studies again.

I can relate. New York is the most fused ethnic global city in our globalized world. New York is a condensed microcosm of America. A place where the great talents of the world arrive brimming with "grand ideas and outsize ambition". Whatever happens in New York usually impacts America and the world. The September 11 attack on the World Trade Center affected families throughout America and the world. The families of the pilots, crew, passengers and victims in the Twin Towers. Even the families of the hijackers. Thousands of sons and daughters of small knit families throughout America – and more than 80 other countries – lost their lives. Tragedy caused people to unite globally. A local New York disaster became an international trauma. New York, like America, is populated by the sons and daughters of people who surrendered their homes and crossed a terrifying ocean to reach a rugged and inhospitable frontier in order to escape religious persecution and to seek religious freedom. There are more Jews in New York City than in Israel!

E.B. White, a New York native and author of *Charlotte's Web* and *Stuart Little,* gave the everlasting definition of New Yorkers. The city of the immigrant who "came to New York in quest of something... Commuters give the city its tidal restlessness; natives give it solidity and continuity; but the settlers give it passion," he wrote. A city with Muslim bagel sellers praying at 4:30 am, substituting a piece of carboard box for a carpet before they start selling bagels and other baked goods to fellow New Yorkers, next to fancy stretch limousines with sleeping Asian drivers across from the multi-racial homeless bundled in the doorways of fancy buildings is what makes New York the unique city it is.

First Lady Hillary Rodham Clinton used the theme during her successful New York Senate campaign. "What's so great about being a New Yorker or defining a New Yorker is that New York has always been a magnet for people from literally all over the world. People are drawn to New York because this is the place that you can stake your claim, you can build a future, you can dream your dreams." All Americans dream. Shaquille O'Neal dreams of Anna Kornakova for a birthday present.

Diversity and Misunderstanding

Paul Randt and his experiences are a good example of global American babies living cultural contradictions. He was born in the U.S. but has spent most of his thirteen years in Hong Kong. "Back in the States," he jokes, "the only thing I've been called is a weirdo from Hong Kong." But the eighth grader's musings echo those of his Internet counterparts. "Home is where I happen to be," he says, adding that he prefers to tell children in the U.S. that he's from Ohio – both to fit in and to discourage the usual set of ignorant inquiries. "People want to know if I've ever tried ice cream or been to the movies," he says of peers with whom he clearly feels out of synch. "Kids back home always tell me that I look for cars down the wrong side of the road. But I know there is no wrong side of the road." I can relate because it has happened to me on more than one occasion. I always seem to be on the wrong side of the road.

California and New York have the two largest Asian populations in America. The Chinese-Americans represent the largest grouping. In tight elections, such as the last presidential election of the 20th century, they, like their Latino and African-American counterparts, can make a difference. In California, Silicon Valley is the place to view a microcosm of America's "majority minority" makeup. Whites make up 49.9 percent of the population while Hispanics, Asians, Pacific Islanders and African-Americans make up the balance. Democrat Mike Honda, a Japanese-American who was interned in a Japanese concentration camp in America as a child during World War II, won the hotly contested 15th Congressional District in the 2000 election. This microcosm mirrors the makeup of California, the state with the most electoral votes. On a statewide scale, the 2000 census showed that 47 percent of the state's 33.9 million inhabitants were white, 32 percent were Hispanic, 11 percent were Asian and seven percent African-American. This cultural mix accounts for the world's sixth largest economy.

Similar cultural mixes hold true for Hawaii, New Mexico and Washington DC! Florida and Texas are close behind. Yet the governors of these states, and most other states, are lily white. There are no African-Americans. New Mexico's Bill Richardson was the sole Hispanic governor at the turn of the century. Washington State's Governor, Gary Locke, is the nation's first Chinese-American governor. His mother is from Hong Kong.

The San Fernando Valley in Los Angeles County is the West Coast equivalent of New York. One third of the population is foreign-born and nearly 40 percent is Latino. It is a place where Ukrainian-Americans, Cambodian-Americans, African-Americans and Armenian-Americans have one thing in common. They all speak Spanish by necessity in order to do business the capitalistic American way. Latinos outpace blacks as the nation's largest minority population. They are an integral part of the Spanish Roman Catholic West, just as Europeans are an integral part of the Dutch British Christian Judeo West, and all of us have a bit of Genghis Khan's "Tartar-Mongol yoke", according to DNA findings. Genghis Khan's Golden Horde planted their seeds widely and indiscriminately. Most Asians, Europeans and Americans are genetically connected to the Mongols. Buddhists, Christians, Hindus, Jews and Muslims.

By 2020 the number of people of Asian descent will double from 10 million to 20 million. By 2050 whites will make up a slim majority of 53 percent. Cultural "code switching" is not limited to the ghetto. The millennium ended with America having its first female Secretary of State. The 21st century started with the first African-American Secretary of State, Chinese-American Secretary of Labor and Japanese-American Secretary of Transportation. The George Dubya appointments at the dawn of the 21st century resulted in the most diverse cabinet in U.S. history and represent modern-day America.

A new study of census data shows that the number of immigrants living in the United States has almost tripled since 1970, rising from 9.6 million to 26.3 million, far outpacing the growth of the native-born population. The latest estimates from both the U.S. Census Bureau and the Department of Planning suggest that sometime in 2001, four out of 10 New Yorkers were foreign-born, the highest figure since 1910.

In 1860 there were only three census categories: white, black and "quadroon". In 2000 there are 30! Asian to Other Pacific Islander. There are 11 subcategories under "Hispanic ethnicity". The categories today accurately reflect what America has always been.

Saint Augustine in Florida is a great place to eat and visit when tired of Mickey and Minnie. It is the oldest city in America. Founded in 1513 by Spanish explorer Ponce de Leon, the Spanish built a wall in 1672 to stop the British, who had torched the city five times, from doing it again.

Take the oldest Spanish-built city in America and add to that the theory that the Chinese beat Columbus to America by 72 years and also circumnavigated the globe a century before the Magellan voyage, as retired British Royal Navy submarine commander and navigation expert Gavin Menzies claims. This raises the prospect that the white European history of America is suspect. In the early 15th century China was the world's greatest naval power. Chinese Admiral Zheng He is believed to have taken his fleet of large ships through the Indian Ocean to Africa, Europe and America. Pre-Columbian maps show the results of Zheng's voyage. Ancient Chinese artifacts found in the Americas and the remains of gigantic wrecks of ships that only the Chinese built in Australian and Caribbean waters lend credible support to the theory.

Standing in the "United States Citizens" immigration line whenever I return to America, I can't help notice how WASPs have become a minority. Even from Europe! When it comes to entry points from Latin America or the Asia Pacific region they are so insignificant that they are barely noticeable. Forgetaboutit! Doing so at the Tom Bradley International airport in Los Angeles, named after the city's first African-American mayor, really brings the point home. The same goes at New York's JFK. One hears every language except English. Queens, the borough where JFK is located, is home to 167 nationalities and 116 languages. It is the world's most diverse county. It even has its own Chinatown. At the dawn of the 20th century New York had one Chinatown in lower Manhattan. At the dawn of the 21st century it has four! There are two more in Brooklyn.

The United States welcomes more than 900,000 legal immigrants annually. Immigrants make up 11 percent of America's population, the largest share since the 1930s, and nearly one in five Americans does not speak English at home.

The Stars and Stripes no longer represents just the colonies and states. It represents the different divisive cultures that make up America.

Diverse and Divided

The political see-saw state of Florida brought America's changing political and racial landscape and antiquated political system to the world's attention in the Gore-Bush election. It also highlighted the fact that culturally and politically the United States is anything but united. It is One Country with Several Cultures. A country split asunder by cultural divides. A new contemporary civil war is looming on the horizon because of the racial and cultural divides fuelled by the ongoing feuds in Washington. One that makes Hong Kong's "One Country, Two Systems" look very progressive. White Southern social conservative good ole boys, African-Americans, immigrants from the Caribbean, South and Central America and the Middle East. Osama bin-Laden disciples training in simulators how to crash jet liners into buildings. American retirees from the North East. All have contributed to today's political reality in the Democratic and Republican duopoly. It reflects the national duopolistic bipartisan anarchy. The political system the two parties have created doesn't give *We The People* much choice. Bush and Gore "were political equivalents of genetically modified food. Both men were devoid of any natural ingredients," Thomas Friedman pointedly observes. Their mutual admiration society imposed by the events of September 11 was nothing short of self-serving nausea.

The U.S. civil rights commission concluded the Florida election was tainted by "injustice, ineptitude and inefficiency". The report goes on to say: "Despite the closeness of the election, it was widespread voter disenfranchisement and not the dead-heat contest that was the extraordinary feature in the Florida election." Racism denied many African-Americans and Hispanics their constitutional right to vote. There weren't enough ballots...The vote was both "confusing" and "illegal" with many questionable practices. The Reverend Jessie Jackson said it best. "For democracy to be credible and free, it must be open and fair," he said. "We take that message to Asia, to Africa, to Europe and to the entire world."

How diverse and divided is America as it enters the 21st century?

It's clearly divided. Is a new cultural and political civil war looming on the horizon?

Jeff Yang, the Chinese-American publisher and founder of *A. Magazine: Inside Asian America,* says, "I am an Asian seed sown and sprouted in American soil. I grew up eating rice in a white-bread neighborhood...I have spent a great deal of my life answering questions about my cultural legacy, from those for whom Asia is still an exotic mystery provoking fascination or disgust."

We non-Japanese-Americans can't really imagine how our interned neighbors felt when they were herded into concentration camps just because of their heritage and race. However, it was a common feature of all the East Asia territories that the Japanese overran that Japanese residents had been spies. This was especially true of Hong Kong residents.

It was doubly so for Arab-Americans, Muslims and Christians, after September 11. Jeff Yang recalls a conversation with his mother when he was eight years old and abused by local bullies. "'Mom', I sobbed, 'why do we have to be different?' 'Don't worry,' she said. 'In America, everyone is different'." Yang's Thanksgiving was also different, "We"d have roast turkey stuffed with sticky rice, water chestnuts and black mushrooms."

"Are you in the Chinese Air Force?" asked an elegantly dressed lady sitting next to U.S. Air Force Captain Ted W. Lieu. He was wearing his blue U.S. Air Force uniform, complete with captain's bars, military insignia and medals.

"Most of the discrimination I have encountered centered on the view that I am not a part of this great nation, even though I grew up in Ohio, graduated from law school in the District of Columbia and received my commission in the U.S. Air Force in 1991." Nevertheless his Chinese features made him suspect and un-American.

Caroline Hwang summed up the emotional confusion American children of immigrants experience: "They do not see that I straddle two cultures, nor that I feel displaced in the only country I know. I identify with Americans, but Americans do not identify with me. I've never known what it's like to belong to a community – neither one at large, nor of an extended family. I know more about Europe than the continent my ancestors unmistakably come from. I sometimes wonder if I would be a happier person had my parents stayed in Korea..."

Congressman David Wu, the first Chinese-American elected to the House of Representatives, was denied entry to the Department of Energy by security guards who demanded to know if he was an American citizen. His congressional identity card made no difference to the guards. What Congressman Wu found most upsetting was that he had been invited to speak at the department's celebration of Asian American Heritage month, but was only allowed in when his hosts vouched for him.

Wang Zhizhi, the first Chinese NBA player, has been referred to by radio personalities as a "Chinaman". His fellow countryman Zeng Zhe, a qualified emergency medical technician, who was on his way to work when the bombers hit the Twin Towers, gave his life to rescue Americans from the burning inferno even though he was not a citizen. In recognition of his bravery New York State authorities granted permission to drape Zeng's coffin in a U.S. flag prior to his cremation.

How will NBA giant Yao Ming be referred to by sport commentators in the 21st century? The jolly "Ching Chong" yellow giant? From basketball to politics, Chinese and Asian-Americans are taking America by storm

"It's time we were treated as first-class citizens," said Shanghai-born physics professor S. B. Woo, the former deputy governor of Delaware. Any wonder there are now over 250,000 Asian-Americans hooked up by e-mail to a cyberspace action group formed to lobby career politicians? Chinese form the largest segment of the Asian population in the U.S., accounting for about 23 percent of the total. There are over 11 million Asian-Americans. Over 60 percent of them are switched on and connected and communicating with each other on the Internet.

The only way racism against Asian-Americans can be defeated is through communication, education and reviewing the revisionist history of America. One of the most rabid U.S. institutional examples of racism towards Japanese-Americans culminated in the trial of Iva Toguri, aka "Tokyo Rose". Iva was born in California and became stranded in Japan after traveling there to visit a sick aunt just before the December 7, 1941, bombing of Pearl Harbor. Iva refused to renounce her U.S. citizenship and took up odd jobs to make ends meet. One odd job was as a typist at radio Tokyo where she was ordered to work as a radio announcer on the program Zero Hour. The show was produced by Major Charles Cousens, an Australian prisoner of war who after threats had consented to broadcast for the Japanese, but was surreptitiously trying to sabotage the country's propaganda effort. He had selected Iva for two reasons: she stood on the Allies' side, and had a "gin fog" voice. Iva was one of many Japanese-American women broadcasters. The others had all renounced their U.S. citizenship and never returned to America. When she returned to America after the war she was tried for treason on trumped-up charges, fabricated evidence, lying witnesses and found guilty and sent to jail. She later received a presidential pardon for a crime she never committed but was convicted for solely because she was an easy Japanese-American target for America's racism.

Let us remind ourselves of the Japanese-American soldiers of the 442nd infantry battalion, the most highly decorated combat unit in World War II, who gave their blood to America while their families were kept in American internment camps. Let's also remember that the army Chief of Staff at the dawn of the new millennium was of Japanese-American descent. General Eric K. Shinseki received the appointment while many cities in California still had laws on their books from 1943 questioning the loyalty of Japanese-Americans after the bombing of Pearl Harbor and opposing their release from internment camps. The city of Upland was prompted by the release of the movie *Pearl Harbor* to rescind the law and alerted other cities to check their records and do the same. They did this in 2001, only months before September 11.

General Shinseki, in the tradition of the Japanese-American soldiers of the 442nd infantry, bravely questioned and challenged Defense Secretary Rumsfeld and the George W administration on their conclusion on the number of troops that would be needed in Iraq to win the war and the peace. His correct analysis was rejected to the dismay and tears of the hundreds of American families whose brave sons died in vain in Iraq.

American insensitivity to fellow non-European-Americans is best exemplified by the continued use by America's sports teams of European-American racist descriptions of Native-Americans. "Redskins", "Braves"... America's racist lack of sensitivity towards Native-Americans whose country was taken away from them by force is going to be a 21st century issue that can no longer be avoided. The 21st century Colorado intramural basketball team, the "Fightin' Whities", are a millennium reminder.

American Prejudices

The bustling streets of New York's Chinatown were among the neighborhoods worst hit by the economic slump that followed the September 11 attack on the World Trade Center. More than 8, 000 jobs – almost a quarter of all jobs in Chinatown – were lost and over 24,000 were disrupted or dislocated. Wages fell by 50 percent. The two biggest employers, the garment industry and the tourist-dependent shops and restaurants, saw business drop by as much as 70 percent. Yet Chinatown was initially ignored when the federal government gave $20 billion to New York for redevelopment. It took local politicians several months to attract government attention to their plight.

One in four Americans holds "very negative attitudes" towards Americans of Chinese ancestry, and one third questions their loyalty to the United States, according to a nationwide poll completed in the opening segment of the 21st century. One in four Americans is opposed to intermarriage with a Chinese-American. Twenty-three percent are uncomfortable with the idea of voting for an Asian-American candidate for president, compared with 15 percent uncomfortable with voting for a black candidate, 14 percent for a woman candidate and 11 percent for a Jewish candidate.

Thirty-four percent said Chinese-Americans have too much influence in the U.S. technology sector. Almost the same proportion, 32 percent, said Chinese-Americans are more loyal to China than to the United States.

"Chinese are cockroaches" is a common racist slur Chinese-Ameri cans endure. People are encouraged by white racists "to get them where it hurts, rip them off, spit on them, flip them off, anything, but do something...demand that they either get a Green Card or go back from wherever they crawled out." Words that are echoed by Argentinians and Indonesians who attacked Chinese and looted their stores when Argentina and Indonesia faced a financial and political crisis at the dawn of the 21st century. Any wonder Chinese-Americans don't trust mainstream American media that don't report these repeated incidents?

Chinese-Americans have been called "chink" and "coolie" since they first started arriving in America to build the railroads and work the gold mines. This only got worse during the Communist Red Scare of the fifties that linked "Red Communist China" and its Chinese-American children in America. Chinese in America were subjected to the same witch-hunts African-Americans, Japanese-Americans and more recently Arab-Americans have experienced. During the 1950s, the U.S. Immigration and Naturalization Service invoked the almost forgotten Exclusion Act of the 1880s that prevented Chinese immigrants from becoming U.S. citizens. Chinese who sent money home to Red Communist China to support their families were suspected of supporting communism. Not very different to what Arab-Americans who send money to support their families have been subjected to since September 11. They are suspected of supporting terrorism.

Asian-Americans are experiencing the same discrimination that African, Arab, Indian, Italian, Irish and Latino-Americans experienced. America's racist roots were really brought home after September 11. Arab and Muslim Americans were subjected to the same violent racist discrimination expressed towards other non-European white Protestants. Thank God for the post 9/11 Arab, Iranian, Muslim and Indian comics in New York City and throughout America that perpetuate their multi-ethnic comic forerunners that make racial profiling the depressingly funny stand-up comedy that is America. The racist killings of Muslims and Sikhs, mistaken for Muslims, after September 11 were just a 21st century reminder of America's racist foundation stone.

Gullible Misled Media

Most of the media were a total lap dog to President Bush and the American Congress not only after September 11, but also over the Cox report on China's spying capabilities.

U.S. investigators targeted the physicist Wen Ho Lee as an espionage suspect largely because he is Chinese-American. They did not have a "shred of evidence" that he leaked nuclear secrets to China, according to the former chief of counter-intelligence at Los Alamos National Laboratory. Racial profiling at its racist best. FBI agent Robert Messemer admitted he gave false testimony that was the basis for which Lee was arrested and placed in solitary confinement. U.S. prosecutors claimed he might have been planning to pad his resume rather than spy.

Dan Stober of the *San Jose Mercury News* and Ian Hoffman of the *Albuquerque Journal* co-wrote *A Convenient Spy* to point out how the case was driven by Notra Trulock, the chief of intelligence and counter-intelligence for the Department of Energy's nuclear laboratories and factories. His flawed logic and open racism were unchallenged or questioned until it was too late. Sinophobia abetted by numerous politicians, Democrats and Republicans alike, and by key elements of the news media, which rather than challenging the charges, added to the atmosphere, forgetting that in such times their role is not to perpetuate a particular spin but to defend civil liberties.

Breaking a long public silence, Robert Vrooman also said he does not believe that China obtained top-secret information about U.S. nuclear warheads from Los Alamos or any other laboratory belonging to the Department of Energy. The stolen data could have come from documents distributed to "hundreds of locations throughout the U.S. government" as well as from private defense contractors.

"This case was screwed up because there was nothing there – it was built on thin air," said Vrooman, a former CIA operations officer. The affidavits of Charles Washington and Vrooman concluded: "If Dr Lee had not been initially targeted because of his race...he may very well have been treated administratively like others who had allegedly mishandled classified information." Why wasn't former CIA Director John M. Deutch arrested and confined in solitary confinement for downloading national defense data on to an unclassified computer? Shouldn't he also be required to plead guilty to a felony? Lee had to plead guilty to a charge of downloading classified information on to his computer. He was charged with 59 felonies! He was never charged with espionage! Judge James A. Parker who heard the case is right when he said the case "embarrassed this entire nation".

Edward Curran, a longtime FBI official serving in the Energy Department's top anti-espionage post, accused congressional critics, especially Chairman of the Senate Select Committee on Intelligence, Richard Shelby, Republican of Alabama, of failing to attend briefings on some of "our most sensitive" counter-intelligence cases. He was also accused of failing to respond to a report in 1997 that contained 26 recommendations for security improvements prompted by reports of spying by China at the labs. "His staff wouldn't even accept our briefings," Curran said. They would "get up and walk away".

When China released American spies Li Shaomin and Gao Zhan a lot quicker than America released Wen Ho Lee, an imaginary spy for China, the media failed to point out the ironic comparisons and contradictions in justice systems.

According to a team of foreign policy analysts at Stanford University, the Cox Report was misleading, inaccurate and damaging to Sino-U.S. relations.

The FBI investigators in New Mexico told their headquarters the same thing. This information became public just before Senator Arlen Specter, Republican of Pennsylvania, was to begin hearings. He dismissed the FBI doubts and proceeded while Lee continued to languish in solitary confinement. This is America? The American public perception is that Lee is guilty. Why? The American public is simply instructed that he is. After all, he is only a Chinaman. That was what happened with Julius Rosenberg. He was a Jew. Jews were suspected of being Communist sympathizers. Why wasn't Deutch, the former CIA chief who couldn't find his computer disks, treated with the same disrespect?

John Barrett, a former U.S. prosecutor who teaches law at Saint

John's University, said: "Wen Ho Lee now stands in the place of every defendant who claims to be wrongly charged or wrongly overcharged. That's a good climate for a defense attorney and an unfortunate one for the country."

Zhao Qizheng, an official Chinese spokesman, said that the power, weight, dimensions and other details of the seven types of U.S. nuclear weapons that China was alleged to have stolen were openly published in the United States. They are available on the Internet.

As John Pike, an expert on the Chinese military at the Federation of American Scientists in Washington, notes, "It's far from demonstrable that China has acquired anything of material significance."

Even where China obviously stole highly sensitive information, it is far from clear whether it could be used. China's indigenous nuclear weapons industry uses computers that are largely incompatible with those in U.S. weapons labs.

The double – make it triple – irony here was demonstrated when the U.S. State Department charged Hughes Electronics and Boeing Satellite Systems with illegally sharing sensitive space technology with China in the 1990s that may have helped Beijing fine-tune its missiles. The media didn't give that story half the play Dr. Lee received because Hughes and Boeing had high-priced spin-doctors that Lee couldn't afford. A year earlier, Loral Space & Communications agreed to pay $14 million in fines to settle charges that it had provided sensitive information to Beijing. Loral neither admitted or denied wrongdoing but agreed to pay the penalty and spend $6 million a year over seven years to improve its compliance procedures. In other words, U.S. companies that are known to have given sensitive rocket and missile technology to China merely pay a fine. Their executives get off scot-free while Dr. Lee spends time in jail just because he is Chinese.

The same happened to Muslim cleric Captain James Yee. He was accused of espionage, arrested and kept in solitary confinement 23 hours a day. He was then released and re-assigned without being charged for espionage. He was charged with adultery and storing pornographic material on his computer.

"A cookbook does not make a great chef," notes Pike. The U.S. government disagrees. Danny Stillman, who once directed intelligence at the Los Alamos nuclear laboratory and worked there for 28 years before retiring, was barred from publishing his book *Inside China's Nuclear Weapons Program,* because he concludes that China made its nuclear breakthroughs on its own. This is contrary to the U.S. accusations that China stole American secrets. Stillman contends the government blocked publication for political reasons rather than national security. In other words, the government wants to maintain its misleading spin.

As columnist Flora Lewis says, "Mr. Cox's paranoia is epitomized by his peculiar accusation that Hong Kong is China's high-tech spy and smuggling capital. 'Hong Kong is the whole ball game',"according to Cox.

Hong Kong hotly disputes those charges, and contends that its own export controls are tougher than those of the United States. The sanctity of its border is central to the terms under which the British territory was returned to Beijing's rule. Hong Kong customs officials periodically seize Soviet-era weapons bound for China.

Edward Yau, a top Hong Kong trade official, called the accusations "unfounded" and "utterly absurd". The U.S. Bureau of Export Administration, the Commerce Department division in charge of enforcing U.S. export controls, argues China's critics have gone too far in trying to implicate Hong Kong in the espionage scandal. After all, once you've purchased the commodity there are a thousand ways of getting it into China, North Korea being the most obvious. Hong Kong is old hat.

Some powerful Americans are striving to make China an active enemy that looms as an imminent military threat. In reality, China is not now, and is unlikely to be, a credible threat to the United States or even to its allies in Asia for some time to come.

Nonetheless, many professional "strategic thinkers", deprived of their reason for being by the lack of a major enemy such as the former Soviet Union, have cast China in that menacing role, regardless of what Asian specialists might say, and regardless of obvious reality. Career politicians like Cox and his spin-doctors are one example of the many racist misperceptions created at taxpayer expense that are widely disseminated by the unsuspecting media.

Labor Secretary Elaine Chao was subjected to similar yellow journalism and outbreak of "yellow fever" in *The New Republic* magazine and the *Courier-Journal* newspaper of Louisville. Her Chinese background and Chinese connections to Jiang Zemin and other Chinese leaders were portrayed as undermining America's foreign policy. Her husband Senator Mitch McConnell was characterized as a disloyal American for accepting campaign contributions from the U.S.-China Business Council. "The U.S.-China Business Council is made up of mainstream American businesses, such as Coca-Cola, Levi, Mary Kay and Sara Lee. What could be more American and less communist than Coca-Cola, blue jeans, make-up and apple pie?" the Senator asked. "Even if one assumes all of the...facts are true, they have demonstrated nothing more than, at best, a naked political vendetta and subtle racism," McConnell said in defense of his wife.

Why didn't the media give as much coverage to the U.S. government's attempt to suppress the book written by retired U.S. scientist Danny Stillman? He made nine trips to China between 1990 and 1999 to visit secret Chinese nuclear weapons facilities and held extensive authorized discussions with Chinese scientists and generals. Is it because Stillman said he believed the Chinese nuclear program made important advances without resorting to espionage?

Why didn't the media also give reasonable coverage to Professor Yang Fujia, the first Chinese nuclear physicist to become the Chancellor at Nottingham University in England? Professor Yang was the director of the Shanghai Institute of Nuclear Research at the Chinese Academy of Social Sciences and an academic of international standing. Is it possible that such stories would create a positive image of Chinese nuclear physicists that would not be in the interest of career politicians and their spin-doctors?

Is it any wonder then that ethnic minorities in America do not trust mainstream media because of their perceived bias? Contrary to popular media spins, America is not a melting pot. It is made up of islands of ethnic communities that turn to their ethnic media for reliable reporting.

Civil Rights

America has racist roots because some of America's Founding Fathers were slave owners and they accepted slavery as a state right to be administered as each state saw fit. Nevertheless, the principles and moral standards they adopted in America's founding documents uphold the rights and liberties of all. It just takes a long time to implement because *We the Apathetic People* don't care.

The state's rights doctrine survived the Civil War. The abolition of slavery at the end of the Civil War did not provide freedom to free African-Americans. Slavery was replaced by sharecropping and segregation. In theory they were to share in the profits of the crops they raised. The 1896 United States Supreme Court case of *Plessy v Ferguson* legalized the southern practice of imposing second class citizenship on emancipated slaves "denying them basic civil rights and barring social interaction with whites." This was nothing less than South African-style apartheid legalized by the Supreme Court.

The only good thing to come out of segregation was The Harlem Globetrotters formed in 1927. Generations of African-American men, whose team was formed because of and against racial segregation, turned out to be one of America's greatest symbols of freedom, expression and self-realization. The Globetrotters have played in 117 countries, entertaining over 120 million people.

The Democratic "Dixiecrats" dominated Southern politics after the Civil War until the 1940s. They were first challenged by President Franklin Roosevelt in the 1938 Democratic primaries. He wanted to purge them from the U.S. Senate because of their repeated success at challenging or blocking his economic and social reforms whenever they joined forces with their Republican colleagues.

Disenfranchised freed slaves and their descendants in the Southern states of America started gaining their civil rights in 1948 after President Harry S. Truman decided to take an active stand against the lynching of blacks and the hijacking of civil rights by establishing the President's Committee on Civil Rights. The Committee's manifesto, *To Secure These Rights,* was released by the White House in October, 1947. The committee called for an immediate end to any form of legal segregation, recommended the passing of an anti-lynching law and federal action to curb police brutality. It called for the repeal of the poll tax and the elimination of discriminatory voter registration requirements and numerous other practices, as Harry S. Ashmore, a Southern-born and raised journalist in his brilliantly researched and written book, *Civil Rights and Wrongs*, explains as he walks the reader through the history of the civil rights movement.

The civil rights legislation and movement matured and was brought to public conscience in the 1960s by Martin Luther King and President Lyndon Johnson. Television, the new mass medium, played a critical role in waking America and the world up to the segregation practiced in the Southern States after the 1954 Supreme Court decision of *Brown v Board of Education* ended segregation in public education.

Civil Rights observer and scholar Harry S. Ashmore accurately concludes, "In the early days of the Kennedy administration the return of activist government to Washington served to re-energize the Democratic organizations in the great cities – which included the black political leadership. This had the effect of containing the spread of the Muslim and Black Nationalist movements among rank-and-file blacks."

Five days after the John Fitzgerald Kennedy funeral, Lyndon Johnson went before a joint session of Congress to declare: "No memorial oration or eulogy could more eloquently honor President Kennedy's memory than the earliest possible passage of the civil rights bill for which he fought so long. We have talked long enough in this country about equal rights. We have talked for 100 years or more. It is time now to write the next chapter – and to write it in the books of law."

The Civil Rights Act of 1964 was passed in the Senate by a vote of 73 to 27 after 115 amendments were defeated on the floor. The U.S. Justice Department was empowered to initiate class-action suits and became the principal means of ending discrimination in housing, employment and public accommodations.

Johnson, who then went on to declare and launch his War on Poverty, brought America back to the ideals and principles of the Founding

Fathers. He reversed the discriminatory practices of two centuries in a couple of years. He took the Truman theme of *To Secure These Rights* and added his spin of *To Fulfill These Rights.*

The "long hot summers" that started with the Watts riots in 1964, the year I arrived in America, fused with the violence of the jungles of Vietnam where a disproportionate number of African-Americans were fighting and dying. Martin Luther King made the connection between the streets of the black ghetto and the jungles. "I criticize America because I love her, and I want to see her standing as a moral example to the world," he said. But that was not possible while she continued to wage war that "exacerbated hatred between continents, and worse still, between races."

I was in agricultural high school in Israel in the early sixties driving tractors and addicted to the music and moves of the delivery truck driver Elvis. I went to Elvis movies dressed like the King and Elvis parties to show off his sexy moves and my white shoes. His songs and moves hit me like a lightning bolt. The rebellious mixture of country, gospel and blues brought black America into the white mainstream and the world to America. Elvis was the embodiment of the post-World War II American dream and the civil rights era of the early sixties. This was one of the many magnets that drew me to America in 1964.

Racial Profiling
Americans were sensitized to America's insensitivity and racist underbelly after the air-borne bombings of the World Trade Center and Pentagon. American-Arabs, Muslims and Indian Sikhs were subjected to unnecessary racist violence, abuse and profiling.

I encountered it first hand when sitting next to a beautiful woman dressed in black in a bar in Grand Central Station in New York. Black hair, black top, black jeans, white face. Born and raised in America to a Moroccan father and Algerian mother. "You're an Aaraab! I'll be damned," said the man sitting on her other side as he picked up his drink and walked away in disgust. It turned out he was a co-worker she had known casually for a couple of years because they took the same train home. She was visibly hurt and worried. I put my hand on her arm and told her not to worry and that I'd escort her to her train.

The Daily Californian, published in the birthplace of the Free Speech Movement, ran an editorial cartoon that depicted two bearded men in turbans and long robes, standing in the devil's hand with a flight manual at their feet. They are in hell, though they believe they are in heaven. "We have made it to paradise!" one exclaims to the other. "Now we will meet Allah, and be fed grapes, and be serviced by 70 virgin women, and..." Students protested claiming the cartoon encouraged violence against Arab-Americans and is tantamount to hate speech.

Three Middle Eastern-looking men were denied permission to board a Northwest Airlines flight after several passengers complained about their presence. An Arab-American member of President Bush's personal Secret Service team was denied access to an American Airlines flight after the pilot questioned the validity of the agent's credentials. All the pilot had to do was to check with the Secret Service as the agent suggested. Bassem Youssef, a U.S. citizen of Egyptian descent, the FBI's top Arab agent, has sued the agency for discrimination, claiming he was excluded from September 11 investigations and denied promotions because of his ethnicity. Mr. Youssef is the only FBI agent able to conduct polygraph tests in Arabic. He was also prevented from serving as a translator when an Arabic speaker walked into an FBI field office claiming to have information about Osama bin-Laden's al-Qaeda network. The man left the office and stopped co-operating with the FBI. Is this any way to encourage Americans with Middle Eastern backgrounds to come forward and work as analysts and translators in the war on terror?

African-Americans and Hispanic-Americans who understand and have been subjected to racial profiling themselves admitted to doing what they despised being done to them.

During World War I, Dachshunds and German Shepherd dogs were kicked and abused because of their German names. In fact German Shepherds got renamed Alsatians to avoid such abuses. It's a good thing that the smallest animal with the word Arab in it is a horse. It can probably do more damage kicking than a racist provocateur.

"Think what it really means," said Nadeem Salem, a second-generation American who leads the Association of Arab-Americans in Toledo, Ohio. "People's civil liberties are being tarnished, compromised. That's not what this country is all about." A CNN/ USA Today/Gallup poll taken a few days after the attacks showed that Americans were supporting special measures intended for those of Arab descent.

Louisiana Congressman John Cooksey said during a radio interview, "If I see someone that comes in that has a diaper on his head and a fan belt wrapped around the diaper on his head, that guy needs to be pulled over and checked." He later apologized but added the war on terrorism can't be won "if we have to stop every five minutes to make sure we're being politically correct." A career politician elected to represent *We the People!* His conduct and behavior fly in the face of what America is. A diverse nation made strong because of the diversity of its citizens.

Watching Rageh Omar, pronounced "Ragee Omar", the BBC correspondent covering the Iraq War from Baghdad on the big screen TVs at the FCC Main Bar, generated many periodic reminders of the Congressman's diaper remark. What were his parents thinking? Naturally, they got culturally confused. I can relate. Immigrants and fans of Johnny Cash's "A Boy Named Sue" which was humorously harmonized by intoxicated journos frustrated they couldn't be there with their embedded "glassmates".

During World War II Native-Americans were used to transmit messages in their native tongues which no Japanese or German code breaker could break. They had no one who spoke Cherokee, Sioux or any other language spoken by Native-Americans. Today America finds itself facing the same problem its World War II enemies did. Arab-Americans are not queuing up to volunteer to help America fight the war on terrorism because of the racism they have encountered. With all the raids, detentions, denial of constitutional rights is it any wonder America is the loser?

More than 270 violent incidents against Arab-Americans were reported in the aftermath of September 11, including five murders. Over 1,000 complaints were filed by Muslims with the U.S. Equal Employment Opportunity Commission alleging workplace bias in the first 18 months following 9/11, double the previous 18 months prior to 9/11. Allah only knows how many incidents were not reported.

These incidents took place while the victims' children, brothers, sisters and neighbors serve in the U.S. military and are on the war front fighting Muslim terrorists. Sound familiar? Sound American? When are We going to learn? Why should any American be subjected to racial profiling or fear and hatred from fellow Americans in the 21st century?

Arabs in general, not just Arab-Americans or Muslims, admire and respect America. Rami Khouri, an American-educated journalist from Jordan and a senior analyst with the International Crisis Group, says: "Arabs love American culture, the rocket to the moon, technology, fast cars. They love going to America. Now they feel like jilted lovers."

Racism and racial profiling pushes its angry victims to extremes as Robin Reid, father of the "shoe bomber", explains. "I became a Muslim because I was fed up with racial discrimination," Reid told reporters. "I suffered in the streets, even though I was born in London. About 10 years ago, I met up with Richard after not seeing him for a few years. He was a little downhearted. I suggested to him, 'Why don't you become a Muslim; They treated me all right.'

"I don't feel guilty about encouraging him to be a Muslim because the sort of Islam I encountered wasn't about blowing up planes – it was about loving mankind." Any wonder Islam is the fastest growing religion in America?

If we continue to act out of hate, rage and react to abominable acts in the 21st century as we have, rather than carefully think of the cause and reasons, we all lose. If we just hate, instead of learn, teach and feed, We and our children lose.

SARS

Our children and the magnitude of our loss, personal and economic loss, were brought home during the SARS pandemic. Airlines, hotels, retail establishments and business in general suffered globally. So did our children. The Chinese, American, Eurasian, European and South Asian students from mainland China, Hong Kong, Taiwan and Singapore were banned from schools or quarantined and thus prevented from attending classes out of fear that they may be infected with SARS. Unfortunately, the SARS virus highlighted how easily the fear of a disease can generate into racist antipathy toward Asian people and their business establishments, especially restaurants, whether they are in Hong Kong, New York, London, Montreal, Sydney or Paris. The fact that a New York or London Chinese restaurateur is third generation local and never been to Asia is irrelevant. The reality is our ingrained subconscious racist conditioning by historic prejudices perpetuated by the political-bureaucratic establishment and media makes us instinctively become racists. I was stunned. Concerts and conventions were cancelled in China and Hong Kong. International conventions banned people from the mainland, Hong Kong, Taiwan and Singapore from attending.

I can relate. People did the same to me when they knew or heard I was from Hong Kong during the SARS pandemic. No one wanted to see me, have me stay with them or even talk to me on the phone! I felt like an isolated Eurasian Arab leper. And I'm not even Asian-looking. I can only imagine how much worse Asians felt.

The SARS fear and blanket ban and boycott of Asians are blatant racist discrimination under the guise of prudent and cautious health concerns. I do not want to in any way minimize the health issues and concerns which I will shortly address. However, the fact is that SARS was not an airborne pandemic and fewer people died of SARS than people who died of pneumonia, car accidents, common colds, alcoholism, flu, smoking, TB and of course wars!

Anti-Chinese propaganda under the guise of health concerns is nothing new. In 1875, the American Medical Association sponsored a study to investigate assertions that Chinese women were spreading a unique, "Chinese" strain of syphilis. Though the study found no evidence to support the claim, one medical publication, *The Medico-Literary Journal,* nevertheless accused the Chinese of "infusing a poison in the Anglo-Saxon blood".

The American press fanned the flames by portraying the Chinese as an insanitary and dangerous race. An editorial in *The Santa Cruz Sentinel* in 1879, for example, described the Chinese as "half-human, half-devil, rat-eating, rag-wearing, law-ignoring, Christian-civilization-hating, opium smoking, labor-degrading, entrail-suck ing Celestials." *The Dutch Flat Forum,* another California paper, echoed the anti-Chinese racism. "Women of California," it asked, "why do you persist in having your dirty linen fouled by unclean hands, under the pretense of having it cleansed? Do you not know that (in these exciting times when the Chinese are losing employment, and naturally mad at the white race) you are taking desperate chances of having disease introduced among us that will render desolate our firesides? And in fact we don't know but that the diseases among our children during the past year, which have baffled the skill of our most eminent physicians, and depopulated many households, have emanated from the Chinese."

In 1910 the Federal government set up a special immigration center exclusively for Chinese at Angel Island in San Francisco Bay. The site was the former quarantine station that fumigated foreign ships and inspected passengers for signs of contagious diseases. Officials claimed that the physical isolation would stop the epidemics that they had been led to believe were "prevalent among aliens from Oriental countries".

The most severe example of medical panic transforming itself into racial prejudice took place in 1899, when bubonic plague broke out in Hawaii. Though the disease struck whites as well as Chinese, the local board of health focused its efforts on the Chinese alone, placing them under quarantine, preventing them from traveling to the continental United States and burning down parts of Honolulu's Chinatown. In 1900, San Francisco followed Hawaii's example, closing Chinatown businesses, forcing Chinese residents to submit to inoculation and cordoning off the neighborhood with a nine-foot fence – a quarantine that a federal court later ruled unconstitutional.

Iris Chang, author of *The Chinese in America: A Narrative History,* reminds us that "suspicion of Chinese-Americans has waxed and waned over the 20th century, but it has never completely gone away. It is no wonder, then, that given this not-so-distant history, Chinese-Americans are uneasy about the way in which people have responded to the threat of SARS. While we are right to expect the government to take all necessary steps to slow the spread of the disease, we are also right to demand more careful reasoning from American institutions."

Racism

Racism is a reality in America. The 2002 Academy Awards when Halle Berry became the first African-American woman to win the golden Oscar statuette was a prime time media reminder. On the same night Denzel Washington received an Oscar that was nearly 40 years overdue – almost four decades had passed since Sidney Poitier was honored for *Lilies of the Field* in 1964. All the major media outlets were quick to trumpet these victories while reminding us that African-Americans are running major Fortune 100 companies as well as winning Oscars. That doesn't negate the fact that racism is still alive and prospering in America today. Jeffrey Sterling, a former CIA agent, is suing the agency for racism and says other black case officers shared his feelings about discrimination but were afraid to speak up. When he was denied an assignment he was trained for he was told by his white supervisor, "You kind of stick out as a big black guy," Sterling recalled. "I said, 'When did you realize I was black?'"

Racism is not just a white-black issue but a Jewish, Muslim and Asian, especially Chinese, issue as well. By 2020, Asians are projected to make up six percent of the nation's population. Incidents of racism are on the rise. Holy racist wars and shootings are still with us. Look at what happened to Yoon Won Joon, a Korean doctoral student who was killed by a white supremacist who fired into a group of people leaving the Korean United Methodist Church in Bloomington, Indiana, over the 4th of July weekend.

A black man was also apparently killed by the same gunman, and seven people – including six Orthodox Jews and a second person of Asian descent – were wounded in separate drive-by shootings. "For us, we don't know who is racist and who is not," said Hwang Hye Joung, a secretary who studied English in America. "That's why it's hard for us to get close to foreigners."

"Whenever we went to bookstores, we were constantly watched by the shop owner," said Jung Min Ah, 24, who visited America for a year to study and travel. "We never knew if it was because we were Korean or Asian, but it was so unpleasant, in the end we had to leave the store. We told the owner we were not thieves." During the 1992 Los Angeles riots some 2,000 Korean-owned businesses were burned and looted.

Before he killed himself, Benjamin Nathaniel Smith also murdered a black man out jogging with his children. Elizabeth Sahr, a former girlfriend of Smith's, told the University of Illinois' student newspaper that "this is his Independence Day from the government, from everything. He is not going to stop until he is shot dead."

Racists are not all white. Racism is not monopolized by whites. In fact the number of black racists is growing thanks to Louis Farrakhan, leader of the Nation of Islam, for whom the white man is a "devil by nature."

White separatist Buford Furrow shot six-year-old Jewish children in a day care center in Los Angeles as "a wake up call for America to kill Jew!" An hour later he killed Joseph Ileto, an American-Filipino postman, as an expression of his hatred for the Federal Government and to make sure his prejudices had a clean sweep.

Considering the number of crazed locals rattling around LA with loaded guns, that must have been one heap of hate.

Modern anti-Semitism can be traced to 1449 when the city council of Toledo in Spain decreed no Jewish converts to Christianity could hold public office. Jews became defined not by religion but by blood. The Crusades, Inquisition and finally the fusion of anti-modernism by the Catholic Church, racism and anti-Semitism resulted in Adolf Hitler. "He was as much a creature of the racist, secular, colonizing empire builders who preceded him on the world stage as he was of the religion into which he was born, and which he parodied. But in truth, the racist colonizers, before advancing behind the standards of nations and companies, had marched behind the cross," James Carroll reminds us in his book *Constantine's Sword The Church And The Jews: A History.* Hitler, like many of his generation, believed that imperialism was a biologically necessary process which, according to the laws of nature, led to the inevitable destruction of the lower races. He merely practiced what Darwin preached. In *The Descent of Man,* Darwin wrote, "The civilized races of man will almost certainly exterminate and replace throughout the world the savage races."

Hatred of immigrants is a form of racism. Immigrants are constantly the targets of racist attacks and harassment. Immigrants are the recipients of a double-barreled racist shotgun. They usually leave their country of birth because of racism and then face it again in their adopted country. America is home base for immigrants fleeing racism and has a duty to prevent the racism to which they are subjected. But that is why they marry inter-racially.

Mixed Marriages-Racial Choice?

Inter-marriage is on the rise. There were some 1.3 million such unions in 2000, and the numbers are likely to roughly double in each decade of the 21st century. Yet for more than 100 years between 1862 and 1965, White Americans were prohibited from marrying Asian immigrants. The prohibition is still in effect today in the states of Florida and New Mexico.

About one in six Asian-Americans is married to an Asian of a different ethnic background. About 40 percent of Asian-Americans and six percent of African-Americans had married white Americans at the dawn of the 21st century. Latinos are inter-marrying in similar numbers. "Because we're a society obsessed with race, inter-ethnic marriages fall under a cloak of invisibility," says demographer Larry Shinagawa. "Let's face it. After the third generation they are all Americanized," says Song Tsai, whose Chinese-American daughter married a Japanese-American.

Scientists who study the human genome say that race is mostly a bogus distinction reflecting very little genetic difference, making up perhaps one-hundredth of one percent of our DNA. Skin color differences are recent, arising over only the last 100,000 years or so, a twinkling of an evolutionary eye. That is too short a period for substantial genetic differences to emerge, and so there is perhaps 10 times more genetic difference within a race than there is between races. An important fact for racist career politicians, religious leaders and their spin doctors to keep in mind as they campaign in the 21st century.

Making a political issue of the "mongrelization" of America only breeds pit bulls. The pressure of being a mixed-race kid in a hostile environment was brought home by Richard Reid, the "shoe bomber". It does not have to be that way. It was really hammered home at the FCC Main Bar when I realized on one of my frequent sojourns that I was surrounded by mixed-marriage couples. Dr. Feng Chi Shun, a prominent local physician, was with his blonde white-skinned Canadian wife Cathy. Neil, a WASP technology editor of the leading English language daily, was with his dark brown Latina-Filipina wife, Lucy. Larry, a light brown Sri Lankan banker with a top international bank, was with his Chinese wife, Caroline. Michael, a bald headed Aryan German reinsurance broker, was with his Sri Lankan wife, Atasha, and Peter Makant, an Englishman with a U.S. bank, was with his Filipina wife, Puri. Sitting across from us was Hugh Van Es, a white Dutch photographer, with his Chinese wife, Annie. The color blind mixed bag of religions harmoniously discussing the political repercussions of a war on Iraq over whiskies, martinis and champagne was a refreshing reminder of how easy it is to relieve pressure from mixed-race children. Pictures of mixed-race children and grandchildren were proudly shared and giggled over.

I shook my head and gulped my drink at the thought of how prevalent mixed marriages are as I walked over to a nearby table where Philip Curlewis and Ben Pasco were seated to discuss our upcoming business trip to China – two other half-breeds whose fathers were English. Phil's mother is Chinese and Ben's Burmese.

Culture is a human evolutionary process that evolves naturally. Emotionally, consciously and unconsciously. Race and religion mix just like the blood of mixed marriages and make Americans what they are today. A multi-layered nationality. Mixed marriages, religious as well as cultural, make for interesting American holidays. Menorahs, Christmas trees and references to Kwanzaa and "Feliz Hanukah".

Foreign-born Asians and Hispanics "have higher rates of inter-marriage than do U.S.-born whites and blacks." Probably because they are "exotically" better looking. By the third generation, one third of Hispanic women are married to non-Hispanics, and 41 percent of Asian-American women are married to non-Asians, Gregory Rodriguez reports in an article written for the *National Immigration Forum*. Rodriguez notes that children in remote villages around the world are fans of Arnold Schwarzenegger and Garth

Brooks, yet "some Americans fear that immigrants living within the United States remain somehow immune to the nation's assimilative power."

The new figures dramatically affirm that America is going through a remarkable transformation in just a generation, one that will reshape its demographics and social landscape for years to come. As a percentage of the population, immigrants now account for nearly one in ten residents.

During the last census of the last century people could choose from six racial categories, which created a matrix of 63 possible racial choices, compared to five a decade earlier. The results show that more Americans than anticipated belong to more than one race.

We must all build together to achieve our full human potential. Build on the traditional foundations laid by our Founding Fathers. By adding on the layers of values of every ethnic group to the American foundation, America can only grow stronger.

Even America's National Pastime is heavily sprinkled with ball players from Asia and Latin America. Rookie of the year 2001 Ichiro Suzuki, as well as Hideo Nomo, Hideki Irabu, Hideki Matsui, Masato Yoshi, Chan Ho Park, Byung Hyun Kim, Masanori Murakami, Sammy Sosa... Over 40 percent of the 70,000 players under contract in American professional baseball are foreign born. The same holds true in the NBA. In 2003 there were 73 players from 33 countries.

America welcomes 100,000 refugees a year. Over 650,000 immigrate legally each year. It is estimated there are over five million illegal immigrants in America today. Half of all immigrants are also Spanish-speaking – 27 percent coming from Mexico alone. Most of these Latinos are descendants of native aboriginal Indians brutalized and forcibly converted to Catholicism. California, New York and Florida have all seen enormous increases in their Hispanic communities. In fact, the Hispanics outnumber blacks as the largest minority group in America. They make up 13 percent of the U.S. population. Any wonder the most popular name for boys in California and Texas is Jose and that tabasco now outsells catsup in America? The Hispanic population of America grew by 60 percent in the last decade of the millennium. They are already shaping pop culture and presidential politics. The Latin wave will change how the country looks – and how it looks at itself. Hopefully, it won't reflect Los Simpsons, the most popular English-language show among Hispanic households.

In the first major city election of the 21st century, Antonio Villaraigosa almost became the first Hispanic-American mayor of Los Angeles, America's second largest city, since the 19th century. LA's myth of golden blondes frolicking in the Golden State's surf has been replaced by beautiful Chinese-Latinas. Miss Hawaii, Angela Perez Baraquio, who became Miss America 2001, is of Philippine ancestry. She was the first Asian-American to be crowned Miss America. Miss California, Rita Ng, was the first runner-up. Both are representative of the 21st century American beauty.

George P. Bush, son of George W.'s brother, Florida Governor Jeb and his Mexican wife, Columba Garnica, tried to get Republicans to understand this at their opening convention of the millennium. "You see, I am American, but like many, I come from a diverse background. And I'm proud of it."

It is little wonder that Latin pop is riding the wave of success and welcoming the new millennium. Latin pop draws different cultures, it also has the power to bring people together. "Latino people have a golden key in their hands, a common treasure," says Colombian-born pop-rocker Shakira. "That treasure is fusion. The fusion of rhythms, the fusion of ideas. We Latinos are a race of fusion, and that is the music we make. And so at the dawn of a new millennium, when everything is said and done, what could possibly happen besides a fusion?"

Puerto Rico, the former Spanish colony and American appendage, is where it all started. Here, in an island inhabited by the descendants of black slaves and Spanish conquistadors, cultures have collided, rhythms intermingled and salsa emerged, inspired by Africa and Europe and New York City. A typical New World Order recipe.

As the recent genome study revealed, there is no scientific basis for categorizing humankind according to racial differences. It is therefore up to *We the People* to work on creating racial and ethnic harmony in the 21st century. Fairness, equanimity, civil liberties and social justice are universal values embedded in the U.S. Constitution.

Unjust Bust Because of Race

In the mid-1980s America apologized to Japanese-Americans for their internment and unfair treatment during World War II. Congress and federal courts reversed earlier convictions of those imprisoned. However, what is disturbing is the U.S. Supreme Court's language justifying such incarceration. The court justified such arrests and convictions on the basis that "residents having ethnic affiliations with an invading enemy may be a greater source of danger than those of a different ancestry."

In another Supreme Court decision, Justice Robert H. Jackson dissented and argued that such an opinion has far more far-reaching consequences. "A military order, however unconstitutional, is not apt to last longer than the military emergency...But once a judicial opinion rationalizes such an order to show that it conforms to the Constitution, or rather rationalizes the Constitution to show that the Constitution sanctions such an order, the Court for all time has validated" that rationalizing principle. And that "principle then lies about like a loaded weapon ready for the hand of any authority that can bring forward a plausible claim of an urgent need."

Justice Jackson reminded us that the federal judiciary has always been reluctant to restrain executive branch excess: "If the people ever let command of the war power fall into irresponsible and unscrupulous hands, the courts wield no power equal to its restraint. The chief restraint upon those who command the physical forces of the country, in the future as in the past, must be their responsibility to the political judgments of their contemporaries and to the moral judgments of history."

Thirty years later, Jackson's argument was validated by the post-humous confession of the man who, as governor of California, had been, in the words of his biographer, "the most visible and effective force behind the internment of Japanese-Americans: the legendary Chief Justice Earl Warren." Warren professed himself "conscience-stricken" about his role as chief jailer. "It was wrong to react so impulsively, without positive evidence of disloyalty, even though we felt we had a good motive in the security of our state," he wrote in his memoirs. "It demonstrates the cruelty of war when fear, get-tough military psychology, propaganda, and racial antagonism combine with one's responsibility for public security to produce such acts." I had the privilege of meeting Chief Justice Warren when he spoke at the law school I attended where he made similar remarks during the Vietnam War.

District Judge Marilyn Hall Patel, writing in 1984 when the case was reopened, agreed with Justice Jackson and Chief Justice Warren that the legal legacy of the Japanese internment reached beyond racism and illuminated a greater danger: "It stands as a caution that in times of distress the shield of military necessity and national security must not be used to protect governmental actions from close scrutiny and accountability. It stands as a caution that in times of international hostility and antagonisms our institutions, legislative, executive and judicial, must be prepared to exercise their authority to protect all citizens from the petty fears and prejudices that are so easily aroused." Let *We the Apathetic Maids* not forget these judicial warnings while Arab-Americans suffer the same fate as we move on into the 21st century. We must sweep these repeatedly hijacked powers away from the career politicians' corner and get them back in ours.

American Flag

The American flag ties and unites Americans' constitutional beliefs and convictions. A symbol of equal rights and justice for all under the law, it stands for the fulfilment of the American dream and the honoring of our ideals. It is a cultural icon that forever baffles cultural and political prognosticators. The baby blanket that wrapped the newborn child of the mixed marriage between the native-American model of confederation and the European enlightenment named America. Stars were added as the child grew. It remains the primary symbol of democracy for all Americans regardless of their color, sex or religion. A democratic cloak that is today primarily manufactured in China. Patriotic Americans attack China and Chinese for being Communist, yet the flags they fly on their front porches and cars, like the flag lapel pins and the Fourth of July fireworks, are increasingly made in China.

The flag is a unique American evolutionary art form that acts as both political bandage and bandana. In time of war it is both and serves all American communities throughout the world. It has been waved, burned, worn, flown, torn, spat at and trampled upon, just as many Americans basic rights protected by the Constitution, the Bill of Rights and Declaration of Independence have been too.

We the Apathetic People cannot ever forget to be proud of our Red, White and Blue again. The white stars that represent the states that created the deep blue federal government where career politicians bury our hard-earned dollars. The red stripes that represent the blood spilt by George Washington's bootless ragged foot soldiers in the terrible winter of 1777-1778 in the snows of Valley Forge, represented by the white strips.

In the United States, Americans still raise the flag, but aren't sure how to properly salute it, except after a national disaster. September 11 saw America wave its flag patriotically to symbolize union and determination to fight and win. Since the fall of communism, the absence of a superpower enemy and the advent of an all-volunteer military, American's feelings about their own country have little to do with battlefields and are no longer so easy to define. Ethnic groups all have their own political agendas that benefit them or their countries of origin. Elian Gonzalez and the Cuban-Americans reminded us of this in the closing year of the millennium. The bombings of the World Trade Center and Pentagon at the dawn of the 21st century saw Arab and Muslim Americans isolated and stigmatized as terrorists and suicide bombers. America's political agenda has become complicated by domestic debates about race, immigration and environmentalism. Kevin Mathey, a 43-year-old bricklayer and school board member, saw hypocrisies and more than a little irony in a nation of immigrants slamming the door shut.

"People came to this country from Europe because of religious persecution, and now the religious right wants to dictate the way people should believe," he said. "And then people want to put up the gates and fences around our borders," fearing that an influx of newcomers will mean native-born Americans will be forced to do with less.

The late Theodore H. White wrote: "Americans are held together only by ideas...." The conservative scholar George Weigel writes: "The continuity of America is not the continuity of race, tribe or ethnic group – the continuity of blood, if you will. Rather it adheres in the continuous process of testing our society against those defining public norms whose acceptance as defining norms constitutes one as an American. In other words, American continuity is the continuity of conviction." Weigel refers to "the concept of America-as-experiment".

Foreign observers have often echoed this American self-definition. The Austrian visitor Francis Grund wrote in 1837: "An American does not love his country as a Frenchman loves France, or an Englishman loves England: America is to him but the physical means of establishing a moral power... 'the local habitation' of his political doctrines." Subsequent visitors have agreed. "Every American is... in his own estimation the apostle of a particular political creed," wrote another 19th century visitor, the British journalist Alexander Mackay.

"I'd like to name the baby America, but I have to talk to my wife and parents first," said an overwhelmed Naim Karaliju, a Kosovan refugee, of his son born in America less than 24 hours after his mother arrived from a camp in Macedonia. A child born on United States soil is automatically an American citizen.

To be American, according to these diverse observers, is to believe in a particular political ideology. In the words of Robert Penn Warren, "to be an American is not...a matter of blood; it is a matter of an idea – and history is the image of that idea." "The genius of this country – which cannot and does not wish to treat its citizens like plants rooted in its soil – has consisted in a citizenship that permits reflection on one's own interest and a calm recognition that it is satisfied by this regime," wrote the late Allan Bloom.

According to the editors of *The Economist,* the U.S., as a non-national idea state, has the potential to become literally a universal nation: America is an immigrants' land, open to anyone of any race or culture who accepts the ideas of the European Enlightenment on which it was founded. Provided the ideas remained intact, an America populated with Martians would still be America.

"The United States truly has not been like other nations, because it is not a historical nation by origin. It was not 'there'. It was made. It was a construction which rested on certain principles and beliefs derived from the Scottish and French Enlightenments, and from the Christian cultures of England and Colonial America," says William Pfaff.

The same can be said about Hong Kong. Hong Kong as a foundation was not a political philosophy but it grew to be an idea, the idea being that it was better to be there than a lot of other places. In its proportion it was almost as spectacular an immigration phenomenon as the United States. You could be a suited European trader or Chinese factory worker and though you couldn't communicate you had one thing in common: Hong Kong was where you could do your own thing by your own lights.

America is a state of mind. One where all people are created equal. "Americans" don't have to be citizens. Pseudo-Americans, wannabees, are people who identify with, have a link, or are connected to the American ideal. The dream. The American Spirit. That is why all "Americans" throughout the world took such great interest in the debacle of the last American presidential election of the millennium and such compassionate pain and ethos with the incidents of September 11. The American presidency, like America, belongs to all Americans. To *We the People.* Not to the individual who holds the office. Is the Home of the Brave turning like its baseball caps: backwards?

"Americans" wear American fashions and baseball caps, listen to American music, eat hamburgers and American fast foods for the same reasons American citizens do when they travel and get food sick. They hunger and dream of coming to America. The magnified and glorified American ideal perpetuated by movies and the media has created "American" addicts. The same culture so many love, also created the Muslim extremists that want to destroy it.

Arab-Americans worked with Osama bin-Laden to bomb the World Trade Center and Pentagon, and to blow up the USS Cole. Arab-Americans also fought with the Taleban against U.S. Special Forces. Cambodian-Americans attacked the Cambodian Ministry of Defense, Albanian-Americans fought and died in Kosovo, and various other militant groups, sympathetic to other political struggles, have followed suit throughout the world. They are "Americans" with American passports. Citizens, yet they are still passionate about their roots and beliefs.

America was founded as an abstract experiment in political philosophy. So far it has worked. It is up to *We the Maids* to make sure it continues to in the 21st century. We have to sweep out all the mildew and dust that has covered the American ideals the Founding Fathers created in the Constitution and the Declaration of Independence.

Praying Yankees
America is the most progressive all-inclusive civilization known to humanity. Individuals are free to pursue their original dreams creatively. It is a nation of cultural contradictions continuously coming to terms with itself, every race, rap, recipe and religion, and it continues to recruit. New York City is the recruiting office that involuntarily assigns newcomers to their battle stations of survival throughout the Disunited States of Apathy. States that unite in wars against convenient foreign enemies but remain disunited in cultural wars on the home front.

"A Prayer for America" in Yankee Stadium in honor of the victims of September 11 represented what America is all about. Hindus, Muslims, Sikhs, Jews, Roman Catholics, Eastern Orthodox Christians, Coptic Christians, Unitarians, Buddhists, Methodists, Lutherans, Protestants, Calvinists, African, Italian, Latino, Chinese, Irish, Indian, Arab, Asian, European and Native-Americans all coming together as the Founding Fathers intended and envisioned.

What do *We the Apathetic People* do after the fervor of patriotism and flag-waving fades to sustain that spirit of living patriotic cultural contradictions together? Patriots who cherish the ideals America stands for and represents should first and foremost take a careful look at America, question and debate its shortcomings. A national self-critical analysis. An honest patriotic dialogue about America's ideals and inspirations in the 21st century. Strengths, weaknesses and necessary improvements.

Cultural Diversity, Fusion or Graveyard?

A weakness that must be addressed in the 21st century is America's shortcomings in speaking and understanding foreign languages. 9/11 highlighted the CIA's and FBI's foreign language defects. Congressional officials expressed concern for years that intelligence agents do not have nearly enough officers who speak Arabic, Farsi or Pashto, languages needed to gain reliable information in the Middle East and South Asia. This critical weakness resulted in the defective and unreliable information America gathered on Iraq's weapons of mass destruction program.

As an infant, I grew up in Switzerland tobogganing down the hills of Bern. Russian and Bern Deutsche became the first languages I spoke. I cursed my parents every opportunity I had for not continuing to speak to me in Russian and German while growing up. Any wonder America is described as a "graveyard" of languages? I hope all American children of the New World Order keep their mother tongues. Many don't and can't even communicate with their non-English-speaking parents. There are American families in which parents and children have not spoken for years. A family of strangers. Not out of anger but lack of knowledge of a common language. This is especially the case among Asian-Americans. Many first generation Asian-American immigrants work so hard that they never get a chance to learn English or spend the necessary time with their children. Their children grow up learning English and thus the barriers go up. The children of today's immigrants are losing their parental languages much faster than second-generation children did a generation ago.

Linguists estimate that in 100 years, fewer than 500 of the world's 6,000 languages will be in use. The rest will be as dead as Ancient Greek and Latin. Hopefully it will be a peaceful communicating world. In 1227, Genghis Khan's son avenged the death of his father by ordering the slaying of the Central Asian Tangut people. He destroyed their culture and their language. Globalization is the 21st century equivalent. A language is the living tongue of a culture, tradition and system of beliefs. So, when a language dies so does the traditional lifestyle and culture it represents.

Chaya Venice is a restaurant near the shores of the Pacific Ocean that blends the best of Asia and America. The cuisine is reflective of this cultural bridge. Nuevo sushi! Much like Baang in Greenwich and Aspen and Vong in New York and Hong Kong. Restaurants that have created, in Noah's words: "Culturally blended cuisines." How about individual and institutional blending similar to cuisines? Just as long, like many unfortunate "fusions," Afghanistan being a recent example, it's not the worst of different worlds, but blending the best America and beyond have to offer. Take as prime examples, the Tea House Restaurant in Torrance, California, a Chinese restaurant that serves up the blues with sweet and sour pork, or Ten Penh, which stands for 1001 Pennsylvania Avenue in Washington DC, which serves a sake martini served with pickled baby octopus.

Cultural fusion and indoctrination subconsciously affect the way we all interact with each other, especially when dealing with the opposite sex.

The fine line between dating and courting, the Anglo-Spanish definitions of trying to get laid, are examples of how frustrating the lack of understanding of the other culture can be. It was in the colonial days and is even more so today in our electronic New World Disorder.

An FCC bar story that summarizes the cultural differences which America has to integrate and overcome in the 21st century comes to mind. On a group of beautiful deserted islands off Thailand, the following people are stranded:

Two Italian men and one Italian woman;
Two French men and one French woman;
Two German men and one German woman;
Two Greek men and one Greek woman;
Two English men and one English woman;
Two Bulgarian men and one Bulgarian woman;
Two Japanese men and one Japanese woman;
Two Chinese men and one Chinese woman;
Two American men and one American woman;
Two Irish men and one Irish woman.

One month later on these absolutely stunning deserted islands off Thailand, the following things have occurred:

One Italian man killed the other Italian man for the Italian woman.

The two French men and the French woman are living happily together in a *menage-a-trois.*

The two German men have a strict weekly schedule of alternating visits with the German woman.

The two Greek men are sleeping with each other and the Greek woman is cleaning and cooking for them.

The two English men are waiting for someone to introduce them to the English woman.

The two Bulgarian men took one look at the endless ocean and another long look at the Bulgarian woman and started swimming.

The two Japanese have faxed Tokyo and are awaiting instructions.

The two Chinese men have set up a pharmacy, liquor store, restaurant, laundry, and have gotten the woman pregnant in order to supply employees for their stores.

The two American men are contemplating the virtues of suicide, because the American woman keeps on complaining about her body, the true nature of feminism, how she can do everything they can do, the necessity of fulfillment, the equal division of household chores, how sand and palm trees make her look fat, how her last boyfriend respected her opinion and treated her nicer than they do, and how her relationship with her mother is improving, and how at least the taxes are low and it isn't raining.

The two Irish men divided the island into North and South and set up a distillery. They do not remember if sex is in the picture because it gets sort of foggy after the first few liters of coconut whisky. But they are satisfied because at least the English aren't having any fun.

Cultural diversity is not only to be respected, it is to be rejoiced in. Coming from a reasonably privileged white man, that is probably easy to say. But how else do we make a decent balance of the times, whether we are couples, or business people or politicians trying to cut a deal? Is it the Anglo, the Hispanic, the Chinese or African-American rules of dating that dictate the night or the imperatives of 2000 AD plus? How many couples scream for each other, how many business people lust for a deal and politicians scratch themselves raw for an agreement whilst half of the brain is balancing tribal rules against today's imperatives? The Foreign Corrupt Practice Act is a good example. Who is foreign and who is corrupt?

The New World Order is no different than the old world order of Shakespeare's time. A dark, uncompromising and very modern view of the world as an irrational place, ruled by violence and chance, a place in which "it is the clowns who tell the truth." Shakespeare's world, like the New World Order, reflected the decline in the values and factionization of the aristocracy that lay beneath the domestic peace of the reigns of Queen Elizabeth I and King James VI and I.

Bridging the medieval and the modern, the age of Shakespeare was a time, as Joseph Papp and Elizabeth Kirkland observed in their 1988 book, *Shakespeare Alive!,* when "nothing seemed stable or reliable anymore; the old ways were disappearing fast, and the search for a fixed point of moral reference was a futile one – everything depended on your point of view, for as Hamlet says, 'there is nothing either good or bad but thinking makes it so'."

It was an age, in Jan Kott's words, when people were forced to grapple with "the divergence between the greatness of the human mind" and "the frailty of the moral order", an age of melancholy and Machiavellianism, an age marked by a taste for violent entertainment and anxiety about the accelerating pace of social and cultural change. In short, an age oddly similar to the New World Disorder.

Peter F. Drucker, author, teacher and consultant to global business and Southern California resident and himself an immigrant, believes it is the sons and daughters of immigrants who will make the difference in the 21st century. He says, "They are hybrids of two cultures, and they have the energy and determination to show that they can do better. They are innovative."

America's immigrants are like the English-Chinese hybrid rose, found growing wild on an island in the Indian Ocean two centuries ago. Combining the best elements of genera from opposite ends of the world's largest land mass, and discovered by a French botanist under Napoleon, the bloom spawned a breeding revolution in Europe, opening new possibilities in color, shape, fragrance and vigor. Many of today's most beautiful varieties are its descendants. The saga of the bi-cultural rose species serves as metaphor and inspiration for a remarkable cross-pollination of cultures and civilizations that celebrates the meeting of East and West both in America and Hong Kong. The American bridge that unites Hong Kong and America is California. The bridge that brings America and China together is Hong Kong.

Inherent Fear

America's heritage is deeply rooted in the fear of terror. George Washington's Patriots who fought for independence were labeled terrorists by the British. Many Americans have a family heritage of fleeing religious or political terror, of having been forced to live it, "back home" or indeed in America itself from the day America was discovered. All Americans crave the freedoms America promises. Including the freedom of fear. The flicker of fear inherent in Americans was explosively rekindled on September 11. The fear of terror is one most Americans erase from their memories because of the erroneous belief and conviction that freedom-loving America is terror-free. For most Americans, the fear that terrorist violence could erupt out of nowhere, with no obvious enemy and no certainty about the day after tomorrow, feels completely new.

Ariel Dorfman, a playwright, essayist and novelist, was forced to flee his adopted country of Chile after the bloody coup led by General Augusto Pinochet. "For me, it's like living it for the second time," said Dorfman, who was born in Argentina, fled to New York with his family and ended up in Chile when Senator Joseph McCarthy set his sights on Dorfman's father. He said the attacks were particularly bizarre because September 11 was the anniversary of the 1973 coup in Chile which brought Pinochet to power and resulted in thousands of Chileans being imprisoned, tortured and killed, and "was, of course, sponsored by the United States".

Dorfman sees the attacks as a chance for countries to work together. "I hope Americans realize that this is not unique to them. This has been done over and over and over, often with the connivance of the United States – which in no way justifies the loss of even one human life," he said. "Just as fire rains down on our sky, it rains down on their sky. It's a common sky." Just because terrorism has struck innocent victims in America doesn't in and of itself justify the escalation of killing and rushing to war. All war does is create more terror and fear and create more "collateral damage" – more innocent victims.

Rejection of Election

Yet the sons and daughters of these immigrants and refugees who sought a better future for themselves and their children don't bother to exercise the rights their forbears fought and died for. Less than half of eligible Americans vote. That means that America's democratically elected president is a minority president. A president elected by less than 25 percent of the electorate. President George Dubya Bush was put in the White House to govern *We the People* by just 23 percent of eligible voters – and the Supreme Court. The Federal Election Commission figures show that ballots for 67.5 percent of registered voters were cast in the Bush-Gore presidential election – which is only 51.3 percent of eligible voters over 18. There were approximately 204 million eligible voters for Election 2000. Of these, 63 million were registered Democrats, 47 million were registered Republicans, 32 million were registered as Independents or with a minor party and over 62 million were not registered at all.

What is surprising is that the voter "turnout was unexpectedly high at 51 percent". There were 99.4 million ballots cast. Now really? Just because in 1996 "only" 49 percent of the eligible 205 million Americans voted! Even more surprising is that a poll a month before Election 2000 found nearly a third of people under 21 who were eligible to vote couldn't name any of the presidential candidates.

Voting seniors outnumber the under 30s by two-to-one. Thus the issues that dominate political campaigns and Capitol Hill are skewed in their favor. If current trends continue, the number of people of 65 and older who vote in midterm elections is likely to exceed that of young adults by a ratio of four-to-one by 2022. This is a disturbing statistic because people under 30 outnumber the over

65s, according to the Census Bureau. Younger voters are just turned off. Survey after survey only confirms that most young people cannot relate to any of the mainstream parties or their candidates. The chasm is expected to expand unless younger voters tune in.

Consequently, voters under 30 are virtually ignored by mainstream candidates because of the high cost of TV ads. Is this democracy? "It's generational profiling," said Rich Thau, president of Third Millennium, a non-profit organization that conducted a study named "Neglection 2000". Thau's group is trying to shift politicians' focus from "the next election" to "the next generation." Considering how much longer the next generation is going to live, this is quite a challenge since most people are withdrawing from politics and don't believe the political system is working. In Britain, a survey released in 2002 revealed that only two percent of the population believed the political system worked! Greater numbers now vote for reality-TV shows. "More people vote in Big Brother than in many elections. Why? Well, perhaps it's because when you vote in Big Brother, you think it will affect the outcome," said former Conservative Party chairman Theresa May.

The 21st century promises to be the golden age for both men and women. The scientific and economic changes in store give us that ability. Dr. Michio Kaku, a theoretical physicist at the City University of New York, interviewed more than 150 of the world's leading scientists for his authoritative look at the future, *Visions: How Science Will Revolutionize The 21st Century and Beyond.* He addresses menopause: designer oestrogens, bone density, pregnancy, fertility, depression, brain function, teeth, cancers, sexual health, urinary incontinence, hair, and longevity. We are going to live longer than any previous generations. We might as well learn to enjoy the extra years we are going to gain and make sure we live with a political system and process that is enjoyable.

Now if doctors can just reverse the aging process!

"I think the life cycle is all backwards. You should die first, get it out of the way. Then you live in an old age home. You get kicked out when you're too young, you get a gold watch and you go to work. You work forty years until you're young enough to enjoy your retirement. You do drugs, alcohol, you party, you get ready for high school. You go to grade school, you become a kid, you play, you have no responsibilities. You become a little baby, you go back into the womb and spend your last nine months floating... and you finish off as an orgasm." A George Carlin fantasy that *We the Maids* must keep in mind as we sweep in a political system that truly belongs to *We the People.*

People Power is a powerful and effective way to communicate with career politicians without a shot being fired. Without a person being killed. Edsa II, or People Power II in the Philippines, was a reminder in the opening year of the 21st century. Corrupt career politicians and their moneyed cronies were swept out by *We the Maids* old and young. Honking horns, nationwide strikes, office and street walkouts, student boycotts, community barricades and massive rallies and demonstrations by seniors and their children are more effective than guns. Peaceful, spontaneous, indignant, united Filipinos protesting, singing, dancing and texting (SMS) friends to join eventually got the generals, military leadership and national police to resign from government and join *We the People* to force a corrupt president to leave office and his vice president to be sworn in as president.

Some people argue it was a millennium coup similar to the one perpetrated by the political and military establishment of its former colonial parent, America. Two presidents who did not get popularly elected were sworn in on the same day. Both are children of former presidents.

Election Day
Every four years Americans, American wannabes and those having a link and connection to America, get together in a Hong Kong hotel at "Election Central" to watch the returns of the presidential election. Elsewhere, TV monitors are also flickering in clubs and offices in Hong Kong as millions of eyeballs anxiously await the returns. The sighs of disbelief at the outcome of the last presidential election of the 20th century echoed those heard when the American government shut down in 1995 due to the partisan civil war and anarchy created by the Republicans' "Contract With America". Embassies and consulates around the world, including in Hong Kong, were closed.

The Americans in Hong Kong mirror their diversity in America, where European-whites are a minority. The Asian-Americans, Filipino-Latinos and African-Americans at Election Central, both men and women, far outnumber European-Americans. They also reflect their diversity at one of Hong Kong's social season highlights: the annual Ivy Ball where graduates of America's Ivy League Universities get together to share memories of what America was. I often wonder what the Founding Fathers would think. After all, they gave only white male property owners the right to vote. Women and non-whites who did not own property were denied the right to vote when the great democracy of America was founded. Americans forget that although the Declaration of Independence of 1776 declared that "all men are created equal", African-Americans gained the right to vote only in 1870, women in 1920 and Native Americans in 1948. It wasn't until the voting age was lowered to eighteen in 1971 that the right to vote became universal.

Watching the 2000 election returns at the FCC with fellow Americans, Democrats, Republicans and Independents, we were repeatedly stunned by the media's wrong projections. Hearing that Vice President Al Gore had called to rescind his concession while waiting to hear him concede left everyone speechless. The Republicans were gleefully toasting their win when the color of their faces changed to match that of their wine, whether red or white. But then again, never in American history has a presidential candidate called to rescind an earlier concession. The millennium American political and cultural civil war had reached an abominable high. The eerie silence was pierced by hundreds simultaneously asking, "What now?"

A July 2001 study by the California Institute of Technology and MIT concluded that as many as four to six million votes cast in the 2000 presidential election may not have been counted. There are over six million eligible American voters overseas. Many were disenfranchised when their absentee ballots were discarded because the ballot envelope was unstamped – due to them being sent by diplomatic pouch or courier. Many choose not to even bother voting because of the hassle of identifying the local district where they last voted and sending in a Federal Post Card Application to register and receive an absentee ballot. Each state has different registration deadlines and notarization requirements. Why can't American citizens just go to their embassy or consulate and register to vote like the Australian and French nationals do?

Election night emphasized the need to adjust and correct the ailing political American institutions if the country is to effectively confront the 21st century. The divide and confusion in America were reflected in the extremes voiced by Americans throughout Hong Kong. The color maps repeatedly aired showed a country clearly divided. Politically and culturally. A country spinning in a political simulator that needed to be reoriented in the right direction. Hong Kong, the heart of the Orient, naturally comes to mind.

Hong Kong's "One Country, Two Systems" overshadows its "One Country, Two Cultures". Like America, Hong Kong has two cultures. The Chinese and the non-Chinese. They mirror America's bifurcated cultures. Religious rural white and non church-going urban African-Asian-Latino. Although Hong Kong has the same two cultures we see in America, in Hong Kong they are much less polarized and more harmoniously fused. However, like America, the Hong Kong public are disillusioned with politics and complain that no political party represents their interests.

Robert Lovett said: "Good judgment is the result of experience. Experience is the result of bad judgment." Will *We the Apathetic People* develop good judgment – and what forms will it take – in the new millennium?

Political Schism
Any wonder people have become apathetic and hate politics? In the 1988 election between Bush Senior and Dukakis, half the voters didn't vote, producing the lowest turnout since 1924. Two-thirds of the voters, according to a New York Times/CBS News poll, wanted choices other than Dukakis and Bush. At the time it was the highest level of dissatisfaction with the available choices ever recorded. Things only got worse as the second millennium came to a close.

The civil rights movement of the sixties created a religious conservative backlash that decided to capitalize on the new mass medium – television. Pat Robertson and Jerry Falwell led the charge that created the political schism and apathy that prevail in America today. Conservatives argue that everything wrong with America today is because of the permissive sixties and seventies. The Liberals argue the troubles are due to the selfish eighties. Both extremes are playing the blame game ad nauseam. "If conservatives and liberals have trouble facing the future, it is because doing so will require both to face up to the flaws in their world views," E.J. Dionne, Jr. reminds us and the polarized extremes. "In essence, liberals and conservatives disagree over what are the most important sins. For conservatives, the sins that matter are personal irresponsibility, the flight from family life, sexual permissiveness, the failure of individuals to work hard. For liberals, the gravest sins are intolerance, a lack of generosity toward the needy, narrow-mindedness toward social and racial minorities. Since the 1960s, American politics has been a war over which set of sins should preoccupy government. Conservatives preached that the good society would be created if individuals could be made virtuous. Liberals preached that the good society would create virtuous individuals," Dionne observes.

The political schism between black and white America is best highlighted every four years during the presidential election. In the race to the White House, Republicans win the majority of the white support while the Democrats win the black votes.

Until the 1930s, most blacks voted Republican out of loyalty to the party that had brought them emancipation. Franklin D. Roosevelt's New Deal permitted many African-Americans to start voting Democratic. Jeremy D. Mayer, in his book *Running On Race: Racial Politics in Presidential Campaigns, 1960-2000* addresses the history and significance of the black-white political schism in America.

The black vote was up for grabs in the 1960 election between John F. Kennedy and Richard M. Nixon because both had promised to improve the lot of African-Americans. However, when Martin Luther King Jr. was arrested in Georgia, Kennedy telephoned King's wife, Coretta, to express sympathy. This calculated gesture motivated a majority of blacks to vote Democratic. After Lyndon B. Johnson signed the 1965 Voting Rights Act the Democrats locked up the black vote. The result was that both black and white registration to vote surged. The whites, particularly Southerners, eventually switched their allegiance to the Republican Party.

The Southern right "combines the political economy of plantation owners with the fundamental religion of hillbillies," Michael Lind points out. "In the 21st century, the right in Texas and the South remains a museum of 17th and 18th century rural British traditions that died out long ago in Britain itself and in other parts of the English-speaking world. The reasons for the persistence of these archaic, pre-modern British cultural traditions in Southern states like Texas have been poverty, social conservatism, and the lack of immigration of the kind which created diverse melting-pot cultures in other regions of the United States," Lind astutely reminds us.

When George H.W. Bush won the presidential election in 1988 it was in no small measure due to the millions of dollars spent by the GOP to make Willie Horton a household name. The racial overtones of the Horton political commercial of the 1988 campaign mushroomed through the midterm elections of 1990 and 2002. Mudslinging has become such a political art form that it is not done by the candidates but by their parties. The candidates are aware that voters despise negative advertising and therefore stick to positive messages. This is the legacy of politics in America from the sixties. E. J. Dionne Jr., in his incisive book *Why Americans Hate Politics,* asks: "A polarized politics that highlights symbolic issues, short circuits genuine political debate, gives discontent few real outlets, allows money a paramount role in the electoral process, and leaves the country alarmed over whether it can maintain its standard of living. Is it any wonder Americans have come to hate politics?"

Crushed Majority
"Chinese people face enormous hurdles trying to balance their duty to the nation and their individual values. Those who toe the line are crushed to death," said Gao Xingjian, the Chinese Nobel laureate. What he said about the Chinese also applies to America. Apathetic people being crushed because they just toe the line.

America is a misrepresented silent majority that has accepted apathy as a cultural imperative. Is this what America's cultural heritage is all about? Hopefully, Norman Lear and David Hayden will change that dismal statistic with their traveling show based on the Declaration of Independence, though that looks increasingly unlikely unless *We the Maids* sweep in changes to the current system. These people came to America for real representation, prosperity and security – not to join a Gadarene rush to vote for human sedatives like Bush and Gore. Dolly Parton summed the "least worst option" best. "It comes down to a choice between the redneck and the no-neck." Or is it stiff neck? Is this democracy? Ralph Nader said it best when accused of being a spoiler. "You can't spoil a system spoiled to the core." This is not "smash mouth" politics. This is political reality.

The Dixie Chicks are on the right track working with Rock the Vote and asking them to send representatives on their "Home" concert tour to encourage young people to register to vote and speak up on issues of concern. More artists should do the same if *We the Maids* are to sweep in change. Let's not forget the words of Thomas Paine: "The cause of America is in great measure the cause of all mankind." Today it is an "electoral joke".

The Florida Tidal Basin legal swamp over which the United States Supreme Court presided in order to appoint America's 43rd president has many precedents on display in Washington DC. They show what can happen when career politicians and jurists ignore the plight of *We the People.* The Hillwood Museum near the National Zoo, the former home of cereal heiress Marjorie Merriweather Post, has on display rare Faberge Eggs, a crown worn by Alexandra during her wedding to Nicholas II and other priceless ceramics, crystal, portraits and opulent items. They represent the arrogance of the Czarist regime before it was overthrown by the people.

Dumbarton Oaks in Georgetown, formerly owned by the Robert Woods Bliss family, houses extensive Byzantine and pre-Columbian art collections deeded to Harvard University. The pre-Columbian gold, silver, stone, jade and ceramic pieces are from the Mayan, Aztec and Olmec cultures.

The pre-Columbian, Byzantine and Czarist empires evaporated because of their failure to recognize and come to terms with political reality. Their presence in Washington is a daily reminder that the same can happen to these "Disunited States" if *We the Maids* remain apathetic in the 21st century.

Just like the Oldsmobile, America's first mass-produced car, America's Oldpolitix, the first mass-produced democratic political model, is no longer functional. *We the Apathetic Maids* have to sweep out the old, defective, retread career politicians with their worn-out labels of liberalism and conservatism and sweep in truth and reality. This is a political truism. It is inevitable that a country that tolerates and encourages racial prejudice, hatred of others and contempt for its political system because it tunes out the voices of the majority of its citizens while it professes to be open and democratic will continue to breed countless Timothy McVeighs and Osama bin-Ladens whose terror tactics will further isolate Americans in self-defined cocoons of fear in the 21st century.

To overcome this fear *We the Apathetic Maids* have to sweep in the constitutional self-evident truths that all men and women are created equal and that we have nothing to fear but fear itself. Fear, prejudice and hate can be eradicated if *We the People* start practicing what the Founding Fathers preached. Equality, justice, liberty and freedom for all people and beliefs. We have to acknowledge and accept our diversity. Knowledge, tolerance and the understanding of others rid us of insecurity, paranoia and unnecessary aggressive behavior that more often than not turns deadly.

We the Maids have to sweep in the social activism necessary to wake up the silent majority required to bring about the necessary reforms needed to marginalize the ruling extremist tyrants now shaping our lives and world. *We the Maids* have to stand up and be counted to make politics relevant, responsive and fear-free. The current passionate politics of violent gun law advocated and practiced by McVeigh, bin-Laden and Bush disciples has to be terminated if there is to be a New World Order.

Hong Kong Buffet
Back in the hot Thai sun, I continued to daydream on the veranda. The sound of the sliding door opening and Julia's voice announcing that "Austen is asleep and lunch is ready" brought me to my feet. Auntie Mame was right. "Life is a banquet and most poor sons

of bitches are starving."

"Le Chaim – To Life," Julia toasted as we all got ready to ravage the food to satisfy the appetite the clean ocean air had re-ignited. "To new life," I responded.

It is inevitable that there will be starvation, confusion and ignorance well into the new century. That I can clink glasses with a fed family in a beach house in the hot Thai sun whilst children starve in ghettos in America, Afghanistan and Africa is not going to end quickly. Nor can I rave against it and stay sane. If our children peacefully and consciously work to the acceptance of the universality of people and insist upon it as a foundation of the New World Order, we may get through the veil of tears. Confucius will help. Anglo-Saxon Protestantism will help. Muslim charity will help. Buddhist spirituality will help. Hindu compassion will help and that mad and wonderful Latino-Filipino Catholicism will help too. And one place to find reference to all that is in that noisy little brat – Hong Kong.

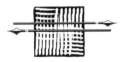

Chapter Three

Fundamental Religious Crusades

Imagine - John Lennon

Religious Harmony

Hong Kong has roughly six hundred temples, monasteries and shrines. Most are small. Some are enormous, including a high rise Zoroastrian Temple in Causeway Bay, the Jamia Mosque on Shelley Street, Ohel Leah Synagogue on Robinson Road, Saint John's Cathedral on Garden Road, the Po Lin Monastery on Lantau Island, the Temple of Ten Thousand Buddhas at Shatin and Wong Tai Sin Temple in Kowloon. The 26-meter tall, 220-ton Tian Tan Buddha at Po Lin is the world's largest outdoor bronze Buddha. One the Taleban would love to dynamite. An ideal setting for an Al Gore fundraiser. The hair-raising bus ride along the steep and narrow road to the Buddha takes the traveler past Christian monasteries co-existing off the same road, and reminds one of how different religions can co-exist harmoniously as they do in Hong Kong. On any day one can see Buddhists, Christians, Hindus, Jews, Muslims, Taoists and a variety of other traditional and new age believers all interact. They shop, eat, do business and play together. The God most Hong Kongers believe in is Mammon, the God of Gold, but Buddha, God and Allah also play a spiritual role.

Confucianism is not a religion. It embraces ancestor worship and in pure Confucianism there is no supernatural element involved. It is a political philosophy designed to create a stable society based on filial piety, a system where the older generation expects to be obeyed. The staunch Confucians were the literati who were the ruling class. The nearest of these gentry in Hong Kong were the Tang clan who controlled the lands around Kam Tin in the New Territories. However, there were no literati living on Hong Kong Island when the British took over in 1841 and many of the population worshipped the old Earth Gods.

A giant park with a Christian theme is being built on Ma Wan Island. "Rainbow Paradise" was inspired by the tale of Noah's Ark and is being funded by Protestant groups. They hope it will complement the Hong Kong Disneyland.

Robert Hendricks, the exuberant professor of religion at Dartmouth College in New Hampshire, who was raised as a Lutheran, says: "In Christianity, we grow up to think in very moral terms: what to and what not to do. With the Tao, virtue is invisible. Virtue is energy, a force. According to the book, it is the creator of ten thousand things, it pushes you to grow and nurture yourself not through rules but according to your nature."

Western religions base themselves on a negative attitude towards humanity – whether via the Christian notion of original sin or the Jewish contract with the Ten Commandments. Taoism, says Hendricks, "takes a more golden view of people. The Tao says that if people are left to their own devices, if they simply let their own nature take its natural course, then people will be actually good."

Climbing the stairs towards the Tian Tan Buddha, in company with many people of different faiths – some come to pray and burn incense, others to sightsee – I couldn't get out of my head how peaceful religious co-existence is in Hong Kong. It contrasts markedly with the religious conflicts in America and elsewhere. The mellow faces of the monks and initiates, clad in their saffron robes, swim tolerantly in a sea of Chinese and Barbarian faces of all colors and creeds.

When the monks' oasis was threatened by a government mass transit redevelopment project that would bring a cable car and mega-tourist bazaar with bars and restaurants to their remote outpost, the monks threatened to close off the monastery grounds to the thousands of daily visitors for a week. The monks, strict vegetarians who have succeeded in persuading local vendors not to even sell seafood in the vicinity, were horrified at the prospect of losing money from tourists chomping on Big Macs and chicken legs as they walked past the holy relics.

They took out full page ads in several Chinese-language newspapers asking the public to support their demand that the government reconsider the proposed development. The threatened closure and publicity worked. The government reconsidered the project.

These same saffron-clad monks shivered as they gaped in amazement at the snow spewed out by snow machines at the Euro Christmas 2000 display on a Hong Kong promenade. Children, many of whom had never seen snow, made snowmen and had snowball fights. European customs were on display and European foods served. Midnight mass was non-denominational. The Chief Rabbi, Muslim Mullah, and all Christian and non-Christian denominations were invited to participate. This was before 9/11.

Studying, the cheerful faces of locals and visitors alike as they enjoyed the Great Buddha or the snow, I couldn't help but reflect on how brutal religions have been and wonder why all religions cannot co-exist as peacefully as they do in Hong Kong. Why do Christians and Muslims have to continue their vengeful religious crusades in the 21st century? Why does religion have to continue being the root of all evil in the 21st century?

Burning Religious Zeal
Religion remains the root of much of the suffering and pain at the dawn of the new millennium. War, hunger, divorce, hypocrisy, illiteracy, prejudice and hatred. These anguishing issues with religious roots have to be addressed directly if we want everlasting solutions. Religion can be the most unifying force on earth instead of the most destructive.

How different are extreme Christian fundamentalists from Muslim fundamentalists? How different are Pat Robertson and Jerry Falwell from Osama bin-Laden and the Taleban's leader Mullah Omar? Extreme Christian beliefs brought about the Crusades. Extreme Muslim beliefs brought on 9/11. Religious zealots embracing ideas that are dated and not in tune with the reality of the 21st century.

Franklin Graham, Billy Graham's son, called Islam a "very evil and wicked religion". Pat Robertson said: "To think that Islam is a peaceful religion is fraudulent." Robertson went on to call the Prophet Muhammad "an absolute wild-eyed fanatic...a robber and brigand...a killer." Pat Robertson, Jerry Falwell, Osama bin-Laden and Mullah Omar claim God has been insulted by those that do not adhere to their interpretation of the message of God. God's anger against America was the reason for the bombings of September 11, according to televangelists Jerry Falwell and Pat Robertson. Osama bin-Laden and Muslim fundamentalists agree. Now who is on which side?

The Bible, Koran, American Constitution and Declaration of Independence express and echo the language and prophesies of the prophets and sages who recorded their messages of peace, harmony and understanding, not hatred and bigotry.

Why do mainstream religious teachings in America and the Muslim world instill fear of their own God and his damnation, fear of other religions, fear of mixed marriages and fear of co-existence? If I have to answer my own questions, I have to recognize that, for poor and working class people, with nothing else to brighten up dull lives in grubby places, sectarian religious organization is an excitement, something of a rush, a harbinger of violence and a definition of themselves. God, Christ and Muhammad were much more tolerant and understanding than their extremist self-serving apostles advocate to inspire their misguided followers.

How any of these extremists can implicate Allah or God in their extreme beliefs is absurd yet understandable. Governor Ventura tried to make this point in his Playboy interview. "I was commenting on the fact that organized religion gets misused a lot. In the hands of the corrupt, it can become a way of controlling people, when people with religious authority start to pretend they speak for God. Worse still is when corrupt people with religious authority also start courting political authority. The combination can be deadly." For a wrestler he makes more sense than most priests, and certainly more than career politicians. Some are so fiery and scalding one would think they must have been burned at the stake in a former life.

Hypo-Christians and hypo-Muslims, the extreme hypocrites in both faiths, have to be removed from the current New World Disorder and put in their place if we are to have a functional 21st century. It is up to *We the Maids* to sweep them aside.

The picture of President George W. Bush standing next to a Muslim cleric and Jewish rabbi in Washington National Cathederal on the Day of Prayer and Rememberance for those killed on September 11 is what America is all about. Tolerance of all religions and beliefs. No religious extremes.

Religion and Politics – A Lethal Combination
In Hong Kong there is a separation between Church and State and different religious groups live harmoniously. People of all religions have been working together for over a century and a half. One's political beliefs and affiliation have no bearing on what is important – business.

Historically, religion, politics and business in America have been intertwined. Unfortunately, *We the Apathetic People* have paid the price. "The First Amendment offers the same protection for religious freedom – even the freedom not to be religious if we don't want to be – as it does for freedom of speech and thought. The First Amendment basically says that religion is none of the government's business," Governor Ventura reminds us. Atheists and Pagans are also protected under the First Amendment. Business, like politics, works best without the interference of the divine. Hong Kong is a divine example.

There has to be a clear-cut separation of religious and governmental authority. Feudal religious-political marriages of convenience have no place in the New World Order the 21st century promises. Is America a democratic republic or a Christian fiefdom?

The decision by Turkey's highest court in the last decade of the 20th century to ban the country's largest political party on the grounds of subversion was a positive step. The court ruled its political agenda sought to replace the secular order, created by the founder of modern Turkey Kemal Attaturk, with one based on Islam. The court also banned the leaders of the religious Welfare Party from all political activity. When the party renamed itself, and declared itself secular and promised not to mix religion with politics, it was allowed to retain the political offices it won in the 2002 national election. Isn't it time America did the same?

To American Democrats, banning a party with a religious platform is undemocratic. In Turkey, Kemal Attaturk brought the rump of an empire out of decadence and humiliation and set in motion his vision of a secular and progressive nation. Attaturk abolished the Islamic Caliphate and replaced it with the Turkish Republic in 1923. He dissolved religious courts, secularized schools, replaced Arabic script with Latin script, replaced the fez with the homburg, adopted the Swiss civil code and granted women the right to vote. Isn't that what America's Founding Fathers had in mind? Isn't it the model other Islamic Republics should emulate?

The U.S. federal court was right to reject the Virginia-based Family Policy Network suit against the University of North Carolina for teaching Islam on the grounds it was unconstitutional for a publicly-funded university to do so. The Family Policy Network continuously lobbies for taxpayer dollars to fund its activities. A classic example of a white Christian religious pot calling Islam a black kettle.

The idea of a White House Office of Faith-Based and Community Initiatives to expand charitable choice is unconstitutional and a feudal regression. Why should any religious organization in America get federal funds? Why don't they provide food, jobs, shelter and education with all the tax-deductible donations they collect directly every Sabbath – and at every other opportunity – from *We the Apathetic People?*

To add insult to injury, the faith-based program bill proposed allowing religious groups that receive federal funds to discriminate in hiring and firing based on religious beliefs!

Religion should not be a department of state and used as a political or military tool to expand the interests of the state. There has to be a separation between church and state. There is no room for religious parties, or religious extremists who dictate a party platform, to play a role in any government in the New World Order. Not in the United States, Israel, any of its Muslim neighbors or any forward-thinking country. And just as important, religious organizations should be self-sufficient. They cannot and should not be supported with taxpayer's money in the New World Order. *We the Maids* can no longer be taxed to clean up continued religious mistakes and failures.

Married Priests

Catholic priests who want to get married, and are open and honest about it, can be found by the thousands. Church bells in the opening year of the millennium rang the echoed marriage vows of Catholic Archbishop Emmanuel Milingo of Lusaka who "placed himself outside the church" by marrying. The 71-year-old Archbishop said God wants him and the Catholic Church to abandon the celibacy rule. The interfaith melodrama he created between the Catholic Church and the Unification Church when the Archbishop decided to leave his wife and return to the Catholic Church only highlighted the absurdity of celibacy.

Consider these terms in the 21st century: Padre and Grandpadre. In the Philippines, like all former Spanish colonies, padre, or father, has always had a double meaning when applied to priests. Many Latinos have holy blood. Spanish blood from a priest was an honor because it improved the lineage and looks. The most famous descendant of a priest is former first lady Imelda Marcos. "I don't understand what the fuss is to have a priest as an ancestor. It was something we took for granted," she said.

It gets better. When a secular priest tied the knot with his partner of 25 years, formalizing a relationship that has given them two children and two grandchildren, members of the 1,000-strong Philippine Federation of Married Catholic Priests attended the ceremony. Since married priests have no authority to solemnize a marriage, a Regional Trial Court judge administered civil rites. At the rate they are going, there won't be a priest left in the church to solemnize a marriage in the Philippines.

The Pope and the Vatican are dangerously out of touch with their priests and congregations. According to Father Ed Kelly, a non-practicing Irish priest based in Manila, "the majority of Catholics favor letting their priests marry. Surveys in Ireland put 82 percent in favor and in America it is 69 percent." How appropriate a number. Why isn't the church listening?

According to Justino Cabazares, the president of the Filipino chapter of the International Federation of Married Catholic Priests (IFMCP), about two-thirds of the priesthood there, some 4,000 of the 6,700 men, have a lover. Most love in secret, though in many countryside communities it is an open secret.

Why is the celibacy vow enforced more than the vow of chastity? Many priests throughout the Philippines and the Latino world are of the opinion that hypocrisy is an evil bigger than optional celibacy. They contend they can count on their fingers how many priests, at least in their diocese, are truly chaste and celibate. Is that any different in America?

Catholic priests everywhere are getting married. Not just in the Philippines. About 20,000 former priests in Spain and Italy are now married, according to Spanish and Italian organizations of married priests, and another 80,000 elsewhere have left the ministry to marry. God knows how many there are in America.

The Spanish Church – traditionally one of the most steadfast pillars of Catholicism – is rapidly running out of clerics, ordaining around 200 priests every year as 400 retire or leave, according to the weekly *Cambio 16.*

Celibacy became commonplace by about 300 AD., when the Spanish Council of Elvira mandated that bishops, priests and deacons who were married refrain from sex with their wives. Stricter Church laws were enacted by the First Lateran Council of 1123 and confirmed by subsequent councils. The crackdown was a response to widespread corruption, as priests and bishops openly took wives and had children who then inherited their property – thus taking land away from the Church. Celibacy has been mandatory for Catholic priests only since the Second Lateran Council in 1139. It was believed it would increase the number of candidates fourfold and would prevent priests from impoverishing the Church by leaving property to their children.

The child molestation-sex abuse victims of priests argue that priests and bishops who are sexually active with adults create a web of dishonesty in the Church. These men are reluctant to reveal wrong-doings by fellow clergy, including child molesters, for fear of being exposed themselves. Sexually active priests-heterosexuals, pedophiles and gays living and protecting each other in a hypocritical web of divine heavenly deceit. Dean Hoge, a professor of sociology at Catholic University, in a 1985 study of college men, concluded that making celibacy optional, as it is for Eastern Orthodox and Protestant clergy, should be considered.

Alfredo Romualdez, a doctor and former Philippine health secretary, says: "Celibacy may pose some risk to health," claiming that chastity can increase the risk of cancer. Graham Giles of Australia's Cancer Council says that research shows that Roman Catholic priests are 30 percent more likely to get prostate cancer. It is not only the health of the priests at stake but the health and very survival of the Church. Who will administer the Catholic Church's last rites? According to a two-year study presented to the National Conference of Catholic Bishops in 2000, more American priests died in 1999 than were ordained. As a result, 3,000 of America's roughly 19,000 parishes were left without a resident pastor and about 2,400 have to share one. The study also pointed out that the average age of priests in America is 57. Even more troubling, of roughly 27,000 active priests only 298 were under 30. The exodus from nunneries is even more spectacular.

Sexual Abuses – Wired Apology

A month doesn't seem to go by without reading about some case being settled somewhere by the Church or a court awarding a judgment against the church for child abuse by clergymen. Since 1978, over 3,000 Catholic priests have been accused of sexual assault in America alone. Maybe it's just the legacy of prospective Popes having their testicles checked by a young Cardinal, while seated in the sedia stercoraria on their coronation day, to confirm that the future Pope is a male after Pope Joan and her child were killed. More on Pope Joan later!

Church, or Canon, law, which is published in Latin, went through its last complete revision in 1983. It requires all cases of sexual abuse by priests to be referred to the Vatican alone instead of being handled locally. Historically, the Vatican distanced itself from such cases because it believed the problem was limited to America. Now that Austria, Australia, France, Ireland, Portugal and even Pope John Paul's Poland are embroiled in sex scandals the church is acknowledging it is not just an American problem. Pedophilia and homosexuality are global Catholic problems.

Father Patrick O'Neill, a high-ranking priest in the Miami archdiocese and former University professor, was arrested and charged with soliciting sex after he pulled his Mercedes to a stop and propositioned a male undercover cop.

Phoenix Bishop Thomas O'Brien was under so much criticism for knowingly re-assigning known priestly sex offenders that he was forced to resign, not for his re-assignments, but because of a fatal hit-and-run. He left the scene of a traffic fatality after he killed Jim Reed.

In earlier days, like today, Catholic priests were merely transferred to other parishes. One of the older cases I enjoyed reading about, actually the first recorded case of sexual harassment, and the first where the woman won, occurred in the Philippines. Loreto Lucero, who was 16 in 1894, slapped Padre Santiago Perez, parish priest of Sta. Ysabel, Bulacan, and pushed him down the stairs of her father's house. He had made advances and used vulgar language, and she had the courage to express her indignation in positive action. She went to court and won. The friar was transferred to another town.

The Pope apologized to nuns and other people who have been sexually abused by Catholic clerics in his first address to the world via the Internet. He acknowledged the Church's failure to stop abuse and asked for forgiveness. Why hasn't he used the same strong words of apology addressed to all the innocent children who were abused and suffered because of the Church's shortcomings? To read that as the Vicar of Christ "knows what's been happening in the U.S. but we don't think he needs to know all the gory details" is astounding. Why not? Is it because at the height of the sex scandals he truly represented the Church he led? Frail and sick?

The scarlet color of Cardinals' hats and robes represents blood, the willingness of the cardinals to make the ultimate sacrifice. What will their ultimate sacrifice be in the 21st century?

In Hong Kong priests that engage in pedophilia and are reported to the diocese get fired, suspended, or in the case of one minor infraction, removed to duties not involving contact with children. The head of the Catholic Church in Hong Kong, Cardinal John Baptist Wu, said: "The diocesan authorities cannot and will not tolerate pedophile practices in any shape or form, whether of the serial or singular kind, least of all among those in the sacred ministry, in whom the faithful in particular and the public in general place a special trust." Police arrest the priests in question when the abuse becomes public. Isn't this what the Catholic Church in the Vatican and America should be saying and doing?

Kevin Sinclair, an FCC regular, broke the Hong Kong church sex story. While being debated at the Main Bar and compared to the injustices in America and the Vatican, Stuart Wolfendale regaled those gathered with a joke he had just heard from a friend in America with his best Irish accent.

Tommy Shaughnessy enters the confessional box and says, "Bless me Father, for I have sinned. I have been with a loose woman." The priest asks, "Is that you, little Tommy Shaughnessy?" "Yes Father it is." "And who was the woman you were with?" "I can't be tellin' you Father. I don't want to ruin her reputation." "Well Tommy, I'm sure to find out sooner or later, so you may as well tell me now. Was it Brenda O'Malley?" "I cannot say." "Was it Patricia Kelly?" "I'll never tell." "Was it Liz Shannon?" "I'm sorry, but I'll not tell her name." "Was it Cathy Morgan?" "My lips are sealed." "Was it Fiona McDonald then?" "Please Father, I cannot tell you." The priest sighs in frustration. "You're a steadfast lad, Tommy Shaughnessy, and I admire that, but you've sinned and you must atone." He gave Tommy penance and dismissed him. Tommy walks back to his pew and sits down. His friend Sean slides over and whispers to Tommy, "What'd you get?" Tommy said, "Five good leads."

More seriously, though, Catholic dioceses and their insurers have had to pay out billions of dollars to victims. The Church would like the world to think all this is a media-honed misconception, of course. But if officers of a corporation or a business were repeatedly found guilty of such offenses, the company would be banished from the community or forced into a bankruptcy court and required to restructure, and its officers would be jailed. Why should churches be any different? Especially, since they receive our hard-earned tax dollars from the government. Tax exemptions do not exempt religious figures and their churches from criminal prosecution. Pedophile priests should not be sent to a different playpen. They belong in jail.

Former Oklahoma Governor Frank Keating resigned in June 2003 as head of the Church's sexual abuse oversight panel after his blunt criticism of the Church's attempts to thwart his group's inquiries. Keating compared some Church leaders to the Cosa Nostra for hiding information on the pedophile sex scandal. Yet several cardinals and bishops continue to suppress damaging information in spite of pledges in June 2002 to be more open.

The Massachusetts Attorney General, Tom Reilly, accused the Boston Catholic Church of perpetuating a "culture of secrecy". "The mistreatment of children was so massive and so prolonged that it borders on the unbelievable," Reilly said when he released his report in 2003 on a 16-month investigation into sexually abusive priests in the Boston archdiocese. The archdiocese's own records documented that 789 victims had come forward since 1940 with allegations of abuse against 237 priests – numbers that highlight the "inexcusable failure" of Church leaders to put a stop to the mistreatment. "When information from other sources is considered, the number of alleged victims who have disclosed their abuse likely exceeds 1,000," the report said. And that is just for the Boston area.

The report detailed a "culture of secrecy" within the archdiocese that was more concerned with protecting abusive priests and the reputation of the Church from scandal than protecting the children at risk.

The Catholic Church's Sexgate cover-up is more contemptible than Monicagate because the victims are young and innocent. The Church's refusal to recognize that the world has changed and that people are not as ignorant or gullible as they were in feudal times is just as pathetic and has to be registered loudly and clearly. Mel Gibson is to be applauded for criticizing the Catholic Church. "I believe in God," he told the newspaper *Il Giornale*. "My love for religion was transmitted to me by my father. But I do not believe in the

Church as an institution."

Sex-offending priests should be treated no different than anyone else. The First Amendment guarantee of religious freedom does not protect or exempt priests who are pedophiles or sex criminals. It is not a liability shield behind which any church is allowed to hide any more. Men and women of the cloth of all religions can no longer be allowed to hide behind the facade or vestment of a church in the 21st century. The Catholic Church in America does not have diplomatic immunity. Priests should be treated no different than doctors, teachers and others who come into daily contact with children. They can no longer be exempted from any state mandatory reporting law in the 21st century.

Breach of Faith
Religious slush funds serve a myriad of purposes. Monsignor Emilio Colaiovanni, who lives in Rome and has counseled Pope John Paul, was charged with fraud and conspiracy by U.S. federal prosecutors because he pledged $1 billion from the St. Francis of Assisi Foundation charitable foundation that he ran as collateral to Martin Frankel's insurance scam. The Monsignor had his own slush fund set up with the $40,000 he received from Frankel as the down payment for the additional $5 million he was promised.

What about the suicide, murder and gay sex that belie the pomp and circumstance of the 500-year-old Swiss Guard? In their dated uniforms designed by Michelangelo, the private army is dedicated to ensuring the Pope's personal safety. It arrived in Rome in 1506 to protect Pope Julius II from infidels. Today it is protecting itself from the events of May 4, 1998, when the bodies of the newly appointed commander of the guard, Alois Estermann, his Venezuelan wife and 23-year-old Vice-Corporal Cedric Tornay were found in the Estermanns' Vatican flat.

The discovery of the body of Roberto Calvi, "God's Banker", found hanging on Blackfriars Bridge in London on June 15, 1982, has led investigators into the close-knit web of the Vatican's criminal dealings with Italy's prime ministers, bankers and mafia godfathers. The murdered body of Calvi, disguised to look like a suicide, led police investigators to the secretive right-wing Masonic lodge called Propaganda Due, or P2. Calvi was a member of P2 which has been linked with Nazism and by some theorists to the assassination of Prime Minister Aldo Moro and the unexpected death of Pope John Paul I, both in 1978.

Gone With the Wind in the Vatican is an account of intrigue, homosexuality, money smuggling and corruption within the Vatican bureaucracy. Written by Father Morinelli, who worked in the Vatican, the book and writer clashed head on with Vatican censors.

"The book does not question the sanctity of Jesus Christ, the Eucharist or the Catholic Church," Morinelli said. "It just points out that the Vatican is made up of men, who, like me, are flawed." So flawed that they even refused to admit that the Vatican radio antennae may have spread cancer faster than religion. The residents of Cesano, a suburb north of Rome, were subjected to emissions from Vatican Radio transmitters that broadcast Roman Catholic programs to five continents. The Vatican, invoking its status as a sovereign state, refused to comply with Italian safety regulations until the Italian government threatened to cut off power to the station.

If the flaws of the Catholic Church are to be remedied in the New World Order, American Catholics have to take the lead, just as they did in the pedophile sex scandals. The American Roman Catholic Church is the third largest in the world. It has over 63 million members. It is unlikely that an American will be elected Pope. It is therefore up to *We the Maids* to sweep the Vatican clean of feudal ideals in the 21st century.

The Reformers
It is the South and Central American prelates along with the English, Dutch and Germans who are the reformers dealing with reality. They have in the past and will continue to do so in the 21st century.

Historical religious abuses and mis-steps are not limited to Catholics. Buddhist monks, Jewish rabbis, Muslim mullahs and men of the cloth of all religious beliefs are fallible human beings. In Japan a Buddhist priest was arrested for forging minutes of the religious corporation's board meeting in order to assume the presidency.

The Taleban leadership in Afghanistan was a current prime time 21st century New World Disorder example of a religious one-hit wonder. They hanged television sets and draped trees with videotape pulled from cassettes. Computers were "executed" on the spot with rifle butts to the monitors. The Taleban and technology were enemies from the start. Except when it came to air-conditioned SUVs. They were a lot cooler and faster than the camels and donkeys they were preaching everyone else should use. "Do you know why they don't teach sex education and drivers education in Afghanistan the same day?" was a popular question circulating around the FCC Main Bar after the U.S. bombing raids on Afghanistan started to flush out Osama bin-Ladin and Mullah Omar. "Because it's too hard on the camels!"

Chevrolet Suburbans are Osama bin-Laden and Mullah Omar's vehicle of choice and Toyota Land Cruisers are an acceptable backup. Preferably the ones with the smokestack-like air inductors running up the windshield pillars. The minimum cost is $50,000 for the basic package – and then there are the extras to be tacked on. But, what the hell, like other religions the mosque and the believers will pay. Wade Hoyt, Toyota's spokesman in New York, put the best corporate spin. "It is not our proudest product placement," he said. "But it shows that the Taleban are looking for the same qualities as any truck buyer: durability and reliability." What happened to the camels? Probably smoking them.

All religious leaders, regardless of their religion, succumb to human nature and temptations. Even their teachings cannot stop them from being human. So why do they insist everyone else should practice what they preach and cannot practice?

I have never been able to understand the logic of people who go to priests to confess or seek counseling for problems of the heart or family. How can unmarried, chaste priests, or surreptitiously unchaste priests for that matter, really understand confessions relating to sexual matters, personal family problems and the torment of extra-marital relationships? Do they really understand?

What is it going to take for *We the Maids* to sweep reform in to organized religion and force reform so that organized religion has the tools people need as we face the realities of the new millennium?

Sex, Pill, Abortion, In-vitro and Cloning
Abortion is a reality in both Hong Kong and America. In fact Hong

Kong has one of the highest abortion rates in the world. This is because of the Chinese cultural attitudes towards children born outside an acceptable family structure. As a result, only two percent of babies in Hong Kong are born outside marriage, compared to more than 30 percent in the United States. Abortion is the reason for the disparity in numbers.

The Pope and the Catholic Church's position on celibacy, sex, birth control, abortion, in-vitro fertilization and cloning have done more damage to the Church's relevance in the 21st century than anything else

The Catholic Church's ultimate excessive religious reach and interference beyond the bounds of basic human decency was its pronouncement condemning the raped Kosovar women who wanted to abort their unwanted Serb offspring.

The Vatican reiterated its condemnation of all such efforts by volunteers and international organizations, no matter how desperate the women were. "The 'morning after pill' does not exist," declared Monsignor Elio Sgreccia. "This is an abortion." Most of the Kosovar rape victims are Muslims, not Roman Catholics, but that detail doesn't alter the Church's stance. I hate to think what they will say and do now that the abortion pill RU486 has been approved by the FDA.

People in the Philippines, like their brothers and sisters in Latin America and the U.S., are too poor to follow the dictates of the Catholic Church to the letter, especially when it comes to contraception. If they listen to the church they won't be able to feed all their children. That is why there are so many abandoned street children in Catholic countries. The overriding pre-occupation to procreate more Catholics seems to override and obviate the concern that they may be poor and suffer. But then again, that fits in with the teachings of the Church. Listen, suffer and a better world awaits in the hereafter. Any wonder the masses welcomed Geri Halliwell, the Goodwill Ambassador for the International Advocacy Campaign for Reproductive Health Care, Gender Equality and the Empowerment of Women throughout the world, while the Church protested? Why is the Church doing nothing to house and feed the homeless and hungry children created by its own dictatorial practices? Not just in the Philippines but in all Catholic countries in the New World Disorder?

Catholic Church leaders in the Philippines were outraged at the former Spice Girl's trip to promote safe sex and birth control. She was greeted at a Manila high school by adoring screaming crowds. "It was like sending Salman Rushdie as an ambassador of goodwill to a Muslim country," Monsignor Pedro Quitorio, spokesman for the Philippines Catholic Bishops' conference, said. What hypocrisy! Most Catholic Filipinas practice birth control otherwise their families would starve on the street!

The Catholic Church's teachings in Africa and the Catholic developing world banning the use of condoms to prevent the spread of AIDS by pronouncing condoms to be porous and the tool of Satan for spreading AIDS is reprehensible. The Church is consciously killing millions of innocent believers with its deceitful hypocritical propaganda. The Church's blind determination to ban all forms of contraception is not only unethical, but criminal.

On the flip side, the Catholic Church is opposed to in-vitro fertilization that some of its devout followers advocate and practice because they want children and cannot have them the "church's way". When it comes to cloning there is nothing to discuss. Kind of ironic that the foremost advocate and practitioner of cloning is an Italian Roman Catholic. In-vitro and cloning are issues the Church has to address and come to terms with as it must with birth control and abortion in the 21st century.

Jerusalem
Joseph Farah, an Arab-American journalist, reminds us that East Jerusalem was not captured from Yasser Arafat and the Palestinians during the Six Day War. In fact Arafat was not born in Jerusalem either. He was born in Egypt. Jerusalem was captured from Jordan's King Hussein. "The truth is that Palestine is no more real than Never-Never Land. The first time Palestine was used was in 70 AD when the Romans committed genocide against the Jews, smashed the Temple and declared the land of Israel will be no more. They promised from then on the land of Israel would be known as Palestine – a name derived from the Philistines, a Goliathian people conquered by the Jews earlier. Palestine has never existed before

or since as an autonomous entity. There is no language known as Palestinian. There is no distinct Palestine culture. Palestinians are Arabs, indistinguishable from Jordanians, Syrians, Lebanese or Iraqis. There has never been a land known as Palestine governed by Palestinians. It was ruled alternatively by Rome, by Islamic and Christian crusaders, by the Ottoman Turks and, briefly, by the British after World War I."

Arthur Hacker was listening for a change. "What about Islam's holy sites? There are none in Jerusalem. Shocked?" Farah continues. "You should be. I don't expect you will ever hear this brutal truth from any one else in the international media. It's just not politically correct. It's not true that the Al-Aqsa Mosque and the Dome of the Rock in Jerusalem represent Islam's third most holy site. In fact, the Koran says nothing about Jerusalem. It mentions Mecca hundreds of times. It never mentions Jerusalem. With good reason. There is no historical evidence to suggest Muhammad ever visited Jerusalem.

"So how did Jerusalem become the third holiest site of Islam?" Arthur asked. "Muslims cite a vague passage in the Koran, the seventeenth Sura, entitled 'The Night Journey'. It relates that in a dream or a vision Muhammad was carried by night to heaven 'from the sacred temple to the temple that is most remote, whose precinct we have blessed, that we might show him our signs... In the seventh century, some Muslims identified the two temples mentioned in this verse as being in Mecca and Jerusalem. And that's as close as Islam's connection with Jerusalem gets – myth, fantasy, wishful thinking. Meanwhile, Jews can trace their roots in Jerusalem back to the days of Abraham," is Farah's response.

The Israelites sanctified the Jerusalem hilltop 3,000 years ago by building a temple on it. Jews continued to pray there until the Romans laid waste to Jerusalem. The Al-Aqsa Mosque and the Dome of the Rock were built by the Arabs after they captured Jerusalem in the seventh century. They were situated on the esplanade, which had been built by the Jews to hold the Temple and its outer court.

Let's not forget that the holiest of Christian sites are also in Jerusalem. Christ was arrested, tried and crucified there. Does that mean Jerusalem should come under the sovereignty of the Vatican or other Christian state?

The Temple Mount in Jerusalem is the foundation of the first Temple built by Solomon. It is the holiest site for Jews. For there to be a long-lasting solution to the violence in the Middle East, we need to begin with fundamental truths.

Religious Co-Existence
Religions have a lot more in common than differences. They can and must learn to co-exist in the 21st century.

John Naisbit succinctly summarizes the similarities between Western Christianity and Islam. "While there appears to be a clash between Western Christianity and Islam, a special report on Islam in *The Economist* notes that they 'have more in common with each other than either has with the Confucian world or the Hindu one...' Both have their origins in religions that believe in a single God...' Few westerners believe that God dictated the Koran, and no Muslim believes that Jesus was the Son of God. Those are important disagreements, but they sit alongside a large number of shared convictions. A Muslim and a westerner both believe, more clearly than most other people, in the idea of individual responsibility. They can exchange opinions about the nature of good and evil, or property rights, or the preservation of the environment, in something like a spirit of brotherhood. To say that the West is evil and materialistic, in comparison to Islamic belief, is incorrect. Both the Koran and Muhammad himself assumed a system based on individual enterprise and individual reward".

Let's not forget that the cornerstones of all three monotheistic religions, the Ten Commandments, Koran and Bible, all mirror each other: individual enterprise, judgment, harmony, spirituality and honesty.

Islam is the largest non-Christian religion in Europe, and the fastest growing.

Throughout Asia, including Hong Kong, there is a growing number of corporate leaders who have converted to Islam. A fact unknown to many is that Islam is generally not incompatible with trade and commerce. The overland Silk Road trading route from Mecca to China and the maritime Silk Road from Arabia to Canton via Hong

Kong brought many Arab merchants and traders who intermarried with Chinese and settled permanently. The Prophet Muhammad, himself a merchant trader in earlier days, has been reported to have said, "A truthful and trustworthy merchant will be gathered together with the prophets, martyrs and truthful." Traders and businessmen of all religions co-exist harmoniously in Hong Kong. Why can't they do the same in America and Europe?

God's Law?

Religion cannot be practiced arbitrarily in ways that is devoid of people, place and circumstances. If we lived today according to "God's Law" then the calendars of the local courts and the International Court of Justice in The Hague would be booked solid into the next century.

Is homosexuality an abomination (Leviticus 18:22)? Is eating shellfish an abomination (Leviticus 11:10)? Which is worse? Homosexuality or eating shellfish? Should men rape a young girl (Deuteronomy 22:28)? Should we burn a bull on the altar as a sacrifice because it creates a pleasing odor for the Lord (Leviticus 1:9) even though it might upset our neighbors? Should we sell our daughters into slavery (Exodus 21:17)? Leviticus 25:44 states that we may buy slaves from the nations that are around us. Does that mean Canada and Mexico?

Exodus 35:2 clearly states one should be put to death for working on the Sabbath. Should we kill those we know who work on the Sabbath? Leviticus 20:20 states that we may not approach the altar of God if we have a defect in our sight. Does that mean all those wearing glasses and contacts should stay away? Leviticus 15: 19-24 prohibits contact with a woman while she is in her period of menstrual uncleanliness. How does one tell beforehand without offending? Especially if the woman wants the contact? Most people I know trim their hair, including the hair around their temples, even though this is expressly forbidden by Leviticus 19:27.

How should they die? Leviticus 11: 6-8 says that touching the skin of a dead pig makes one unclean. Does that mean football players have to wear gloves? What about farmers who violate Leviticus 19:19 by planting two different crops in the same field, as do their wives who wear garments made of two different kinds of thread (cotton/polyester blend)? Now we know these farmers and their wives also tend to curse and blaspheme a lot. Is it really necessary that we get the whole town together to stone them as per Leviticus 24:10? Couldn't we just burn them to death at a private family affair like we do with people who sleep with their in-laws as prescribed in Leviticus 20:14? God help rednecks.

The criticism Dr. Laura was subjected to in Canada for quoting the above verses of the bible on her talk show paled in comparison to the criticism Canadians were subjected to at the FCC Main Bar for her remarks. Michael Ceurvorst, a former U.S. Foreign Service diplomat who heads Democrats Abroad in Hong Kong, brought diplomatic calm and smiles to all faces when he quoted George Bernard Shaw and toasted America's northern neighbors.

"Mr. Shaw and cronies were tippling into the dawn hours, having like us dedicated the evening to discussing the influence of the Bible on the development of Western Civilization. After one more wee drop, Mr. Shaw observed summarily, 'When I think of all the evil that the book has wrought on mankind over the centuries, I truly despair of ever writing anything to equal it'."

"God made man in His image and likeness. Man being a gentleman and not to be outdone, has done the same for God," retorted a chorus of slightly tipsy Canadians.

Homosexuality

Rabbi Harold Kushner, a co-editor of *Etz Hayim (Tree of Life)* a new Torah and Commentary published at the dawn of the 21st century, who dealt with Leviticus 18:22, said the Torah's prohibitions on homosexual relations "have engendered considerable debate" and that the Conservative synagogues should "welcome gay and lesbian congregants in all congregational activities."

The rabbi's words echoed those of the Reverend Troy Perry, an excommunicated Pentacostal Minister I met in West Hollywood during my politically active days in the 1970s. The Reverend had gathered a dozen gay congregants in his living room in 1968 to sing hymns. Today his Universal Fellowship Metropolitan Community Church has over 44,000 members in 23 countries. The Church was founded a year before the Stonewall riot in New York

City that gave rise to the gay rights movement.

The Reverend Perry's political endorsement was highly prized by candidates seeking political office in Los Angeles. Listening to political candidates trying to convince the reverend why they would make a difference in the lives of gays brought the same cynical smirk to the reverend's face that I had expressed to the candidates in preparation for the meeting seeking the endorsement. Gays have been used by politicians and then abused and persecuted politically and religiously almost as genocidally as Jews.

This truth was brought to the forefront in 2003 when Gene Robinson, a homosexual, was appointed Anglican Bishop of New Hampshire, and Canon Jeffrey John, also a homosexual, was appointed Bishop of Reading in England. The resulting controversy merely reminded people that there are a large number of gay believers in all communities. Vicars, rabbis, mullahs, clergy of all religious denominations, just like their many gay congregants, politicians, soldiers, teachers...

America was settled and built by people fleeing religious persecution in Europe. The church of the Founding Fathers was the same Episcopal Church that appointed Gene Robinson Bishop of New Hampshire. Isn't it time America start honoring the founding principles of the Founding Fathers and accept all people regardless of their religious beliefs and sexual orientation? The Episcopal Church of the Founding Fathers also acted as the government in the puritan colonies during the British colonial days. Politics and religion were inseperable. That is why the Founding Fathers consciously and deliberately separated the Church from State in the Constitution. There is no room for politics in religion or religion in politics in 21st century America.

"Trembling Before G-d" is a film that describes the anguish of men and women trying to reconcile their homosexuality and Orthodox Jewish religion. The director, Sandi Simcha DuBowski, an Orthodox Jew who explored the plight of Orthodox Jews both in America and abroad, says that what he discovered and the film explores also applies to gay Catholics, Mormons and members of other religions worldwide. Is it right in the eyes of God for gays of any religion to continue to be subjected to religious discrimination in the 21st century?

God?

Does God exist or is he a figment of our imagination? Scientists in the new field of Neurotheology are seeking the biological basis of spirituality. What mystics call nirvana and what Christians describe as a state of grace, scientists are trying to explain in terms of neural networks, neurotransmitters and brain chemistry. The frontal lobe, parietal lobe and temporal lobe each play a role in spirituality. Could the flash of wisdom that came over Siddhartha Gautama – the Buddha – have been nothing more than his parietal lobe quieting down? Could the voices Moses and Muhammad heard on remote mountaintops have been just a bunch of firing neurons – an illusion? Could Jesus' conversations with God have been a mental delusion? Andrew Newberg, a scientist studying religious experiences, says: "The brain is predisposed to having those experiences and that is why so many people believe in God."

No matter what scientists find out and tell us, people of all religious beliefs will continue to believe what they want and find the arguments to support their convictions. That's all right as long as they don't try to impose them on others holding different beliefs, especially by force. Dogmatic beliefs are the cause of religious wars, fanaticism and intolerance. Including the bombings of September 11 and the resulting war on terrorism. Christian crusaders, Muslim martyrs, Hindu clerics and Jewish rabbis have all preached religious dogma that killed millions of innocents and destroyed many civilized contributions to human development. Who gave them the right to preach the absolute truth? *We the Apathetic People!* This human and cultural genocide must end in the 21st century.

Judaism

Judaism is based on monotheism, democracy and the teachings of Moses and the Talmud. The Chosen People believe people make their own heaven or hell here on earth. Not in the afterlife. God, the supreme power, can be whatever *We the People* want to believe he or she is.

The Ten Commandments Moses brought down from Mount Sinai after the Israelites left Egypt are the underlying cornerstones of the Talmud and the Torah – The Book Judaism revolves around, including the Old Testament. Jews read The Book, discuss and debate its contents, meaning and what the various writers of the scriptures meant and whether interpretations are still relevant. Questioning and conversing about God in an inclusive participatory democratic process in pursuit of the truth are an integral part of Judaism.

The central premise of Judaism is the Jewish view that history was a meaningful story, providentially ordained, a cosmic drama of the unfolding design of the one, omnipotent God for His chosen people. Through His covenant with that people could be found guidance for right action, and it lay in adherence to His law. The breaking of that law had always brought punishment; it had come to the whole people in the deserts of Sinai and the waters of Babylon. This great drama was the inspiration of Jewish historical writing, in which the Jews of the Roman empire discerned the pattern which made their lives meaningful.

That mythological pattern was deeply rooted in Jewish historical experience. The Exile which began in 587 BC when the Babylonian conquerors took many of the Jews into slavery after the destruction of the Temple was the last crucial experience in the molding of the Jewish character and national identity.

The Persian overthrow of Babylon in 538 BC allowed Jews to return to Jerusalem. The Temple was rebuilt and Judah became a Persian province, a sort of theocratic satrapy, effective administrative power being in the hands of the priestly aristocracy, which provided the political articulation of Jewish nationhood until Roman times.

Different interpretations result in different Jewish groupings. Orthodox, Conservative, Reform, Kabala and Jews For Jesus. Jesus and his disciples and followers were a group of Jews questioning and discussing The Book. A Jewish offshoot discussing God, love and tolerance of neighbors. They also questioned a totalitarian Roman Caesar and why Caesar is not God. Why God is the one and only Almighty, who is above all religions and beliefs. Including Rome. The Jewish offshoot became Christians. Their religion spread after Roman Emperor Constantine converted to Christianity and made it the religion of the Roman Empire.

The concept of property rights dates back to biblical times in the land of Israel. Christian teachings adopted and modified the Jewish concept of property rights to suit the Church's needs. The Israelites' concept and definition were developed to protect their property from autocratic rulers, including their own, that they had been subjected to in Egypt and the desert. David S. Landes, in his scholarly study of property painstakingly detailed in *The Wealth and Poverty of Nations,* cites two examples, where the response to popular initiative is directly linked to the sanctity of possessions. "When the priest Korach leads a revolt against Moses in the desert, Moses defends himself against charges of usurpation by saying, 'I have not taken one ass from them, nor have I wronged any one of them'." (Numbers 16:15).

The tradition of property belonging to people distinguished the Jews from the other kingdoms around them and earned them the hostility of nearby rulers. Who needs such troublemakers? But it tended to get lost in Christianity when the community of faith became a church, especially once that church became the official, privileged religion of an autocratic empire that wanted to control property. "One cannot well bite the hand that funds," Landes correctly concludes.

The illiterate masses of the time outside the land of Israel knew nothing of the Jewish concept of property rights. The Church decided to keep it that way. The best way to do so was to let only "qualified" people, religious leaders and clerics, know the Bible. The Good Book, with its egalitarian laws and morals, its prophetic rebukes of power and exaltation of the humble, invited questions, challenges, and invited "indiscipline among the faithful and misunderstanding with the secular authorities". Only after censorship and elucidation could it be communicated to the laity.

It was not until the appearance of such heretical sects as the Waldensians (Waldo, c. 1175), the Lollards (Wiclif, c. 1376), Lutherans (1519), and Calvinists (mid-16th century) that the Judaic-Christian tradition entered explicitly into the European political consciousness. These "heretics" put the emphasis on personal religion and the translation of the Bible into the vernacular which reminded rulers that they held their wealth and power thanks to God, and then on condition of good behavior. This was, and continues to be, a very inconvenient doctrine for the Catholic Church, its leaders and Islamic Republics and Saudi royals. Isn't it time *We the Maids* again sweep out the rulers who have forgotten this fundamental property right of ours?

Islamic Democracy

When Napoleon Bonaparte proclaimed the French revolutionary slogans of Democracy and People Power when he conquered Egypt no one had a clue about what he was talking about. Not many do today either. Islamic fundamentalism has been changing slowly since then. Very slowly. To put things in perspective, let's keep in mind that not one of the 22 Arab states represented at the Arab summit held in Beirut in 2002 had a democratically-elected government. Including those that walked out! Archaic totalitarian regimes govern one-fifth of the world's population and control roughly a quarter of our energy resources.

However, there is hope in the New World Order. Reformist Islamic intellectuals are openly talking about new interpretations of the holy word. Political power, they argue, should rest with *We the People.* The clerics should not believe that they have a mission from God to run peoples' affairs. Some even appear to question the Islamic republic's most sacrosanct concepts – and one has been put on trial in Iran for his audacity. But the rethinking has started. The phrase Islamic Reformation is now sometimes even heard in Iran. Reformasi has also been heard loudly and publicly in Muslim Indonesia and Malaysia. These non-Arab Muslim countries, with their Asian brothers and sisters in Pakistan, India and Bangladesh, are Islam's center of gravity. They are home to over 60 percent of the world's Muslim population. A Muslim population that is moderate, tolerant and becoming democratic.

The Islam practiced by the Taleban was an extreme mixture of religion and politics recognized by only three Muslim countries. "The whole policy of the Taleban was opposed by the vast majority of Muslim and Arab countries," Amr Moussa, Secretary-General of the Arab League, said, "so the cause of supporting bin-Laden and so forth by the Afghan regime was a strange cause..."

The tiny Arab state of Qatar adheres to the same Wahabbi strain of Islam practiced in Saudi Arabia. Yet it has managed to modernize the practice. Alcohol is openly consumed, women drive, vote and run for office and its Al Jazeera TV station openly criticizes Arab leaders.

In the Muslim world, however, only 23 percent of countries are democratic. Eleven of the 47 countries that are predominantly Muslim are democratic. "Since the early 1970s, when the third major historical wave of democratization began, the Islamic world, and in particular its Arab core, have seen little evidence of improvements in political openness, respect for human rights and transparency," concluded the Freedom House survey, Freedom in the World 2001-2002.

"In countries where there is an Islamic majority, there is just one free country, Mali, while 18 are rated partly free and 28 are not free," the report said. The most democratic nations after Mali are Bangladesh, Indonesia, Jordan, Kuwait, Turkey and Morocco.

In the final years of the last millennium, 100 Arabs from 15 countries did meet, at great danger to themselves, to send a cry for Arab rights to the world, which eagerly avoided it, and to their own people, those who somehow get word despite censorship and the religious police.

The statement deals bravely with the "grim" truth that even the few scraps of liberties Arabs do hold are declining. Saudi Arabia and some Gulf States, it says, lack even the symbols of democracy – no constitution, parliament or modern legal system. Countries that had made progress are back-pedalling – Tunisia, Egypt, Yemen, Jordan. In Iraq, Syria, Sudan, Bahrain there are "massive and dangerous human rights violations". Only Morocco got some praise for a "relative improvement" this past decade. A present for the host but a very conditional one.

The statement attacked armed Muslim groups for physical and intellectual terrorism. Going further, the signatories denounced regimes that used "Islam's specificity" as an excuse to reject reform. This was an overt attack on fundamentalism.

Is it because of religion that Islam has so miserably failed to create democracy and tolerate human rights? The Crusaders and the Catholic Inquisition acted in a similar spirit, but this kind of fanaticism gradually became less fashionable in Europe as the Enlightenment and modern science began to undermine traditional religious certainties.

Catholicism, Orthodox Christianity and particularly Protestantism often overcame bigotry and the calls for eyeball-plucking in their own pasts and have produced representative government through debate as well as war. Isn't it time Muslims, American-Muslims in particular, peacefully bridge the misperception of their fellow Muslims? Isn't it time that they share their knowledge and benefits of balancing the best of Islam and other civilizations? Isn't it time they actively engage in overcoming the propaganda of the extremists?

Listening to Fareed Zakaria, Editor of *Newsweek International,* speak to the Manhattan Institute For Policy Research about his book *The Future of Freedom* at the Harvard Club in New York City on May 29, 2003, right after America's "victory" in Iraq, I decided that democracy and Islam are compatible if allowed to develop the Islamic way. After his lecture, I had the pleasure of chatting briefly with Fareed and asked him why he thought America's policy-makers don't understand that their policies are misunderstood and misinterpreted in the Muslim world and why they unwittingly contribute to America's sad state of affairs with Muslims by not introducing democracy in an acceptable way. "Americans, the Christian world in general, forget that Islam and the Muslim world never had a Pope against whom kings and royalty could rebel to bring about a reformation the way they did in Europe," Fareed replied as Lawrence Mone, the President of the Manhattan Institute, reminded Fareed we had to move on to the next room for dinner.

The Papacy allowed the kings in the Christian world to rebel and the reformation to flourish. The Ayatollahs in Iran created the moral and religious equivalent of the Papacy and created an Islamic Reformation by the people instead of royalty. U.S. policy-makers and the Muslim monarchs and dictators America coddles should take serious note of this reality. Orderly and non-violent change will come to the Muslim world when the Western equivalent of either a constitutional monarchy or a religious equivalent of the Papacy, as was the case in Iran, are in place which will allow for an orderly reformation and transition to democracy.

Democracy and Islam can co-exist in the New World Order. Not only in America, Bangladesh, Indonesia, Turkey and Qatar, but throughout the entire Muslim world, including the Arab Middle East. Jordan is a fledgling example. The 2003 parliamentary election saw 25 to 30 parties compete and a higher voter turnout than America. Nearly 59 percent of eligible voters went to the polls. Granted that democracy in a Muslim country can be a double-edged sword. It can bring extreme fundamentalists to power – it almost happened in Algeria and some argue it has already happened in Turkey. It happened in Pakistan in the 2002 parliamentary elections where Islamic fundamentalists won 48 seats and formed a ruling coalition with former Prime Minister Benazir Bhutto's Pakistan People's Party.

In a young Muslim democracy it is inevitable that extreme Islamic fundamentalist parties will win office. That is a short-term sacrifice that is much more desirable than military or monarchical dictatorships. Islam's democratic nature is all inclusive. In time the moderates will prevail as they are doing in Iran.

"No one has a divine right to rule," Iran's Mohammad Khatami said, taunting the theocrats who claim they do. Khatami's election twice as President of Iran by 80 percent or more of the votes cast shows that democracy exists and can prevail even in closed Islamic societies. This was confirmed in the parliamentary election of March 2000 when the reformers took control of Parliament. Even the grandson of the late Ayatollah Ruhullah Khomeini, Sayyd Hussein Khomeini, welcomes the long-awaited freedoms democracy can bring. He even went so far as to welcome U.S. intervention in Iran to bring about democracy. He labelled Islamic theocracies as misguided.

The reformers are up against the wall from conservative mosque pressure but in Iran there has always been a balance to be held between the secular ruler and the mosque. The Shah allowed it to be skewed radically. The theocratic mullahs are repeating the Shah's blunder. If a balance can be found again, Iran is set to become a regional power and alternative beacon of secular democracy to Turkey's for the Arab Middle East to emulate. Indigenous and established by popular mandate instead of being imposed by force as was attempted in Iraq.

In Muslim Malaysia, the Muslim world's first truly multi-racial and sectarian party, The People's Justice Party (PKP) – a cross-section of Malaysian society with Muslim clerics, Indian workers, Chinese businessmen and Eurasian professionals – was formed in 2003 and can be the model for the rest of the Muslim democratic world.

India, with the second largest Muslim population in the world, has a Muslim president because of its secular democratic framework. Over a billion people with a bewildering range of differences spanning religion, ethnicity, culture, language and caste are coming to terms with the forces of modernity and globalization in a participatory political process.

Benjamin Barber, author of *Jihad vs. McWorld,* wrote: "In the long run, war cannot defeat terror alone because violence cannot defeat fear. Only democracy can do that."

U.S. foreign policy was a major contributor to the quashing of democracy in the Muslim world, a result of its confused petro-dollar policy that conveniently fused with its Cold War policy.

Political Islam became a convenient tool of American foreign policy to fight communism. Saad Mehio, a regular contributor to *The Daily Star* in Lebanon and *Al Khaleej* in the United Arab Emirates, correctly points out that: "The alliance between Western democracies and local despots, whether Saudi royals or Saddam Hussein in his early years, had two results: the destruction of democratic openness in the Arab world, and the obliteration of any chance for a liberal Arab nationalist movement that could act as a bridge to the modern world."

This misguided and shortsighted foreign policy not only brought fear to America's shores, but quashed democratic movements in the Muslim world. *We the Maids* have to hoover out this oil-colored policy in the New World Order and sweep in democracy and American values.

Let us not forget that the Athenian ideal of self-rule once had an uncertain hold in the world beyond a handful of Western European nations, America, Canada, Japan, India, Australia and New Zealand. Only a generation ago, Spain, Portugal and even Greece were ruled by the same sort of dictators that ruled Africa, Latin America,

Asia and the Communist world.

Americans faced similar doubts about the universality of democracy in Japan after World War II. There was little in Japanese history that led experts to believe it was ready to embrace democracy after a suicidal war of conquest similar to the one embarked upon by Saddam Hussein when he invaded Kuwait. But just as Japan did, Iraq and its nearby desert sheikhdoms will and can embrace democracy on their own terms, not America's. Even conservative Saudi Arabia has reluctantly announced it will hold municipal elections in the future. Freedom of expression is enshrined in the Universal Declaration of Human Rights. That doesn't mean that democracy can be parachuted or bombed into a country overnight. It takes time and education for democracy to take root in any culture. It evolves and builds according to each country's unique traditions and values.

Fear of Democracy

The Saudi government, through various charities including U.S.-based charities, has continuously funded terror and anti-Semitic hate groups because of its inherent fear of democracy. They funded anti-Semitic groups in America in the hope they could break down American support for Israel. After the fall of communism, the Saudis took over funding the most militant terror organizations for direct attacks against Jewish and Palestinian supporters of the peace process. Oliver North wrote in his autobiography that every time he tried to do something about terrorism, he was told to stop because it would embarrass the Saudi government.

The Saudi government secretly funded al-Qaeda, Hamas and Islamic Jihad for two reasons: the destruction of the State of Israel and the prevention of the formation of an independent Palestinian State. Hamas and Islamic Jihad were specifically chosen and funded by the Saudis because of their willingness to undermine Arafat's Palestinian Authority. The Saudi goal is to create such animosity between Israel and the Palestinian Authority that it would wreck any chance for the creation of an independent Palestinian state. Their tactics specifically called for the intimidation or murder of those Palestinians who were willing to work with Israel for peace. The covert Saudi network funded the murder of fellow Muslims for the crime of wanting to create the first democratic Arab state. Whatever harm the Israelis may have done, they did build an excellent public education system, including several universities, for the benefit of their Palestinian neighbors. That was a problem for the Saudi Wahabbis.

The government of Hosni Mubarak in Egypt is also afraid of democracy because it will bring an end to his lucrative family business. Like other dictators in the Arab world he is grooming his son to take over as president. The fact that America has kept him in power at the expense of U.S. taxpayers is an embarrassment. It should therefore come as no surprise that the Egyptian Mohammed Atta led the kamikaze attack on September 11 because of his anger at America's support of Mubarak's repressive dictatorship in Egypt.

September 11 and the harsh prison sentence handed down by an Egyptian court against American human rights activist Saad Eddin Ibrahim for his criticism of the repressive Mubarak regime are 21st century reminders of why America has to fight for and defend democracy in the Arab world if it is to be respected there in the new millennium. Even if democracy yields some extreme Muslim governments, this is a short-term risk worth tolerating. Iran has shown us that time and education lead to moderate democracies.

The literacy rate in the Arab world is below 50 percent. In Israel it is 97 percent. Israel is the only place in the Middle East where an Arab woman can vote. In 50 years, Israel has created the first Arab class to be exposed to democracy, literacy and Western values. To the Saudis and Egyptians, a democratic Palestinian nation would be a cancer in the Arab world, a destabilizing example of freedom that would threaten Arab dictators everywhere. Next to the Jews, the House of Saud and Mubarak hate the Palestinians the most.

Open Mind
My parents decided, because of their different religions, to expose me to both of theirs and those of our Muslim and Orthodox Christian neighbors and let me make up my own mind. Consequently, I believe I am a little more open-minded and receptive to honest religious discussions and the pros and cons of Judaism, Islam and Christianity. I went to Anglican Sunday school and church and Jewish temples, Orthodox, Conservative and Reform, depending

on where I was. Turkish neighbors took me to the local mosque. I celebrated both Christian and Jewish holidays. Christmas and Hanukkah were just a rolling holiday.

My father's family tree has been traced to 600 AD Sweden where my forefathers were Vikings who marauded, raped and pillaged Europe. From then on the family moved wherever there was a good fight to be fought or an army to modernize, from Germany to Russia. My father was born in Russia.

My mother's family tree has been traced to the Tribes of Israel and specifically the tribe of Cohanim – the Jewish priesthood, founded by Moses' older brother Aaron. Her family fled the various wars and pogroms everywhere and wound up in Russia where her father was a textile merchant and local lay rabbi. Like my father she was also born in Russia.

Both fled the Bolshevik revolution. My mother's family wound up in Palestine and my father in England. He was sent to Palestine with the occupying British forces to fight the "terrorist Zionists" and my mother worked for Israel's independence. They met and as they say the rest is history – and collaboration.

Growing up in Cyprus and Israel, I was raised on religious war stories going back to biblical times. Vikings, Alexander the Great, Muhammad, Saladin, Attaturk, Phoenicians, Crusaders, Romans, Cleopatra, Ottomans and modern day Israeli-Arab and Greek-Turkish conflicts. I experienced first hand the horrors of religious conflicts. I read the romanticized versions of many religious wars. My parents, friends, teachers, priests, Muslim clerics, rabbis and neighbors, Greeks, Turks, Arabs and Israelis, all had self-serving biased interpretations. They all repeatedly fought over and conquered and recaptured Cyprus and the Holy Land, the land of Israel.

Because Cyprus is so strategically situated in the Mediterranean, it has experienced most religious and political trends that have blown across the region.

The Byzantine and Crusader walled cities of the Middle East are all around. They were built upon and modified by each conquering civilization, especially Muslim and Christian. Walking to the beach always involved circumnavigating the walls of the "Old City".

The story- telling about the history of each city and the region have different versions and interpretation depending on whether told by a Turk, Greek, Arab, Israeli, Bedouin or European. The Indian and Pakistani tailors and merchants had their own saucy take on history.

The war in Kosovo between Orthodox Serbs and Muslim Kosovars reminded me of what happened in Cyprus between Orthodox Cypriot Greeks and Muslim Cypriot Turks, with the support of Greece and Turkey respectively. Ethnic cleansing took place in Cyprus in 1963 when the Greek Cypriots cleansed neighborhoods of Turkish Cypriots. The religious hatred between the two groups is passionate and unswerving.

Stories of Serb and Kosovar boys disappearing reflect the experiences of Greek and Turkish neighbors who all had similar stories of military age children disappearing. Children I played with while we were growing up were ethnically cleansed.

Story-telling and backgammon were the primary pastimes in the fifties and sixties in the Middle East as TV was still relatively new. Few people had access to one. We took long walks, hitchhiked and went on camping trips for recreation through the Negev and Sinai deserts, visiting the Dead Sea, Mount Sinai, the alleged Burning Bush, Bethlehem, Nazareth, Jerusalem, Masada, Galilea and all holy sites in between. We explored, learned religious histories and communicated with each other. On street corners, bazaars and homes. With no TV or Internet we had no choice. Shouldn't we try to plan more quality time with our children teaching them history, geography, religion and positive story-telling – or do we just leave them to Star Wars, the chaos of the dot.com world and the fantasies of Harry Potter?

Camping in a desert for several days is a cathartic experience. Swimming in the Sea of Galilee, River Jordan, waterfalls of Ein Gedi, the Dead Sea and the Red Sea with all its underwater wonders, one can understand why the roots of Judaism, Islam and Christianity lie under the sifting sands and gentle waters of the warring Middle East.

Spiritual Search

Jedi is the mystical faith followed by some of the central characters in the Star Wars films. More than 70,000 Australians upset Australia's statistics agency by identifying their religion as "Jedi." How many Americans do? The Star Wars mania is a liturgy of Asian mythology for people seeking a better life. A mish-mash of recycled comic strips, dreary Saturday-morning serials and half-baked mysticism and mythology for a generation alienated and spiritually lost. Americans are spiritually starved thanks to their churches and to religious leaders they cannot understand or relate to.

Maybe that is why the 20th century ended with a global religious revival. Search and convert missions. Take all prisoners. Religion is offering "refuge" and "identity" and offers answers to needs lost in this drug trip called "post-industrialization", "service industry", and "information highway". More broadly, the religious resurgence throughout the world is a reaction against secularism, moral relativism, self-indulgence and a reaffirmation of the values of order, discipline, work, mutual help and human solidarity. Religious groups meet social needs left unattended by families and state bureaucracies.

Parents who grew up in secular homes are sending their children to religious schools. They are seeking moral guidance for their children. Adults of all denominations are turning away from secular classes. Affiliated schools of all religious denominations are turning students away!

Young people today are rebelling by seeking refuge in religion. To grab them, religions are reviving the ancient practices, exploring Gregorian chants, Kabala, the Latin Mass. Our children are looking for their religious roots. Tradition. The truth. Hell, John Lennon and Paul McCartney found each other and the truth having met at a church in Liverpool as searching lost teenagers.

Money and materialism cannot buy individual fulfillment. Ever see an armored truck follow a hearse?

Maybe that is why alternative New Age religions reviving ancient Hindu and Buddhist sex practices such as Tantra are gaining popularity again. Who says one is limited to practicing traditional single-deity worship? After all, religious freedom is guaranteed to all by the Constitution. Tantra is Goddess worship that evolves around sacred sex. It is definitely less violent and more loving. How you differentiate between a sacred orgasm and a secular one has got to be worth finding out! If we are to be tolerant of all religious practices in the new millennium, we must allow others to pray to any God or Goddess they choose. Tolerance, understanding and love is the cornerstone of all major religions and the American Constitution and Declaration of Independence.

Tantra, like Confucianism, is not a religion. Nevertheless, like Islam it is gaining followers among Americans at an astonishing rate. Tantra made its first splash in America in 1981. Its chief apostle was the Oregon commune leader known as Bhagwan Sri Rajneesh. Many today in America see the mix of sex and New Age cachet as an irresistible selling point to Americans shedding their inhibitions and willing to treat their sex lives like their tennis games – something to be worked on, preferably with the help of a pro.

The Baha'i faith founded in the 1800s is also gaining followers in the U.S. It emphasizes racial unity, even to the point of encouraging interracial marriage. Isn't this what every religion in our New World Order should be doing?

Maha Kumbh Mela saw many American celebrities and the Dalai Lama join 25 million Hindu pilgrims in the opening year of the millennium in India purifying themselves in the River Ganges. The event takes place every 12 years. The 21st century dawned with the 144th-year alignment of the planets.

While celebrities embrace Hinduism, many Hindu Dalits – or Untouchables – are escaping from the clutches of their religion to Buddhism. They change religion and names to escape the caste system. Ram Raj, leader of the Dalit group, the Confederation of Scheduled Castes and Scheduled Tribes Organizations, said: "I am walking out of Hinduism because the 3,000-year old caste system will never allow me any respect or dignity. There is no future for us in it." Shouldn't more of *We the Maids* be questioning the organized religion we know and compare it with what we really think?

Religious Revival

Hong Kong, like America, is experiencing a religious revival. More and more people are converting and re-prioritizing from Mammonism to religion. Money is no longer the only god. Buddhists, Taoists, Mormons, Muslims and Jews are seeing their numbers rise. Falun Gong, Christian Scientists, Baha'i and numerous New Age spiritual groups are also feeling the upsurge. But, then again, Hong Kong and America have always been spiritual. They are the front lines of peaceful religious expansion in the 21st century.

Hong Kong is still a missionary launch pad. Not just for China but Asia. In Asia, Christianity is also emerging as one somewhat surprising religious option. David Barrett, editor of the *World Christian Encyclopedia*, estimates that around eight percent of Asia's population is Christian. Each day some 25,000 Chinese join the Protestant faith. Three new churches open every two days. One of the major factors in the growing number of converts is the film *Jesus* which has been translated into 830 languages and seen by over five billion people, more than have seen *Gone With The Wind, Titanic* and *ET* courtesy of the missionary zealots from the Campus Crusade for Christ International.

Christianity claims nearly a third of the world's population as adherents. Most of the credit goes to women. Christianity's appeal for women was a major reason that it grew so rapidly in competition with other religions of the Roman Empire. Then, as now, most Christians were women. The new religion offered women not only greater status and influence within the church but also more protection as wives and mothers. Many became church leaders. We saw it happen again in the late 20th century in the Soviet Union after the collapse of communism. Women, young and old, flocked to join convents and the church even though many do not initially believe in God. They seek His sanctuary from the harsh realities of life.

There were women priests and bishops in the first five centuries as well as cross-dressing saints, according to Peter Stanford in *The She-Pope*. Shades of *Yentl*, the 1983 movie in which Barbra Streisand plays a Jewish girl who disguises herself as a man to learn the Talmud. If the Roman Catholic Church in the middle of the ninth century (853-855) was headed by Pope Joan, a woman disguised as a man as Stanford claims in *The She-Pope,* why can't women be priests in the 21st century?

Chaucer's Wife of Bath was right on when she said, "Christ was a maid, and yet shaped like a man." The church has continuously reinforced the idea that women are inferior, and scare the hell out of men to believe, fear and deny the very qualities Jesus promoted.

Women were the first to recognize and accept Christianity as disciples, prophets, and the first to recognize Jesus as the Messiah. Nevertheless, the macho world of the first few centuries after Jesus died did everything to suppress and deny the role of women. So what else is new? Robert McElvaine, a professor of history at Millsape College, focuses on the fact that "although three of the Gospels plainly state that the risen Jesus first appeared to Mary Magdalene, and women are prominently mentioned throughout Gospel accounts of the cruci-fixion and resurrection, Saint Paul's account of the first Easter and its aftermath sounds as if it took place in a men's club."

The church also protected children from the whims of tyrannical fathers. Under Roman law, fathers could and often did commit infanticide. Female babies were especially vulnerable because they were nothing but an expense. Sound familiar?

Over the past few years, Islam has become one of the fastest growing religions globally. Many adherents in the United States are more devoted to their religious practices than those in their homelands because they studied and embraced the Koran while in refugee camps waiting to come to America. No different from Mike Tyson when he was in jail.

In the United States, Muslims in the not too distant future will outnumber Jews. One critical reason why, and a point to keep in mind, is that of the three monotheistic religious faiths it makes the least demands on the newly converted at the beginning. Great marketing. Once hooked, reel them in. About half the Muslims in the United States are African-Americans. Only 12 percent are Arabs. The rest are Asian, Anglo and Latino. It is ironic that it was usually Arab traders who captured and shackled their forefathers and delivered them to the slave ships in West Africa.

The language of choice of Latino Muslims is Spanish. Mariam Montavio explains why. "I had a lot of problems with the church. One Bible says one thing, and another Bible says something different."

Scores of Latinos throughout the U.S. – specifically in New York, New Jersey, Chicago and Miami – have fled the church of their birth and embraced Islam as their newfound faith. Women converts to Islam outnumber men by four to one. Islam has adherents throughout Latin America and the Caribbean as well, with especially strong followings in Argentina, Brazil, Colombia and Panama.

A 1998 Georgetown University study of people aged 20 to 39 found that eight percent of the Latinos had joined another denomination or religion. Of those, at least 65 percent left for the evangelical Protestant groups, Pentecostal churches or Mormonism. A smaller percentage accepted other religions, including Islam and Buddhism.

Mark Twain's proposed solution for missionaries at the turn of the century still holds true today.

"Let us import American missionaries from China, and send them into the lynching field," he wrote.

"With 1,511 of them out there converting two Chinamen apiece per annum against an uphill birth rate of 33,000 pagans per day, it will take upward of a million years to make the conversions balance the output and bring the Christianizing of the country in sight of the naked eye; therefore, if we can offer our missionaries as rich a field at home at lighter expense and quite satisfactory in the matter of danger, why shouldn't they find it fair and right to come back and give us a trial?

"The Chinese are universally conceded to be excellent people, honest, honorable, industrious, trustworthy, kind hearted, and all that – leave them alone, they are plenty good enough just as they are; and besides, almost every convert runs the risk of catching our civilization. We ought to be careful. We ought to think twice before we encourage a risk like that; for, once civilized, China can never be uncivilized again..."

With the growth of Islam in America today his call rings truer than ever if we are to believe the Christian extremists. Moreover,

if America is to continue pursuing its role of terrorist exterminator
and global peacemaker in the religious conflicts of the 21st century,
it has to first get its religious house in order.

In the wake of the Catholic Church's sex scandals in America,
it has to heed Twain's admonition if it wants to stop closing rural
churches and maintain enough priests to tend to its flock.

Shamans and Virgin Dragon Lady

Following the rise of Chinese-style capitalism, China like America
has become a nation of spiritual seekers. The Communist Party
advocated atheism because Marxists regarded religion as "the opium
of the people."

The shamanistic religion called Dongba boasts the last living
hieroglyphic language known as Naxi. It is a Tibeto-Burman language
whose unique script has 2,400 characters and a 1,000-year recorded
history. It is a nature-worshipping faith that believes the Earth's
original people were not living "righteously" if they chopped down
trees and polluted waters. Such activities would prompt angry gods
to send down floods to wipe out the population. In the old days,
anyone who cut down a tree near a river was ostracized from the
village until he planted an orchard to replace it.

The shamans dance to the beat of drums, cymbals and conch horns
to pay homage to the gods. The robed priests dance together stooping
forward and rearing back, twirling to the trance-like rhythm much
like Native-Americans. Young helpers wave burning branches of
spruce to purify the air. Farmers line up to collect holy branches
they will burn to ward off evil.

The Black Dragon Pool Temple in Zhenchuan was built around
a natural spring during the Ming Dynasty, nearly 500 years ago.
The story of the temple's founding is tied to another traditional
belief: an immaculate conception and the birth of five dragon kings.

A maiden, the story goes, was washing clothes by a creek when
she spied a peach bobbing downstream. She ate it and found herself
pregnant. Sound familiar? Ultimately, she gave birth to five dragons
– black, green, yellow, red and white – that emerged from her
mouth, nostrils and ears.

The maiden was proclaimed a goddess – the Niang Niang goddess – and became a symbol of fertility. The Black Dragon made his home in the valley that ultimately took his name. Thousands of farmers, farmers' daughters, mothers, nephews and nieces make the pilgrimage to pray and burn incense at China's Bethlehem.

Robert Hendricks reminds us that Chinese religion can be classified as a series of "folk religions". One does not "join" them or go on certain days. "Instead, there are core beliefs. You are raised in these beliefs. The Taoism of the Tao temple isn't the same as the original philosophy. That I suppose is true for every religion."

Being Honest

Historically, intolerance was dictated "by the fears of the clerical hierarchy, by their distaste for the findings and paradigms of a science that negated religious doctrine," David Landes reminds us. As the English chemist and Unitarian minister Joseph Priestley put it, the pope, in patronizing science, "was cherishing an enemy in disguise", for he had "reason to tremble even at an air pump, or an electrical machine".

Thomas Cahill, the author of *The Hinges of History* series and *Pope John XXIII,* asks what changed Christianity? How did Christians learn the virtue of tolerance? "Centuries of bloody religious wars and persecution finally convinced most Christians that there must be a better way to organize society, a way that did not involve quite so many burning bodies, human charnel houses and corpse-strewn battlefields. The slow germination of this revolution in consciousness can be traced at least to the 18th century, toward the end of which a country finally emerged – America – that officially refused to play the old game of whose religion was true. It took a generously agnostic view of religious truth: you may believe what you like, and so may I, and neither can impose belief on the other." Isn't it time *We the Maids* sweep this constitutional cornerstone clean to make sure it is not forgotten in the 21st century?

We've come a long way since 1600 when Giordano Bruno, a defrocked priest from Naples, was burned at the stake for espousing, among other things, his belief that there might be other worlds and other life-forms beyond Earth. The U.S. government still does its best to belittle that view, even though it spends billions of dollars supporting

NASA's quest to find life on other planets. In 1633 Galileo-Galilei championed the Copernican view that the Earth revolves around the sun, and is not the center of the universe. This "heretical" assertion brought him into conflict with the Roman Inquisition which forced him to appear and, under threat of torture, recant his opinions. He refused and spent the last years of his life under house arrest.

Father Tissa Balasuriya was excommunicated by the Vatican for denying the Catholic dogma of original sin and because he also denied the immaculate conception, that Mary was a virgin and that her body was assumed into heaven after death. Significantly, he also questioned papal infallibility. Should creative religious leaders like Bruno and Father Balasuriya be excommunicated for being honest and creative and saying what they believe is in the best interest of the church?

Leonardo Boff, a Franciscan friar in the Brazilian Catholic Church, clashed with the Vatican and was also punished. "Human rights should apply within the church," he stated. "I strongly question the church as an institution. It is a vestige of feudalism. It claims to know the absolute truth, and to have a monopoly on salvation. I feel I work within the Christian ideal. The hierarchy is one thing, another is the church as a community of the faithful. I am completely comfortable with the community of the faithful. I define myself more as Franciscan Catholic than Roman Catholic. Never forget, Saint Francis was a layman, he wasn't a priest or part of the hierarchy. This is possible within the Christian faith," he said.

"The great theme of our day is not about the future of Christianity or the future of the church, but the fate of the planet, and of humankind. And by liberating the poor, everyone will achieve liberation. For 20 years we have worked among the poor who live off scraps in a garbage dump in Petropolis [outside Rio]. The Vatican is frightened of this approach, because there is a part of the church that is an accomplice to this unjust social order. We want to break that complicity. One of our errors was that we concentrated heavily on politics and economics."

If Catholics like Father Tissa Balasuriya and Franciscan Leonardo Boff are excommunicated why weren't Hitler and his Catholic

Nazi henchmen? Hitler, Goebbels, Himmler, Bormann were all Catholics. How about the Catholic primate of Germany who ordered the Requiem sung after Hitler's suicide? Why are their names still on the rolls of the Catholic Church? The Catholic Church had no compunction in excommunicating every Communist party member after World War II ended. Why not Nazis? Why did the Vatican and the Catholic Church compound their offense by offering the Nazis the Croatian Rat Line and other escape routes, operating in Rome from a Vatican Catholic college, to flee Europe to Catholic havens in South and Central America? Why did the Catholic Church protect these war criminals and hide them from the Nuremberg war crimes tribunal?

Is it because Hitler's slogan of *Totalitatsan spruch* "claim of the whole" was music to the Catholic Church's ears? A promised return to the medieval ideal of one nation and one church? Is it because the doctrine of the separation of church and state was as detested by Hitler as by the popes?

Is it because the Vatican declared the Magna Carta (1215) null and void because the Vatican detests the foundation of constitutional government and enjoys the company of dictators and wants to return to the Roman Catholic Empire's heyday of glory?

When Hitler came to power the Vatican signed its concordat with the Third Reich. The Catholic Church was the first foreign power to enter into a bilateral treaty with Hitler. In 1933 the Roman Catholic hierarchy in Germany had overridden an earlier ban on Catholic membership in the Nazi party.

Dr Konrad Adenauer, the first post-World War II German chancellor, was an early critic of the Roman Catholic hierarchy for its failure to oppose Nazism. "I believe," he declared in 1946, "that if all the bishops had together made public statements from the pulpits on a particular day, they could have prevented a great deal. That did not happen, and there is no excuse for it. It would have been no bad thing if the bishops had all been put in prison or in concentration camps as a result."

The Pope's visit to the Holy Land in the closing year of the millennium in an attempt to bring reconciliation among all three Abrahamaic faiths, Judaism, Christianity and Islam, and peace, the duty of anyone who would call himself the vicar of Christ, is a giant step all his successors and followers should follow in the New World Order. What a contrast to Pope Paul VI's same trip in 1964. I was in Israel at the time and remember his insensitivity when he managed to insult the Israelis by never referring to Israel once as a state, and the Jordanians by implying Israel was the only Holy Land.

Hopefully the successor to Pope John Paul will set a tone for honest atonement, address the realities Catholics face in the new millennium and will be more receptive and open to the wishes of Catholic congregations worldwide. We the Believers, people and maids, religious leaders, as well as political leaders, have to be receptive in order to survive in the New World Order!

The Anglicans are coming clean. The Archbishop of Canterbury Rowan Williams has been made an honorary white druid in an ancient Celtic ceremony. He said the suggestion that the honor was linked to paganism was offensive. Richard Burton, Queen Elizabeth and the Queen Mother were also white druids.

The former Archbishop of Canterbury, George Carey, leader of the world's 70 million Anglican faithful, triggered a religious storm after questioning the resurrection of Jesus Christ. "I can tell you frankly that while we can be absolutely sure that Jesus lived and that he was certainly crucified on the cross, we cannot with the same certainty say that we know he was raised by God from the dead."

The Archbishop's "Jesus 2000" message went on to launch a broader attack on the Church's record through history, stating it "defamed the name of Jesus" by contributing to the Jewish Holocaust.

Poor Man's Sword
In the Philippines, the Moro Muslim rebellion that started in the early 1970s in southern Mindanao is a blend between traditional pirates, modern-day terrorists and a modern-day Christian Muslim crusade. The Abu Sayyaf, which claims to be fighting for an independent Muslim state, appears more interested in kidnapping foreigners and wealthy Filipinos for ransom payments.

Politically motivated religious kidnappings are a common Muslim practice even today. That is why the new millennium started much like the last two ended. Kidnappings for money. Armed rebels in Algeria kidnapped 14 European tourists in the Sahara desert in 2003 and demanded 4.6 million euros for their release. Africans and Chinese were kidnapped and sold as slaves. American and European sailors were also obtained through kidnappings. Not much has changed at the dawn of the 21st century.

Today slavery still exists. Muslim raids to capture slaves and hostages in the Philippines, Indonesia, parts of Africa and many other countries, have gone on for millennia. Ferdinand Magellan brought slaves with him when he circumnavigated the world and discovered the Philippines.

Tourists and reporters are constantly kidnapped. In 2000, hotel guests and workers were abducted by boat from an island resort hotel in Malaysia to which Muslim extremists in the Philippines make claim. War-like Moro Muslim clans in Zamboanga, Basilan and the Sulu archipelago in the Southern Philippines today, much like their Bedouin forefathers in Arabia, carry on the tradition of banditry and vendettas as cherished local customs and practices. The various Abu Sayyaf factions brought this to the world's attention with their kidnappings of millennium global rainbow hostages. The reality is that they were kidnapped for ransom by bandits. Not political activists. These criminal kidnappings under the guise of religion continue in the 21st century.

This is nothing new. That is why the Spanish and Filipino Christians built Fort del Pilar in Zamboanga and Fort San Pedro in Cebu and why old church and convent walls in the Southern Philippines are so thick. A case of "Praise the Lord – and pass the ammunition." Not only in the Philippines, but all colonies of the Roman Catholic Spanish Empire.

Low-level wars for Muslim converts and independence have raged for years in Asia. Muslim Mindanao, in the Philippines, Aceh in Sumatra and the southern provinces of Thailand.

Horrific stories of religious persecutions are still prevalent today in the remote areas of the Malukas in Indonesia. There, several thousand villagers are practicing Muslims during the week. On

Sundays they secretly attend Christian services in nearby hills far from the eyes of strangers. Otherwise, like their priest, they will be killed. Jihad holy wars follow medieval practices of forced conversions in the name of Islam. Destroy churches, crosses, change names because Christian names are "not good". All men in the village are circumcised with a single, blunt razor blade.

Nobel laureate V.S. Naipaul points out the "calamitous effect" of Islam on the peoples who converted over the last two millennia. Naipaul referred to Western civilization as "our universal civilization'. The beauty of this civilization is that it enshrines "the idea of the pursuit of happiness...the idea of the individual, responsibility, choice, the life of the intellect, the idea of vocation and perfectibility and achievement." Such a society, he said, "cannot generate fanaticism". To be fanatical would be intellectually dishonest and sterile. Well guess what? There are a lot of intellectually dishonest and sterile career politicians and religious leaders that plan our daily agendas.

Naipaul is disturbed by Islam's textual rigidities and by its inability to allow the word to slip into secular grasp. Above all, he is disturbed by that religion's tendency to turn men into "nothing" and by the willingness of that religion's adherents to "allow themselves to become nothing". In his *Beyond Belief: Islamic Excursions Among the Converted Peoples,* Naipul reminds us that the conquests and conversions of Islam, conducted by Arab armies in lands to the east of Arabia, were more destructive of local histories, and of local self-images, than even the worst excesses of Western colonialism. It is not uncommon to hear Pakistanis, for example, describe dates as their favorite fruit, instead of the local mango. In this cultural genuflection to the desert lands of Arabia, one sees trivial, but telling, evidence of what Naipaul detests – the deracination of Islam of "converted peoples". The Taleban reminded the world of their destructive religious fervor with their cultural and civilizational genocide of Afghanistan.

The Taleban's religious conquest of Afghanistan posed a threat not only to America and Western civilizations, but to all neighboring Muslim countries, especially Pakistan where they were first trained and sent from to Afghanistan.

Pakistan's decision to support America and the coalition to destroy the Taleban was a politically astute decision to preserve the country from the clutches of the Taleban and other religious extremists. Contrary to its track record in the region, America took care of the political threat to Pakistan as promised.

Kashmir has become the latest frontier of Muslim guerrilla excursions. Pakistani Kashmir volunteers, and veterans of the Afghan Mujahedina now lead the rebellion.

The Muslim fringe of the former Soviet Union, the Uzbeks, the Kazakhs, the Tajiks and the Turkmens, all seem vulnerable to Taleban contagion. One fatal flaw for them is that their borders are largely artificial. The area is much more of a trading crescent. The governments in the tawdry national capitals have a difficult misperception to maintain. On the other hand, trade is vigorous, traditional and potentially rich. If the borders, including Pakistan's, soften and continue to talk money and politics rather than religion then what the Taleban offer is very unattractive.

Afghanistan in its ferocity and aridity has few equals. The Taleban are unschooled fundamentalists coming from distant towns in the driest and hardest parts of Afghanistan. What they have, even for modestly angry anti-American lower and middle-class Muslims, is uniquely unexportable. No different than any extreme interpretation of any religion.

"Islamic movements today are driven more by appalling local social conditions than by some all-pervasive ideology," Khalid Ahmed, a Pakistani writer on Islam, reminds us. He goes even further in saying that "in the Islamic world, by and large, the ruling elites have failed to deliver the goods to the people, and the end of the Cold War has only stripped off the veil. The growing gap between rich and poor, runaway inflation, unemployment, massive corruption, and widespread disillusionment with the mainstream parties and their leaders are the core issues in the Islamic world." That was made crystal clear in Indonesia with the removal of Suharto and Wahid and in Pakistan when both Benazir Bhutto and Nawaz Sharif were removed from office and charged with corruption. Although fragile and slow, democracy does bring change to countries ruled by Muslim dictatorships. This is something that cannot be forgotten or done away with in America's new war on terrorism. Democracy cannot be compromised for oil or political support from dictators supporting the war effort.

Muslims clearly have problems living peacefully with their neighbors. Muslims make up about one-fifth of the world population but in the 1990s were far more involved in intergroup and intragroup violence and wars than any other group of people. "Quite clearly," James Payne concludes, "there is a connection between Islam and militarism." Richard Nixon also pointed out that "Muslim-versus-Muslim conflicts have cost ten times as many lives as the Arab-Israeli conflict."

Let's keep in mind what Islam stands for. Obedience and submission to Allah, not to any mortal who comes around the corner. It is to be distinguished from fanaticism. Will Rogers reminds us that "a fanatic is always the fellow that is on the opposite side."

Self-Destructive Jews
The cultural war between secular and orthodox Jews in Israel could nudge towards internal strife that will only hasten a self-fulfilling prophesy – Armageddon. The destruction of the Third Temple.

The debate in Israel on who is a Jew in the late 20th century and 21st century is also revolting. The burial of Staff Sergeant Michael Oxman in a section of the military cemetery set aside for non-Jews was not only revolting but tragic. He was an Israeli citizen who considered himself Jewish. He fought for Israel and died at the hands of a Palestinian fighter defending the country he loved. Yet he could not be buried as a Jew because his mother was not a Jew.

What right do the Orthodox Jews have to dictate who is a Jew? Do they want to again bring about the implosion and destruction of the Third Temple? Are they determined to create an internal Holocaust whereby Jews do to themselves what the Parses have done? Eliminate themselves by a self-destructive definition and behavior?

They almost succeeded in the eighth century B.C. when the 10 tribes of Israel disappeared after being driven out of the land of Israel by the Assyrians. Luckily, they were recently discovered through DNA testing and are now living in an Indian community on the Burmese border. Some Israeli rabbis believe the descendants of the lost tribes number more than 35 million around the world today. Shouldn't these Jews be welcomed with open arms back to Israel?

Religious Poverty

Piety and poverty have a direct correlation. The more religious people become, the poorer they are. This is an overall generalization which economic, political and religious history supports. There are exceptions. Religious and political ignorance continues to perpetuate self-serving religious and political leaders. This has to change in the New World Order if poverty is to be eliminated.

A few modern-day extreme examples can be seen in the city of Sofia in Bulgaria, the village of Sasgargram in Madhya Pradesh and the practice of Devadasism – the religiously sanctioned consignment of girls to a lifetime of sexual slavery – in India. Mutilating a corpse is a crime. Unless of course you are the Pope of the Catholic Church. According to the Rome daily *La Republica,* an undisclosed body part of the exhumed dead Pope John XXIII was removed and wrapped in a medieval cloth and delivered by Pope John Paul to Sofia's new cathedral during his four-day visit to Bulgaria in 2002. It will be kept in the cathedral as an object of veneration. One of the more popular popes of modern times, he is revered in Bulgaria, where he served as a priest from 1929 to 1934.

In India gods give their blessing to sexual slavery of poor girls. Members of the Banchhara caste, one of the poorest in the country, encourage their elder daughters to become prostitutes at the age of 12. These girls support entire families and are worshipped as living goddesses. "It is only in India where girls are worshipped and marketed...prostitution is part of their religious cult," said Justice Gulab Gupta, head of the human rights commission in the region. "They believe that they have divine sanction to initiate their daughter into the flesh trade...They don't see it as ruining their daughter's life. For them, it is God's will. Ironically, it is not a male God who ordains this prostitution, it is a Goddess."

In India, 15,000 girls are also sexually abused by Hindu priests and then "dedicated to god" in temples each year in the southern states of Andhra Pradesh, Tamil Nadu and Karnataka. Devadasism thrives on a regular supply of girls belonging to the lower castes who are systematically suppressed by the higher castes in India's traditional social hierarchy. The girls' "marriage" ritual to a god is performed in a temple where priests take turns raping the girls while their families are engrossed in ceremonies and a banquet to mark the occasion.

Samuel Huntington in his *Clash of Civilizations* points out: "Indeed, outside of North America, the most prosperous, least crime-ridden and most educated countries are the post-Protestant societies of Northern Europe, in which traditional Christianity is in serious long-term decline, and the highly secular Confucian societies of East Asia. Conversely, the parts of Europe and the Americas in which institutional Christianity has been strongest in recent centuries, the Catholic and Orthodox countries, have been characterized by poverty, tyranny, and political instability, which exist to an even greater degree in the Muslim world. The most religious part of the United States, the South, has long been the poorest, most violent, and most illiterate section of the country."

As Ignace Lepp points out: "Miracles, which used to be regarded as the chief guarantee of the truth of Christianity, are today its main stumbling block." Lepp goes on to say: "Christ was always said to be on the side of the poor and the oppressed, but those who claimed to speak in His name taught them that their chief duty lay in resignation – a resignation which played into the hands of the rich and powerful." The same holds true in India and many developing countries obsessed with traditional religious practices that suppress the progress of ignorant illiterate peoples.

All great religious teachers from the last Buddha to The Prophet confronted the conventions and corruption of the day. In the present day, any one of them, including Jesus, would have a U.S. Federal warrant out against them for being subversive. *We the Maids* had better start separating the wheat from the chaff in this political and religious New World Disorder.

Today's religious leaders, and their career politician spokesmen, perpetuate the historical lie of the poor and lower classes being predestined to their misery and that the only way to salvation is strict compliance with their religious dogmas. Heaven awaits them if they listen and dutifully comply. The alternative is the Great Satan's hell, which is even worse than their current plight.

We the Maids have to take a careful and honest look at the infallible truth and what the scriptures of both Christians and Muslims say about the seductive devil infidels, and make sure We sweep out the hypocritical self-serving untruths.

Politicized Religious Penis

Christianity declared a division between man and beast in the realm of sexual behavior. To be human was to contain one's animal passions; to accede to them was to sink to the level of a brute. But the Western imagination, shaped in Greece and Rome, was still haunted by pagan myths that spoke of satyrs, centaurs, and other beings half-man and half-beast. Implicit in those myths was the idea that to be closer to nature was to be closer to sex – and farther from civilization. I highly recommend David Friedman's *A Mind of Its Own, a cultural history of the penis,* for those who want to have a better historical perspective of how the Church politicized the role of the penis.

After white Europeans reached black Africa, the Greco-Roman images of natural sexuality were revived and infused with the Christian notion of sin, then projected onto Africans, people who, by European standards, seemed to live with no sexual inhibitions. Few Europeans objected to this because blackness was already loaded with negative meaning. It symbolized filth and death, while whiteness stood for purity and life. Christians linked blackness with sin and lust even before the myth of The Curse of Ham became part of their oral tradition.

The Curse of Ham occurs in the ninth chapter of Genesis:

> The sons of Noah who went forth from the ark were Shem, Ham and Japheth...These three were the sons of Noah; and from these the whole earth was peopled. Noah was the first tiller of the soil. He planted a vineyard; and he drank of the wine and became drunk, and he lay un-covered in his tent. And Ham, the father of Canaan, saw the nakedness of his father, and

> told his two brothers outside. Then Shem and
> Japhet took a garment, laid it on both their
> shoulders, and walked backward and covered
> the nakedness of their father's their faces were
> turned away, and they did not see their father's
> nakedness. When Noah awoke from his wine
> and knew what his youngest son had done to
> him, he said, "Cursed be Canaan; a slave of
> slaves shall he be to his brothers."

"Nakedness" is clearly a euphemism for penis. By staring at his father's penis, Ham mocked both patriarchal authority and the Mosaic laws of sexual modesty. His actions showed him to be a son without respect, a crosser of moral boundaries, someone unwilling to contain the erotic beast within, according to the Christian interpretations and oral tradition.

The English, when they became richer and stronger imperial rulers, began to see themselves as God's Chosen People. This elevated The Curse of Ham into a divine rationale for enslaving hundreds of thousands of black Africans, then shipping them off to work the tobacco, cotton and sugarcane plantations in the English colonies in America, just as the Spanish, French, Portuguese and Dutch did for their colonial holdings in the New World.

Nearly every "witch", European women burned at the stake for consorting with the Devil, described his penis as black. Their crime, knowledge of the Demon rod. The Christian witch burnings brought out the entire community. Church bells rang and priests led the masses in prayer.

All penises are ultimately tools of the Devil, taught Augustine, the Church's most influential theologian. But now some of them – those on Africans – were declared more satanic than the rest. The proof was in their size and color, each a punishment from God. It was not long before other experts, using the secular language of science, reached a similar conclusion.

Anti-semitism campaigns in Europe often presented cartoons depicting Jews with massive syphilis-spreading erections lusting after Christian virgins. The Nazi party newspaper *Der Sturmer* was rife with such cartoons. Making this libel even more odious was the widespread belief that Jews themselves were immune from syphilis. It was the Jew's nature, his diabolical mission, such racial thinkers believed, to foster racial corruption by creating hidden Jews among the larger population with large diseased penises. One cure for this threat to the Christian body politic was castration, which was occasionally administered to Jews via vigilante justice in a fashion not unlike lynchings in the American South. Just like the African penis, the Jewish penis was racialized, criminalized, and, on occasion, excised by the Christian believers.

Holy Peace-Seductive Devil

Political Christian and Muslim religious leaders created an illusory evil tempting seducer who represents all things distasteful to their respective political and religious agendas. The Devil in the New Testament became the Seducer in the Koran. They allegedly tempt people who pursue desires that are distasteful and threatening to the political agendas of religious leaders. Freedoms of expression, religion, culture and desire are freedoms that threaten religious teachings and political power. Jews were an easy and convenient target to identify with the Devil. Even for the tolerant Reverend Billy Graham. The great American evangelist told Nixon the nation's problems lies with "satanic Jews", according to Nixon aide H.R. Haldeman.

Today the Seducer to Muslim fundamentalist leaders is represented by American culture and conveniences. The Devil to Christian fundamentalists is any freedoms they disagree with. Eternal damnation became the creative tools to scare the bejezus out of true believers.

Whose God decides anyway? Doesn't God belong to all of us? Who decided God advocates war, death and destruction? *We the Maids* must never forget it was religious political leaders that have advanced and justified war for a variety of self-serving political and religious reasons. Not God or Allah! The Almighty never advocated war and never took sides when religious and political leaders started them in God's name.

According to both the Bible and the Koran, God calls for justice and love for all, even the unjust, regardless of political or religious agendas or affiliation. That is what Jesus preached and why he was respected and accepted by all. His message is universal.

No country, political party or organization has the right to claim a monopoly on God. Conversely, no one can accuse those with different religious beliefs of being the Seductive Devil.

America, true to the constitutional mandate of its Founding Fathers, has embraced, if sometimes reluctantly, all religions, including Islam. Why is it therefore necessary for both Christian and Muslim fundamentalist extremists to continue on their religious crusade in the 21st century?

Yankee Evil Dollar

The U.S. Constitution was adopted in 1789. Washington was elected President and he invited Thomas Jefferson to be Secretary of State. Alexander Hamilton was appointed Secretary of the Treasury. But when the first federal Congress came together in 1789 the mood was one of anticlimax. Few delegates bothered to make it to the official opening in New York, and it took another three weeks to reach a quorum. Nobody was sure how a federal government ought to behave, or even what to do next. Washington presided over dinners where no one was allowed to talk, and "played on the table with a knife and fork like a drumstick". Delegates didn't know what to call him. Washington was no wiser as how to address them, and had no clear idea of their powers. The one thing they agreed on was God had none! Is this the Evil Satan many Moslem extremists rave about?

Money, and the U.S. dollar in particular, is accused of being the root of all evil. When the U.S. declared independence in 1776 it issued 10 million dollars to be used throughout America as the official currency. Sinister messages may be hidden in the Great Seal of the United States, which appears on the back of the dollar bill. A popular theory fingers a Masonic sect called the Illuminati, whose aim is to overthrow governments. It is so secret and ruthless that nothing more is known about it. The first American to become frightened by the Illuminati was a Boston preacher called Jediah Morse, whose more famous son was the inventor of the Morse code. Another obscure belief of occultists is that a mysterious man in black appeared one day at Thomas Jefferson's elbow and told him how to reproduce the symbols of the Great Seal. Anyone with a ruler, compass and a taste for voodoo can use a dollar bill to design the nine-pointed star traditionally associated with calling up the Devil.

George Washington made his way on to the dollar bill in the 1920s, before the Great Depression, before World War II. The same face on the same greenback. "It was produced in the Roaring 20's, the age of skyscrapers, mass production and design consultancies: an 18th-century portrait among the laurel leaves and table mirrors of a fancy whorehouse," Jason Goodwin tells us in his book *Greenback*. He's looking at us through tired eyes, a stubborn commander who won his war by refusing the possibility of defeat. He kept his army together for eight years until the enemy's army – the world's best-trained, best-paid and most powerful force – finally gave up.

Today there are seven trillion greenbacks in circulation. It is the world standard. The great majority of these dollars exist electronically, but about $666 billion's worth, in denominations from $1 to $10,000, are printed on 22 billion paper bills, of which almost a third are held outside the United States. This means there are more dollar bills in existence than any other branded object, including Coke cans. George Washington and Mammon are America's idols. I personally know the power of those idols. When all reason fails with career politicians or customs officials anywhere, a few greenbacks get the job done.

Lucifer
Thanks to Bush and his Christian Coalition, the removal of the Saddam regime brought to light the Yezidi tribe living deep in the Sinjar highlands of Kurdish-dominated northern Iraq. They have a 2,000-year-old shrine dedicated to Lucifer, the chief angel of their religion. A black stone snake, which they stroke for good luck, slithers up the wall by the front entrance. Inside, a sarcophagus containing the 1,200-year-old remains of Shaykh Adi, one of the great thinkers of the Yezidi religion.

At sunrise and sunset, the Yezidi face the sun to pray. They do not wear blue clothing or eat lettuce – both are forbidden for reasons that have been lost. They do not believe in heaven or hell because Adam, the first man, never left the Garden of Eden. Belief in the afterlife, while central to the philosophy, is not essential for the million or so Yezidis scattered around the world. Makes me wonder if my neighbor in Rivas Canyon, Los Angeles, with a Lucifer license plate on his red Ferrari was a Yezidi. Probably not, he acted like a Jewish turd – not a Kurd.

The Yezidis are so relaxed about religious obligations that they can nominate proxies to pray and fast for them, paying their stand-ins for each sin they ask forgiveness for. "Is there paradise or not? It is very difficult to say," Prince Tasin Beg, chief of the Yezidi tribe, says in an agnostic uncertainty. "It is not necessary to believe in paradise or hell. All people are free to believe as they choose. Some do, some don't."

Far from being evil incarnate, Lucifer, according to the Yezidis, was not cast out of heaven by God but was forgiven and restored to his position as chief of seven angels. Yezidis deny they are devil-worshippers and are forbidden from referring to Lucifer as Satan, but they are part of an ancient sect which reveres him as the archangel and creator of the material world. Lucifer, Adam and Gabriel are regarded as pretty much the same being rolled into one chief divine figure called Malak Taus, or the peacock angel, who rules the universe on behalf of God, who lost interest after creating it.

Suicide and Unjust Wars
Suicide bombers don't just kill Americans and Jews. The September 11 attack on the World Trade Center was a grim reminder. The suicide bombings in Israel, Saudi Arabia, and Turkey don't just kill Americans and Jews. They kill Arabs, Muslims, foreign workers and tourists.

Suicide is not condoned, sanctioned or approved by either the Torah or Koran. The descendants of both sons of Abraham abhor and prohibit suicides. Life belongs to God who grants it, not to mortal men who are its trustee. Both Judaism and Islam celebrate life and promote its enjoyment.

Martyrdom – istishhad – is an old and esteemed idea in Islam. It took root in 680 when Husayn, the son of the Caliph Ali and the grandson of the Prophet Muhammad, died at Karbala in southern Iraq. Shiite Muslims, who see rightful rule in Islam descending through Ali's bloodline, permanently embedded the death of Husayn, "the prince of all martyrs", into the broader Muslim consciousness. Shiite Iran's revolution in 1979 and the Iran-Iraq war between 1980-88 electrified and made modern the concept of martyrdom and holy war throughout the Muslim world.

The ancient Roman proverb, "Beware the man of one book," seems to grow more urgent by the month when the book is a Holy Scripture. Killing in the name of God is hardly unknown in history, but the extent of freelance religious violence committed around the world lately might cause a Borgia Pope to blush. The Talmud, which is the Jewish oral tradition, asks: Why did God test Abraham? So the world would know that if anyone tells you they are committing murder in the name of God they are a liar. No Jewish religious court has had the power to levy a death sentence since Jesus' time. It was Romans, not Jews, who crucified Jesus. The Fifth Commandment proclaims "Thou shalt not kill." How can Christians then justify their support of the death penalty?

Sheik Muhammad Rafaat Othman, who teaches Islamic law at the most prestigious Islamic school in the Middle East, Cairo's Al-Azhar University, unequivocally states the Koran prohibits suicide, even as a tactic in a legitimate holy war. "As I interpret our religion, I don't see any evidence of exception to this rule...You can expose yourself to a situation where you might get killed. But you can't knowingly take your life." Sheik Muhammad added: "Attacking innocent, unarmed people is forbidden. Prophet Muhammad demanded that we not kill women, children or the elderly. Attacks should be against soldiers and armed civilians." Even the Grand Mufti of Saudi Arabia, Sheik Abdulazia bin Abdallah al Sheikh, said: "Jihad for God's sake is one of the best acts in Islam, but killing oneself in the midst of the enemy, or suicidal acts, I don't know whether this is endorsed by Sharia or whether it is considered jihad for God. I'm afraid it could be suicide." He added that such suicide bombers do not die as martyrs but as suicides.

Islamic law forbids harm to non-combatants. Verse 190 of the second chapter of the Koran reads: "Fight in the path of God those who fight you, but do not transgress limits. God does not love transgressors." Even in war, Islamic law and tradition clearly prohibit any transgressions, including any damage to property. This injunction is partly based on a famous saying of the Prophet: "Do not burn a plant, or cut a tree in the territory of combatants."

These eminent Muslim scholars echoed the words of their fellow imams in America. "It violates the very foundations of Islamic law," said Imam Yahya Hendi, Muslim chaplain at Georgetown University, a Jesuit school. "We respect your faith...Its teachings are good and peaceful, and those who commit evil in the name of Allah blaspheme the name of Allah," President George Bush correctly declared.

Muslim extremists, like Christian extremists, have hijacked the teachings of the Prophets. No different than what the career politicians have done to the teachings of the Prophets of America – The Founding Fathers.

"It doesn't take a rocket scientist to see that a guy who went to bars and strip clubs down in Florida isn't a good Muslim. And the intentional killing of civilians isn't permitted under Islamic law. So whatever these guys are fighting for, it isn't classical Islam," said Cleveland State University law school professor David Forte, whose language about Islam being hijacked by the September 11 kamikazes was used by President Bush and is still remembered as one of his most memorable lines.

The Catholic Church came up with the just-war theory in the mid-19th century to justify the wars the Vatican supported. To hear Pope John Paul II say there is no such thing as a holy war in Kazakhstan and Armenia as America was preparing to go to war in Afghanistan, words he used when the American-led coalition went to war against Iraq, was another millennium reminder that war cannot be justified by any religious teachings or religion. "Religion must never be used as a reason for conflict," the Pope proclaimed at an outdoor mass attended mostly by Muslims.

For Holy Peace to replace Holy Wars all religions have to acknowledge and respect other religions. Pronouncements such as those made by Cardinal Joseph Ratzinger's dictum, "Dominus Jesus", of August 6, 2000, that the Catholic Church is "the only true church" are not only offensive and disrespectful but perpetuate religious hatred and unnecessary wars in the new millennium. Fighting evil with violence cannot contribute to Holy Peace.

Abort Fundamentalist Crusades

President George W. Bush launched a "crusade" in response to September 11. "Operation Infinite Justice". As Sheik Taha al-Alwani, chairman of Islamic jurists in North America, pointed out, the term could be translated to "absolute justice", which is something that only God can deliver. Could it be that President Bush thinks he is God in America, like Caesar, Muhammad's successors and the Chinese emperors?

The Iraq War underscored the dangerous religious fundamentalist crusade undertones our Founding Fathers cautioned us to look out for and avoid. The Iraq War became a religious war. America's born-again Christian president peppers his speeches with religious terms and almost always ends them with a solemn "God Bless America". The U.S. Congress passed a resolution calling on President Bush to order a nationwide day of prayer for the country. U.S. soldiers in Iraq had been asked to pray for President Bush so that "God's peace be [his] guide". Meanwhile secular Saddam Hussein put Islam at the heart of his victory and survival. "Oh Arabs, oh believers across the world, oh enemies of evil, God is on your side," he said. "Rely on God and the soldiers of the merciful on our land will be granted victory."

Does this religious fundamental crusade between Muslims, Christians and Jews dating back to the first Crusade have to continue in the new millennium? America has to be proactive to ensure this ongoing clash ends.

Do the new form of Crusades or Fatwas disguised as ethnic cleansing or terrorism have to continue in the New World Order? Is it really necessary for Osama bin-Laden's disciples to pursue the World Islamic Front for Jihad against Jews and Crusaders? Likewise, is it necessary for America and its allies to pursue their democracy crusade in Muslim countries? Algeria, Bosnia, Kosovo, Indonesia and Afghanistan can do fine without an American-imposed political structure. America will be better off getting its democratic house in order first. The mullahs' offer to send observers to future U.S. elections is a reminder of how much *We the People* have to do at home first to implement the Founding Fathers' constitutional principles.

The millennium ended with the "Good Friday" peace accord in Ireland and its architects John Hume and David Trimble justly earning a Nobel Peace Prize for their efforts. Hopefully, it will stand the test of time. Their example, like those of Sadat and Begin, Rabin and King Hussein, should shame the dictators and the mullahs into pursuing peace and prosperity. If they don't, *InShallah,* God willing, their successors will.

America has been a key broker in bringing different warring religious factions together. In Ireland, Bosnia, Kosovo, Afghanistan, Israel and Palestine. Christians, Muslims and Jews. To continue being an honest credible impartial "peace broker" in the 21st century, America has to first get its religious house in order. Then Americans can learn, understand and appreciate the different religious cultures around them and be accepted as the impartial country the Founding Fathers intended.

A splendid working model to achieve better understanding has been adopted by the Marks & Spencer retail chain in Britian. It takes management trainees from Israel, both Jewish and Arab Israelis, in an attempt to use business to build bridges across the divide. This is a ritual that takes place every day in Hong Kong. People with different beliefs work together side by side every day. Shouldn't more companies and communities be doing the same with all remaining religious combatants?

The religious strife at the dawn of the 21st century in Nazareth, a once sleepy town populated by Arab Christians and Muslims, over the Muslims' plan for a large new mosque to be built with funds donated by the Gulf states, near the Christian Basilica of the Annunciation, where tradition says the angel Gabriel told Mary she was pregnant, is another millennium reminder of how religious bonds in the New World Order still transcend national and local boundaries, even ethnic groupings.

"There is no argument in the world that carries the hatred that a religious belief does. The more learned a man is the less consideration he has for another man's belief," Will Rogers reminded us early in the 20th century. He went on to say: "I have sometimes wondered if the preachers themselves have not something to do with this. You hear or read a sermon nowadays, and the biggest part of it is taken up by knocking or trying to prove the falseness of some other denomination. They say that the Catholics are damned, that the Jews' religion is all wrong, or that the Christian Scientists are a fake, or that the Protestants are all out of step.

"Now, just suppose, for a change they preach to you about the Lord and not about the other fellow's church, for every man's religion is good. There is none of it bad. We are all trying to arrive at the same place according to our own conscience and teachings. It don't matter which road you take." Isn't it time we all tried to converge on to the same road in the 21st century?

Religious Impartiality and Neutrality

I understand, but have difficulty accepting, the lack of tolerance Christians and Muslims have for each other which has been increasing over the centuries. Russia, like Slavic Serbia, conducted one of the biggest anti-Muslim purges after World War II. In its predominantly Muslim areas of Russia, Central Asian and Soviet areas of Turkestan, Kazakhstan, Turkmenistan, as well as in the Crimea, including Chechnya, Russia expelled Muslims from their homes and replaced them with Russians. It repeated its ethnic cleansing of Chechnya at the sunset of the old millennium and continues to do so at the beginning of the new.

This intolerance took new turns in the closing decades of the millennium. In addition to the bombings of the World Trade Center, the Pentagon, American embassies in Africa, the USS Cole, terrorist bases in Afghanistan and Sudan, there were cases of destruction of churches and mosques in India, Pakistan, Indonesia, Bosnia, Georgia and Kosovo and growing anti-semitism in the Western world against Arabs. The Islamic participants plot the assassination of CIA officials, prominent Westerners and the bombing of civilian aircraft like the Pan Am airliner over Lockerbie, Scotland. The United States plots the overthrow of extremist Islamic regimes. During the 15 years between 1980 and 1995, according to the U.S. Defense Department, the United States engaged in 17 military operations in the Middle East, all of them directed against Muslims. No comparable pattern of U.S. military operations occurred against the people of any other civilization.

Religion has played a critical role in the evolution of humanity and the world as we know it today.

The Catholic Church's active opposition to communism in Poland, Russia and Italy is suspect. Communism was a threat to Catholicism.

The Pope – a Pole – and the Catholic Church actively fought communism after the post-war establishment of the Eastern bloc, not only in Russia, Poland but in Italy where the Communist party almost came to power.

John Paul II's Polish nationalism and his fearless anti-German position as Bishop of Cracow, as well as acts of courage towards Polish Jews, are well-known. Equally well-known has been the Church's unwillingness to castigate conciliatory right-wing regimes in Catholic nations. In that John Paul II has been complicit – especially in South America. In a New World Order the Holy See should interfere in foreign matters of brutality and deep disgust but it must do so with disinterest and not socio-political partiality. What Sister Gertrude, a former mother superior, and Sister Maria Kisito, two Rwandan nuns at a concentration camp where thousands of Tutsi refugees were slaughtered, did to facilitate the genocide is inexcusable in the New World Order. Their prison sentences are justified.

The Catholic Church in Hong Kong has balanced its role in the community. Catholic Bishop Joseph Zen Ze-kiun said the clergy has a duty to denounce injustice in Hong Kong. "We have a role as a prophet in society. We have to judge whether things happening in society are right or wrong. It is the church's teachings that we should uphold, those that are just, and condemn those that are unjust." The church was outspoken against government decisions and comments on the controversy over which mainlanders should get right of abode in Hong Kong, over the Falun Gong and Article 23, the new security law. It criticized outgoing Chief Secretary Anson Chan Fang On-sang for not speaking up against Beijing, saying she does not deserve her reputation as "Hong Kong's conscience." When the government declared the children of parents seeking right of abode in Hong Kong could not attend local schools until their legal status was determined, the Catholic Church stepped in and defied the government by enrolling them in church schools.

Bishop Zen joined other Christian leaders in Hong Kong who called on their 600,000 church members to join the campaign against the proposed national security legislation because it would harm civil liberties and religious freedom. More than 50 prominent figures from the Anglican, Baptist, Catholic, Methodist and Presbyterian churches joined forces in their personal capacity to protest against the legislation. Over 500,000 people joined the protest. Almost 10 percent of the population. Imagine what would happen in America if church leaders got 10 percent of their apathetic followers to take to the streets and protest the Patriot Act!

The Catholic Church in Hong Kong counts among its members influential and prominent figures such as the Chief Secretary, Donald Tsang, the Secretary for Housing, Dominic Wong Shing-wah, and former Democratic Party leader Martin Lee Chu-ming. Bishop Zen said the church could lobby such prominent members to put forth the church's position. However, "Is it suitable to lobby them frequently and in high profile? I think it should be avoided because people might then say the Church wants to control Government," Bishop Zen rightly cautions. Shouldn't all church leaders be doing the same in the 21st century?

The Pope and Church's refusal to condemn fascism was political. Its refusal to condemn genocide was wrong. No political movement should be opposed or supported by any religious leader or religious organization. Acts of barbarism against humanity, no matter what religious reason is cited, must be condemned by all religious leaders. Separation between State and Church must be pursued and enforced as a universal goal in the New World Order if humanity is to survive.

Religious Nuclear Fallout
The U.S.-led bombing of Afghanistan was followed by a massacre of 16 Christians in Islamabad, Pakistan. Four of the dead were children under 12, four were women and eight were men. One of the men was Father Emmanuel, the minister conducting the morning service. "Graveyard of Christians – Pakistan and Afghanistan," said the gunmen and: "This is just a start."

A few weeks later Muslim terrorists based in Pakistan attacked the Indian parliament on a suicide mission to wipe out the leadership of India. The attack took place as the U.S. was flushing Osama bin-Laden from his Tora Bora hideout and almost led to religious nuclear fallout. Tensions between India and Pakistan, who have fought three wars since 1947, have to be contained now that they run the risk of testing their nuclear devices on each other.

Pakistan has to contain the thousands of Taleban and al-Qaeda fighters who have taken refuge there and are re-charging for their next fight. Kashmir is a logical target. A target India will not give up without a fight.

Hindu nationalists must also separate Church from State in the New World Order. The Hindu-Muslim and Hindu-Christian sectarian strife has escalated at the sunset of the 20th century and the dawn of the 21st. Hitler is presented to millions of Hindu school children as a heroic figure in Gujarat state, the birthplace of Mahatma Gandhi. Gujarat borders on Pakistan and Muslim-Hindu violence is endemic. Muslim Kausar Bano, eight months pregnant, was allegedly dragged out of her home and gang-raped in front of a frenzied Hindu crowd after an arson attack on a train carrying Hindus killed 59. One of the rapists then reportedly slashed her stomach with a sword and pulled out the fetus. According to witnesses, he displayed it to the crowd, then poured fuel over mother and unborn child and set them alight. Thousands of Muslims were slaughtered in the violence that followed the fire bombing of the train. Rioters also destroyed some 230 unique Islamic monuments during the rampage.

In India a sleeping priest was beaten to death with pump handles, Christian graveyards were dug up and tombstones smashed and bombs exploded in churches around the country. Hindus killing priests like Graham Staines and his innocent sons, Philip, 10, and Timothy, 6, and setting Christian churches ablaze is just as intolerable as Indonesians killing priests and nuns in East Timor and burning Christian churches. India's Hindus must also attempt to minimize the potential nuclear conflict with their Muslim neighbor Pakistan. The thought that India may change from a secular state to a religious Hindu state is chilling. India will be the most populous nation in the 21st century. Let's not forget India still has the second largest Muslim population in the world, even after Muslim Pakistan and

Bangladesh were carved off as independent nations.

"Can you get me a copy of the video I've heard about made in India that's a Hindu rock video honoring their nuclear explosion?" my ex-brother-in-law Don Richstone asked. "I hear it's real freaky. It glorifies nuclear weapons and India's nuclear explosions," he continued. "Have you seen it?" "Yes, it's actually aired on MTV Asia," I told him. "Isn't that a scary thought, India and Pakistan going to nuclear war?" he asked no one in particular. "No! What is the downside, I ask you?" interjected Matt Billet who was putting another log on the outdoor fire as we toasted in the New Year. "You must be joking?" I said knowing he wasn't.

The serious and dangerous potential of a religious nuclear conflict between India and Pakistan is a reality in the new millennium. FCC member and novelist Humphrey Hawksley outlines a realistic scenario of a nuclear conflict between India and Pakistan in his novel *Dragon Fire*. I hope nobody dismisses *Dragon Fire* as one more work of fiction. The political and historical backdrop against which he writes is real.

Hawksley spoke at an FCC luncheon about his experiences research-ing the book. After his speech, his book and nuclear scenario became the topic of animated discussion at the Main Bar. Luke Hunt, who covered the Kashmir conflict for AFP and spent time in Afghanistan and in Pakistan shortly after the coup, said: "If anyone really thinks Hawksley is a dimwit, then be careful – there is a real risk you will choke on the words 'he told you so'." Luke put his money where his mouth is. He placed a HK$500 bet predicting a nuclear war between India and Pakistan, arguing "dipping into someone else's wallet is a nicer way of saying 'I told you so'." Hopefully, India's election of President A.P.J. Abdul Kalam, a Muslim scientist widely hero-worshipped as the godfather of the country's nuclear missile program, will keep the silos buried.

Church and State have to be separated and respected by all religions in the 21st century. Religious figures and places of worship, no matter what the religion, have to be respected, maintained and preserved by *We the Maids*. America's example must be emulated by all. America has gone to great lengths to avoid damaging or destroying places of worship and holy sites. We saw this most recently during the Iraq War and Afghan War. Holy shrines and mosques were avoided even when legitimate military targets were set up nearby to provoke a destructive attack. During World War II we saw America avoid bombing Kyoto, Japan, out of concern of damaging the numerous historic Buddhist temples there.

The elusive "peace train" that has ridden the tracks of time has to be caught by all religious civilizations in the new millennium. The religious tools used to create conflict for millennia have no place in the New World Order. God has to be demilitarized. The alternative is a nuclear fallout.

New Jerusalem-City of Peace and Religious Harmony
Jerusalem, the center of the Western world's three major religions, the fabled city where David ruled, where Jesus died, where Muhammad allegedly ascended to Heaven, might be obliterated in a final battle brought on by religious hatred. Given the mileage between capitals and groups it would be like dropping a nuke on yourself – even a battlefield tactical device. But then again, what do suicide bombers care? It would certainly be a clearing of the decks. The Goyim would shrug their shoulders and say: "Well, there you go!"

The sword carriers of Muhammad, or rather the explosives and nuclear bombs of the fundamentalist suicide bombers, trying to blow apart the "infidels" by "jihads" or "fitnas", have to be replaced by the peaceful readers of the Koran. The ensuing result is peaceful commerce, prayer and mutual respect Why can't this be pursued as a continuous global goal? If even the Irish Catholics and Protestants manage it in the near future, there really can be no excuse for anyone else.

God is One to Christians, Muslims and Jews. All three believe in monotheism – single deity worship. "Let everyone," as Will Rogers said, "arrive at the same place according to our own conscience and teachings!"

Buddhists, Christians, Hindus, Jews and Muslims are cousins. Jews and Muslims are first cousins. Why do they have to continue being killing-cousins rather than kissing-cousins in the 21st century?

Jerusalem has historically been the birthmark of good behavior between Christian, Jew and Muslim. It has also on many occasions been its cancer. The problem with Jerusalem begins with its name. The word evokes more than 4,000 years of history and the spiritual heritage of three great religions. But only a tiny part of what is today called Jerusalem is in fact connected to that holy city.

Until 1860, Jerusalem was confined within the kilometer-square walls of what is today called the Old City. The holy places are almost all within those walls and in a smaller area outside embracing the Mount of Olives and Mount Zion. Today's Jerusalem, however, is more than 100 times the size of the Old City. "The sacredness of this modern city has been built by political rhetoric," says Abraham Rabinovich. "If peace can be made to work in Jerusalem, it might even become contagious. Failure certainly will be," Rabinovich correctly opines.

The debate in Israel on whether the Israeli authorities can place a second door in the Church of the Holy Sepulcher is an ideal snapshot of religious mania of the New World Disorder.

Most Christians believe Jesus was crucified, buried and resurrected at the site of the Church of the Holy Sepulcher. Three denominations – Roman Catholic, Greek Orthodox and Armenian – have principal custody of the Church under an edict issued in 1852 by the ruling Ottoman Sultan and known as the Status Quo. Three additional denominations – the Copts, Syrian Orthodox and Ethiopian Christian – are given space within the church, portions of which date to the fourth century.

The purported tomb of Christ, the centerpiece of the church, remains encased in rusted scaffolding erected more than half a century ago by British Mandate governors seeking to repair earthquake damage. The factions cannot decide how to go about removing the scaffolding, even though it is a harsh blemish on the one feature the pilgrims will queue for hours to behold.

The definitions of The Almighty, The Prophet, True Path and Peace have many parallels to the debate about Jesus. Theological scholars still debate who Jesus was.

There are three proofs that Jesus was Mexican. His first name was Jesus. He was bilingual. He was always being harassed by the authorities. But there are equally good arguments that Jesus was black. He called everybody "brother". He liked gospel. He couldn't get a fair trial.

But then there are equally good arguments that Jesus was Jewish. He went into his father's business. He lived at home until he was 33. He was sure his Mother was a virgin, and his Mother was sure he was God.

But then there are equally good arguments that Jesus was Italian. He talked with his hands. He had wine with every meal. He used olive oil.

But then there are equally good arguments that Jesus was a Californian. He never cut his hair. He walked around barefoot. He started a new religion.

But then there were equally good arguments that Jesus was Irish. He never got married. He was always telling stories. He loved green pastures. But perhaps the most compelling evidence is ... the three proofs that Jesus was a woman. He had to feed a crowd at a moment's notice when there was no food. He kept trying to get the message across to a bunch of men who just didn't get it. Even when he was dead, he had to get up because there was more work for him to do.

The play "Corpus Christi", which presents Jesus as a lusty, hard-drinking foul-mouthed homosexual, has again tested and survived the First Amendment in Indiana. Jesus is controversial. A continuing controversy over power and rights.

As the controversy over the door shows, the Church of the Holy Sepulcher is really a modern-day metaphor not only for the region, but the New World Order, over which diverse people and religions have struggled for a share of land and political power. No faction is willing to cede anything that might take away from its own position or give another faction an advantage.

During the time of the Crusades, the Church of the Holy Sepulcher had a dozen or so doors. The bloody Crusader reign came to an end when the Muslim warrior Saladin recaptured Jerusalem in 1187. He expelled the Crusaders but allowed a limited number of Christian priests to continue to work from the Church. However, to keep tabs on who entered the church, he ordered all its doors sealed, except half of the main portal. In addition he entrusted the single key to the single door to a single Muslim family, ensuring control over access – and avoiding having to favor either Latin or Eastern Christians.

The exchange of gunfire between Palestinian gunmen in the church and the Israeli army in Manger Square resulted in fires that further charred Christ's birthplace while the U.S. Catholic Bishops were being summoned to Rome to discuss the pedophile sex scandals that had engulfed the Church. At the same time, Muslims slaughtered Christians in Indonesia, Muslims and Hindus butchered each other in India while fires there burnt out entire communities; sectarian religious conflicts continued in Africa; and the global crusade against terrorism expanded. These simultaneous events were millennium reminders of how hypocritical and destructive religious fervor and fundamentalist political fires have become at the dawn of the 21st century. They have created the bonfires of hell here on Earth. Fires that *We the Apathetic Maids* have to put out if we are to evolve as a harmonious and peaceful community in the spirit and vision of Christ and Muhammad.

The only momentary respite for humor during the turmoil surrounding Bethlehem's Church of the Nativity were the two Japanese tourists so engrossed in their guidebooks that they did not notice they had wandered unwittingly into a war zone. They were probably looking at the complimentary map of the world without Israel that Fuji Co. gives its customers. According to Fuji, Israel doesn't exist. Local women and children simply gazed at the Japanese in disbelief. Shouldn't we all?

If the Irish and English cousins manage to kiss and make up in the sunset of the old millennium after centuries of mutual hatred and attempted extermination, I fail to see why others of all religious denominations can't follow in their exemplary footsteps in the 21st century! Why don't all religions try to open up a second door for all of us? "Go back far enough and all human kind are cousins," Naomi Mitchison reminds us. Do we really have to experience Armageddon before the coming of a Messiah?

The cancellation of Christmas celebrations in Bethlehem, Jesus' birthplace, in the last year of the millennium, because of the violence between Israelis and Palestinians, is also symbolic of the religious conflicts worldwide, whether in Indonesia, Kashmir or Chechnya. Bethlehem must keep its doors open at all times in the 21st century as a symbol of religious tolerance and harmony. That is what Yeshu, the Jewish revolutionary guru, died preaching. The city of peace has to lead the long peace march of the 21st century.

Global Religious Council

All religions of the world should make a concerted effort to work together to search for the truth in the New World Order and bring about a better understanding, tolerance, love and peace to the world. Bring an end to religious wars. A Global Religious Council with representatives of all religious groups that want to participate should be established in Jerusalem, or other acceptable city, as the Jews, Christians and Muslims did in Cordova at the dawn of the 12th century. It must be self-sustaining with each religious denomination paying its own dues. There cannot be any government or taxpayer support of the GRC. The world's major religions, Buddhist, Christian, Hindu, Jewish, Muslim and so on, would be represented on the Council. An assembly of all other religions of the world willing to pay their fair share of dues shall debate and discuss the issues of mutual concern and pass resolutions on a majority basis to be recommended for consideration by the Council. They take effect only if adopted by the Council.

The 21st century should encourage different religious groups to work with each other and attempt to resolve misunderstandings as God intended. With love and compassion.

Abuse of Faith

President Bush believes his actions, domestic and foreign, are justified "because of the power of prayer". David Frum, who was the Bush speechwriter who coined the phrase "axis of evil", recounts in *The Right Man: The Surprise Presidency of George W. Bush* what the President said at a meeting in the Oval Office when talking to a group of reverends from the major denominations: "There is only one reason that I am in the Oval Office and not in a bar: I found faith. I found God. I am here because of the power of prayer."

America's political leaders abuse and violate the Constitution when they invoke the name of God to justify their actions or lobby for political support. A country, political process and foreign policy cannot be run on faith and prayers. President George Dubya is an extreme example of such blatant abuses. President Bush, it was reported, told Prime Minister Mahmoud Abbas that he had gone to war in Afghanistan and Iraq on instructions from God. Is this a justifiable reason to go to war, especially for a secular nation? After all, it is mere mortal taxpayers who pay the costs of war and send their children to fight and die. Not God, Jesus or the Holy Ghost.

Michael Lind correctly concludes in *Made In Texas* that "The Texan conservatism of George W. Bush combines 17-century religion, 18-century economics, and 19-century imperialism. The United States in the 21st century can do better than this."

Separation of Church and State
George W. Bush said Jesus Christ was the historical philosopher he admired most. Which one? The blonde version perpetuated by the Church for centuries or the real one with dark Semitic features? Al Gore has declared himself a born-again Christian. Senator Joe Lieberman says "miracles happen" when he accepted Gore's invitation to be his running mate in a speech that took religious-political rhetoric to soaring new heights. At one point he invoked God's name 13 times in 90 seconds!

Politicians have to separate their private beliefs from public duties, just as the Founding Fathers did. The "Magnificent Seven" were religious men. God-fearing praying Christians. Nevertheless, they separated their personal beliefs and practices from their vision of America. A country where religion and God had no role. The number of Americans belonging to churches during the American Revolution was only 17 percent! According to a 2002 *Newsweek* poll, 45 percent of American society defined the United States as "a secular nation"; only 29 percent of Americans view the United States as "a Christian nation" and only 16 percent as a "Biblical nation, defined by the Judeo-Christian tradition". America is the Enlightment's secular child.

The United States Supreme Court in the case of *Board of Education v. Everson* ruled that the non-establishment clause prohibits the State from setting up a church, passing laws which aid one religion, or all religions, or prefer one religion over another, and from participating openly or directly in the affairs of any religious organizations or groups and vice versa.

The "Star Spangled Banner" is what Americans sang until Irving Berlin, a Jewish immigrant from Russia who entered the United States at Ellis Island, wrote "God Bless America" in the 20th century. Irving Berlin was born Israel Baliner in 1888. He also wrote, "White Christmas" and "Easter Parade".

The Anti-Defamation League of B'nai Brith was correct when it objected to Senator Joe Lieberman's insistence that, "as a people we need to reaffirm our faith and renew the dedication of our nation and ourselves to God and God's purpose." This appeal to belief in God, the agency argued, is contrary to the First Amendment and to the American ideal. Nor did the agency agree with the senator's belief that "morality cannot be maintained without religion". American atheists, the ADL declared, "should not be made to feel inferior, or left out of the political process".

It can be argued that atheism is also a religion. Madalyn Murray O'Hair, the atheist leader who played a key role in banning mandatory prayer in public schools in the 1960s, argued that one did not necessarily have to believe in any deity. That was an individual religious choice. For the state of Florida to label a personalized license plate with the word "Atheist" as obscene, 16 years after it was issued, is a dire warning of how far we have drifted from the fountain of the Founding Fathers' vision.

Most Americans agree with Senator Lieberman, which is why he said what he did. After all that is what political rhetoric is all about. America is the most religious of Western democracies, and believers who feel excluded from the political process either withdraw or find a way to polarize the parties. "Religious people are all members of a minority religion," says Yale Law School professor Stephen Carter. "To think otherwise is like black folks looking at white and thinking they are all the same."

Why should any political candidate's religion be brought up in an election? The last presidential election of the last millennium was a religious nightmare. A religious slugfest. The delicate line between church and state was crossed. The Founding Fathers warned us about crossing the line because America is a country where all religious beliefs can be practiced openly and freely. America is not a Christian country that must elect the best Christian. The Religious Right cannot change this constitutional cornerstone. Americans are atheists, Muslims, Jews, Hindus and adherents of many more beliefs. Not just Christians.

Religion in America has developed as a highly anti-intellectual farce. Along with the "sports" ethic and rampant materialism it has helped push America on its way to becoming a land of profound spiritual illiteracy.

That the U.S. Attorney General presides over a Pentecostal Christian Bible study every morning within the Justice Department that employs 135,000 people with hard-earned dollars collected from taxpayers of all religious denominations is not only outrageous but unconstitutional. "The source of freedom and human dignity is the Creator," John Ashcroft says. "All people are called to the defense of the grantor of freedom, and the framework of freedom he created...And this is our responsibility: the guarding of freedom that God grants is the noble charge of the Department of Justice. It is a cause in which all people may participate."

The devotionals by the chief law enforcement officer of the land are just as illegal as it is to fund-raise for political races on Federal property. The fact that he is the deeply conservative son and grandson of an Evangelical Christian preacher who believes "for every crucifixion a resurrection is waiting to follow" – especially after he lost his Senate re-election campaign to a dead man – does not give him the right to impose his religious beliefs in the U.S. Justice Department.

Religion in public affairs, government buildings, parks and schools in America must suffer the fate of the Dead Sea, the lake in the bosom of the birthplace of the world's three major religions – become lifeless.

Where was God when Ashcroft lost to his opponent Governor Mel Carnahan, who was killed in a plane crash? If the people of the state of Missouri rejected him and his beliefs and principles, why should *We the Apathetic Maids* have them imposed on all taxpayers in America? If Ashcroft spent the time he does praying and preaching on the duties and responsibilities of his taxpayer-salaried job and departmental duties he was appointed to do, the Immigration and Naturalization Service and FBI, which he oversees, would have connected all the dots that were in their and his face before September 11. According to the Founding Fathers, connecting the dots is more important than connecting with God. Isn't it time people like that are swept out of office the way our Founding Fathers intended?

Swept out like Pat Robertson was from the presidency of the Christian Coalition for his endorsement of Jerry Falwell's justification of the September 11 bombings. The bad news about the fallout of the collapse of the Christian Coalition is that Robertson's old lawyers are now working at the Justice Department. If one of the most influential men in U.S. politics in the 20th century can be removed by people expressing their outrage at his comments, why can't *We the Apathetic People* sweep out the rest?

George Dubya is a burning bush. He has scorched the Constitution and burned America economically and geopolitically. It is time *We the Maids* sweep out the ashes and Ashcroft-minded burning bush career politicians.

Why do we have congressional chaplains when America is supposed to be a secular country? There have been over 61 Senate chaplains and 48 House chaplains, and all, save a lone Catholic, have been Protestant. Other religions have been represented on the Hill in the form of visiting clergymen, starting in 1860 when Rabbi Morris Jacob Raphall prayed at the opening of a House session. In 1971, Congress played host to a Native-American holy man and in 1992 Imam Wallace D. Mohammed became the first Muslim to open a congressional session.

The U.S. Attorney General told graduates at Bob Jones University that America was founded on religious principles, and "we have no king but Jesus." For the enforcer of the Constitution to have such a distorted view and to be running the Justice Department like a church is disturbing. For him to prohibit any correspondence from the Justice Department bearing his signature, to use the word "pride", which the Bible calls a sin, and the phrase "no higher calling than public service" must have America's Founding Fathers spinning in their graves.

The 200 gay and lesbian employees of the Department of Justice went into a definite spin when Attorney General John Ashcroft denied them the right to hold their annual meeting in the department's Great Hall where it has been held for several years. The decision violates the Justice Department's own non-discrimination policy which promises to eliminate discrimination on the basis of sexual orientation.

Fundamentalists push to become part of the state. Religious agendas have to be kept separate and apart from politics and entertainment! The declaration of Ohio's 41-year-old motto "With God, All Things Are Possible" as unconstitutional in the closing year of the old millennium is a constructive good beginning.

Lejla Sehovic, crowned Miss Croatia, was asked to give up her title because of her religion. She is Muslim. She was correct in saying "In future they should list the real criteria for the contest: nationality and religion." However, I hope they don't. Non-PC criteria like brains, tits and ass should be the only criteria. Even mullahs make love. The example set in Israel in 1999 is the one to follow in the New World Order. An Arab woman was crowned Miss Israel for the first time. "It is not important if I am Arab or Jewish," said winner Rana Raslan. "We must prove to the world that we can live here in coexistence. They wanted a beauty queen, not a political queen."

Incoming German Chancellor Schroeder's refusal to invoke the name of God or make any religious reference when taking his oath of office because of his desire to further distance the church from politics is to be applauded and replicated by all progressive states in the New World Order. Religion has to disavow its once ordained and now just knee-jerk interference in national politics and private sex. It cannot help, and should interfere in the face of deep cruelty, wrong and evil; but that will take men of intellect in the New World Order to gauge when and where.

Jefferson rode horseback through all 13 colonies, the founding states, preaching the importance of the separation of church and state as the basic foundation of America. There was no room for religion in politics then and there is none today.

Watching once anti-semitic Evangelical Christian Conservative Republicans support Israel and urging the White House to refrain from exerting pressure on "God's Chosen People" to surrender land to the "Palestinians," – some like House Republican Leader Dick Armey of Texas suggest that it should be the Palestinians that surrender land to Israel in the quest for peace – is just another millennium reminder of how far America has drifted from the founding cornerstone of separation of church and state.

Shouldn't we all be wrestling the Religious Right to separate church and state as the Founding Fathers intended? The devil and the occult aren't just limited to The Exorcist. In 1986 there were only 20 church-appointed exorcists in Italy. Today there are about 300. How about using them to exorcise religion from politics in the 21st century?

It is time for a modern-day Enlightenment. An American Reformation. Freedom and equality for all religious beliefs, including atheism, the occult and devil worship. The pursuit of knowledge of other religions and a real separation of church and state as our Founding Fathers dictated must be foremost on our agenda in the 21st century.

Why do *We the People* pay lip service to religious extremists in America and allow them to dominate the country's political process? That is not what the Founding Fathers had in mind when they consciously and deliberately separated church from state. Unfortunately, the original spirit and written gospel of the Founding Fathers – like Muhammad's – has been hijacked by religious extremists.

John Adams wrote, "I will insist that the Hebrews have done more to civilize men than any other nation." He wrote as a Christian but added that even if he were an atheist and believed in chance, "I should believe that chance had ordered the Jews to preserve and propagate to all mankind the doctrine of a supreme, intelligent, wise, almighty sovereign of the universe, which I believe to be the great essential principle of all morality, and consequently of all civilization."

President George Washington wrote a letter to the Hebrew Congregation in Newport, Rhode Island, on August 21, 1790, in which religious freedom is laid down as a basic principle of the New Republic.

> To the Hebrew Congregation in Newport, Rhode Island Gentlemen.
>
> While I receive, with much satisfaction, your address replete with expressions of affection and esteem; I rejoice in the opportunity of assuring you, that I shall always retain a grateful Remembrance of the cordial welcome I experienced in my visit to Newport, from all classes of citizens.
>
> The reflection on the days of difficulty and danger which are past is rendered the more sweet, from a consciousness that they are succeeded by days of uncommon prosperity and security. If we have wisdom to make the best use of the advantages with which we are now favored, we cannot fail, under the just administration of a good government, to become a great and a happy people.
>
> The citizens of the United States of America have a right to applaud themselves for having given to mankind examples of an enlarged and liberal policy: A policy worthy of imitation. All possess alike liberty of conscience and immunities of citizenship. It is now no more that toleration is spoken of, as if it was by the indulgence of one class of people, that another enjoyed the exercise of their inherent natural rights. For happily the government of the United States which gives to bigotry no sanction, to persecution no assistance requires only that they who live under its protection

should demean themselves as good citizens, in giving it on all occasions their effectual support. It would be inconsistent with the frankness of my character not to avow that I am pleased with your favorable opinion of my administration, and fervent wishes for my felicity. May the children of the stock of Abraham, who dwell in this land continue to merit and enjoy the good will of the other inhabitants; which every one shall sit in safety under his own vine and fig tree, and there shall be none to make him afraid. May the father of all mercies scatter light and not darkness in our paths, and make us all in our several vocations useful here, and in his own due time and way everlastingly happy.

G. Washington

Michael Novak, a Roman Catholic theologian at the American Enterprise Institute, says: "The best kept secret of American history is that the favorite language of the republic's founding generation came from the Torah. The founders referred to their own experiment as the Second Israel."

Benjamin Franklin proposed as a motto of the republic "Rebellion to Tyrants is Obedience to God." It fit the American circumstance. The signers of the Declaration, after all, were committing treason. They needed some sort of moral warrant. They faced the most powerful army and navy in the world. It helped that they believed that Providence had created the world so that liberty would in the end prevail. For without liberty, how could the creator, who desired the friendship of free women and men rather than the worship of slaves, fulfil His eternal purpose?

Michael Novak adds: "Most historians lazily say that the founders were Deists, because they did not use Christian names for God, like Trinity and Savior and Redeemer. They miss the crucial point. Three names for God in the Declaration – Creator, Judge and Providence – are unmistakably Jewish names for God. This language did not come from the Greeks or Romans. If the schoolchildren of America were to say a daily prayer entirely in the language of the Declaration, Jews, Christians and Muslims could happily join in."

The Pledge of Allegiance and U.S. currency did not use the phrases "under God" or "In God We Trust" until 1954 when Congress, at the urging of President Dwight Eisenhower to demonstrate to the godless Communists during the Cold War "the dedication of our nation and our people to the Almighty", inserted them.

The "Establishment Clause" of the First Amendment to the Constitution requires that Congress "make no law respecting an establishment of religion." The Establishment Clause has already led to a series of debates over the separation of church and state, with cases ranging from publicly-funded Christmas displays to school prayer. The Federal Ninth Circuit Court was right to rule the words "under God" in the Pledge of Allegiance are unconstitutional. America managed fine by reciting the Pledge of Allegiance without the words "under God" for almost 200 years as the Founding Fathers intended. They got inserted in the 1950s because *We the Apathetic People* were too busy enjoying America's new peace and prosperity after the Great Depression and World War II to object.

All politicians in Washington grappling with the issue should, in the words of Senator Barry Goldwater, try to be "men of conscience" and vote their American constitutional mind, not that of their constituency. They must lead their people to heaven. Lead their people back to the founding cornerstone of America that exorcized religion from politics and the national landscape.

Alexis de Tocqueville warned that "religions should be more careful to confine themselves to a proper sphere, for if they wish to extend themselves beyond spiritual matters, they run the risk of not being believed at all." Nixon admonished that "this is a warning that militants on both the religious right and the religious left would do well to heed. A clergyman's mission is to change people, not to change governments."

Tibetan Buddhists, including those in northwest Yunnan and western Sichuan which were once part of the Tibetan province called Kham, are much more traditionally Tibetan than many in present day Tibet.

They drink from cups made of human skulls and listen to the bleating of the kangling, a trumpet made of a human thigh bone, a stark reminder of how inhuman theocracies can be and why religion has to be separated from politics in the New World Order.

People who believe the clergy should play an active role in politics ought to review the dismal record of theocracies, most recently the Islamic theocracy in Afghanistan. Today even the mullahs in Iran are arguing how to separate church from state. Why can't members of Congress in America?

We have to separate religion from politics in the new millennium. It can no longer be allowed to permeate domestic or international political agendas in the New World Order. The space shuttle Columbia, which disintegrated upon re-entry at the dawn of the 21st century with astronauts whose countries, America, India and Israel, represent all major religions, is an example of how the different major religions must explore together how new frontiers can be collectively conquered in the interests of humanity.

What is clear is that the Founding Fathers wanted God's existence to be free of entanglements in the state. The Founding Fathers wanted a country where all people could freely pursue their religious beliefs. An America where there is a clear and distinct separation of church and state. Isn't it time we got this constitutional cornerstone repolished and updated? If we allow this fundamental article to fade away through communal sanctimony and emotionalism then we might as well take the whole Constitution and toss it in the air and see where it falls. Chances are *The Handmaid's Tale* of the 21st century in the Republic of Gilead – the country formerly known as the United States of America – will no longer just be seen in theaters.

Chapter Four

Karma, Luck and Timming - Gambling For Change

The Gambler - Kenny Rogers

Chinese Junk

When the breeze is just right and it's not too hot is when Hong Kong is really special. The sun, cool, breathy winds and a cloudless sky make for a perfect day in paradise. Rare, but it does happen. The ideal time to be on your back up front on a Chinese junk leaning against the cabin window on a pillow, sipping a beer, smoking a joint or a cigar, preferably a bit of each, taking in the sights of Hong Kong's fragrant harbor while chugging off to one of the outlying islands for lunch or dinner. The average junk accommodates up to 30 people. Whether or not the passengers are old friends or newly introduced business acquaintances, it matters not. All eyes focus on the sights and sounds of Hong Kong harbor. It's an incredible experience. Tankers, cargo ships, ferries, yachts, junks, hydrofoils, fishing boats, destroyers, garbage and aircraft carriers move through Hong Kong waters like a Broadway musical. They somehow manage to avoid hitting each other – well, most of the time. The only sad spot is the rush to reclaim so much of it.

Earl Klein is a retired banker. He left his former wife and three children in Los Angeles when he moved to Asia. On this junk trip, Earl was hosting a small group of several friends with his girlfriend, Catherine. Earl publishes *The Hong Kong Racing Journal.* He is an avid punter and was born and raised in Los Angeles in a household that was intimately involved in the gambling world. He loved going to the racetrack and decided to publish the journal with Catherine when he found that other local publications lacked the basic information that punters need.

Earl had just returned to Hong Kong from the U.S. where several North American racetracks had signed on to subscribe to his journal online for their late night casino punters wanting to bet on the Hong Kong track. He had joined me up front on his junk for a cigar. We had just left the Aberdeen Yacht Club and passed the famous floating restaurants. We were maneuvering to avoid hitting any of the other junks and yachts heading out to sea.

I had just returned from New York where I met with clients, including Donald Trump, who had asked Julia and me to visit his Penthouse at the top of Trump Tower. Marla was re-decorating. What a place! What a view. "Oh, hi," Marla said as Donald introduced us. Julia's American name is Tiffany and everyone in the U.S. calls her by that name. "What a great name. Our daughter is named Tiffany," Marla said as she came down the stairs having dismissed the decorator and army of lieutenants. I was describing the views from Trump's Penthouse when Earl interrupted. "Now there is a man with incredible karma, luck and timing. Talk about a survivor who managed to surprise all the pundits and his bankers. He also has great gambling palaces in Atlantic City. What an ego..." We were joined by Ted McFarland. Ted had driven us to the marina in his wife's Rolls-Royce. She and the kids had preceded him back to Hawaii and Ted was savoring the weather, the wine and freedom. "This is what Hong Kong is all about," he said as he sat down next to Earl. "Want to trade the junk for the Rollie?" Ted was trying to sell his car. "When the karma and timing are right they line up to buy Rolls-Royces. This is the Rolls-Royce capital of the world. Things get shaky and you can't give the damn thing away," Ted lamented as we headed out to sea.

Karma

Tom Southwick, the founder of *Cable World* magazine, was in town and I had invited him to come along for the ride. We moved about to make room for Tom as he joined us. I dropped my cigar, which rolled off the side into the water. "This is incredible!" Tom exclaimed as he waved his arm out towards the harbor and the myriad vessels making their way to wherever. "I think I may move to Hong Kong for a while if this is how you guys live. I thought life was tough here," he said as the boat boy replenished everyone's refreshments. Tom had worked for Senator Edward Kennedy as his press secretary. As the conversation got back to people, luck and timing, it was inevitable that the subject of the Kennedy family's bad karma would be discussed. "Now there is a family with no luck or good karma. In fact if it wasn't for bad luck they'd have no luck at all," Earl started in on Tom. "Hold it Earl. You're a Republican who has it in for every Democrat, especially a Kennedy," I interrupted. I had heard Earl's harangues on the Kennedys on more than one occasion.

"You know the first day I arrived to America back in 1964, I was walking in New York City with my girlfriend, Barbara Rosner, who came up from Philadelphia to meet me. I met Robert Kennedy who was campaigning for the Senate!" I was being emphatic to damp down Earl. "There I was, admiring the great skyscrapers of the city with my girlfriend. First day in America and I meet Robert Kennedy. He shakes my hand and wants my vote. Hell, I just got off the boat about five hours earlier and wasn't even a U.S. resident yet alone a voter," I continued. "Like I said," Earl jumped in, "the Kennedys have no luck or karma. What a schmock. He wasted his time on a non-voter," he continued as everyone shared a chuckle. "That's not true, Earl. In a funny kind of way it was good karma...," I said as I tried to light a new cigar by facing away from the wind. "You see, I was so impressed with the man and what he said, even though I can't remember exactly what it was, that when his son Joseph Kennedy ran for Congress I didn't even hesitate when asked to host a fund-raiser at Scratch. It was his damn highest netting fund-raiser during his first campaign. Both he and his brother, Michael, could never thank me enough. Had I not met Robert Kennedy I probably wouldn't have hosted the event." Earl and Ted both blew their cigar smoke my way. Ted was also a Republican.

The deaths of Michael Kennedy in a skiing accident and JFK Jr's in a plane crash are fresh reminders of the Kennedy bad karma that started with the death of Joseph Kennedy Jr. in World War II. The Kennedy family tragedies are a constant reminder of Karma,

Luck and Timing. The deaths of JFK Jr. and Michael are a reminder that taking unnecessary risks and not getting rid of bad karma can be deadly.

The Kennedy bad karma is much like that of their Boston Red Sox and the once powerful Chiang Dynasty. Chiang Kai-shek ruled China until he lost the Chinese civil war to Mao Tse-tung and fled to Taiwan. There he slaughtered the local indigenous people that resisted his establishement of the Republic of China on Taiwanese soil. Like the Kennedy family, the Chiang family appears to have been cursed. Almost all the males from the first three generations died of cancer or other serious disease. His eldest son Ching-kuo died from complications of diabetes in 1988. A year later, his son Hsiao-wen died of heart failure after being stricken with cancer of the oesophagus. The second son, Hsiao-wu, died three years later of pancreatic cancer. The third son Hsiao-yung died in 1966 of cancer of the oesophagus They were all in their late forties and early fifties. Another son, Winston Chang Hsiao-tzu, born out of wedlock, died in Beijing while attending an academic conference.

The bad karma of the Boston Red Sox has become baseball folklore. It is legendary, especially during the playoffs against the New York Yankees. According to New England legend, the Red Sox, who had won three World Series in six years behind the bat and pitching of the legendary Babe Ruth, were cursed by the Babe after he was sold to the Yankees in December of 1919. Since that day, the Yankees have won 26 World Series and the Boston Red Sox have won none.

Hong Kongers deal with *feng shui* and karma daily. They look for luck and try to get rid of the bad karma. That's why when John Lennon thought he had bad karma, his wife Yoko Ono sent him to Hong Kong to exorcise his demons. Looking at the moon and stars above I couldn't help but think, hum and mumble the words of John Lennon's "Instant Karma".

Shirley McLaine has written and lectured on Karma and Reincarnation extensively. So has Tina Turner. The Thai writer Chatchai Wisetsuwanabhum, not as well-known, despite his 38 novels, 12 short stories and numerous non-fiction works, shows how people, no matter how different they appear to be, are connected to each other in some way.

Karma is the dynamic of cause and effect. What goes round comes round. "You receive from the world what you give the world." You hate you are hated. You love you are loved. While on Earth we create our own negative or positive karma. Karma governs the balancing of energy within our system of morality. It doesn't always occur in one lifetime. The karma of our soul is created and balanced by its multiple personalities. Former and current. That is why some people's karma is imbalanced.

We are the product of the karma of our soul. Our soul is at the core of our being. It is the harmonious human force within our heart that deals with the dynamics of our daily activities unconditionally, without restriction or judgment. It is the intellect of our heart, not our mind. It contains our Divine Intelligence. It flows continuously towards wholeness without a beginning or end. Its personality – its persona – is a natural force in touch with its physical incarnation that interacts with all matters physical. Each is unique because each soul is unique. It operates cohesively with the soul. Name, time and place of incarnation, relationship to planets and energy environment all impact on its formation and wholeness. The karma of the soul determines the personality. Physical, emotional, psychological and spiritual. Reality. How the personality reacts to its experiences creates more karma.

When a person is in full balance, in touch with their spiritual depths, "the personality is soothed because the energy of consciousness is focused on its energy core and not on its artificial facade, which is the personality," Gary Zukav, the author of the bestseller *The Seat of The Soul,* says. Understanding the soul allows non-judgmental justice to flow naturally. Non-judgmental justice allows us to experience life without any negativity. Especially, negative emotions.

America's addiction to political apathy is a collective choice. Conscious and unconscious. "Test your power of choice because each time you choose otherwise you disengage the power of your addiction more and more and increase your personal power more and more," Zukav correctly points out. Isn't it time apathetic America did? "What choose you?" asks Zukav. He continues: "The first time that you challenge your addiction, and the second, and the third, you may not feel that anything has been accomplished. Do you think that authentic power can be had so easily?" You and I, all of us, have to work at it. "The choice not to choose is the choice to remain unconscious and, therefore, to wield power irresponsibly," Zukav concludes. Apathy is the result of insecurity and choice consciously made through fear and doubt instead of wisdom.

"Consider the United States, for example, as simply one unit of energy that is evolving with a particular consciousness. The individual souls that pass through this collective consciousness expand it, create actions, create thought forms, create causes and effects, and that is how it accumulates karma. The relationship of these souls to their nation is like that of cells to a body. Your consciousness affects every cell in your body, and every cell in your body affects your consciousness. There is mutuality. Each individual in the collective consciousness that is called the United States can be thought of as a cell in that nation, in dialogue," Zukav tells us. Do *We the Apathetic Maids* continue to be apathetic or authentic and active in the 21st century?

We have to start evolving into complete human beings and species in the New World Order. We have the power to make conscious decisions which align themselves with what we choose unconsciously. Thus we create our reality. That is our intention. Our collective choice. "The choice not to choose is the choice to remain unconscious and, therefore, to wield power irresponsibility," in the words of Zukav. That is how our choice to become apathetic evolved. Isn't it time we changed? Made more conscious decisions to learn about our political system, process and consciously change what we don't like? When we choose to learn wisely we gain power. Authentic power rather than apathetic. "Authentic power is acquired. It is built up step by step, choice by choice. It cannot be meditated or prayed into being. It must be earned," Zukav correctly concludes.

As the new millennium dawns, the human species, Americans in particular, are again given the chance to choose how we will learn and evolve. Americans can choose again. Differently. To choose a conscious growth and conscious life.

The cycle that ended in the last millennium and therefore is beginning in the 21st century is unique because it is a moment in which three cycles come to conclusion and begin again. These cycles act one inside of the other. Just as the moon orbits the earth, which orbits the sun, there are orbits within orbits, so, too, there are cycles within cycles. We are coming to the close of a grand cycle astrologically, a 2,000-year cycle, and an even grander cycle, where a 25,000-year cycle is linking with a conclusion of a 125,000-year cycle. That is why these things, within this moment in our evolution, are happening now. This is when they were meant to be. Maybe that's what Dubya's "Three finger W" symbolically represents in the New World Order.

The negativity of the last 2,000-year cycle is being collected now so that it can be discharged and transformed, so that the next cycle of 2,000 years which starts with the next beginning cycle of 25,000 years and the next beginning cycle of 125,000 years, all three simultaneously, can begin fresh. A New World Order!

This is what the present situation and moment upon our earth is about: the birth of very different opportunities, opportunities to release patterns that are no longer necessary. The more Light, literally, the more en-Lightened that *We the Apathetic People* are, the more *We the People* will choose different ways.

We the People have the power within us to change the political system. "Power is energy that is formed by the intentions of the soul...There is no power in fear, or in any of the activities that are generated by fear. There is no power in a thought form of fear, even if armies support it. The armies of Rome disappeared more than a millennium ago, but the force of the life of a single human that Roman soldiers put to death continues to shape the development of our species. Who had the power?" Zukav correctly asks. *We the People* have the power within us to change the system.

American Muslim Hasim Rahman, the 20-to-one underdog against Lennox Lewis, just kept swinging even though he couldn't see out of his left eye until he landed the one knockout punch at the opening bell of the 21st century. Karma, luck and timing. Shouldn't *We the People* be doing the same with career politicians? The poster in the gym where he trained bears the slogan "The harder you train, the luckier you get." Shouldn't *We the Apathetic People* be learning harder to get luckier with the political knockout necessary to get rid of career politicians? "Someone once told me that luck is being prepared when opportunity presents itself, and I feel we were ready and prepared," Rahman said after his win. The underdog pulled one of the biggest upsets in boxing history. Bigger than Evander Holyfield's over Mike Tyson, James "Buster" Douglas's over Tyson, Muhammad Ali's over George Foreman and Cassius Clay's (Muhammad Ali's) over Sonny Liston. If they can take out their superior opponents why can't *We the Maids* clean out the political mess? Like them we are underdogs that can deliver a political knockout.

Feng shui

Superstition has a long history in China and Hong Kong. For instance, before Yiching launched his counterattack on Ningpo in 1842, he spent so much time and conspicuous effort selecting an auspicious date for the attack that Gutzlaff's spies found out. After China failed in its attempt to stage the 2000 Olympics in Beijing it was generally accepted in Hong Kong that there was absolutely no possibility of it bidding for the 2004 Olympics, simply because four is an unlucky number. The Simpsons was initially a flop in China and Japan because the characters have only four fingers.

U.S. House Resolution 4444, granting permanent normal trading relations (PNTR) to China, could not have been tagged with a more ominous number. In both Mandarin and Cantonese, the number four is a homonym for death, and so believed to be extremely unlucky.

It is claimed that the Bank of China building was deliberately designed to destroy the feng shui of Government House to the extent that the Governor Sir David Wilson was obliged to plant a row of trees to shield the building from bad luck. After the handover, Tung Chee-hwa, who is Western-educated and had spent some years in America before becoming Chief Executive, refused to live in Government House on the grounds of the bad feng shui . This was considered a perfectly acceptable reason by the Hong Kong people, the opposition politicians and the local media.

Chinese *feng shui* is based on the essence of a balanced life. The yin and yang. The yin and yang are further divided into five elements – fire, earth, metal, water and wood. Wood, conquers earth. Earth conquers water. Water conquers fire. Fire in turn conquers metal and metal wood to complete the cycle.

The *Tung Sing,* also known as the Chinese Bible and "Chinese Almanac", has been in existence since the Hsia dynasty, from around 4,000 B.C. Millions of Hong Kong citizens rely on the book to run their lives. When to travel. When to wash their hair. When to leave the house. When to visit sick relatives. What to wear. Hong Kong's windsurfing queen and Olympic gold medal winner, Lee Lai-shan, followed its advice in order to marry on a lucky day.

It is based on calculations of the positions of the sun and moon and the five elements to help people keep in harmony with nature, to pursue good fortune and avoid evil.

I'm glad to see feng shui is being embraced across America. The hard sciences support feng shui's viewpoint that all matter is imbued with energy – indeed, is energy – and that seemingly insignificant occurrences can have large consequences.

In LA a feng shui master who also knows Jewish laws and traditions advises people to use the ancient Chinese practice to harmonize energy at Passover. Consultants employing the ancient Chinese philosophy are shaking up the Southern California real estate market, prompting some buyers to cancel sales and unnerving skeptical brokers. LA Lakers coach Phil Jackson got a feng shui millennium haircut and shave so he could make the transition to the new millennium with luck. He capped the old with a championship ring with the Lakers and wanted to ensure he added another in the new millennium, and did.

In Britain, Tony Blair's official residence at Number 10 Downing Street brought in a feng shui Master to do his thing. Is the White House far behind?

The Catholic Church probably would have considered feng shui a heretic spiritual practice. Thank God the Crusaders and the Inquisition never made it to Hong Kong.

"Us ignorant people laugh at spiritualists, but when they die they go mighty peaceful and happy, which after all is about all there is to living, is to go away satisfied." Will Rogers did have a take on matters.

Coincidence

Some people call it "coincidence". "Of all the gin joints in all the towns in all the world she walks into mine." But was the arrival of former love, Ilse Lund, at Rick's bar in Casablanca really such an amazing coincidence? Questions like this come up every day in all of our lives. Meeting an old friend or relative at the oddest place. Just like Earl and I did in LA during one of our separate trips to the U.S. We found ourselves in the same restaurant seated next to each other. Pure coincidence.

9/11 is no longer just the local emergency number in America. The 9/11 suicidal meltdown of the Twin Towers has made the number a universal synonym for disaster. The 9/11 disaster warning went out again in 2003 in room 911 of the Metropole Hotel in Hong Kong. That was the room in which the doctor who brought SARS to the world's attention stayed when he came to Hong Kong from China to warn the world about the new pandemic. Coincidence?

Did Mark McGuire's slamming his 61st home run on his father's 61st birthday count as coincidence? How about Lindsay Davenport winning the women's U.S. Tennis Open on her mother's birthday? How about liver transplant recipient Chris Klug who won a bronze Olympic medal in the snowboard parallel giant slalom 18 months after the transplant on February 15, National Donor Day? Coincidence too?

How about this U.S. historical coincidence. Abraham Lincoln was elected to Congress in 1846. John F. Kennedy was elected to Congress in 1946. Abraham Lincoln was elected President in 1860. John F. Kennedy was elected President in 1960. The names Lincoln and Kennedy each contain seven letters. Both were particularly concerned with civil rights. Both wives lost their children while living in the White House. Both Presidents were shot on a Friday. Both Presidents were shot in the head. Lincoln's secretary was named Kennedy. Kennedy's secretary was named Lincoln. Both were assassinated by Southerners. Both were succeeded by Southerners named Johnson. Andrew Johnson, who succeeded Lincoln, was born in 1808. Lyndon Johnson, who succeeded Kennedy, was born in 1908. John Wilkes Booth, who assassinated Lincoln, was born in 1839. Lee Harvey Oswald, who assassinated Kennedy, was born in 1939. Both names are composed of fifteen letters. Lincoln was shot at the theatre named "Ford". Kennedy was shot in a car called "Lincoln", which is a Ford. Booth ran from the theatre and was caught in a warehouse. Oswald ran from a warehouse and was caught in a theatre. Booth and Oswald were assassinated before their trials. And here's the kicker. A week before Lincoln was shot, he was in Monroe, Maryland. A week before Kennedy was shot, he was with Marilyn Monroe.

A more serious and relevant point is the Iraq War. America's Bushes have a lot more in common with Mongolia's 13th century Khans than meets the eye. Both attacked Iraq twice. The Mongol attacks were separated by 13 years while the Bushes by 12 years. Between the Mongol wars, Baghdad was weakened by a devastating series of floods. At the end of the 20th century it was U.N. sanctions and "no-fly zones" that weakened Baghdad's defenses.

Jack Cohen, who co-wrote an article *Explaining Coincidence,* is a reproductive biologist. He was asked to explain two very curious statistics. While in Israel, he was told that 84 percent of the children of Israeli fighter pilots are girls. "What is it about the life of a fighter pilot," he was asked, "that produces such a predominance of daughters?" The second statistic arose in connection with in-vitro fertilization. IVF clinics use ultrasound to monitor ovulation, and so can determine whether an egg – and the resulting baby – comes from the left or the right ovary. One clinic discovered that most of the girl babies came from the left ovary, and that most of the boys from the right. A breakthrough in choosing the sex of your children? Or just a statistical freak? How about Cindy Goh who was born in her father's car giving birth to her son in a taxi? Another statistical freak?

Synchronicity is meaningful coincidence – "meaningful sequences of unusual accidental events." A coincidence "is a sequence of events which occur in close proximity to each other and which by chance are related to each other through some kind of notable similarity."

Day Dreaming

Take Mickey Kantor. There is a guy with bad karma, I thought to myself. The conversation had moved on to the U.S. – China trade relationship and how Mickey was handling the Chinese. I met Mickey when he first came to Los Angeles to run Senator Alan Cranston's campaign. We traveled in some of the same political circles and on occasion supported the same candidate. He lived in the Pacific Palisades where I lived and our children went to the same high school. He lost his first wife in a plane crash and then lost a son in a car accident. I had been with Valerie, his first wife, at a political function a few days before her plane crash in San Diego. My daughter and son had been with his son earlier the evening of his fatal accident at a Pacific Palisades street festival.

That power wielders in Asia, from Shih Huang-di, China's first Emperor, to the Asiaweek Power 50, wear the trappings of the higher forces or causes should come as no surprise to those who know the Asian psyche. While Westerners celebrate personal will, Hong Kongers find peace and security in submitting to an entity larger than their separate selves. To many it would be karma or fate; to others, a religion, a nation, a corporation or a charismatic person. Hong Kongers also define themselves as their fellows regard them: by the face society gives them. And for most people, it is the family that best cradles both fate and face. Building a prosperous, honorable family is the best way to also be in harmony with the larger order, and the social world.

On the junk in Hong Kong harbor, Earl and Ted were pointing out to Tom the different landmarks passing by. One is the "bite" taken from Tai Sheung Tok. It is a 10-metre excavation in a quarry that will expand to 40 meters. Raymond Lo Hang-lap, a local fung shui master, claims the prominent rock-faced peak was part of the "Dragon Arm" that maintained energy and prosperity in the western harbor area. "If you diminish the height it means the energy will be leaking." The Dragon Arm was associated with man and its shrinking could lead to a strengthening of the position of women in Hong Kong.

Listening to them describe the other landmarks, I started to California daydream. I got to think about my former partner, Tim Tierney.

He and I traveled the state representing "Red Neck" mobile home park owners. Tim was married to Janice, a beautiful and lovely African-American lady. "People used to spit at us when we dated and called me nigger-lover," Tim once recalled sadly as we were sharing drinks in Santa Cruz. Tim and Janice lost their only baby daughter to a drowning accident. Several years later Janice lost her eye, and almost her life, when she and Tim were standing in a movie line and were hit by a car whose driver lost control. They had bad karma, luck and timing.

My mind drifted back to China and a story Julia told me about her grandfather. He was a successful textile entrepreneur. He loved music. So he decided to open a radio station to pursue his hobby. The station became a success and the triad gangs demanded protection money. After a while he got tired of paying protection money and decided to do something about it. He got the Kuomintang government to make his station a government station. A sign went up declaring the station a government station. The triads left him alone and his problem was solved. So he thought. When the Communists came to power they arrested him for running a Kuomintang radio station and sent him to jail for 25 years. That is real bad karma, luck and timing.

Karma or Coincidence?
From time to time karma, luck and timing are seriously adverse. They can cause awful loss to befall individuals and communities.

Ted McFarland, the passenger with the Rolls-Royce, lost his wife Kippy within three months of that junk boat ride to bacterial pneumonia in Hawaii. She had been misdiagnosed. They thought she had the 'flu.

What about Callie Marie Johnson who was accidentally switched at birth? When the mistake was discovered through genetic testing, it turned out her real parents had been killed a month earlier in an automobile accident. What about Donna Fasano, who is white, delivering a black baby that belonged to Deborah and Robert Rogers, who are African-American, because the fertility clinic mistakenly implanted the wrong fertilized egg? That is an easy mix-up to detect. What about all the other same race implants that may go undetected similar to Callie Marie Johnson?

Think on the three generations killed in the Omagh bombing in Northern Ireland. Mary Grimes, 65, her daughter Avril Monaghan, 30, who was pregnant with twins, and her 18-month-old daughter Maura. Or An Luan Phi Dawson, killed when hit in the face by a piece of metal torn from a tall ship at Frontierland in Disneyland one Christmas Eve. Or Mara Bitros, a passenger in a New York taxi who died down the street from my office on 42nd street in mid-town Manhattan when the taxi driver lost control. Her head slammed against the plexiglass partition, injuring her severely and causing cardiac arrest.

Then there are the two Hong Kong taxi drivers killed while dining when a fellow cabbie stepped on the wrong pedal as he was parking his cab to join them. Or Heather M. Vitarelli, 29, a tourist from Hawaii killed instantly by a stray bullet fired by robbers while standing near the main casino cage at Harrah's. Or Nicholas Bourdakis, Christopher Divis, Elie Israel and Ruth Levy, the four UC Santa Barbara freshmen killed in Isle Vista when David Attias deliberately drove his vehicle into them. They died needlessly like the 10 people killed while shopping in a Santa Monica farmers' market when an elderly driver lost control of his car. Or Wa Yeung, a 33-year-old chief operating officer of a high-tech company who died in a Wan Chai, Hong Kong, office building fire after he had been with the company for less than a month.

How about the Beijing married couple who had wooed each other online and set a time and place for a romantic date, only to start a fight when they found out they were about to cheat on each other? Or the man in Germany, who went to the red light district in search of a good time, only to find his wife working hard there? Or Guillermo Sobero, who told his wife he was going to a friend's birthday party in Arizona, but instead went with his girlfriend to the Philippines only to be kidnapped by Muslim rebels and beheaded? What about Australian Evelyn Bassett, who was killed in a crash when a train plowed through her car while on her way to pick up winnings from a lottery ticket? How about 74-year-old Yoshinori Niiya, who fled a hit-and-run accident in a panic only to find out later he had killed his own son? How about Egyptian tax official Waheeb Hamoudah who had been feeding his sheep tethered on the rooftop destined for sacrificial slaughter at the Muslim Eid al-Adha feast? The sheep pushed him to his death off the three-story building in Alexandria.

Then there was Dharmarathna Thero, chief priest at a Sri Lankan temple, who was gored to death by a bull as he fed it bananas. He had saved the bull from the slaughterhouse. A Chinese peasant was bitten by a viper when he uncorked a bottle of snake liquor. The snake, bottled in the wine, not only survived but reared out to bite the tippler on the neck before he could taste his drink. What about New Delhi's Catholic Archibishop, Alan de Lastic, 70, who was killed near Krakow, while on a visit to Poland, when a cyclist crashed through his car's roof from a bridge?

How about gun control advocate New York City Council member James Davis who unwittingly assisted his assassin gain entry to City Hall to kill him? Councilman Davis had been beaten by two white officers in 1983 when he was wrongfully accused of stealing a car. Ten years later he became a policeman. He became part of a system that eventually killed him.

What about all the innocent victims of 9/11 who were in the wrong place at the wrong time? Such as Mark Bingham and Jeremy Glick, two of the many unsung heroes of flight UA-93 as it headed for Washington DC? Mark overslept on September 11, missed his scheduled flight and got on the ill-fated 93. Jeremy was scheduled to fly on September 10 but had to delay to September 11 because a fire at Newark cancelled his scheduled flight.

What about John O'Neill, the top FBI counter-terrorism agent in the FBI's New York office, who ignored the now notorious Phoenix memorandum that warned the FBI of the potential danger of al-Qaeda terrorists taking flying lessons at U.S. flight schools? He retired from the FBI in late August and had just begun a new job as the security chief of the World Trade Center when he was killed by pilots trained at U.S. flight schools!

What about New Yorker Mark Sokolow? He survived the September 11 World Trade Center bombing only to be bombed again by the first female suicide bomber on January 27 in Jerusalem, and survived that as well. Did he have good or bad karma? These are some of many cases of very sad bad karma and timing stories.

Is it symbolic coincidence that the letters approving visas for terrorist leaders Mohamed Atta and Marwan al-Shehhi arrived at their flight school on the six-month anniversary of the September 11 bombings? Is it coincidence that the September 11 kamikaze squads led by Atta that operated in the U.S. as part of the "Hamburg cell", originated in Germany, the same country the first crusade originated? How about the New England Patriots winning the Super Bowl after September 11?

Conversely, when karma, luck and timing are with you ...You can do no wrong. It just flows and clicks, like the antique Box Brownie camera U.S. camera collector Don Roccoforte got as a gift. The camera was bought at a charity shop in England and contained an undeveloped film which had a picture of his British wife's family with whom he is friends.

When the force is with you things just happen. For example, FCC regular Richard Warburton was sitting at Paddy's bar in Bali and bent down to pick up his change from the floor when the terrorist bomb went off killing hundreds of people. He survived with a few shrapnel wounds on his leg while those around him, seated at the bar, perished. Then there was the 13-month-old "miracle baby" whose heart stopped after she wandered outside her home in Edmonton, Canada, in minus 20-degree weather and survived without any brain damage. How about Sukhlal Gautam, who was declared dead in hospital, was removed to a mortuary, but when his body was being picked up to be taken for cremation, gasped for air and was re-admitted to hospital and his death certificate cancelled?

I reflected on an Eric Clapton concert I wanted to see in LA. I couldn't get a good seat for love or money. About a year later, I went to London with Nelson Wong, a friend and client, who was the CEO of a real estate consultancy. We caught up with Sir Harvey Goldsmith for drinks because Harvey and I were exploring some business opportunities in China. Harvey is one of the premier concert promoters in the world. After we finished our drink and conversation Harvey casually asked: "What are you doing? Do you have any plans? If not you are more than welcome to join me in the Prince of Wales' box at the Albert Hall to see Eric Clapton perform. He's doing a gig for the Prince's Trust." Needless to say we went. When your luck and timing are right you can do no wrong. But you have to be in touch with yourself and nature for your karma to capitalize.

Shah Cyrus Karma

When Los Angeles County Supervisor Zev Yaroslavsky decided to first run for a Los Angeles City Council seat, his campaign was launched in my law office. When he won the council seat, we remained friends. We would bet on political races on which we could not agree on the outcome. We bet dinners, drinks and breakfasts.

One of the bets that I lost meant I had to take Zev and his wife Barbara to Chasens. It was a very popular and expensive "chili joint" in Los Angeles. It was actually a very fine restaurant that had started as a chili stand. As Gail and I pulled up to the valet we noticed several Secret Service agents outside. As we were taken to our booth, where Barbara and Zev were already seated, we noticed that in the private dining room in the back there were many celebrities and politicians. Gregory Peck, Farrah Fawcett, Mayor Tom Bradley to name a few. "What's going on back there?" "The Empress Farina from Iran received an honorary doctor's degree from U.S.C and she and the Iranian government are hosting a dinner for the entertainment community," Zev replied. "Look at those mountains of caviar," Gail exclaimed. Gail loved caviar. "Let's see if we can get in," she said to Barbara, grabbing her arm. "The Mayor knows you. Maybe he'll get us invited." Gail wishfully dragged Barbara towards the party.

They returned dejected after the mayor's security men, whom Barbara knew, turned them back. However, they indicated they would let the Mayor know the Councilman was here. As we were getting ready to order, the Mayor approached the table with Ambassador Zaeidi to introduce him to Zev. I reminded the Ambassador that we had been introduced by President Jimmy Carter during the Rostropovich recital in the presidential box right after he negotiated the release of the Bnai Brith hostages from Muslim extremists. He insisted "that you, your wife and guests come meet my Queen and join us for dinner!" Gail went straight to the caviar after we were introduced to Her Majesty. "Damn, de Krassel, when you pay off a debt you do it in style," Zev remarked as we laughed and helped ourselves to the caviar.

Can you believe my luck? I mean, what are the odds on that happening? I meet the guy once while I was with President Carter then I meet him with his Queen after our women want caviar. Talk about good karma, luck and timing. I couldn't have planned it any better if I'd tried.

Here I was in the midst of mounds of caviar, crabs, lobster and bottomless glasses of champagne with the wife of the new world megalomaniac moralist. The man who lectured America and the industrialist nations it led whenever he raised oil prices in the early seventies. "They will have to realize that the era of their terrific progress and even more terrific income based on cheap oil is finished. They will have to find new sources of energy. Eventually they will have to tighten their belts; eventually all those children of well-to-do families who have plenty to eat at every meal, who have their cars, and who act almost as terrorists and throw bombs here and there, they will have to rethink all these aspects of the advanced industrial world. And they will have to work harder.... Your young boys and young girls who receive so much money from their fathers will also have to think that they must earn their living somehow," was my personal favorite lecture. What goes round sure comes round as the Shah and the world were soon to find out.

"Ironic, isn't it?" I asked Zev who was a history teacher before winning public office as the "people's candidate" against much wealthier opponents as we refilled our plates with more caviar. "Here we are with the wife of the man who spent somewhere between $100 and $200 million to have Maxim's of Paris cater the most lavish party back in 1971 to entertain 50 heads of state at Persepolis, the capital of the ancient Persian empire that was sacked by Alexander the Great in 330 B.C., to celebrate the founding of the Persian empire twenty-five hundred years ago by king Cyrus the Great. Do you understand why he would celebrate a decimated empire instead of a new one?" "Not really. Doesn't make much political sense. Maybe he is King Cyrus reincarnated," was all Zev could say as we walked towards the Empress. "Is his karma such that he is doomed to the same ignominious end?" I whispered as we were ushered towards the Empress.

"One of the things my husband likes in life," said the Empress, "is flying, driving, driving boats – speed!"

Unfortunately, the Shah's karma was not as good as the Yaroslavskys', Gail's and mine who managed to crash his Empress' lavish party. He crashed his country by applying his love for speed to greed and the modernization of Iran. In his haste to make Iran "one of the serious countries in the world", he drove his souped up wreck into the hands of the fundamentalist Ayatollah. He and his plane were not welcome anywhere once he left Iran. His father, Reza Shah, had found refuge in South Africa. Not so the son, who, in his own exile, turned into a modern version of the flying Dutchman. "He could find refuge in no port and seemed cursed to wander forever," Daniel Yergin reminds us in his own witty way in his Pulitzer Prize-winning book *The Prize*. Egypt, Morocco, Bahamas, Mexico, America and Panama – countries where no one wanted him to stay. Others wouldn't even allow his plane to land to refuel. At least he was doing one of the things he liked. Flying.

Oil Coincidence
Oil shortages and energy crises seem to be common occurrences ever since oil was discovered. The more oil replaced coal the more the crisis that repeatedly justified the new increase in the cost of oil at the well and the gas pump. The nationalization of oil fields, Middle East wars, oil spills, environmental regulations, OPEC, emotions and panic buying all deserve their fair share of the credit. Every crisis had its humorous sidebars. The 1973 energy crisis saw Japan run out of toilet paper because Japanese housewives bought "upwards of a two-year supply". Toilet paper became more expensive than oil. The price quadrupled. Now for a country that imports 100 percent of its oil that is some serious....

The energy crisis of 1979 raised my ire because it had too many historical coincidences. Starting with the Shah, like his father and King Cyrus, being removed from Iran which brought an end to Iranian oil exports starting in December 1978 to the autumn of

1979. Since Iran was the second largest producer after Saudi Arabia, the concern and emotions are understandable.

Then the Saudis, who had made up the initial shortfalls from Iran, cut their production in the second quarter of 1979. A variety of reasons were offered for the cutback. "Were the Saudis trying to send a conciliatory and neighborly signal to the new Islamic regime of Ayatollah Khomeini by making room in the market for returning Iranian production and thus avoiding a regional confrontation? Or were they seeking to express their dissatisfaction with the Camp David peace accords between Israel and Egypt, which had been signed on March 26?" Daniel Yergin asks. I am of the opinion it was the latter, which had been the Saudi government policy ever since the State of Israel was founded.

Then, "in one of those coincidental tricks of history, several hours after the latest OPEC meeting had adjourned, in the early morning of March 28, a pump failed and then so did a valve at the Three Mile Island nuclear plant, near Harrisburg, Pennsylvania," Yergin reminds us.

The resulting gas lines and political crisis were nothing America or the industrial world had experienced before. That's when I decided to make a political statement and ride my Arabian horse from my home in Pacific Palisades to my office in Beverly Hills and name him OPEC for the day. My partner and staff joined the ride. We protested our dependence and reliance on Middle East oil and encouraged conservation and alternative environmentally friendly sources of energy.

Japanese TV asked us to partially re-enact the ride for a special on our widely covered ride that became the lead news story of the day. When I repeated the story 23 years later during a sake-besotted business dinner in Tokyo as oil prices were climbing because of the impending war on Iraq it really pulled their chain. "You lide Alab hols plotest oil embalgo? Hay? I lemember! Ah so!" our dinner host remarked as we downed another round. "Did he just call you an asshole?" an American TV executive on his first visit to Japan asked. Thank God Japan didn't run out of toilet paper this time round.

Coincidence or Karma?

Trying to hitch a ride out of Eilat on the Red Sea at any time of the day is a nightmare. It can take days. Hitchhikers line the roads out of town for hundreds of yards trying to thumb down one of the rare vehicles making the desert crossing.

Some, especially trucks, stop at the gas station on the outskirts of town to fill their tanks for the ride across the desert. Hitchhikers line the pavement for hundreds of yards, either side of the gas station. It is strictly forbidden for hitchhikers to try to beg for rides in the gas station as it disrupts business. I mean "Strictly Forbidden," "Verboten," ... I grabbed Gail by the arm. I decided to go into the gas station. "Out, out, immediately," a gas station attendant yelled in Hebrew and English. "Do you have a map of the desert?" I asked in English. I knew that if I acknowledged speaking Hebrew he would yell at us even louder. However, Israelis are a lot more polite to perceived tourists. Before he could answer, someone yelled in Hebrew "Hey Peter, is that you with long hair?" I turned around towards the direction of the salutation and my eyes fell upon a schoolmate from a year behind me in high school leaning out of the window of an 18-wheeler. "Yeah, how are you Tzvika?" I replied hastily in Hebrew as the gas station attendant started cursing me, or, more accurately my mother and certain parts of her anatomy. "Hey, Moishe, it's OK this guy is an old friend of mine. Hey Peter, you need a ride?" I nodded. "They are riding with me so leave them alone," yelled my schoolmate at the attendant. What coincidence, karma, luck and timing!

Some of the stories of the survivors of the September 11 attacks are even more amazing. How about the one of the Port Authority police officer who fell from the 86th floor and survived with just a broken leg? Or his fellow officer, Sergeant John H. McLoughlin, who also rode the building down from the 86th floor and suffered only an injured kidney? Or the people that got laid off the day before, delayed getting to the buildings, or just slipped out to have a cigarette when the planes hit the Twin Towers?

Reading about Lamja Jaha and her husband brought shivers to my body. They were evicted from their home and herded away with thousands of other fellow ethnic Albanians, along with a memento of her dead father in her pocket.

She had taken a copy of a certificate bearing her father's name. That piece of paper took the Jaha family full circle. It was the copy of a certificate issued by the Yad Vashem Holocaust memorial in Jerusalem, commending her parents, Dervis and Servet Korkut, both Muslims, for risking their lives to save Jews during World War II, during the Nazi occupation of Yugoslavia, and honoring them as "righteous among the nations".

Now it was Mrs Jaha and her family who were expelled from Kosovo. Jaha showed her father's commendation to officials of the Jewish community in Macedonia. They helped her and her husband, Vllaznim, to join a planeload of Kosovar Albanian Muslim refugees accepted by Israel.

More than fifty years after her parents sheltered Jews in their home, she found shelter in the Jewish state. "I don't know how to express how much this means to me," she said. "My father did what he did with all his heart, not to get anything in return. Fifty years later, it returns somehow. It's a kind of a circle." Talk about karma, luck and timing!

I had an engaging discussion about karma with Pilar Pilapil one evening during dinner. Pilar is a well-known Filipina movie star who has made over a hundred movies. She is also a Christian missionary who spends her free time in the provinces helping the needy. "Karma does not believe in forgiveness. That is why people hope to have a better life in the next world. Christianity believes in forgiveness." My surprise at her comment must have been quite visible. "What's the matter? You don't believe that is the case?" Pilar continued. "No, it's just that I am trying to understand the relevance of forgiveness. If forgiven, you go to heaven, and if not you go to hell, according to Christianity. In either case, I believe you get reincarnated and it is just a question of whether you'll have a good or bad life. Karma, right?" Wrong. "If you do not ask for forgiveness you are cursed and the curse continues until you do. The only way you can end the curse is to ask for forgiveness," Pilar explained. We tossed that around into the wee hours of the morning. Catholicism, I concluded, had usurped and interpreted karma to suit the church's needs. Thank

God the Inquisition made it only to the Philippines in Asia.

Gambling

All sorts of people who can believe in anything from Christ through Zen to feng shui come out with fatalistic cliches like: "What goes around does come around," "when your number is up, it's up,"and "when it's your turn to get your ticket punched," and so on.

I hear Earl ask Tom, who had been questioning him about Hong Kong racing, the Hong Kong Jockey Club and what it does for the community, "Did you hear the story about the habitual horse punter who had a dream?" Tom hadn't.

"Well, God spoke to him in the dream and said 'tomorrow is going to be a very lucky day for you at the track. Bet on any horse that has a name that means hat'."

The punter went to the races and in the first race bet on Stetson. The odds were 10 to one but the horse won. He took all his winnings and in the second race put it all on a horse named Beret. The odds were 20 to one. It won. This went on through all the races. There was a horse in every race named after a hat. Derby, Helmet, Tam, Fedora, Sombrero and so on. By the time he got to the final race he had a couple million dollars and bet it on a horse and lost. He couldn't believe what happened to him and went to the bar. As he was drowning his sorrows, the bartender, who knew the punter, asked what happened. The punter relayed the story and told the bartender he bet all his money in the last race on a horse named Chateau. The bartender looked at the punter in utter disbelief and said. "You fool! The French word for hat is Chapeau not Chateau!" The punter slowly lifted his head and responded: "It doesn't matter, a Japanese horse named Yarmulke won." Yarmulke, for the unintiated, is a Jewish skull cap.

People do gamble and they all have their "method" or "formula" to win. Most lose. Human nature is to gamble because life is a gamble. People gamble in life for its rewards. If anyone has a doubt drive through Las Vegas, Macau, Monaco or Atlantic City and look at the ever increasing number of expanding and new casinos. They were all built with the proceeds from gamblers. When it comes to gambling, all people do it. Not just the Chinese. At casinos, racetracks, lotteries, Indian reservations, riverboats, living rooms and school toilets. On the Super Bowl, local high school or college game, people gamble. They test their karma, luck and timing to the limit. Most lose.

"Do you realize that 95 percent of the punters at the track here in Hong Kong as a general rule lose?" Earl asked after I bragged about a recent win. I didn't and felt even luckier.

America's Gambling Philosophy

Las Vegas is the gambling capital of the world and embodies the American philosophy of taking risks. Some argue that poker, and not baseball, is America's real national game. The kind of risk America took when it went to war with Iraq. It was a poker play. The Texas cowboy's high stake poker game was played with bluff, deception, and a 55-card deck with pictures of Iraq's top leadership.

The virtuous conservative right-wing gambling "whale" William J. Bennett epitomizes America's deceptive and hypocritical gambling spirit. He gambles away millions of dollars while moralizing against the private misconduct of individuals. Bennett was a hypocritical "minnow" when compared to fellow arch-conservative Rush Limbaugh, who gambled and built a syndicated radio empire by attacking liberal drug-crazed hippies, while being addicted to drugs himself. The bad karma these two holier-than-thou American idealists created for themselves came home to roost.

The same happened to baseball's Pete Rose. He not only lost to his bookies, but the right to play the game he loved. Rose not only gambled on baseball but on forgiveness of his lifetime ban to be involved with the game and admission to the Hall of Fame.

Gambling, like war, brings people of all walks of life and incomes together. Millionaires share gaming tables and slot machines with welfare recipients and together they try to beat the system. Shouldn't *We the Maids* of all walks of life and incomes join forces and take the risks necessary to sweep in the political system created by the Founding Fathers?

It was therefore appropriate for the 28th annual convention of the Society for the Advancement of American philosophy to hold its three-day conference in Vegas at the dawn of the 21st century.

"Las Vegas is a realization of the kingdom of God on earth," said Mark Taylor, who teaches philosophy and religion at Williams College in Massachusetts. "The culture of simulacra has become all-encompassing and inescapable." For philosophers, a simulacrum is a reproduction that some may see as surpassing the real. Taylor added: "You cannot understand America today if you don't understand Las Vegas. And you can't understand the world today if you don't understand America. So if you want to understand the world, you've really got to come to Las Vegas."

The faces and reactions of Chinese or Mongolian delegations when they first visit Las Vegas say it all. I make a point of taking such delegations to Vegas so they can understand America and the world. Upon disembarking from the plane we would take the longest stretch limo to Caesar's, Mirage or the Hard Rock. The shows, tours and shopping consumed most of the day. The rest was spent in the casinos either learning the different games or betting on the ones they already knew. Slot machines are easy. Especially when you are on a limited budget. Forget sleeping! The convergence of Chinese and American yen for gambling, karma, luck and timing happens in a casino.

Instead of allowing gambling money to pad the pockets of illegal operators, local hustlers or organized crime, why not have the community benefit from it? Especially in today's wired cyber-world. Internet gambling makes it easier for punters to try their luck without even leaving home. Trying to legislate morality doesn't work. Yes, addiction and the damage and consequences to family, community and society are terrible! But gamblers will gamble if they are so inclined no matter what their family, friends, religious support group or local government tell them. So why not keep the money in the community and tax it in a way that the community as a whole benefits? At the same time addicts can be healed in a community that faces the truth of human frailty.

Gambling, like food, drugs, anger, alcohol or sex, is an addiction. As such it has to be treated spiritually. A spiritual journey through the defenses of denial and beyond. A conscious journey to experience the nature of the addictive personality. Deal with it. Face what it has produced and change that. Banning gambling is not the cure for gambling addicts.

Gambling Meccas do have high suicide rates. Real gamblers go for broke. Nevada, like Hong Kong, has a very high suicide rate. In fact Nevada has the highest suicide rate in America. Nevada suicides run at more than twice the national average. Hong Kong has one of the highest suicide rates in the world. In Hong Kong, someone commits suicide every 10 hours. Hong Kong is the suicide capital of Asia. One in five Hong Kong teenagers has thought about or attempted suicide. Suicide is the leading cause of death among 15 to 24-year-olds in Hong Kong. This compares favorably to America where 28 percent of youths thought of or attempted suicide, compared to 21 percent for Hong Kong.

A University of Sydney study published in the *Journal of Epidemiology* and Community Health concluded that suicide rates in Britain and Australia surged in the 20th century whenever conservative governments were in power. When conservatives ruled the local, state and national federal governments, men were 17 percent likelier to commit suicide than when a Labor government was in power. Women were 40 per cent likelier to kill themselves.

John D. Donahue points out in *Disunited States:* "The Continental Congress fed and armed Washington's army, in part, with revenues from a lottery, and state-sanctioned games of chance financed the early growth of Harvard and other colleges."

The total annual amount wagered legally in America is about $500 billion. For a sense of scale, consider that America's entire economic output is in the range of $11 trillion a year. American states take in over $27 billion from lotteries per annum and have, on average, over $9.8 billion in revenues left over after paying off winners and covering administrative costs.

Hong Kong Ponies
As our junk cruised the islands, I couldn't help reflect on the history of gambling in Hong Kong and how much it has contributed to the welfare of the community. Governor Sir John Bowring (1854-1859) believed that almost all crime originated in the illegal gaming houses in Tai Ping Shan. Gambling Ordinance No. 14 enabled the police to raid these Chinese gaming houses. There were stiff

penalties for owning, operating or "haunting" such places. The ordinance proved unenforceable, mainly because of police corruption. To bring the situation under control, Bowring suggested that the Hong Kong Government should follow the example of Macau, where gambling houses were licensed.

His pragmatic suggestion was rejected outright by three successive Secretaries of State for the Colonies. Where Bowring failed, Governor Sir Richard Graves MacDonnell (1865-1872) almost succeeded. However, during discussions with Westminster, the Tory government was voted out of office and replaced by the Liberals. The new Government was largely Nonconformist and a group of militant missionaries known as The Moral Six, branded poor MacDonnell an anti-Christ and managed to wreck the scheme.

Nobody seemed to worry very much about betting on horse racing, possibly because there was only one race meeting a year; but probably because several Hong Kong governors in the 19th century were Irish racing men. The first races were a shambles. The horses, like their owners and jockeys, were of many nationalities. Australian Walers ran against pure bred Arabs and there were wild China ponies from the steppes of Mongolia. There were army cavalry horses and broken down old hacks. There was even a 50-yard race where a man ran against a horse. The man won by a short head, probably because the horse got off to a bad start. The Governors, the taipans (big bosses) of the big hongs (colonial trading houses) and the various national communities were expected to present cups and prizes. The first 40 years of racing in Hong Kong were chaos. Ironically, one of Hong Kong's oldest racing trophies with the inscription "Won by 'Cockspinner' at the Hong Kong Spring Race Meeting, 1852. Owner: W. Lamonde" came back to Hong Kong after a 150-year odyssey that took it to Peking during the Boxer Rebellion, then on to Uruguay to the home of the Uruguayan ambassador to China in 1901, and back to Hong Kong when soccer betting was legalized in Hong Kong in 2003. Karma or coincidence?

In 1884, the top racing men of Hong Kong got together and founded the Hong Kong Jockey Club (HKJC). The races were held once a year during the Chinese New Year holidays in Happy Valley, which became a fairground. The great racing clubs of China, like

Shanghai and Peking, sent horses and jockeys down by steamer to compete against Hong Kong's finest. The annual race meeting was a great party that went on for three days.

In December 1891, a new Governor, Sir William Robinson, conscious of questions asked in the House of Commons by the anti-gambling lobby, announced just before the February race meeting that gambling would not be allowed. As one commentator wrote: "The meeting indeed was a model of morality. It was worthy of a Bishop's own heart. Had there been no ponies, as one gentleman remarked, it would have been perfect."

Almost all members of the Legislative and Executive Councils were dedicated racing men and the new Governor was given an extremely rough time. Eventually the pressure became too much. He capitulated and lifted the ban on gambling. In the early days the earnings from the tote, the Race Fund, were very small and were spent on prize money and the social event of the season, the Race Ball. The puritanical Victorian argument that it was improper to use money raised by a vice, in this case gambling on horse racing, for public purposes carried on well into the 20th century. However in 1930 a small betting tax of 2 percent was imposed. By the advent of World War II, HKJC proceeds to charity were totaling about $ 50,000 a year.

After the establishment of the People's Republic of China in 1949, hundreds of thousands of refugees poured into Hong Kong. With little entertainment available, enormous crowds turned up at the race meetings. Suddenly the HKJC was turning over $400,000 every race day. The Chairman of the Club, Sir Arthur Morse, one of the architects of Hong Kong's spectacular recovery after World War II, and the Governor, Sir Alexander Grantham, got together. There was still no way that a direct betting tax of any size could be imposed that would be acceptable to the British parliament. Sir Arthur Morse suggested to Grantham that the HKJC should give over one-third of its takings to civic and social undertakings and that the Government should advise on which projects it felt worthy of support. It was a simple gentleman's agreement and there was absolutely nothing in writing, so there was nothing that the puritanical do-gooders in London could do about it. In the first year the fund came to around $700,000.

Morse and Grantham envisaged that most of the money should be spent on development. There was a shortage of hospital beds so one of the Club's first projects was to build the Tsan Yuk Maternity Hospital. It also funded 13 Jockey Club Clinics and launched a Floating Clinic that toured the outlying islands. Although it supported hundreds of small projects, it generally had one or two enormous projects in hand, designed to promote the quality of life. In the 1960s it was Victoria Park, a green lung in busy, congested Causeway Bay; in the 1970s it was Ocean Park, a wildlife-related theme park; in the 1980s, it built the Academy of Performing Arts and the Hong Kong Government Stadium, home of the Hong Kong Rugby Sevens. Today, the HKJC is among the world's five largest philanthropic organizations. Over the last decade of the last millennium it donated over HK$1 billion to improving the lot of Hong Kongers.

Sometimes as much as $327.75 million is wagered on a single race day in Hong Kong. In turnover terms, the HKJC would place in the top 150 companies on the Fortune 500, ahead of such well-known names as Federal Express, Microsoft and Nike.

The size of HKJC donations ranges from as little as $5,000 to help out a small youth club to $256 million to build the magnificent University of Science and Technology. Most of the donations fall into three categories: medical and health; sports, recreation and culture; education and training. Projects on hand include a new $15 million School of Chinese Medicine.

When soccer betting became popular in Hong Kong, the government legalized soccer betting and granted the franchise to the HKJC. The primary purpose was to curb illegal bookmaking and collect an estimated $128 million or more in additional gambling duties to help narrow the budget deficit.

The Catholic Church in Hong Kong doesn't believe gambling is evil and stays neutral on controversial gaming proposals such as legalizing football or Internet betting. Father Dominic Chan Chi-ming, Vicar-General of the Hong Kong Catholic Diocese, says: "It is meaningless for us to say whether we support or reject soccer betting since we believe gambling in itself is not evil. It becomes a source of evil when people are drawn too much into such activities."

Gaming Reality

Gambling is impossible to banish thoroughly or legislate against. In Hong Kong the drag racing circuit cult uses top-of-the-range cars, with syndicates and triads gambling on the drivers. They are illegal but take place on back roads and freeways at night. No different than illegal gambling in America. Legislation cannot stop human nature.

In America or any country, it is generally accepted that a total ban, like Prohibition, invites crime, and simply creates more problems than it solves. The Hong Kong formula seems a reasonable solution for a small contained urban society. There are three sorts of legal gambling in Hong Kong. Of these, the Hong Kong Jockey Club tote is by far the most popular. The Mark Six, a lottery drawn twice a week, accounts for only 4 percent of the HKJC's turnover. This is surprisingly low as numerology has a considerable history in Chinese culture. There are also licensed mahjong schools. Social games for small stakes at parties, weddings and in social clubs are generally tolerated. However it must not be forgotten that the nearby casinos at Macau provide a safety valve for the compulsive gambler offering blackjack, baccarat, craps, roulette, keno, fan tan, dai siu, sik po, pai kao and slot machines. Even so, Hong Kongers bet on soccer with overseas bookies. Many of the Hong Kong punters are women. "Hong Kong is easily providing us with the greatest volume of business," said Jeff Wells, general manager for British bookmakers William Hill.

Whereas Nevada allows unlimited gaming, many states restrict gambling to horse racing, charitable games and sometimes a lottery. This popular formula is similar to Hong Kong. However there are some states where no gambling of any kind is permitted at all such as Utah and Hawaii. Illegal gambling, like illegal immigration, is dangerous and violent. But it does have a huge upside potential. The reward is worth the risk. Like illegal aliens, *We the People* all have to gamble to win a political change. We, like illegal aliens and gamblers, have to take chances if we want to improve our life. When we gamble and hit the jackpot it's worth it. When you hit, you hit big! If We lose, what the hell, We are losing anyway by being apathetic. What will We really lose as opposed to what We can gain if We win? I can just hear those Methodists shivering.

We have to take a gamble if we want change. Even Las Vegas took its own gamble in electing Oscar Goodman as mayor, a mob lawyer whose clients included Meyer Lansky and Anthony (The Ant) Spilotro. He ran as an outsider. He advocated a populist libertarian philosophy that obviously struck a chord with voters.

We the People, many of us descendants of illegal immigrants, have a grudging subconscious respect for criminals and their lawyers. Maybe that is why we elect them to Congress. The funeral of Dapper Don, or Teflon Don, was a millennium reminder.

The gambling charity carrot is a very effective means of raising money. In Hong Kong around 13 percent of the HKJC's turnover goes straight into Government coffers and just over one percent is spent on charity and community donations. Out of a total betting turnover of $11.8 billion, the government receives about $1.5 billion and charity and community projects get a modest $135 million. This allows the community to take government and tax dollars out of the welfare and social aid business while the community benefits. There is no reason why the percentage that charity receives cannot be increased.

Fifty years ago the Irish Hospital Sweepstake was illegal in every country in the world except Ireland. Today lottery junk mail is a common phenomenon. With the Internet it is possible to place bets in other continents and countries that have far more flexible gambling laws than one's own. Gambling has become internationalized. In a place like Hong Kong where there are no currency restrictions, opening a betting account overseas is not a problem.

"Every State in the Union gambles as much as Nevada does, but they were smart enough to pass a law and get some tax money out of it. If Wall Street paid a tax on every 'game' they run, we would get enough revenue to run the government on," Will Rogers quipped. Why not collect a tax on every game, especially the illegal ones? That will ensure enough income to run a significant number of the government's social, medical and educational programs. Like the Boss Bruce Springstein says in "Roll of the Dice". It's just another role...

Gaming is a $51 billion industry – legal in 28 states. California finally realized it was losing out of huge revenues to Las Vegas and decided in the closing year of the millennium to legalize gambling on its Indian reservations. Over the first five years of the 21st century, Bear, Stearns and Co estimate that Vegas will pull in an additional $1 billion in casino revenues over and above its $9 billion current average. Meanwhile California will take in nearly $5 billion – numbers that surely cannot be ignored.

Detroit's decision in the closing months of the old world order to legalize gambling, thus becoming America's largest city to do so, is an example and trend for the New World Order. The fact that its first casino opened in the former IRS building is a great metaphor for how tax dollars should be raised.

If the New World Order is to eliminate poverty, hunger, disease and illiteracy, *We the Apathetic People* have to gamble for change. Political change and changes in gaming laws. The loss of career politicians, like punters' losses, can only benefit America as a whole. Career politicians and punters' bad karma, luck and timing are the communities' gain, good karma.

Gambling Gazzarri Style
In Los Angeles I became a close friend with my client Bill Gazzarri "The Godfather of Rock'n' Roll'. "Meet my lawyer, he's the only guy I know who can get you on death row when you're offered life," is how Bill would introduce me. Bill used to invite me to join his panel of celebrity judges to judge his "Gazzarri Dance Contests" at Gazzarris on the strip. The panels over the years included Jack Klugman, Telly Savalas, Glenn Ford and George Peppard. The winners included Barbie Benton, who went on to date Hugh Hefner, and Barbara Bach who wound up becoming Mrs Ringo Starr. The house bands that entertained at Gazzarris and played for the contests included Van Halen, Guns N' Roses, Sonny and Cher, The Doors and The Byrds.

Bill invited me on several occasions to join his group of "Vegas Pals" who would go to Las Vegas every week to party with him and Don Costa, the conductor and musical arranger for Frank Sinatra and Paul Anka, and their pals. Bill loved blackjack and taught me the subtle rules of the game whenever he insisted I play a few hands. "Blackjack. Hit him," is something Gazzarri would have yelled on the 21st day of the Iraq War as the U.S. forces took control of Baghdad. I can just see Bill pointing his middle finger at the giant bronze statute of Saddam Hussein in the centre of Baghdad when the Stars and Stripes that flew over the Pentagon on September 11 was wrapped over Saddam's face before the statute was pulled down. Bill was a proud World War II veteran and would have applauded the Iraqis jumping on and kicking the fallen symbol of Saddam's regime.

Whenever our trips coincided with an Elvis performance I tried to get Bill and his pals to join me to see and listen to "The King" perform. "You going to try and serve him papers again?" Bill asked on one such trip in the mid-seventies, a couple years before the King's untimely death. A few years earlier, during a show, I had served Elvis with a summons and complaint in a lawsuit I had filed against him on behalf of a client who had been seriously injured in a car accident. He had been hit by a Stutz Bearcat owned by Elvis that made an illegal turn. Suing the man who had been such a major influence on me during my teens was quite a heady challenge. "We've settled," I responded bluntly as I tried to get the conversation back to catching the next Elvis show. "Aren't you guys tired of listening to Sinatra? Let's go see Elvis tonight for a change of pace," I implored in my most persuasive tone.

On my Vegas trips with Bill and his pals I usually spent the days in meetings with my mobile home park clients. Many of the glitzy hotels and apartment buildings off the Vegas Strip today used to be mobile home parks. Their owners land-banked the properties waiting for the right time to develop them. Many of the mobile home park managers I dealt with were Elvis clones. Elvis was representative of America, and especially its excesses of the 1970s. Bill's "Vegas Pals" were both witnesses and participants of his parody of American success stories. Consequently, they refused to see his show because watching our over-sized idol in gaudy rhinestone outfits hit too close to home.

We were sitting with a few ladies of the night at the Galleria bar outside Caesar's showroom with Don who was getting ready to leave for the Sinatra performance in the showroom. Bill looked at me and made another one of his philosophical pronouncements. "Peter, look at those poor old dumb fat fucks. They remind me of Elvis. Overweight, doped-up and miserable.

"Do you think Elvis or they are happy with those old fat blue-haired broads that probably just came from the Elvis show? Look how the women are holding on to their arms. You'd think the guy was going to run away the way Elvis did from Priscilla the way their wives are holding on. You know those old broads know their old farts would rather have this sweet thing right here holding on to their arm and later holding on to and sucking their dick."

Before anyone could respond, Bill continued: "Hell, that's why like Elvis I got rid of my wife. I took off and said 'later babe!' If I can't have fun with my pals and hang out with women that make me feel good and relax, who needs you and your aggravation all the time? What happens to them once they get married, anyway? You'd think they own you. You know the best way to get a broad to stop giving you good head?" he went on looking around at everyone while people were shaking their head. "Marry her." The group collapsed with cynical animal laughter that only night-clubs can prompt.

Bill, with his Italian-American New York accent, fedora hat and cigarette was a character right out of Guys & Dolls. I can see him saying: "Hey! How come women want to change you after you get married? It's like they love the suit, but once they buy it and take it home, they want to change it. Change the cuffs. Change the collar. Change the length. Change the pleats. So why do they bother buying it in the first place?" No wonder people want to gamble with their relationships and do change them.

I enjoyed being philosophical with Bill because he inevitably came up with socially relevant wisecracks. "You should have a little more respect for women. Did you know, that women hold up half the sky according to Mao Tse-dong?" I asked him on another occasion as we were walking to the Caesar's arena to watch a title fight. He was taken aback by my remark and then without hesitating said: "Is that why Mike Tyson has a fuckin' tattoo of Mao? Because of his respect for women?"

"In Afghanistan women held up the entire sky, but only on Friday mornings. That's when they were allowed to make love by the Taleban. But of course it's their feet that are in the air," Luke Hunt, the AFP correspondent, retorted when I shared the Tyson-Gazzarri story.

Las Vegas has a colony of quickie marriage chapels, including an Elvis chapel, that benefit from the rigidity of marriage laws elsewhere. Why do people have to get married, blood-tested and licensed, after paying for both, just to live together? Why does the state have to regulate and charge license fees and approve peoples' right to co-habitat? This is just another form of tax. People should be allowed to tie their knot their own way. Religious ceremony, civil ceremony or no ceremony. Just live together as long as the relationship lasts. The primary concern of society should be their happiness and welfare of their children, if any, born to the relationship. Why does the state have to regulate how many, and under what conditions, people can live together as husband and wife?

The collapse of the World Trade Center Towers on September 11, ironically, symbolizes the collapse of American-style loving re-lationships and marriage in the 21st century. The message was delivered by polygamous Muslims.

The October 14, 2001, issue of *The New York Times Magazine* was dedicated to capturing the unique rhythms of modern couplehood in the wake of the attack. Matthew Klam contributed an article titled *Love In the 21st Century*. He concludes: "The attack on September 11 makes it brutally apparent that such visions of permanent togetherness are delusions. People die; people break up; people end up alone. Yet humans will always push the fantasy of couplehood to the limit."

Chapter Five

Eve Dominates Adam's Harem-Until Life Do Us Part

Pussy rules the world but I have a dick in my brain - Madonna

Divorce Texas-Style

The sight of windblown snowflakes gliding down the mountains to cover the tree tops left me breathless. Dozens of caribou scavenging through the garbage cans and bins on the grounds of the former presidential summer palace in Ulan Baator, Mongolia, was surreal. Here I was in the land of the military genius Genghis Khan who by the time of his death in 1227 created the greatest land empire the world had ever seen. The Khan took pleasure in raping the wives and daughters of his vanquished enemies; in fact, he went for any female with a pulse and pretty face, says an Oxford scientist. His sons and grandsons were no better. Consequently, no fewer than eight percent of men living in the former Mongol empire have Y chromosomes that may be the hallmark of the Mongol House of Khan. In other words, half a per cent of the world's male population – 16 million, or one in every 200 – can claim descent from Genghis.

I was traveling with Ray Record and Granger McDonald, the "Texas Cowboys" who were having difficulty adjusting to the bitterly cold climate after their relaxed visit to Hong Kong. We had returned from visiting several collective cattle farms that wanted to increase their milk yield with American technology. Embryos from high-yielding American milking cows transplanted into hormonally synchronized local cows would do the trick. Conversely, Buddhist spirituality and Chinese sexual practices transplanted into synchronized Texans.

Ray and Granger had stopped over in Hong Kong to enjoy its massage parlors where petite Chinese ladies walked up and down on their Texas-size bodies. It was a memory they cherished and brought up repeatedly. It was minus 40 degrees Celsius as the howling wind, accelerating out of the steppes and deserts, whistled through everything in its way including our thermal underwear.

It was 1992, the year the Soviet Empire imploded. While traveling between farms we would periodically stop to watch and cheer what seemed to be endless train loads of Soviet tanks, personnel carriers and other military equipment rolling through the landscape from the Chinese border dragging the relics of the Cold War back home to Russia.

The rumbling trains brought back memories of my earlier trips to Mongolia from Beijing on the crowded, rickety-rocking Trans-Siberian Express. Sharing vodka with drunk Mongolians and Russians who belted out patriotic songs and kept disrupting my piecemeal conversation with a beautiful Mongolian princess. Nevertheless, we got to admire Genghis Khan's purple sunset over the Gobi desert. Jimmi Hendrix's Foxy Lady took on a whole new meaning – one the Texans were beginning to grasp in their purple haze.

It also struck me as ironic that in 1991 Saddam Hussein had compared then President Bush to Hulegu Khan, the Mongol leader who sacked Baghdad. When the Mongols invaded Baghdad in 1258, the Mongolian generals so terrified the Iraqis that the Caliph of Baghdad not only agreed to hand over his hoard of gold and treasure, but also 700 princesses as a gift in exchange for his life. Wouldn't work with a Bush. Maybe with a Clinton? When Bush Junior threatened war in 2003 Saddam referred to Americans as the "new Mongols".

That doyenne of the FCC, Clare Hollingworth, should be here reporting, I thought to myself. Her first husband divorced her for desertion. She could jump right in and share her matrimonial experience with Granger, who had just settled a long and ugly Texas-size divorce with his wife. He was now embroiled in another

Texas battle with his girlfriend. You would think it was the Alamo. The conversation had gotten around to women in general and marriage in particular.

Hong Kong and its balanced lifestyle of hard work and relaxation in massage parlors, bars or karaoke lounges were constantly brought up by the Texans who sorely missed them. "Damn, them small Chinese women walking on your back getting all those cricks out are something we need back home," Granger would repeatedly remind Ray. "They sure know how to relieve pressure without all the bullshit we have to put up with to just get off. Hong Kongers with their mistresses and massage parlors sure have it made!

"You know in Texas we have a bounty on coyotes 'cause they kill cattle. I swear if women didn't have a pussy there would be a bounty on their head," Granger pronounced. "Women, especially wives, sure know how to screw you in more ways than one," Granger said as he brought the conversation back to Hong Kongers and their mistresses. "I may move to Hong Kong once this project gets off the ground." To many, marriage is a three ring circus. Engagement ring, wedding ring and suffering. How many more people have to say "She got the goldmine and I got the shaft"?

Divorce American Style

According to the U.S. Census, the fastest growing marital status is divorced persons. Their numbers have more than quadrupled from 1970. In 1970, only three percent of all people under 18 years of age were divorced. That figure has almost tripled today. In the words of Will Rogers, "A Ford car and a marriage certificate is the two cheapest things there is. We no more than get either one than we want to trade them in for something better." Britney Spears' brief marriage in 2004 was a 21st century confirmation on how devalued the institution of marriage is today. Even Barbie and Ken got divorced in 2004.

Rogers' home state of Oklahoma, like the rest of the Bible Belt, has the highest divorce rate in America. The divorce rate in much of the area where evangelical Christianity is particularly strong is roughly 50 percent above the national average. In Arkansas, Governor Mike Huckabee declared a "marital emergency" in 1999. In Oklahoma, Governor Frank Keating diagnosed divorce as a principal cause of poverty in his state. "Seventy percent of our people go to church once a week or more," Governor Keating said in an interview. "These divorce statistics are a scolding indictment of what isn't being said behind the pulpit." More significantly, the fewer American couples who do marry see no reason for religious approval or a religious ceremony. Religious hypocrisy, interfaith marriages and the growing number of people honoring and trying to live up to their personalized ideas of spirituality and personal bond are leading the matrimonial charge into the 21st century.

The institution of marriage is losing ground rapidly. The latest census found that in the 1990s the number of unmarried couples living together jumped by 97 percent in Oklahoma, 125 percent in Arkansas and 123 percent in Tennessee. These increases in the Bible Belt are well above the 72 percent increase in unmarried couples that the census found in the United States as a whole.

For the first time, the census showed that married couples with children made up less than a quarter of the U.S. population (23.5 percent). In Oklahoma, the percentage of such nuclear families was even lower at 23.2 percent. "Those numbers are a total reflection of marriage as an institution that is losing its appeal," said Jerry Regier, Oklahoma's Secretary of Health and Human Services. "Our society has been overwhelmed by divorce." The rate of failed marriages doubled from the early 1960s to 1980, reaching a point where about 43 percent of marriages ended in divorce. A study completed by the universities of Oxford and Limerick concluded that children, once a stabilizing factor in a marriage, now increase the divorce risk.

Americans are less likely to marry than ever before, according to a study released by Rutgers University's National Marriage Project. Fewer people who do marry report being "very happy" in their marriages. The survey found that the nation's marriage rate has dipped by 43 percent in the last four decades of the 20th century – from 87.5 marriages per 1,000 unmarried women in 1960 to 49.7 marriages in 1996, the lowest point in recorded history.

The percentage of couples who reported being "very happy" in their marriages fell from 53.5 in 1973-76 to 37.8 in 1996. Similar statistics are being reported by the Civil Affairs Ministry in China. Marriage is falling out of fashion in the world's most populous country as well.

Men are happiest when they are "serial monogamists" according to researchers from the University of London. Men prefer to have a succession of faithful relationships and avoid marriage. Study author Michaela Benzeval said: "The best mental health was in men who had two or more partnership re-formations."

In America there are more and more divorces every year. In the last 50 years the institution of marriage has become completely devalued. So much so that many couples have regrets and remorse once the wedding invitations have been mailed and never follow through. More married couples wish they had done the same. Many more couples don't even get married at all. They are increasing so fast that they are classified as "Never Married" by the U.S. Census Bureau. Consequently there are millions of single parent families. The argument goes that as it is quite common for a man or woman to be divorced three or four times and have children from each and every marriage, what is the point of getting married in the first place?

Cohabitation, Marriage, Divorce and Remarriage is a report prepared by the Centers for Disease Control and made public in 2002. It concluded that fewer divorced women in America today remarry. Only half of them marry again or cohabit five years after their divorce. This is down dramatically from the 1950s when two-thirds of divorced women remarried. The reason being that today there is less stigma attached to divorced women.

Another study found that young men and women in their 20s, unlike generations before them, are not interested in finding marriage partners when they date. Instead, as the Rutgers University study's title suggests, they favor *Sex Without Strings, Relationships Without Rings.* No different than previous generations. A New World Order balance. "Marriage is like a cage; one sees the birds outside desperate to get in, and those inside desperate to get out," the author of the report astutely observed.

The big social issues change from generation to generation and at some stage modern moralists will be compelled to tackle marriage, which is slipping into a state of anarchy. Most politicians avoid the issue because it is such an emotive subject. Consequently reformation is likely to start as a grassroots movement.

When Arthur Hacker was asked one rowdy evening at the FCC why he hadn't gotten married, he replied: "I didn't want to get a divorce!" He later turned to me and said: "How can people go through several marriages and divorces? It's absurd and unreal." As we continued on the matter I raised the subject of how and why people talk about meeting or introduce women with the caveat "my future ex". "Precisely my point!" Arthur stammered. "You know what Arthur?" I said as I got up to leave. "What?" "That is why people do have to get out of their ruts and into new grooves."

Divorces are the result of "Life" and not "Death". Growing together is difficult and a human condition that must be closely re-examined. The institution of marriage as we know it today is not what it proclaims to be. For centuries the priest up-front and the congregation behind expected the couple to die in misery, if necessary, to honor those vows. That's what the "...or worse" means. After all isn't "until death do us part" about happy companionship? If so, why bother being with someone you can't stand or enjoy? The expression didn't even exist till the latter half of the 19th century.

A Hong Kong joke about marriage vows sums up reality. A minister is reading the wedding service of a Hong Kong businessman and a would-be tai-tai (ladies who live to lunch and shop – expensively – on their man's ticket). "Do you take this woman for better or for worse, for richer or for poorer, in sickness or in health, in good times or in bad..." The tai-tai interrupts in a furious whisper. "Could you shut up? You're going to talk him out of it if you're not careful." He'd probably be better off.

The Jerusalem wedding hall collapse during Keren and Assaf Dror's wedding as they kissed and danced, only to wake up in adjoining hospital beds while fellow wedding guests and family members died, is symbolic of marriages today. They are doomed and most collapse at the outset.

Rod Stewart, who has been divorced twice, suggested that wedding vows should be renewed like dog licenses. He failed to mention with how many bitches. His daughter Kimberly honestly expresses today's reality. "I'm sure I'll get married in my 20s – and I probably won't spend the rest of my life with that person," she said.

Prince married girlfriend Mayte Garcia in Minneapolis, Minnesota, on Valentine's Day. He finally decided to annul the marriage because he believes "contracts are made by man to guarantee the possibility of divorce". At a Madrid press conference Prince explained: "Mayte and I are joined for life, and the best way to demonstrate it is to do away with the legal bonds that people demand."

Hong Kong Mistresses and Misters
Being a Hong Kong mistress has never been a particularly shameful thing. In Hong Kong society, everybody seems to know who's sleeping with whom. Wives seem to be the most accepting, recalling the Chinese saying: "One eye can be open, but keep the other one closed." Most mistresses are in their 20s and 30s – older ones are unusual unless she and her partner have been together for years.

Go to a high society Chinese dinner or flick through the social pages of the newspapers and you can still read all about the mysterious, big-spending companions of Hong Kong's wealthiest men. Even in death, as was the case at the funeral of Swire taipan Peter Sutch CBE, who was also remembered as "the lover". Some step out proudly with their benefactors. The very married chairman of the Bank of East Asia, David Li, is regularly pictured in the papers with his socialite mistress, Peggy, in restaurants and clubs from Hong Kong to Paris. Hong Kong martial arts icon Bruce Lee died in the bed of his mistress, Betty Ting Pui. The movie idol's beloved home was sold a few years after his death and converted into a short-term love hotel where mistresses and prostitutes are taken for sex.

Maybe that is why former Philippine President Joseph Estrada's mistress, Laarni Enriquez, chose Hong Kong when she fled with their three children to avoid being served a subpoena in the president's impeachment trial. Mistresses are comfortable and acceptable in Hong Kong.

The alliance of Macau casino tycoon Stanley Ho and Angela Leung, who is half his age and is often referred to as his "number four wife", resulted in a baby – Ho's 17th child by four women. Illegitimate children, even the result of incestuous relationships in his extended family, are nothing new. Family litigation at the dawn of the 21st century only confirmed how human emotions overcome familial, communal, religious, political and media concerns.

Ho's treatment of the women in his life is rooted in old Hong Kong. Each is given a staff-filled house and due recognition. One socialite said her father-in-law had one wife and two mistresses in his life, and they often dined together and behaved like sisters. Some of Ho's women enjoy a similar relationship.

A leading Hong Kong developer, who appears on lists of the richest men in the world, keeps his mistress and their two small children in a deluxe, Conduit Road apartment in the expensive Mid-Levels area. Neighbors say he calls at least twice a week to see them, shuttling between Conduit Road and nearby McDonnell Road where his "real" family lives.

Numerous high-rise apartment blocks in Hong Kong are known as "mistress villages". When well-connected Ivy League expatriate executives from Fortune 500 companies rent apartments in the same complex it naturally becomes another local joke on the Hong Kong gossip mill which makes SMS look like a slow-burning bush fire.

When a well-known "mistress village" in the Mid-Levels was swept away by a massive mud-slide on a Saturday afternoon after a heavy rain, more than one wealthy well-known gentleman who had been visiting a lady who was not his wife was dug out of the rubble. Caught with a building down was an extreme form of being caught with your pants down. No different than Sumner Redstone being stranded in a hotel on fire a few blocks from his home.

There's also the tale, now woven into Hong Kong legend, of a former beauty queen whose married, billionaire boyfriend wrote her a blank check as a parting gift. She was said to have asked for only HK$10 million – plus a shiny new convertible and a florist's business to keep her occupied.

Shop managers often tell of men who call to buy two of everything – one for the wife, one for the "other woman". It's very common for wealthy Chinese men to buy several HK$100,000-plus baubles at once, presumably for mistresses. Others tell of mistresses going in for the latest designer ensembles, using credit cards they'll never have to pay off. And then there are all the tiny, loss-making, no-name boutiques and beauty salons dotted throughout Hong Kong. Chances are they're little trinkets given by wealthy men to keep the mistresses busy by day.

For all the candor associated with the subject of mistresses, adultery is almost as acceptable in Chinese society as gambling!

Dalliances outside marriage are little more than a tradition passed on. A wealthy restaurateur said: "My father had three wives. He was a property tycoon and money was never a problem. I was close to him and my mother, and his two other wives. Eventually my mother moved to Canada, one wife went to live in San Franciso, and the other is in Hong Kong, but I don't have much contact with her. They are all quite old, but my father travels to be with all of them, and looks after them. Maybe only one of his wives was official, but the other two were treated as wives. They had separate homes, and my father would rotate between all of them."

In many cases a man's wife and concubines became friends, laughing together over the foibles of the man they shared, playing mahjong to pass the time and going shopping or to the movies together. Early Eurasian millionaire Sir Robert Hotung had two wives of equal status, Lady Margaret and Lady Clara. Both women were Eurasians and cousins. The devoutly Christian Margaret introduced the equally pious Buddhist Clara into her husband's household when she could not have children.

In patriarchal China, the reasons for taking a concubine then were akin to those for taking a mistress now: a soul mate, a desire for heirs, a search for pleasure, the drive to show a man's social status, because concubines were a privilege of the rich.

That children born outside marriage might be viewed as illegitimate was irrelevant: any male child would be recognized as an heir.

Concubinage was legally abolished in 1931 but the practice has left a lasting cultural residue. One European woman married to a wealthy Chinese man has a bird's-eye view of Hong Kong high society, and hates what she sees. "Women here feel more for their American Express cards than they do for their husbands," she says. "As long as they have someone to buy them a pair of shoes they don't care what their husbands do. They have gold-plated hearts – platinum if they're lucky. That's Hong Kong romance for you."

Married women in Hong Kong seem more than accommodating if their husbands want to take on other women. "I don't know any man who doesn't have at least one mistress," says a socialite married to a Hong Kong businessman. "One of my husband's friends called me today asking if I could get him a discount on a Cartier watch. I know he's not buying it for his wife," she says, adding that she would never tell the friend's wife because it wasn't her business. "There's like a gang of them, and they all go out together, with their mistresses. Everyone is pretty open about it. Why not? It doesn't mean they don't love their wives," she says. "It's expensive to keep a mistress because you have to pay for everything. But the men say it's better than gambling. With gambling there's no limit. But with a mistress, at least you can control the expenses."

The socialite, who said she had been married off before she had had a chance to become a mistress herself, has been married for several years and has two children. She told her husband early in their marriage that she fully expected him to be with other women. "I told him as long as he was responsible, and his heart was with me, there was no harm. I told him if he was smart, he wouldn't let me find out. But if he did it quietly, I wouldn't mind," she says. She suspects her husband does enjoy "a bit on the side", but because he never lets it affect their marriage, or their children, she chooses to overlook it.

As business ties between Hong Kong and China have grown, so have second families. The two worlds were never supposed to meet. Hong Kong men supported women and children in dirt-cheap China, and their Hong Kong wives never had to let on if they knew. A court ruling threatened to blow the lid off the cosy arrangement by allowing the perhaps thousands of Hong Kong children with at least one Hong Kong parent to immigrate to Hong Kong. Though Beijing overruled the court decision, the lie was exposed. Social workers estimate that as many as 25 percent of married Hong Kong men commit adultery, and many have second wives. "The family is falling apart," says Crystal Kwok, a former radio host who used to take calls from cuckolded women. "The veneer of propriety is being destroyed." In Hong Kong these days, having a mistress at a business dinner has become a mark of wealth and success. "Men think that if you don't have a second wife, you're not a man," says Shirley Hong, a social worker who wrote her dissertation on the second-wife phenomenon.

Just like Eskimos use more than a hundred words to describe "snow", the Chinese have dozens, if not hundreds, of words to describe "women". The term *Ernai* or "second breasts" is a common one to describe mistresses of businessmen, especially those from Hong Kong.

Hong Kong millionaire Ng Ching-poon left his entire estate to his wife. However his mistress Ting Fung-yee challenged the will and claimed she was promised full ownership of four properties. The judge ruled in her favor and awarded her HK$700,000 and one property because the relationship had been "a most intimate one".

Hongkong Telecom hosted an international debate on concubines and mistresses when its Exchange Square office was temporarily transformed into a courtroom. In a satellite link-up, Chinese family law expert Professor Anthony Dicks testified from Britain in a multi-million dollar inheritance case hinging on the legality of concubines. Millionaire Sung So-chun's 90-year-old widow claims the other women in her husband's life were concubines, not mistresses, making them part of a traditional Chinese family.

If the second "concubine", Chu Lee, who was left in charge of his fortune, was declared a mistress, then Sung's widow and family cannot claim his estate because the money, in effect, was given to a stranger.

The judge hearing the case concluded that concubines disappeared in 1931 when lawmakers drafted and enacted a Civil Code reducing Chu's status to mistress! But did the law really bring an end to the practice? Obviously not. A subsequent case in Hong Kong confirms that the practice is still widespread. An accident victim's legitimate son joined forces with his father's concubine and her children to fight for compensation.

My favorite polygamist probate is the estate of Wong Yee-man which took 33 years and a Court of Appeal to settle. The case involved two widows and 13 children in two families, neither of whom knew the other existed until after Mr. Wong passed away. The evidence included 80-year-old immigration records and polygamy laws in China and the study of the Chinese horoscope, after a lower court judge miscalculated the Year of the Rooster.

One family lived in America and the other in China. The property they were fighting over was in Hong Kong. After DNA tests proved the siblings of the two families shared the same father, the Court of Appeal ruled they should share the property of the estate equally. The court concluded Mr. Wong was allowed to have two wives as he technically resided in China, a country which recognized polygamy when he wed for the second time. Can you imagine the day when cases like this will be heard in America?

Extramarital affairs are not only a man's domain in Hong Kong. Women are just as indulgent. While Hong Kong women have long been portrayed as the victims of infidelity, the Caritas Family Service Project on Extramarital Affairs says more men are calling its hotline for help. The number of calls from men has rocketed from one or two per month in 1995 to over 200 today. Not only in Hong Kong, but in urban China!

Any wonder that in 40 percent of paternity DNA test findings, subjects find they're not their children's genetic fathers in Hong Kong? According to a landmark study published in the *Chinese Medical Journal,* the data shows the continuing trend of extra marital affairs.

Women having affairs is far from the traditional image of honorable Chinese women. History depicts married women who had affairs as evil. In ancient times, in some villages an unfaithful wife and her lover would be locked in a bamboo pig cage and drowned in a river. But Chinese societies, which once turned a blind eye to – or even encouraged – men's infidelity while demonizing women who do the same thing, are having their moral ground rules redefined. As in America, the reality of female adultery is becoming more honest and open.

Latino-Filipinos

The South Seas Catholic Filipinos are the largest expatriate community in Hong Kong. Unlike chilly Americans who appear to live out their sexual fantasies only on faraway beaches, under false names, the Filipinos are a great deal more frolicsome than most Americans and live out their sex fantasies daily. It is expected of politicians to have several wives and numerous children with all of them.

When Senator Ramon Revilla's wife died people asked: "Which one?" After all, he has had 72 children with his different wives. "The mother of Governor Bong Revilla" was how the deceased was distinguished from the other wives. It is not unusual for obituary announcements to name wives, children and mistresses.

A Filipino business associate of mine has a close family of two wives and three children. "I have two 15-year-olds. One born to my second wife in February and one with my first wife born in September," he explained by way of clarification when I got confused as to how he could have children born just seven months apart. Being in a Catholic country, he, like all Filipinos, is officially married only to the first wife. The rest are common law wives. "We all go out together and are a close family even though the wives live in separate houses."

"Bill Clinton has the scandals while I have the sex," replied presidential candidate Joseph "Erap" Estrada when asked by a reporter to compare his sexual scandals to Clinton's after the Catholic Church announced its opposition to his candidacy. This memorable comment best describes the different moral standards of politicians in America and Asia. After he was elected the question was how would he adjust to the "Oral Office". The Philippine Presidential Security Group faced a logistical problem: how to protect and secure his families of six women and 10 children. In his impeachment hearing, some of his mistresses were called as witnesses. One thing career politicians do have in common in all countries is the knowledge and ability to self-destruct and to screw *We the People* at our own expense. They bilk us and then we are also stuck with their legal bills.

Fidel Casto wasn't just married to the Cuban Revolution. He

spearheaded the sexual revolution. He has at least nine children from four women. The Catholic Latino political leaders' sexual behavior pales in comparison to their Muslim counterparts. Saudi Arabia's Ibn Saud personally led the great Saudi baby boom. He unified his realm by fathering children with the daughters of as many tribal leaders as possible. Seventy years after he founded the kingdom, the House of Saud counts more than 5,000 princes.

Filipino-Americans have more in common in America with Hispanics than Asians, including religious and cultural values stemming from more than 300 years of Spanish rule. The community increasingly is using Hispanic organizations as the models for its own quest for political power.

Anyone who doubts the cultural affinity between Filipinos and Hispanics should compare the Spanish influence on Latin and Filipino food, music, song, dance, religion, customs, dress and attitude. Mañana has become a cliche for a reason. Hearing an airplane captain say "they're still looking for the bridge operator" 10 minutes after we arrive at a gate and wait while the luggage is being unloaded is a common occurrence at airports in Manila, Mexico City and numerous other Latino countries I have visited. Mañana at its frustrating finest.

Latina-Filipinas seem to be using their imagination to improve on honest patterns of relationships. One evening I was with Helena Arias, Margie Katigbak and Rica Thio talking about honest re-lationships of Latinos versus phoney Americans.

"Of course it's natural for a man to have several wives and girlfriends," Helena lectured me. "Men, like my brother, need several woman companions to fulfill different needs." "Yes that's right," interjected Margie. "One wife for intellect, one for business, one for sex, one for friendship ..." "Look at....." Rica almost screamed as she tried to be heard over the loud exchange of information by the other two vociferous ladies. Helena had been married to a former politican in Panama and has lived in the States and Latin America. Margie was married to a leading local businessman and Rica to a Chinese-Indonesian businessman still living in Indonesia. She has also lived in the States and Indonesia. That's Filipino *Chizmiz!* Gossip. Sometimes I think they have a patent on it! Actually, it exists in most Latino cultures in smaller doses. "Women are no different than men. We line up backups, reserves, volunteers for when we break up with a boyfriend," Rica added. Real life telanovelas. Chizmiz at its finest.

Adulterous Hypocrites

More than half of all married men and more than one-third of married women in America claim they are guilty of it. Adultery. Kobe Bryant became the adulterers' reluctant poster boy.

"Most men are hypocrites. Lying, cheating hypocrites." That's the conclusion of men's magazine *Arena* after publishing its annual sex survey.

Take the question of fidelity. While over half the men surveyed believe being faithful is an important element of every relationship, 62 percent would not think twice about having an illicit affair if there was no chance of being found out.

Sixty-four percent of those aged 16 to 55 admitted they had two-timed their partners. Although two-thirds said they were involved in steady relationships, the same proportion also admitted enjoying the occasional one-night stand. Fifty percent said they never wore a condom during casual sex.

And if casual sex is not freely available, many men are more than happy to pay for it. A third said they had slept with a prostitute and 10 percent said they regularly paid for sex. Others prefer to satisfy their lust closer to home. Thirty percent said they dreamed of having sex with their girlfriend's sister; 10 percent said they had. No percentage is available for those who scored with both at the same time. Too ecstatic to talk about, probably.

About a fifth of respondents saw marriage "not as a word but a sentence". The idea becomes more unpalatable as men grow older, with almost 45 percent of those between 45 and 54 regarding marriage as "inhuman bondage".

Media magnate Ted Turner makes a valid point when he says: "If you're only going to have 10 rules, I don't know if adultery should be one of them."

Men get into an affair for sex while soul-searching, consciously and subconsciously. Most men have affairs with younger women who stimulate them sexually and arouse their inner self. However, today more men are looking for older women with brains, attitude and independence. If a man falls in love with his lover, chances are that the prospect of leaving his family for her are distasteful. The costs of breaking up his family, damaging his reputation, turning his life upside down and possibly losing his children, are too great to even consider. He tries to balance the fulfilling relationships. Quietly. Secretly.

Larry Beinhart, the author of *American Hero,* the book on which the film *Wag the Dog* was based, wrote an article in the *Los Angeles Times* in support of Bill Clinton's behavior.

"Everything I hear and read about the possible impeachment of Bill Clinton starts out with a sentence like 'Nobody denies that what the president did was wrong.' Here comes nobody. I deny that what the president did was wrong. To say Mr. Clinton did wrong requires a set of assumptions. The underlying one is: Sex is bad. That is followed by: Sex outside of marriage is really bad. Which is founded on the idea that the primary purpose of marriage is sexual exclusivity, and that sexual exclusivity is the most significant measure of a marriage...

"All this should be questioned. First, sex is good. And if it is bad, it is because something else is wrong. When we were children, we were told that sex was only for marriage, and marriage only for sex. The adult reality is that married people frequently do not want to or cannot have sex with each other. If, in theory, we can agree that having sex is better than not having sex, what do we do about that?"

Accept the fact that people enjoy sex with multiple partners. In England, Dougie Smith, the respectable co-ordinator of Conservatives for Change (Cchange), the influential Tory think tank, also runs London-based Fever Parties that hosts "five-star" orgies for swingers. Can you imagine any of the conservative Republican think tank co-ordinators doing the same in America? Who knows, some probably do.

In France orgies for swingers have become passe and boring for politicians. Political orgies are sadomasochistic and even involve the killing of a transvestite prostitute who threatened to blow their cover.

Dominique Baudis, the former mayor of Toulouse, an anti-pornography campaigner who also heads up France's broadcasting authority, has been accused of participating in the orgies and ordering the murder of the loose-lipped prostitute. What can we expect of a country where judges are placed under official investigation for "sexual exposure" in a courtroom? The judge masturbated for several minutes after discreetly lifting his judicial robe in open court while a female lawyer pleaded her case. Is that why the French practice civil law as opposed to common law? It certainly sounds more enjoyable.

Adultery and sex are universal. Adulterers are stoned to death in Muslim countries, dentists are free to commit adultery with their patients in Hong Kong as long as it's not under anesthesia, and priests and rabbis find new congregations. "The rabbi gave up his soul and went to this abominable place to check whether students from the seminary go there," a spokesman from an unidentified Jewish seminary in Jerusalem said, explaining why its rabbi had been photographed in a nude bar, dressed as a cowboy. How about all the rabbis and talmudic scholars lined up outside well-known brothels in Israel?

The History of Infidelity
The National Museum in Malaysia opened the world's first known exhibition on marital infidelity. The exhibition's 25 sections covered anti-adultery devices, famous adulterers – excluding government ministers – punishments for infidelity and even culturally acceptable peccadilloes.

The methods exhibited to curb infidelity included the chastity belt, first developed in Asia. In some African societies, men stitched closed their wives' vaginas to achieve the same end. The ancient Chinese custom of foot-binding was also an anti-adultery tactic as it virtually crippled women, confining them to their homes. The exhibition had no step-by-step video on how adultery is practiced nor did it answer the question, does sodomy with another man fall under the heading?

Men of the Wodaabe tribe in Africa who believed themselves ugly permitted their wives to have intercourse with other men to ensure more attractive children. Why haven't the "Ugly Americans" got round to that? In the Aleutian Islands, a woman's hospitality included sexual services, while aboriginal peoples of Australia used wife exchanges as a form of peacemaking after war. This was secretly considered for Japan after World War II but dropped as logistically awkward by MacArthur. Just kidding!

In Shanghai, Professor Liu Dalin operates a private museum chronicling China's sexual history. "Our ancestors were not as conservative [about sex] as we imagine them to be," Liu said. "Though they worked hard, they also knew how to enjoy life and possessed a rich knowledge about sex." The Chinese indulged in communal sex several hundred years BC in the Han Dynasty. Erotic art of the period is on display in the Xindu County museum in southwest Sichuan Province. A large mural portrays a couple having sex beneath a mulberry tree draped with their discarded robes. Birds and monkeys dart around, while another man waits behind the tree with his erect branch. Zhang Yuxin, the museum's deputy director, explains: "The painting has extremely high historical value as it reflects so much of the society of the time. For example, Taoism was very popular in the Han Dynasty. People believed that having sexual intercourse, especially in the wilderness, was a way to cultivate oneself and to prolong one's lifespan by combining yin and yang." In ancient China there were many surprised but contented water buffalo. China has a long and deep history of erotic culture, including "sensual Buddhas", Taoist sex scientists and a landscape of phallic mountains and vaginal crevices.

The subject of sex is a weekly special at the Main Bar. Luke Hunt, an AFP correspondent who was based in Afghanistan, repeatedly challenges those partaking in a discussion of sex in Muslim countries if the public stoning of unfaithful Moslem women is a primitive and perverse sexual orgy: "Being in a stadium full of men watching a woman being stoned to death is a perverse way to get turned on. I was in one in Afghanistan and I swear every guy in the stadium had a hard on," Luke exclaims whenever the subject comes up.

The fact that New York has opened a museum dedicated to the study of sex is a great way to start the new millennium. Inaugural exhibitions included Heels to the Toe – the Fetish and the Fashion; Sex in America: From Puritans to Playboy and Scandal! – Notorious Sex Scandals; Tabloids and Yellow Journalism. Oddly missing from the list is Upstanding Sex: on the Subway and In the Elevator.

American Promiscuity

One little reported incident in the wake of the attacks of September 11 is divorce 9/11. A married man with an office at the World Trade Center spent the morning with his mistress, far away from his place of work. When he turned his mobile phone back on, he got a call from his frantic wife asking where he was. "In my office, of course," he lied. This was a little hard for her to take, since the entire building had collapsed. Isn't it time Americans stop hiding their invisible lovers in our transparent cyber- world? Isn't it time Americans acknowledge their promiscuity? Especially now that there is social and scientific evidence to support promiscuity.

Infidelity may be a family tradition. Scientists have isolated the long lost "promiscuity gene" which encourages people to have sex with a variety of different partners. The research, which will be seized on by lotharios who have long claimed that they cannot control their need for sexual variety, shows that men have a 50 percent chance of being born promiscuous. Although the study was carried out only on men, the findings were expected to be similar for women.

Clinton, Jefferson, Roosevelt and Kennedy represent such macho lotharios fighting life's battles with their legions of apparatchiks and finding refuge in the arms of one or more of the women in their harem.

Hillary Clinton appears to dominate Bill Clinton's harem, just like Jackie O dominated President Kennedy's and Bonnie Livingston dominated Speaker-designate Bob Livingston's. They are clearly "Wife Number One". The Sultan of Brunei, because of his Muslim religion, could showcase his two wives openly at the crowning of his son Crown Prince Al-Muhtadee. His brother Prince Jefri Bolkiah, who has four wives and was known to hire up to 40 prostitutes at a time at London's Dorchester Hotel, used to openly flaunt his harem in Beverly Hills, Manila, London and elsewhere until he got fired from his official positions and had to cut back on some of his extra-curricular activities.

Men like to have a harem from which to pick their lady of the night. Whether it was King Solomon, Chinese Emperors, European Kings, Catholic Popes, American Presidents, or your average Joe Blow. Picking a lady from the endless numbers available, be it from behind shopping windows in Hong Kong, Holland, Thailand, Philippines, Hollywood Boulevard or Times Square or any Vegas casino and other endless street corners and whore houses in America is a 21st century reality.

The countless Johns coming to Hong Kong on business trips, for the annual Rugby Sevens and a variety of other reasons, who then take "sex tours" to any one of the number of Asian countries without their wives or partners knowing about it are daily living testimony of hypocritical sexual promiscuity.

How many more mamas and papas have to continue being rolling stones because they can't resist the temptations the opposite sex offers and have to leave their home and children before we come to terms with human nature?

The ultimate hypocrisy was the secret life of Charles Kuralt, the folksy CBS "On the Road" correspondent. For 29 years, until his death in 1997, he had a mistress and maintained a second family. While his wife remained at their home in the concrete canyons of New York City, he nurtured his second life along a rushing trout stream in Montana. American aviaton hero Charles Lindbergh fathered three children with a mistress he had to fly to visit in Germany.

How about Gordon P. Getty, son of oil baron Paul Getty and father of four adult sons, who disclosed that he has had a secret family in Los Angeles for more than a decade? How many more families like that are there, kept quieter and tighter than the witness protection program?

American politicians, like the people they represent, have been practicing adultery since the Founding Fathers of the United States wrote the Constitution. Presidents Thomas Jefferson, Warren

Harding, Franklin Delano Roosevelt, John Kennedy, Lyndon Johnson, Richard Nixon and, most recently, Bill Clinton, and politicians Wilbur Mills, Dan Burton, Henry Hyde and Gary Hart have all partaken in some type of extramarital affairs. Not only with younger women. President Kennedy, in addition to having an affair with his intern Mimi Fannenstock, seduced Marlene Dietrich aged 60!

Richard Nixon? Yes, even Tricky Dickey committed adultery. It was common knowledge in Hong Kong. Nixon used to hang out at a bar in the Hong Kong Hilton, where he was friendly with a local Chinese female employee. Both were married at the time. He later moved her to the States. A story the American media missed.

The highly publicized politically driven sex scandals of President Bill Clinton in the closing years of the last millennium highlight the modern – day attention brought to the private lives of politicians.

Thomas Jefferson, the third president of the United States, although married to Martha Wayles Skelton, had extramarital relations, which began way before his wife's death in 1782, according to author Wesley O. Hagood. Jefferson had affairs with "Betsey Walker 1768-79, Sally Hemings 1787-1826, Maria Cosway 1786-87, Angelica Schuyler Church 1788, and Dolley Madison 1808." What a role model for his namesake! Makes Bill Jefferson Clinton look like a choirboy.

America's founding Puritans enjoyed having sex with each other, their slaves and indentured servants while their wives and significant others prayed. No different than Strom Thurmond or Bill Clinton.

President Warren Harding's sexual adventurism is also fascinatingly detailed in the Carl Sferazza Anthony biography of *Florence Harding*.

Hollywood, politics and sports, because of the celebrity culture, are always rife with stories of infidelity and damaged children. Whether it is Jackie O and her affair with Gianni Agnelli in 1962 while away on vacation without the president, or with brother-in-law Bobby Kennedy after the president's assassination. No different than what first ladies do in America's former Spanish colonies. Actually, a lot of first ladies. Imelda Marcos was renowned for her affairs, especially the one with George Hamilton, whom she even "loaned" millions of dollars. Loans? How about Hugh Grant and Elizabeth Hurley over a blow job, the less than two-year marriage of Eva Herzigova, wife of Bon Jovi drummer Tico Torres, because of her affair with Leonardo DiCaprio or the highly publicized divorces of Mike Tyson, Elizabeth Taylor, Michael Douglas, Harrison Ford, Rosanne Barr, Tony Curtis, Dudley Moore, Michael Chrichton, Brook Shields and Andre Agassi, Dennis Quaid and Meg Ryan, Kate Winslet and Jim Threapleton, Tom Cruise and Nicole Kidman, Wolfgang Puck and Barbara Lazaroff, or Demi Moore and Bruce Willis just to wallow in a few. Demi caught Bruce in bed with one of their employees. Lisa Marie Presley and Michael Jackson, Nicholas Cage...Billie Bob Thorton and Angeline Jolie couldn't stay together even after they bottled each other's blood in vials around their neck as a commitment of eternal devotion. George Clooney appears to be the most honest. He just keeps changing the glamorous babes while sticking close to his favorite permanent significant other: his potbellied pig, Max, which sleeps in his bedroom.

How about Frank Gifford and Kathy Lee, or Sonny and Cher? Joe DiMaggio and Marilyn Monroe? Jack Welch, the former chairman of General Electric after he had an affair with Suzy Wetlaufer? Media tycoon Rupert Murdoch lived with Wendy Deng while married to his second wife Anna for a year before his divorce and remarriage.

Mick Jagger repeatedly broke up with wife Jerry Hall over his affairs and impregnations, the latest result being his love child with Brazilian model Luciana Gimenez Morad. No wonder he and Jerry didn't get married for several years after they had children! Even that alleged marriage was suspect. At 65, the Czech-born film director, Milos Foreman, had twins with his girlfriend Martina Zborlova. He was still married at the time to former actress Vera Kresadlova with whom he also had twins. How about Will Smith? His second wife Jada Pinkett, while pregnant with their second child, was furious when she discovered that his first wife wanted another child with him because their first-born needed a brother or sister! Then there is Bob Dylan's daughter with his "secret wife"? The Axis of infidelity, a person with a spouse and lover, in America is more alive and real than the Axis of Evil. Why perpetuate the hypocrisy, pain and suffering Kobe and Vanessa Bryant went through and brought to light? How many more Americans have to suffer and cry in private?

Dennis Rodman's outrageous behavior is understandable in the context of his abandonment by his father who preferred to live life with several wives in the Philippines. Philanderer Rodman Jr left his wife Shirley, Dennis and two daughters, Debra and Kim, in 1965 and moved to the Philippines where he has two wives and fourteen children.

Liz Taylor has been married eight times and is still searching. Rod Steiger, Larry Fortensky and Mexican lawyer Victor Luna have courted her in her old age. I met Victor when we traveled to Israel with Liz. I couldn't understand then and I can't now why he is so determined to be her next husband. "I love her with all my heart," is all he would say whenever the subject came up.

New York Mayor Rudy Giuliani, like his opponent Hillary Rodham Clinton, thought he had an arrangement with his wife Donna Hanover. At least he thought so until he pushed his luck and was seen in public with his "very good friend" Judith Nathan. Hillary managed to outsmart Rudy in a state like New York. Not over Yankee baseball but political sexual reality. Mr. Cajones, who made an issue of her husband's sexual dalliances, was struck out by a political woman because of his own womanizing. He was forced to pull out of the New York Senate race against Hillary Clinton after a cancer diagnosis and the admission of an affair.

Bertie Ahern, the Prime Minister of Ireland, is accused of moral failure because of his "concubinage" and "living in sin". The sanctity and value of marriage, especially in Catholic countries, is no longer viable in the 21st century. One-third of Irish babies are being born outside marriage. The statistics for other Catholic countries, especially Latino countries, are even higher.

Do Jerry, Anna, Demi, Donna, Hillary or anyone for that matter really think their men or mankind will really ever change no matter what morality is legislated? Conversely, do Mike, Rupert, Bruce, Rudy, Bill or any macho man think their women will?

Jackson Pollock, generally considered the greatest American painter, suffered a great personal torment because of the women in his life and the resulting conflicts. His wife, painter Lee Krasner fled to Europe to let him resolve his affair with an art student, Ruth Kligman. "Jackson was romantic, not realistic," said Kligman. As for the two women in his life, "it was his fantasy that we could all be together – very grown up." Was he unrealistic?

Novelist Graham Greene's feelings of Catholic guilt because of his obsession and affair with American beauty Catherine Walston inspired his novel *End of the Affair.*

Homecourt Advantage written by Rita Ewing, who separated from her husband, New York Knicks superstar Patrick Ewing, and her pal Crystal McCrary, wife of NBA guard Greg Anthony, point out how virtually all athletes have a "main woman" and a "side girl" and always the twain shall meet. Patrick Ewing split up with his wife of eight years, leaving her with his son by another woman, and began seeing a Knicks cheerleader. Clean and keen Kobe was just the latest to be outed.

The fact that 75 percent of the cases of sudden death during sexual activity involve people who were taking part in extramarital sexual intercourse is doing nothing to slow down extramarital affairs.

New Woman – Chix With Stix
Sexual adventurism has not been limited to men. Elizabeth I could send her lovers off to the Tower of London when they made eyes at her pretty ladies-in-waiting. Catherine the Great had similar options at her disposal, especially if there were horses around. Agrippina and Cleopatra, the other sexually rapacious ancient babes, only laid the groundwork for their millennium successors.

"Isn't it touching that they think we are so under control?" says Helen Fisher, a Rutgers University anthropologist. Isn't it obvious that every time a man is sleeping around, he is sleeping with a woman? Granted there are exceptions. "It's basic math that women are 50 percent of the problem here. Men want to delude themselves into thinking that women are Madonnas and pristine and in control of their sexuality because men have a terrible fear of cuckoldry," Fisher observes. I wonder what the number is of men who support girlfriends and mistresses who in turn support their own boyfriends and toy boys unbeknown to their benefactor? I know quite a few.

A survey by the Institute of Interdisciplinary Psychology in Italy showed that a double life is actually more a female characteristic, especially if it lasts a long time. It showed that married women aged between 30 and 45 were extraordinarily successful at managing two sentimental lives without being discovered by their husbands. "There is a cold, rational approach women adopt in betraying," said survey spokeswoman Miriam Tomponzi. "Only five percent of women compared to an incredible 37 percent of men leave 'risky' objects; only seven percent of women compared to 39 per cent of men, having started another love affair, change their emotional attitude towards their husbands." Female promiscuity was most recently confirmed by the not-so-scientific Russian agency Alibi, whose business is to sell good cover stories for adulterous partners. Most of its clients are women.

Female promiscuity is not all bad, according to scientists, because it helps create healthier offspring – at least in birds. Scientists at the Max Planck research Center for Ornithology in Starnberg, Germany, concluded some female birds preferred more than one mate to improve their chances of producing fitter young. No wonder Europeans refer to women as birds.

Women do behave badly, or at least as badly as men. They drink and go out in packs hunting for members of the opposite sex, even more aggressively than men. Increasing job choices and changes in the education system have given women more independence than ever before and any evening anywhere they are everywhere grabbing the opportunity and men.

I have run into these same hunting herds of women in New York, Greenwich, Los Angeles and countless restaurants and bars in Hong Kong and America. In many Hong Kong bars and discos Wednesday and Thursday nights are ladies' nights. In America it sometimes feels like every night is. Women travel in packs with one thing on their mind. They want to get laid just as bad as men do. Chinese, American, European, Asian and Latinas. Doctors, lawyers, bankers, secretaries, students, wives significant others and singles all have one thing on their mind. The extreme sport of fucking is still alive and well in Hong Kong, America and the global New World Order.

Sex in the City is a crash course on what women really want. Southern Baptists, Daughters of the American Revolution and the Republican Right won't play officially on the record so they "don't get it" – in any sense. Unofficially, they get it in more conceivable ways than *We the Apathetic People* want to know.

Mae Jemison, former astronaut and director of the Jemison Institute at Dartmouth College, says: "It all comes back to power. We have to understand that is our responsibility, and that we have the authority and the permission to work on changing the world."

The price women paid to re-establish their power is high. They are alone, childless and miserable. For Muslim women the road they have to hoe is even more depressing. Egyptian film maker Inas el-Degheidi, whose movies "defend women's rights, women's feelings and dignity" in the Muslim world, reminds us how much more hypocritical the standards are in the Arab Muslim world. Girls "are victims of a society that lives with two personalities: You can do anything wrong as long as it's not in public."

The film *Muriel's Wedding* captured today's woman's desperation. Whereas the traditional old maid tended to have one special gentleman slip away, the current breed of new maids seem to spend their entire lives dropping the ball. What seems to upset the woman left behind the most is the time and effort they've squandered. Women don't understand that usually men really don't know what they want. This is especially true after a man's own failed relationships when he feels he has dropped the ball on his foot and both have rolled into his mouth. Women waste a lot of energy trying to figure men out thumbing through The Rules. Any wonder women blame men for all their ailments? MENtal illness, MENstrual cramps, MENtal breakdown, MENopause, GUYnecologist, and when they have real trouble it's a HISterectomy!

Maybe that is why so many women, especially career women, are seeking religious fulfillment to fill the void in their life. Ahmed Andrews, a sociologist of religion at the University of Derby, believes so. "Disillusionment with Christianity or life, such as a personal crisis, are usually behind a conversion, but for women there appears to be an added element," he says. "It's a search for spiritual enlightenment, to find oneself. A feeling of taking back control of their lives and a freedom of expression from the old boundaries."

Does this mean that as women start outnumbering men in the 21st century more will convert to Islam? Many countries' Census and Statistic Departments, including Hong Kong's, report women will outnumber men dramatically in their country by the middle of the 21st century.

It seems every class I've ever been in from grammar school through law school, the top student in the class is a woman. Now, either I've been in classes with stupid men, am delusional or the simple fact is woman is more developed than man. "I'll bet you the time ain't far off when a woman won't know any more than a man," Will Rogers predicted in 1923.Well that time ain't arrived yet! According to Matt Towery's book *Powerchicks: How Women Will Dominate America* it's still far off! One politician who is proud of his smarter wife is Britain's Tony Blair. "My wife is smarter than me, which is why she chose to go into law and not politics," Blair has said on more than one occasion. One thought I repeatedly reflect on is if women are so smart how come they always seem to be standing in endless lines waiting to get into the ladies room? Geneticists at Stanford University concluded that female genes acquired their modern form some 143,000 years ago. It took the male version another 84,000 years. This overturns the Biblical tale of woman created from a spare rib left over from man.

I was reminded of this fact in 1998 when we purchased an office in Hong Kong for our television distribution business. My two partners in the business at the time were Chinese women. Isn't it ironic, I thought to myself, that here I am buying an office with two women while I am looking to lease an office with two men, my editor of the *Asia Cable and Satellite World* publishing business, and his deputy editor. "Damn," I blurted out loud as the thought crossed my mind at the FCC Main Bar. "You OK?" Ronnie Ling, an advertising executive, asked. "Yeah, just thinking about how dumb we men are when it comes to women!"

Mark Sharp, the local chief police training instructor and coach of Lee Lai-shan, the Hong Kong Olympic windsurfing gold medal winner, put down the paper he was reading as he had clearly overheard my remarks. "Men are a beach and women and life are the waves.

They can keep coming and crashing. It's up to us to grab our boards and ride the waves." Being on his second marriage and numerous relationships, I slowly digested his surprising philosophical comment. My surprise must have been evident because of the sarcastic smile he cavalierly tossed my way as he returned to his paper.

Women in the 21st century will play a much more prominent role in the professions and occupations dominated by men, except the military. It is already happening. Eileen Collins became the first woman space commander in the old century's last Columbia space shuttle. Two grandmas, Senator Patty Murray of Washington and Representative Nita Lowey of New York, were the leading Democratic Party fundraisers in 2002. Sallie Krawcheck became CEO of Citigroup's Smith Barney unit after criticizing Sandy Weill for his acquisition of Salomon. Women soccer players and their sisters in the WNBA brought women from outside the entertainment and business worlds to the forefront of the New World Order.

The women's World Cup soccer final between America and China is a stellar example. The U.S. women won the first cup in China in 1991. Nevertheless, it took them another eight years to garner their mass following. When the American squad took the gold medal in the 1996 Olympic Games, NBC aired a mere 10 minutes of highlights. But in 1999 ABC, ESPN and ESPN2 jointly covered all of the women's World Cup, and the ratings did not disappoint. As the American team swept through the preliminary games, one broadcast on ESPN drew more households than the cable channel's typical Major League baseball game.

The Chinese women soccer team had won two of the three previous matches against the U.S. before the 1999 World Cup championships but the U.S. team won the cup. They tied overall! How symbolic of the U.S.-Sino geopolitical relationship. The final between China and America was an example of how the two global civilizations can compete in a sportsmanlike way. Respectful, friendly, yet competitive, without being enemies.

Women soccer players also showed us that for women, like men, it's sexy to be strong.

What about the great number of female vocalists – girl rockers, rappers and award winning hip-hoppers that pioneered leading, winning, female role models? Used to be male vocalists and bands dominated those categories. Now it's the women's turn. The same with "Saturday Night Live". Today it is the women comics that get the ratings.

The same applies to politics. Democrat Nancy Pelosi became the first woman minority speaker at the dawn of the 21st century. Even in some Muslim countries, women have been elected heads of state. Benazir Bhutto in Pakistan, Khaleda Zia in Bangladesh, Megawati Sukarnoputri in Indonesia and Tansu Ciller of Turkey. Whether it's Clinton, Pelosi, India's "Bandit Queen" Phoolan Devi, who was assassinated after she was elected to parliament because she killed her male abusers and challenged male supremacy, or Wafa Idris the first woman suicide bomber, women are demanding their rightful place outside the home. In Iraq, Huda Amash, dean of the University of Baghdad's College of Science, was the only female named to the inner circle of Saddam's political elite, the Revolutionary Command Council. Saddam Hussein's biological weapons of mass destruction are the creation of Rihab Taha, a woman nicknamed "Dr. Germ". For all his shortcommings, Saddam Hussein, to his credit, did end discrimination against women in Iraq.

Muslim women, like their Western counterparts, are reminding their male-dominated societies that Islam preaches equality. As modernity collides with religious tradition, women have begun to demand a reinterpretation of the civil codes that presume that a woman, in her private life, is a capricious creature in need of a man's guiding hand. Queen Rania Al-Abdullah of Jordan is leading the charge to have women play a greater role. Endon Mahmood, the wife of Malaysian Prime Minister Abdullah Ahmed Badawi, is also challenging and breaking down the male barriers and encouraging Muslim women to fight outdated interpretations of Islamic tenets. She is actively campaigning to establish monogamy for Muslims.

The tragic fire that killed 15 girls in a Mecca school because the fleeing girls were forced to return to the burning building by the religious police to cover their heads highlighted the absurdity of extreme religious enforcement. Isn't it time all Muslim women follow in the kicksteps of the anonymous Jordanian woman in Zarqa, Jordan, who ripped off her cloak and veil and punched and kicked three youths after their repeated cat-calls? The men fled screaming. Witnesses said the woman quoted the song "Patience has its Limits" by late Egyptian star Ulmm Kalthoum before leaving the scene to the applause and cheers of the crowded street. The guys should have turned on the TV and looked at Vida Samadzai, the Muslim Afghan beauty representing Afghanistan at the Miss Earth competition. She was posing in a bikini next to more than 50 other women. "I would like to make people aware that as Afghan women we are talented, intelligent and beautiful," she said posing in her revealing swimsuit. "We are one of the peoples who can make a difference in this world."

In the Muslim world women are the key to modernity because they are unlikely to vote away their own rights. The more rights they acquire the less the chances of success the extreme fundamentalists have. Any wonder that the Saudis and Taleban deny women the right to vote? The United Nations and numerous other private international agencies have produced endless statistics to show that improving the status of women and educating their daughters lead to substantial reductions of poverty. "We can no longer afford to minimize or ignore the contributions of women and girls to all stages of conflict resolution, peace-building, peacekeeping and the reconstruction process," UN Secretary-General Kofi Annan correctly admonishes.

Kim Campbell, former Prime Minister of Canada, offered a solution to today's scandal-riddled world: women leaders. "The qualities that are defined as masculine are also the same qualities that are defined as the qualities of leadership. There is virtually no overlap between the qualities ascribed to femininity and those to leadership." Yet in several studies, Campbell said, "results show that when you have a critical mass of women in an organization, you have less corruption." Peru and Mexico have implemented initiatives based on such thinking. And Campbell warned that "lest you think that all we aspire to for the world can be accomplished by male-dominated organizations, I have only to say to you: Enron,

Taleban, Roman Catholic Church."

At the dawn of the 21st century women brought down the "good ol' boy" network that rewarded unquestioning loyalty. Sherron Watkins at Enron, Cynthia Cooper at WorldCom and Coleen Rowley at the FBI. A trend or coincidence? Perhaps it's more than a coincidence. The first brand-name whistle blower was a woman. In Greek mythology, Cassandra had the gift of foresight. She correctly predicted the outcome of many events, warning the Trojans about accepting a wooden horse as a "gift" from their Greek opponents. "Problem was," Paul Farhi reminds us, "when she spurned the god Apollo as a lover, he retaliated by making anyone who heard her prophesies believe they were lies. It was men, for the most part, who disbelieved her, leading inevitably to disaster and tragedy." Maybe things are changing after all in the new millennium.

Subtle female domination is changing. It is now breaking through the bedroom ceiling to the street and beyond. Some men are now taking the woman's surname and abandoning theirs. Women have gone from dropping their maiden name and taking that of their man for life, to combining it with the name of the man they marry until "life do them part", to choosing the woman's surname over the man's for both partners.

Maybe Aristophanes' famed antiwar comedy *"Lysistrata"*, written more than 2,000 years ago, that portrays how the women of Greece end a cycle of senseless wars by withholding sex until the men stopped fighting, is something women of the 21st century should try if they want to run a peaceful world.

Feminism
Feminism and the sexual revolution are not just sixties phenomena. Feminist revolts and sexual revolutions are common in periods of general disruption, E.J. Dionne Jr. points out. They have been the rule in America since the American Revolution. "If particular care and attention are not paid to the ladies," wrote Abigail Adams to her husband John, "we are determined to foment a rebellion, and will not hold ourselves bound by any laws in which we have no voice or representation."

It is important to understand the deep roots of the feminist revolution in order to see why feminist values became so widespread in the sixties and seventies. Too often in our political discussions, we treat feminism as a sudden development. Understanding that the sixties were not a onetime episode but part of a long and difficult process is one key to dealing with the truth and the real issues of the day and moving beyond the politics of false choices.

Feminism is a gradual process through which society is trying to adjust to a vast array of changes that began with the industrial revolution, including changes in the nature of production and of household work.

E.J. Dionne Jr. pinpoints the development of feminism in America in *Why Americans Hate Politics.* Although feminism has a long history in America, the roots of the current revolt lie in the Progressive Era, which saw the rise of movements for both women's rights and sexual liberation.

Christopher Lasch has argued that the rise of new attitudes toward women and the family after the turn of the 20th century could be traced to radical changes in the nature of production as farms declined and production shifted out of the home and into factories. The new family had a paradoxical effect, since it "simultaneously degraded and exalted women". On the one hand it deprived them "of many of their traditional employments, as the household ceased to be a center of production and devoted itself to child rearing." On the other hand, as child rearing itself came to be seen as more important, society concluded that to carry out that responsibility, women needed more education "for their domestic duties". The Progressive Era, Lasch noted, taught that women "should become useful rather than ornamental," and this created a much broader revolt as "bourgeois domesticity gave rise to its antithesis, feminism." The new domestic arrangements "gave rise to a general unrest," Lasch noted, encouraging women "to entertain aspirations that marriage and the family could not satisfy."

The new attitudes toward family life led to a series of remarkable changes in the position of women in society. Female college enrollment tripled between 1890 and 1910 and doubled again in the teens. There was explosive growth in the membership in women's organizations and a sharp upturn in women's participation in the work force.

Traditionalists had increasing difficulty in holding the line against experimentation in other aspects of family life, notably sex. As the family role in production declined, its new importance lay in providing comfort and intimacy in an increasingly competitive world. As mass production took some of the joy and individuality out of work, the family came to be seen as the primary arena in which individuality could be expressed.

The sexual revolution after the turn of the 20th century, which reached its height in the 1920s, was a natural by-product of these changes. The emancipation of women meant that their own sexual needs and desires suddenly became legitimate. The triumph of the value of "healthiness" over the demands of religion and tradition emphasized individual satisfaction over adherence to communal norms. In their excellent social history of the American family, Steven Mintz and Susan Kellogg reported that the "purity crusade" of the Victorian 1880s and 1890s against prostitution and venereal disease had the ironic effect of vastly liberalizing attitudes toward sex. The crusade "broke the veil of silence that had surrounded discussions of sexuality during the 19th century and inspired pioneering efforts at sex research and sex education," they wrote. For the first time, women's sexuality was publicly acknowledged.

A 1913 magazine cover declared that the hour had struck "sex o'clock in America". Defenders of the family came to realize that full-scale resistance to the new morality would not work. "Instead of trying to annihilate the new morality, they domesticated it," Lasch wrote, celebrating "a freer, more enlightened sexuality within marriage". The result was a new theory of family life, "the companionate family". As Mintz and Kellogg put it, the new theory held that "husbands and wives would be 'friends and lovers' and parents and children would be 'pals'." The companionate marriage, Mintz and Kellogg noted, "placed an unprecedented emphasis on the importance of sexual gratification in marriage."

The triumph of such norms was interrupted by the Great Depression and then World War II. These were followed by the domesticity of the 1950s and early 1960s, a time when the country seemed to be stepping back from an ethic of liberation. In many respects, the 1950s were special, marking a sharp break with the patterns of the previous half-century. Marriage rates during the 1950s reached an all-time high. By the end of the 1950s, 70 percent of all women were married by the age of 24, compared with just 42 percent in 1940 – and 50 percent in the 1980s. The rate of increase in divorce was lower in the 1950s than in any decade of the 20th century.

If the movement of production outside the home changed the nature of household work, so, too, did the technological revolution in housework with the advent of machinery from vacuum cleaners to dishwashers. By reducing the time it took to maintain a home, the new devices contributed mightily to the reassessment of women's roles that began in the 1950s. By the end of the fifties, most Americans took the security that had eluded them during the Depression and World War II for granted again. They were free to return to the struggle to redefine women's roles that had begun at the turn of the century.

Women joined the Civil Rights movement and the class war, which revolved around the abortion issue. In her exceptionally sensitive study of activists on both sides of the abortion issue, *Abortion and the Politics of Motherhood,* Kristin Luker argued that the views of pro-choice and pro-life activists are explained in large part by their radically different interests and life choices. "Pro-life women have always valued family roles very highly and have arranged their lives accordingly," Luker wrote. "They did not acquire high-level educational and occupational skills, for example, because they married, and they married because their values suggested that this would be the most satisfying life open to them." By contrast, "pro-choice women postponed (or avoided) marriage and family roles because they chose to acquire the skills they needed to be successful in the larger world, having concluded that the role of wife and mother was too limited for them." The class war was made ever more bitter by a religious war, since very religious people were much more opposed to abortion, on the whole, than others.

Lost Man
In the early 1990s society celebrated the arrival of the politically correct "New Man" who was not afraid to share responsibility

for children and housework. Women today are demanding their men do a lot more. As a result, young American men are becoming increasingly confused about their identity and seem to be harboring feelings of insecurity and isolation from the rest of society, according to new research.

While their fathers and elder brothers enjoyed the security of belonging to male social groups – what many researchers called tribes – those born since 1978, the so called "Generation Y" men, face a bewildering array of choices from the new "supermarket lifestyle".

Unable to decide whether they were new men, new lads, eco-warriors or global villagers, young men felt they lacked an identity and role. And they could become alienated. The Barclay's Life survey concluded that young men would need to redefine themselves in the 21st century, as did women in the 1960s. "Men have seen the breakdown of their traditional roles but have yet to replace them with anything else. Football seems to have taken over from religion as a way of connecting with other people."

The competitive culture now has new combatants. Women. Men are having a difficult time grappling with intimate sex objects that are independent role challengers. As women rise in the professions, the board room or the classroom, men and boys are sinking in despair. There is a new "gender paradigm" that has the flexibility to accommodate diversity among the sexes as well as common ground, such as the desire in many couples for both partners to have careers and contribute equally to bringing up children.

Lisa Sullivan, the community activist and founder of Listen Inc., concludes: "Black men are having a very difficult time. I tell brothers I know they're going to have to find a way to survive in a patriarchal society that never intends for them to be able to play it out." Any wonder hotmail servers went down when the timeless wisdom of "What might happen if men wrote 'help' columns" circumnavigated the world to the billions of frustrated men? It was funny, but reality is it was a momentary chuckle. The fact is that half the male population suffers erectile dysfunction because of women and the ugly realities men face in today's world. The scary part is the proportion is likely to grow, according to impotence expert Chris McMahon, director of the Australian Center for Sexual Health. Why promote erectile dysfunction and prostate cancer, not to mention their insidious related illnesses, caused by sexual frustration caused by the morality and political correctness dictated by the Church and religious rightous politicians?

The relationship between woman and man has to be honestly re-examined to minimize mental and sexual cruelty in the New World Order. It would greatly benefit the majority of men and women who have already been won over to the principle of equality and are now trying to figure out how to enjoy its benefits. Some men should be freed to find that perhaps football or computers or even other men are more interesting than women are. Women already have.

Real Gentlemen

"The Concert for New York" organized by Paul McCartney in support of the city's uniformed services was a millennium reminder of who real men are. Men who are willing without fear to un-conditionally sacrifice their lives by serving others. Many real gentlemen were finally recognized for what they are as they sat in the most expensive seats in Madison Square Garden. They think about money and stock options later in life only after they have served their community. Real men are not about money. They are about humility, service and caring about family, friends and community.

Many of these men have affairs as they go through life servicing the community. Is that a reason for a community to be deprived of the individual's spirit of public service, talent, chivalry and ability? One such real example of a gentleman that brought this point home after September 11 was New York Mayor Rudy Giuliani.

Multiple Relationships

The Republic of Palau is a beautiful cluster of several thousand rock islands in the West Carolines between Guam and the Philippines. It is heaven on earth. Beneath the waves its coral and underwater sights rank it as the number one "underwater wonder of the world". I met Larry Hillbloom there. A fellow California lawyer and co-founder of DHL. He and I advised different governmental entities in Palau.

Larry didn't believe in the institution of marriage. He preferred to have different "virgin wives" in Palau, the Philippines, Vietnam and any place else he spent any amount of time doing business.

His unexpected death in May 1996 when his seaplane vanished resulted in several lawsuits being filed by the numerous siblings he sired with different women across Asia seeking their fair share of his estate. The "virgin wives" were merely protecting the rights of their children, which is understandable. In life they all knew of Larry's sexual pursuits and accepted them as long as he provided for them. Some lawyers argued that the "virgin wives" were nothing but prostitutes. How do they differ from Nicole Smith? Was her marriage a bond of love or prostitution? What is the difference today in marriages in which the wives stay solely for material security? Are they not prostitutes? Young chicks hoping their old man will die on the job.

Polyamory goes back to the days of ancient Greece and is derived from the Greek and Latin root meaning "many loves". It is not just about casual sex or extramarital affairs. It is about a delicate intimate social network that combines sex and love.

Historically, society condoned polygamy, polyamory, mistresses, misters, concubines and prostitution. In fact a polygamous unchaste life was the general practice. The judiciously fair King Solomon had a thousand wives. Today, Muslims and Mormons are still practicing polygamy openly and frankly.

A brief comparative history of polygamy, mistresses and concubines might be helpful, let alone tasty.

Darwin's *Theory of Evolution* was based on the survival of the fittest. Baboons have harems. If our evolutionary forefathers were not monogamous is it realistic to try to impose monogamy on mankind? Man, Homo sapiens, has a very strong survival instinct, whereas by contrast, the giant panda, *Ailuropoda melanoleuca,* has not. Only some 1,000 giant pandas are left – mostly in the forests and mountain regions of the western Chinese province of Sichuan. Unlike St. Anthony, who had the iron will to resist any form of sexual temptation, human or supernatural, the panda is uninterested in sex and seems to be determined to become extinct in spite of artificial insemination and the efforts of the modern mandarins of the People's Republic of China. Of the pandas in captivity, only 10 percent of the males have ever mated and only 30 percent of female pandas get pregnant. Adolescent giant pandas at the National Giant Panda Reproduction Research Center at the dawn of the 21st century now watch videos featuring pandas having sex in the hope it will stimulate reproduction.

Most animals have a strong survival instinct, including the majority of apes, and are polygamistic. Few animals develop a pair-bond relationship. The law of survival in the jungle is that the male attempts to mate with any available female he can find and the mothers of his offspring will defend their young to the death. These natural instincts for survival are reflected in the behavior of the human species in the form of the promiscuous male and the protective mother.

The strongest male of a pride of lions is able to mate with more females than the weaker males. This is true of many other species of animals including man. Consequently, chieftains, kings, emperors and the extremely wealthy tend to have more women than anyone else.

In societies where ancestor worship is prevalent, conceiving a large number of children in order to achieve an indirect form of imortality is a religious obligation. However, polygamy does not necessarily produce heirs. The Emperor of China, Hsien Feng, had around 70 wives, but when he died at the age of 30 in 1861 he had only one son, Tsai Chun. The child's mother, Tzu Hsi, later known as the Dragon Empress, was a second rank concubine who managed to organize a coup and gained control of the infant. As a result she ruled China for almost 50 years.

In Christian Europe if a king did not have a son it was a national disaster, because it invariably led to a civil war after his death. One son was also not enough; "an heir and a spare" were essential. King Henry VIII of England, a second son himself, married his dead brother's wife Katharine of Aragon. Only one of her children, a girl Mary who later became Queen, survived infancy. In the days of an all-tempestuous monarchy, if a king was succeeded by a female or a child who had not yet reached maturity, it could cause terrible problems. Richard II, Henry VI and Edward V were all child kings and they were all deposed and murdered. Illegitimate children could not inherit. Although many kings of England had bastards, none of them succeeded to the throne. A king needed a number of sons to help him to control power. Even if they could not inherit, illegitimate children often proved invaluable in this respect.

When for political reasons Pope Leo X refused to grant Henry VIII a divorce it led to the English Church's break with Rome. In spite of chopping off the heads of a couple of his queens and two divorces, the House of Tudor ended on the death of his daughter Elizabeth I.

Henry VIII was born 1,500 years too late. According to Julius Caesar, the ancient Britons practiced polygamy. Caesar also claimed that these women shared several husbands. English historians accept reluctantly that their ancestors may have been polygamists, but the suggestion that they may have also practiced polyandry as well is too much of a cultural shock. Even today Caesar's report is frequently dismissed as fantasy by historians who simply don't want it to be true, although they may be quite happy to acknowledge that the foreign Queen Cleopatra VII of Egypt was incestuous and married two of her brothers, Ptolemy XIV and Ptolemy XV, and had a son called King Caesarion as the result of an affair with Caesar.

Casanova upset the church and nobility in Italy when he was found in bed with two nuns. No different than some of today's stories of priests impregnating nuns.

In the Roman Catholic Spanish Empire, because the ratio of male immigrants to female immigrants was around 10 to one, "some of the conquistadors collected veritable harems of Amerindian concubines," David S. Landes reminds us.

Although European royal families seldom committed incest they are in the main all related to each other, to the extent that King George V looked like an identical twin of Nicholas II, the last Czar of Russia. European royalty is basically an extended family. Although these close family relationships were designed to provide some sort of political security, in reality they were redundant in preventing wars caused by national interests.

In societies where polygamy existed such as Imperial China in the Qing Dynasty, the family trees of royal concubines were carefully scrutinized and the Emperors were restricted to marrying only fellow Manchus, which excluded ethnic Chinese. In certain societies, having children did not necessarily ensure that a monarch would enjoy a tranquil old age. Shaka, the founder of the Zulu Empire, refused to marry and decided not to have any children and although he enjoyed the favors of his 600 concubines he practiced contraception. The reason he refused to wed was self-preservation. If he had had children, there was a strong possibility that when he got old and feeble, his sons would kill him to gain power. Ironically he was murdered by two of his brothers.

In Renaissance Italy it was not uncommon for a Cardinal to have an illegal family of illegitimate children by a number of mistresses. When such a Cardinal became Pope his sons would become papal lords and his daughters would be married off to the nobility in order to help him strengthen his power base. The story of Pope Alexander VI and his children, the murderous Cesare Borgia and his incestuous sister Lucrezia, is well known. But Alexander was not the only Pope who behaved in this manner, just the most notorious.

In many countries that practiced polygamy, the eldest son did not necessarily become the next king, sultan or chief. With many children to choose from, the father or the aristocracy was able to select the most capable of the sons as heir. King Rama III of Siam (Thailand) had 22 sons and 29 daughters. However when he died in 1851, his nobles did not choose any of his children to succeed him. Instead they selected his brother Prince Mongkut who was a monk at the Bovorniwet Temple. He'd already been passed over before but he proved to be an inspired choice. As King Mongkut (Rama IV) he kept his country out of the hands of predatory European colonial powers by sheer brainpower and patient diplomacy. Mongkut himself had 37 wives and 67 children and employed an English governess, Anna Leonowens, to educate some of them.

Anna's descriptions of harem life are quite fascinating, but they are seen through the eyes of a Victorian English woman and were considered, even at the time of publication, by Europeans who knew Mongkut and Thailand as prejudiced, highly colorful and alarmingly inaccurate. Thais find the film "The King and I", which was loosely based on her story, extremely offensive, and it is banned in Thailand. This is understandable considering the managed misperceptions it presents. Even the 2000 film "Anna and The King" had Chinese actors playing royals and aristocrats speaking in street market Thai.

For a more authentic description of a sophisticated Buddhist polygamous household one should turn to the *Ching Ping Mei,* which describes in detail the family life of voluptuary Hsi Men and his six wives.

The anti-hero Hsi Men is a rich Chinese shop owner and merchant. Moon Lady, his principal wife, has the unenviable job of keeping the women of his turbulent household in order. His Second Lady, Picture of Grace, is technically a concubine, as are the rest of his junior wives. She was a former singing-girl and her function had been that of a sex toy. When the story begins Hsi Min is already tired of her. Wife three, Tower of Jade, is a widow who is older than Hsi Men. He marries her to look after his household books. Basically she is his accountant. His fourth wife, Beauty of Snow, had been a household servant. He marries her for her cooking. His fifth wife, Golden Lotus, is a beauty who men would kill for to possess. His Men conspires with Golden Lotus to murder her first husband, Wu Ta, so that they can get married. He marries his sixth wife, the Lady of the Vase, who is the widow of his best friend, for her money. She dies early on in the book.

Although *Ching Ping Mei* is set in the final years of the Sung Dynasty (1101-1126), the system hardly changed until the 20th century. In British colonial Hong Kong in the 1930s, tin millionaire Eu Tong-sen had five wives, an unknown number of concubines and 34 children. Each child was looked after individually by a separate English nanny. By the 20th century the status of secondary wives and that of concubines had become separate and although a man's wives might all live under the same roof, a concubine generally had her own establishment and was more like a mistress with a certain legal status.

While creating heirs, sex and prestige were the main reasons for polygamy in China. In more primitive macho rural societies, the wife was the workhorse. Consequently the more wives you had the more laborers you had to till your fields.

Before the Kafirs of Afghanistan were forcibly converted to Islam, wives were little more than field-slaves. "Marriages are simple affairs: they are actually women purchased by men," wrote the anthropologist Sir George Scott Robertson. He goes on to say: "Kafir women are practically household slaves. They seem to have no civil rights of any kind. To all intents and purposes they are bought and sold as household commodities." An orphaned boy would often marry a middle-aged woman simply because he needed someone to till his fields. When he came of age he would buy a younger wife. This would cost him about 8-12 cows. If a man had only one wife he was considered a nobody. A man was also able to buy a wife on an instalment plan, but until the debt was paid, the wife was not allowed to leave her father's house. When a man died his son and heir could sell his step-mothers and his sisters. If his mother remarried he would receive a bride price, which in effect meant he could sell his mother. "Women are rarely actively ill used; they are just despised," concluded Robertson. Has this perception really changed in Afghanistan today?

In most societies where polygamy is practiced, women don't have a great many rights although there are individual exceptions. In Lugu Lake, China, women of the Mosuo ethnic group have the power. It is not only a matriarchal society but a woman's kingdom. Females call all the shots, run all the businesses and dominate "walking marriages". They decide who will sleep with them on a particular night by tickling the palm of their heart's desire. It is not uncommon for a Mosuo woman to have several children all fathered by different men.

In many Muslim countries a marriage can be contracted without the consent of the bride. Traditional Islamic law allows a man to have four wives at one time, and to pronounce talak (divorce) without restriction. Even by mobile phone. However, before the collapse of the Soviet Empire, religious codes in its Muslim states had been replaced by civil laws based on a European pattern in regard to polygamy and divorce. The same is true of Turkey and Albania.

Muslim polygamy varies from state to state, but it does more or less conform to a basic set of rules. However Hindu polygamy in India, with over a thousand different castes, is difficult to generalize. The caste system is such that a Brahmin can only marry a Brahmin and an Untouchable an Untouchable. There are more than a dozen different castes of untouchables and one must marry within one's caste. For this reason the marriage between first cousins is common among Hindus, whereas it is forbidden in many religions. The basic motives for taking a second wife are the same as anywhere else: a sick or barren first wife, prestige, someone to do the household chores or till the fields, or just plain lust. As in Imperial China, the first wife often chooses the second wife. But while a second wife may raise the prestige of the husband in India, she lowers the social status of a family who provides a second wife to a man, when his first wife is still alive. In some castes marrying a widow is taboo, where in other castes it is perfectly acceptable.

Amongst the Nayars of the Malabar coast in Southern India, polyandry was quite common before the advent of British rule. They were also polygamous. Husbands lived in different houses from their wives. This created a situation which occasionally arises in America today, when a divorced or simply an unmarried couple have a sexual relationship, where a man becomes the "social father" of his lover's children. If Woody Allen had been legally married to Mia Farrow, instead of just having a long-standing affair with her, he would probably have been guilty of incest when he married her adopted daughter Soon-Yi Previn.

In most Christian countries it is illegal for a girl to marry her step-father. However there seem to be no laws, other than moral, to prevent a "social father" marrying his lover's adopted daughter when he is the father of one of her other children. It is a situation that would have been unlikely to happen when the laws of kinship and affinity were written.

In the Himalayas, fraternal polyandry exists alongside polygamy today, even among high caste Brahmin and Rajput in the remoter regions of Uttar Pradesh in northwestern India. "In this society a polyandrous union occurs," wrote anthropologist Gerald D. Berreman, "when a woman goes through a marriage ceremony with the eldest of a group of brothers all of whom thereupon become the woman's husbands." The children call all the brothers father, but the firstborn is regarded as the child of the eldest brother, and the second, the child of the second brother, and so on. This custom is fairly flexible. In some villages in the region there are polyandrous marriages, where a commune of men and women share husbands and wives.

Like many ancient peoples the Jews were polygamists. In the Book of Genesis we are told: "Sara, Abram's wife, took Hagar her maid the Egyptian, after Abram had dwelt ten years in the land of Canaan, and gave her to her husband Abram to be his wife." This is a classic case of a barren first wife selecting a second wife for her husband. The rules concerning polygamy are set down in the Fifth Book of Moses, called Deuteronomy. However while the Kings of Israel, particularly Solomon, had harems the prevailing form of marriage was monogamous. The Edict of Worms of 985 imposed a prohibition on multiple-adult, non-monogamous households to avoid persecution by conforming to Christian values.

In the past, difficult divorce laws created a number of quasi-polygamous marriages. Take the case of T.E. Lawrence. His father, Sir Thomas Chapman, was an Irish baronet who established a second family to get away from his wife, whom he called the "Vinegar Queen". He eloped with his daughters' Scottish nanny to England, where he lived under the assumed name of "Mr. Lawrence" and sired four sons, one of whom became a national hero known as Lawrence of Arabia. The fact that Lawrence was illegitimate was not published in his lifetime nor was it generally known. Today if a celebrity like Lawrence was the bastard son of a baronet it would be splashed across the tabloids and more than likely be used as a vehicle for promotion or denigration.

The shame of being a bastard or being a quasi-polygamist has almost disappeared. Billionaire Sir James Goldsmith, the renowned global takeover artist and green mailer, made no effort to conceal that he had a number of quasi-polygamous marriages. At weekends he lived with his second wife, Ginette, and their two children in

Paris and during the week with Lady Annabel Birley, who had two children by him. There was also a third woman, Laure Boulay de la Meurthe, by whom he had two children. In his lifetime Sir James was envied rather than censured. He behaved like the principal male in a pride of lions rather than an adulterer. He was respected for his lifestyle because he dealt with it honestly and openly.

Attempts by Westerners to set up harems have not been particularly successful. Alexander Hare established a harem of about 40 women, who had been given him by the Sultan of Banjermasim. After being hounded out of South Africa in 1825, he moved them to the uninhabited Cocos Keelings atoll, about 600 miles south west of Java Head. All went well for a couple of years until his former partner, John Ross, arrived with 10 young Scottish settlers. Ross' intention was to found a new colony. Unfortunately all he found was Hare who had already claimed the island for himself and his harem. Needless to say they quarreled. Hare, in an attempt at reconciliation, presented Ross' Scots with a roast pig and a keg of rum on St. Andrew's night. The ungrateful Scots got drunk, raided his island and carried off most of his women.

Polygamy American-Style
Twenty-five years after Alexander Hare attempted to establish a polygamous island paradise for himself in the Java Sea, Mormon evangelist Brigham Young and his Church of Jesus Christ of Latter-day Saints attempted to do the same thing on a much grander scale. He set out to build a New Jerusalem in Utah, a bleak territory that was at the time outside the jurisdiction of the United States of America. Mormons embraced polygamy as essential to reach the highest degree of celestial glory. The polygamous element in the Mormon Church's teaching was regarded as an abomination by many American Christians and Joseph Smith, the founder of the church, was murdered in 1844.

In 1848 the U.S. acquired Utah after the ending of the Mexican War and two years later the Territory of Utah was created. The Mormons were basically an isolationist cult and had an aggressive policy towards "Gentiles" or non-Mormons. This unfortunately led to the massacre of 120 immigrants who were passing through Utah to California. The Mountain Meadows Massacre led to the

Mormon War (1857-58). In 1862, polygamy was made illegal by an act of Congress, but it was not until 1890 that the Mormon Church officially banned polygamy, without actually renouncing it, in order to join the Union. The anti-polygamy clause was incorporated in the Utah Constitution as a condition for statehood. Writing in the *Salt Lake Tribune,* Maxine Hanks explains that polygamy is still active.

"Utah usually ignores polygamy, hoping it will go away. But its scope and problems have grown and 'festered like a cancer,' according to an ex-wife... Polygamy is a relic of 19th-century Mormon fundamentalism, still thriving. Today, there are a dozen major clans consisting of hundreds of families. And there are small independent groups. Often the clans are eccentric and insular, while other polygamists blend unnoticed into contemporary American society. Estimates vary wildly, but insiders claim that Mormon fundamentalism may involve 60,000 people scattered from Canada to Mexico across seven Western states. Most of them are practicing polygamy." Seeing the billboards in Salt Lake City promoting the book *More Than One: Plural Marriage – A Sacred Pioneer Heritage* is a millennium reminder that monogamy in Utah, like the rest of the country, is unsustainable even though mandated in the state's constitution.

The Mormon fathers practiced polygamy for religious reasons, but there were practical considerations as well. To build a New Jerusalem in a barren desert you need not only people, but also people who subscribe to your faith. A community that practices polygamy is able to produce more children faster than a conventional monogamist society. The Muslims and Mormons have proven that theory. This must have been a contributing factor.

The pro-polygamy lobby argues that at one time 80 percent of the world's population were polygamists. There are also claims that some early Christians were polygamists. The Emperor Constantine made Christianity the state religion of the Roman Empire in 313 A.D. The Romans were monogamists and the Christians believed in the doctrine of original sin. Linda Grant, like many other writers and philosophers, concludes: "'sin', an invention by the ruling class to suppress the poor."

This combination seems to have been fatal as far as polygamy was concerned. The Romans ruled most of Europe and the subject races of the Roman Empire fell into line. The Jews who had been scattered all over the known world by the Diaspora had to follow the marriage laws of their adopted countries in order to survive.

In the United States there is quietly emerging a subculture known as polygamous bourgeoisie. Politicians should actually support the lifestyle. It makes door-to-door campaigning easier. Each household in a polyfilial household will have numerous voters, up to hundreds rather than the usual two or three.

Polygamy remains a felony in Utah, but is no longer prosecuted, according to Eric Ludlow, the Washington County Attorney in Southern Utah where a number of "plural families" live. He says polygamists get round bigamy statutes by legally marrying only one wife; the others were recognized only by religious leaders or simply by the individuals themselves. "They go under the table, and we don't track it," Ludlow says. It's a consensual relationship between adults. Like all relationships should be!

Increasingly, these families find themselves entering the mainstream, and along with it the middle class. "Our parents had a harder time," says a Mr. Baker, a successful builder who works on construction jobs all over the state. "No one would hire them. Now people don't care about your personal life. They don't ask."

Utah Senator Orin Hatch and Governor Mike Leavitt are descendants of polygamists. Ironic that the Governor's brother David Leavitt prosecuted Tom Green for polygamy at the dawn of the 21st century after looking the other way in the 20th.

There are probably four or five times as many polygamists in America today as the U.S. had in the 1880s, the last heyday of polygamy. Sounds like Hong Kong.

Mary Potter, once one of a Utah policeman's three wives, has formed a group in support of plural marriages. "In polygamy," she says, "men are properly channelled" – and thoroughly, one would have thought.

The practice of having several wives is not unusual. Occasionally it gets brought to the forefront by a news splash on a prominent politician or celebrity. "Dylan had children by two secret wives, says 'lover'," blared a headline on folk rock legend Bob Dylan. The article discussed a newly released biography.

How about world boxing champion Evander Holyfield, whose wife gave birth to their first child in 1998, admitting he had fathered two other children within the past year with two ex-girlfriends? Holyfield himself is one of nine children born out of wedlock. The champion described Janice his wife as "my best friend" but added he regretted marrying her almost immediately.

How about Julius Erving, the Hall of Fame basketball player who had been one of his sport's greatest performers and sturdiest model of personal rectitude acknowledging he was the father of rising tennis star Alexandra Stevenson, whose white mother publicized racism on the tennis circuit? Erving was married when Stevenson was born. He said he had kept his wife informed all along, and that his four other children were aware that he had another daughter.

Sexual Mathematical Alternatives
By God! Even Einstein had an illegitimate child and multiple affairs!

David Buss, a professor of psychology at the University of Texas at Austin and one of the most outspoken of the evolutionary psychologists, says that asking a man not to lust after a pretty woman is like telling a carnivore not to like meat. Even President Jimmy Carter has admitted lusting after spare-rib.

How many nameless hard-working people who are not known and don't make the headlines engage in the practice in one shape or form? Stories periodically appear on the subject which leads me to believe the practice is greater than we want to acknowledge or believe. After all, that is part of our hypocritical managed misperception.

All one has to do, as Will Rogers did in preparation for his shows, is read the daily newspapers. *Mistresses ride Wall Street boom*, declared one headline.

It is often said in Hong Kong that any self-respecting Hong Kong tycoon has a mistress hidden away across the border, and it transpires Manhattan's money men feel the same way. In the wake of several high-profile mud fights involving executives and scorned mistresses, observers are speculating that every Wall Street boom brings with it a corresponding rise in the amount of sugar-daddy relationships with the best models money can buy. If anyone should know, it is celebrity divorce lawyer Raoul Felder, who says he sees a sharp rise in cases involving affairs that have turned sour after a bullish stock market turns bearish.

"I can tell how the economy is doing by how many mistresses come into my office looking for justice. I don't need no [Federal Reserve chairman Alan] Greenspan." No different than what happens to many mistresses Hong Kong men have in China. When the economy tanks, the mistresses get dumped.

During the Hong Kong handover ceremonies, Jake Berman and I were comparing the Hong Kong Chinese and Latino relationships between man and woman to those in America. Jake and I went to high school together and stayed friends over the years. Jake lived in the Philippines at the time but had worked and traveled extensively over the last 20 years to Latin America.

"I have a very simple philosophy," Jake started with deliberation in response to my question why the Catholic Latinos were so open about their promiscuity. "Neither man or woman are monogamous. We have all been conditioned and brainwashed. Left to our own devices, and given the choice to do so freely, we will all screw around. It's OK as long as no one is hurt in the process. Why not just live a sexually fulfilling life and let others do their thing, whatever it may be, even monogamy?

"That is one thing Latinos have really got down pat. The Spanish Catholic influence, the American Puritanical ethic have only made the Latinos integrate religion and ethics into their lifestyle and culture to allow them to honestly and openly live with several sexual partnerships or relationships simultaneously. We would all be better off in the States if we learned from the Chinese and Latinos who can manage it in such a religious society, Catholic church and all."

While showering after playing 18 holes at the Fanling Golf Course, Jake asked me: "Did you hear the one about the guy in the gym who after a workout was spending more time than usual priming himself with after shave lotions, perfumes, body creams? Well the guys in the locker room asked him: 'Hey what's up? You got a hot date with some new pussy tonight?' 'Yeah, in fact I do', he answered. 'My wife!'" I almost choked on the shampoo. I couldn't think of a more timely "spot-on" joke.

On the way home we passed a local wedding hall in Kowloon where a wedding party was preparing to make their entry into the ribbon-bedecked hall. Glacing over, Jake said: "Another mistake in the making. When are we going to learn?"

"I know what you mean. I married a mistake," I responded.

Men usually do get pussy-whipped into marriage. Even Larry Flynt! When he married his nurse, the reason he gave for getting married was: "I put her off for seven years. Marriage is more important to women than to men. I could have done without it, to tell you the truth."

Doubling Up

Jake and I have been playing backgammon since high school. It is the oldest known recorded game in man's history. It is widely believed that its origin was in Mesopotamia in the ancient Persian Empire. The Persians called the game "Takheh Nard" which is Persian for "Battle on Wood". When the Romans conquered Britain in the first century AD, they introduced the game referred to as "Tables". The first use of the word "Backgammon," or "back game", was noted in England. The word comes from the Middle English gamen, meaning game. In 1743 an Englishman standardized the rules of the game. It is a great way to relax and pass time whilst philosophizing about women.

"Going back to your philosophy about human relationships, do you think man and society can stay monogamous and somehow survive the inter-personal wars and acrimonious divorces we see so many people go through?" I asked as he pounded the table in frustration at the terrible numbers he had just rolled.

"No way, there is a lot to be said and learned from the intellectually honest sexual lifestyle of the Chinese and Filipinos. I wish it was like this everywhere, especially back home in the States," he replied.

I doubled him by turning the doubling cube. One can multiply up to 64 times during a game. He accepted the challenge. Human relationships, like backgammon, entail doubling up or more, depending on one's financial circumstance and relationships.

"Did you hear the one where the Arab says, 'I have four children. With one more I'll have a basketball team'?" I asked Jake. He hadn't.

"The American says, 'I have 10 children and with one more I'll have a football team'. The Filipino says, 'I have 17 wives and with one more I'll have a golf course'." Jake dropped his dice as he exploded into a howling laugh.

There is a doctor at Hong Kong University, Dr. Ng Man-lun. He is a member of the Asian Society of Sexologists and a leading expert on the love lives of Hong Kongers and China. His solution to problem marriages is? Polygamy!

It's a remedy Dr Ng Man-lun claims to have successfully prescribed to some of his patients as a cure for their marital ills. The psychiatrist and sexologist offered his framework for legal "multi-model marriage" as an alternative to conventional marriage. "The suggestion is simple: you can allow any combination of men and women to get married, so long as they all agree to it," Dr Ng said. Mistresses would become second wives, illegitimate children would be welcomed into families and jealousy would be rare, he said.

One couple – patients of the controversial psychiatrist – were discovering three is not necessarily a crowd, he said. An accident had left the husband impotent and frail, so he turned homemaker while his wife became the breadwinner. "The conflict, when they came to see me, was that the wife had another sex partner and the husband was very depressed," Dr Ng said. "She was giving money to the other man and she felt guilty. My advice to them ... was to accept the third partner. So, they are living together, although there are still a lot of social pressures." It was therefore only appropriate that the fourteenth World Congress of Sexology, the last one of the last millennium, was held in Hong Kong.

The World Association for Sexology's president, Professor Eli Coleman, said the theme of the Congress was "Sexology in the New Millennium".

"During the new century, we are sure to face enormous social and cultural changes throughout the world. We must anticipate these changes and find ways to promote sexual health in new and significant ways," she said.

If people are unable to fulfill their sexual desire when their significant other has no interest, is not in the mood, lacks passion, has post-natal depression, or when all else fails, a headache, they will remain sexually frustrated and angry. Maybe that is one of the reasons adult video sales are on the rise.

Adult Video News reports a 100 percent rise in American porn-video rentals and sales since 1992. That doesn't include Internet porn. At $4.2 billion, it's a business twice as large as Major League baseball, three times as large as Disney's theme park division, eight times as large as Broadway.

The Scots are the only people who have managed to balance their Christian morality, sexual hypocrisy and human nature. To this very day they honestly and publicly celebrate human frailties and infidelity in every community throughout the world. Their national poet Robert Burns is honored every year for a month or more starting on his birthday, January 25, with a series of Burns Suppers. His affairs, illegitimate children and understanding wife are honored with countless toasts.

Alternative Marriage Options
Sex drive, like hunger, is an appetite that has to be fed. If one's wife can't fulfill the role why force people to resort to adultery or, worse, divorce? As Alma Birk points out: "Except for a minority, sexual monogamy is a myth." The subject of monogamy has been debated for centuries. Plato, in the Republic, forbade marriage and advocated a community of wives.

Linda Grant articulates in a very blunt fashion: "The aristocracy was permitted erotic freedoms and retained the old idea of marriage as power brokering conducted to fulfill certain financial or dynastic needs; they were unions to which no one was bound sexually, an arrangement that neither Princess Diana nor the tabloid press seems to have fully understood in our own day." Diana's cuckolded husband and the entire royal Windsor establishment knew and approved of her affair with James Hewitt.

Monogamous marriage became the norm in the West when certain religious beliefs about the importance of worshipping one God were transferred to the marital relationship. Chivalry required lovers to treat each other like gods. Traditional marriage vows reflect this by compelling spouses to "worship" each other, blatantly ignoring the spirit of Jesus' admonition to avoid calling people master. "The jewel in the crown of marriage vows is the pledge of lifelong fidelity," says Stephen Palmquist, an associate professor in the department of religion and philosophy at Baptist University in Hong Kong. "But faithfulness and exclusivity are separate. In societies where polygamy was the norm – as in the Old Testament – the pledge of fidelity did not imply monogamy. Nor did Jesus acquiesce when religious leaders tried to trap him into deifying monogamy," Palmquist points out.

Marriage is an evolving social institution. That monogamy is now virtually identified with "right" marriage does not rule out the possibility of improvement. What if a woman would rather live in harmony with her husband's second wife than be divorced? When the women's movement has reached full maturity, such a choice will be legal. Statistics on marriage and divorce prove anti-bigamy laws cannot change human nature. Solving the real problem they address – the fundamental difference in the way men and women tend to experience love and life – is not so easy. "Instead of solving the problem, such laws merely replace polygamy with serial monogamy," Palmquist reminds us.

Eighteenth century German philosopher Immanuel Kant proposed a useful principle for designing fair laws: "Any action is right if it can co-exist with everyone's freedom in accordance with a universal law." In other words, what's good for the goose is good for the gander.

One way of revising marriage laws to bring them into closer conformity with Kant's principle would be to legalize multiple marriages for both sexes: allow men to have multiple wives and women to have multiple husbands. To prevent oppression, one's current spouse(s) must agree with any new marriage. Palmquist correctly points out that "although this option maximizes both freedom and equality, many believe its complexities would create social chaos. Maybe so, but the question remains: which form of chaos is less harmful to the people involved – the freedom to love responsibly through multiple marriage, or the restriction of marriage in a way that promotes divorce and broken homes?" Alternative honest solutions to the sorry state of affairs facing the institution of marriage, and the resulting havoc it creates, merit society considering all alternative options.

The institution of marriage was created for our physical survival and evolution. On the farms and frontiers and in cities and villages. Not necessarily as equals. For shelter, food, and defense. Primarily for external reasons. Physical survival. Today our mental and spiritual survival is just as important. Some will argue more so. It is equally important to both parties. Spiritual growth in the New World Order brings people together on a level that was not a factor or consideration in the traditional physical marriage. People get together today to form a spiritual partnership.

Gary Zukav concludes: "Spiritual partners are able to see clearly that there is indeed a deeper reason why they are together and that that reason has a great deal to do with the evolution of their souls...The bond between spiritual partners exists as real as it does in marriage, but for significantly different reasons. Spiritual partners are not together in order to quell each other's financial fears or because they can produce a house in the suburbs and that entire conceptual framework...The commitment of spiritual partners is to each other's spiritual growth, recognizing that that is what each of them is doing on Earth, and that everything serves that." They are soul mates growing together in this life. Evolving to the max no matter how long it takes. Weeks, months, years or forever. Marriage vows cannot deter our spiritual growth. They were only relevant for our physical growth. Concubines, mistresses, girlfriends and prostitutes do not only satisfy physical needs. They fulfill spiritual demands.

Hillary Clinton was subjected to criticism by Republican conservatives during her New York Senate race for staying married while touting the institution of marriage at the same time. If a spouse errs, a perfectly intelligent wife like Hillary might say: "Why should I stop growing spiritually"? Why should the whole family, including the children? Is America better off having women who are upset by their estranged husbands starting forest fires that threaten our cities, like the Colorado fire of 2002 did to Denver? How many more Americans have to suffer, burn and lose because of current matrimonial laws? Are such fiery tragedies really necessary to perpetuate in the 21st century?

Non-polygamous Judeo-Christian Americans in North America, Europe and Asia who constantly bemoan the rapid growth of Muslims in their country can maintain and increase their own numerical superiority in the 21st century by also practicing polygamy and having multiple families like their Muslim and Mormon neighbors. All it takes is a change in the law. There is only one way to outgrow and outpace the rapid multipliers among us. "Go forth and multiply." It is after all a numbers game. How else do *We the Apathetic People* decrease our apathy while we grow in number? *We the Maids* have to sweep in changes that make multiplication a lot easier and as enjoyable as a backgammon game.

Americans should give polygamy and polyandry another closer evaluation and accept them as a viable solution if that's what it takes to make married life more pleasurable in the New World Order. After all, wouldn't society be better off if every time one got into a disagreement with one's significant other they could openly find shelter and refuge in the arms of another loving mate? One can be with the right person to suit one's particular mood and needs. Isn't that more pleasant than being with someone you really don't want to be with until death intervenes? Parents can focus on spending quality time with their children even if they no longer are passionate about each other or even find each other physically attractive any more. They can remain good friends – and good parents raising their children. Sexual desires can be fulfilled by other willing partners, thereby eliminating the need to fight or divorce. As the Eagles say in the song that launched their career, *Take It Easy*, it sure feels better than when you shake it easy.

That's what many Japanese do. *Sekusuresu* (sexless) marriages are a common phenomenon in Japan, according to Dr Teruo Abe, a Japanese psychiatrist, and Tomomi Fujiwara, an award-winning writer. A third of the houses built for young couples have separate bedrooms. One of the main reasons is that wives don't want to be touched by the husband. As a result, Japan's population in the last five years of the 20th century grew at its lowest rate since the end of World War II. A nation entering the 21st century with a predominantly elderly population that it is ill-equipped to support. Do we want this to happen to America?

We the Maids should be more receptive in the new millennium to re-introducing P.P. – Poly Proven family structures to those communities wanting alternative family lifestyles. Incest should not be tolerated in any family, monogamous or polygamous. Those that can stay in a happy monogamous relationship until death do them part should be encouraged to do so. By the same token, those wanting multi-mate relationships should also be allowed to lovingly pursue them.

Shouldn't all American communities in the New World Order benefit from harmonious families, including those dominated by women? Sex can never be immoral. Denying people their right of individual choice is. How else can *We the People* avoid unnecessary conflicts and become a mature, responsible, harmonious and united community in the 21st century?

Chapter Six

Managed Misperception -
Spun Out of Control

What succeeds is correct, what fails is false -
Mao Tze-dong

Body Beautiful

Taking a shower with the boys was something I looked forward to when I was going to the American Academy in the late 1950s. The Academy was a junior high school in Larnaca, Cyprus. The boys were Greek, Turkish, Armenians, Arabs and miscellaneous mutts like me. I transferred to the American Academy after the British Army Childrens' School was shut down after Cyprus gained its independence from Britain.

The showers were weekly excursions to the local bathhouse. "Shower time! Let's go and soak in hot water," I would yell to my roommate Boris Basmajian. Like me, Boris lived in Famagusta. His parents owned a hotel there. Unlike some of our fellow boarders who came from small villages where a weekly shower was a luxury, we were spoiled. Daily showers were something we missed. So who cared if they were communal? The same held true when I transferred to an agricultural high school in Israel in 1960.

The two shower stalls at the old FCC health club were, like the gym, co-educational. It was not unusual to occasionally hear a female member scream when a male member pulled aside the shower curtain to use the shower not realizing that it was in use by a member of the opposite sex. What goes on in the sauna and steam room is another matter.

Showers are something Hong Kongers look forward to especially on a hot humid day after a workout in the gym. Or just a walk down the street.

"Listen to this," I said to Stuart Wolfendale, a long time columnist in Hong Kong as we shared wine, conversation and the day's newspapers at the FCC's Main Bar. "Can you believe what has happened to kids' modesty?" I added after I read out loud the headline and handed him the article.

"Standing around together naked?" Andre Hennig, an 18-year-old senior at McHenry High School in the northwest suburbs of Chicago was quoted as saying. "Oh no, man – people would feel really uncomfortable about that."

Modesty among young people in America today seems in some ways out of step in a culture that sells and celebrates the uncovered body in advertisements, on television and in movies. But some health and physical education experts contend that many students withdraw precisely because of the overload of erotic images – so many perfectly toned bodies cannot help but leave ordinary mortals feeling a bit inadequate. It doesn't matter whether you are hung like a horse or have the usual "wiener". Nerves and the terrible chill of communal showers shrink everything to a mushroom in a bed of seaweed.

"Gay men looking at the buns and pecks perfections of West Hollywood call it body fascism," Stuart retorted after handing the paper back to me in disgust.

Any wonder American children today are confused by the myths conveyed by adults and their spin-doctors trying to create and over-manage perception?

Fast Lane
America's fast food and fast lane culture has evolved to mean instant everything thanks to spin-doctors. Instant gratification. Instant sex. Instant service. Instant communications. Instant food. Instant news. Instant war. Instant patriotism. Instant victories. Instant relief. Instant cure. The cure is up to *We the Maids* to sweep in. Erik Gordon, director of MBA programs at the University of Florida's Warrington College of Business, said it is not that Americans lack

time. "It's because we think we lack time and because we are conditioned to instant everything. Televisions used to have tubes and take time to warm up. Telephones used to have slower rotary dials. Then they got touch pads. Then they got auto-dialers. Web pages used to be a miracle in themselves. Now, if it takes 10 seconds to load, we abandon them."

Some marketing experts are blaming the Internet for America's rapidly growing impatience. "Expectations from our online experience spill over into the real world and we just don't have patience," said Anne Brumbaugh, assistant professor of marketing at Wake Forest University's Babcock Graduate School of Management. The demand for undemanding goods has even some marketers who sell convenience products a little concerned. "We've heard kids say they find it inconvenient to eat an apple or peel an orange," said Steve Luttmann, director of beverage brand development for Lipton Tea. "The convenience trend is starting to become a little absurd. People are looking for instant gratification." Americans "can't abide slowness," said David Shi, president of Furman University in Greenville, South Carolina, and a cultural historian.

Perception
Nothing is quite what it seems in politics, religion and marketing. Everything has a spin: a twist, a turn, a subversive angle. Most of what we read and see is pure popular fiction. Spin-doctors create the misperceptions the media fuel for public consumption. They become the burning fluid that burns and sears in the public mind the misperceptions that spin-doctors want us to believe.

My favorite example is the speech President George W. Bush made in 2003 standing against what appeared to be a backdrop of cardboard boxes stamped "MADE IN USA." The boxes in the Saint Louis, Missouri, warehouse were painted on a large screen behind the president. The real boxes in the warehouse were stamped "MADE IN CHINA" and had white labels pasted over them.

The September 11 World Trade Center deaths are another good example. The total started at 6,700 and then dropped to 2,940 out of public view. World leaders, U.S. diplomats, military leaders, newspaper columnists and radio talk show hosts continued to believe and assert that anywhere from 5,000 to 6,000 people died even though such numbers are wrong and the real much lower number was known. They included General Richard Myers, Chairman of the Joint Chiefs of Staff, Secretary of State Colin Powell and Don Imus. When questioned about the real number, a State Department official in Washington said that he was unaware that the number of people dead or missing in the Trade Center attack had decreased so markedly. "It is not to obfuscate or create any more sympathy, because, regardless of whether or not it is 3,900 or 5,000, the magnitude and severity of the events on September 11 are clear," said the official, who asked not to be identified. Now really?

Over history, early estimates of death tolls in cataclysmic events have had a way of taking stubborn hold. Spin-doctors know this and maximize the high spin to build up the public support to justify why America has gone to war.

In historical terms, it means September 11 can no longer be called the deadliest day in American history. That was September 17, 1862, when at least 3,650 Confederate and Union soldiers died at the battle of Antietam, and thousands were wounded.

The flip side of the coin is the myth of martyrdom created by religious fundamentalist spinners, which, like the myth of heaven and hell, has to be unspun. The best spin is the truth! Truth is reality. Reality can be heaven or hell. That is up to *We the Maids*. We can sweep hell away and sweep in a heavenly paradise here on earth now! All we have to do is keep in mind one of my favorite political jokes of the 2004 election that made the round at the FCC one too many times.

While walking down the street one day, George "Dubya" Bush is shot dead by a disgruntled NRA member. His soul arrives in heaven and he is met by St. Peter at the Pearly Gates. "Welcome to Heaven," says St. Peter. "Before you settle in, it seems there is a problem: We seldom see a Republican around these parts, so we're not sure what to do with you." "No problem, just let me in; I'm a believer." Says Dubya.

"I'd like to just let you in, but I have my orders from the Man Himself: He says you have to spend one day in Hell and one day in Heaven. Then you must choose where you'll live for eternity." "But I've already made up my mind; I want to be in Heaven." "I'm sorry, but we have our rules." And with that, St. Peter escorts him to an elevator and he goes down, down, down, all the way to Hell. The doors open and he finds himself in the middle of a lush golf course, the sun is shining in a cloudless sky, the temperature a perfect 72 degrees.

In the distance is a beautiful clubhouse. Standing in front of it is his dad...and thousands of other Republicans who had helped him out over the years...Karl Rove, Dick Cheney, Jerry Falwell... The whole of the "Right" was there...everyone laughing...happy... casually but expensively dressed. They run to greet him, hug him, and reminisce about the good times they had getting rich at the expense of the "suckers and *We the Maids*". They play a friendly game of golf and then dine on lobster and caviar. The Devil himself comes up to Bush with a frosty drink, "Have a margarita and relax, Dubya!" "Uh, I can't drink no more, I took a pledge," says junior dejectedly.

"This is Hell, son: you can drink and eat all you want and not worry, and it just gets better from there! Dubya takes the drink and finds himself liking the Devil, who he thinks is a really very friendly guy who tells funny jokes and pulls hilarious nasty pranks, kind of like a Yale Skull and Bones brother with real horns. They are having such a great time that, before he realizes it, it's time to go. Everyone gives him a big hug and waves as Bush steps on the elevator and heads upward. When the elevator door reopens, he is in Heaven again and St. Peter is waiting for him. "Now it's time to visit Heaven," the old man says, opening the gate.

So for 24 hours Bush is made to hang out with a bunch of honest, good-natured people who enjoy each other's company, talk about things other than money, and treat each other decently. Not a nasty prank or frat boy joke among them; no fancy country clubs and, while the food tastes great, it's not caviar or lobster. And these people are all poor, he doesn't see anybody he knows, and he isn't even treated like someone special!

Worst of all, to Dubya, Jesus turns out to be some kind of Jewish hippie with his endless "peace" and "do unto others" jive.

"Whoa," he says uncomfortably to himself, "Pat Robertson never prepared me for this!" The day done, St. Peter returns and says, "Well, then, you've spent a day in Hell and a day in Heaven. Now choose where you want to live for eternity."

With the "Jeopardy" theme playing softly in the background, Dubya reflects for a minute, then answers: "Well, I would never have thought I'd say this – I mean, Heaven has been delightful and all – but I really I belong in Hell with my friends."

So St. Peter escorts him to the elevator and he goes down, down, down, all the way to Hell. The doors of the elevator open and he is in the middle of a barren scorched earth covered with garbage and toxic industrial waste...kind of like Houston. He is horrified to see all his friends, dressed in rags and chained together, picking up trash and putting it in black bags. They are groaning and moaning in pain, faces and hands black with grime. The Devil comes over to Dubya and puts an arm around his shoulder.

"I don't understand," stammers a shocked Dubya, "Yesterday I was here and there was a golf course and a clubhouse and we ate lobster and caviar...I drank booze. We screwed around and had a great time. Now there's just a wasteland full of garbage and everybody looks miserable!"

The Devil looks at him, smiles slyly, and purrs, "Yesterday we were campaigning; today you voted for us."

Dramatic early political campaign-minded terrorist claims following highly publicized arrests in the wake of the September 11 attacks were quietly downplayed when the arrested suspects were found to be innocent and released. The injured and maimed American servicemen from Iraq are flown back to U.S. hospitals at night, usually after midnight to avoid the press and minimize the collateral negative spin of the Iraq war. More "collateral damage" being downplayed by spin-doctors. "Collateral damage" being the military term to play down the killing and maiming of innocent civilians in a military attack.

Airplane safety and security was another myth spun by airline spin-doctors until it was blasted home for what it really is on September 11. Spin-doctors had Americans believing and feeling safe from terrorism in America, even though acts of terrorism had been going on for years in America. Against abortion clinics, the federal government, technology and even the World Trade Center in 1993.

The perception that the drink Red Bull had more kick than coffee is another 21st century example of spin-doctors and marketers convincingly planting a false perception. In fact, with 80 milligrams of caffeine per can, it does not even have the caffeinated punch of a small Starbucks coffee, which has about 200 milligrams. Much like the Corona spin the previous century. Add a slice of lime in a clear bottle of beer and its cool even though every beer connoisseur knows that dark bottles better preserve the taste of beer.

It's not just the young public that is influenced by spin-doctors. Even adults and professionals perpetuate myths thanks to spin-doctors. Doctors, for example, perpetuate the myth that drinking and antibiotics don't mix because of their conditioning by pharmaceutical spin-doctors. The fact is this instruction was first given to sailors who had contracted a venereal disease and were taking antibiotics to cure it. They were told not to drink because doctors were concerned they would get drunk and then again seek out a prostitute and pass on the disease before they were cured. Not because antibiotics and alcohol don't mix. They do and can, unless one is going to get behind a wheel.

Perception is created by spin-doctors, pollsters, advertising agencies and marketers. Even the "New Millennium" was recreated and marketed by spin doctors as starting in the year 2000 because commercial establishments and their corporate parents needed to maximize profits a.s.a.p. They couldn't wait a year. Especially if the economy was going into a recession and consumers would cut back spending. Think about it. Since when do new millennia, or centuries for that matter, start in a year ending with zero? Logically, astrologically and honestly they start with the year one. Yet why did "Americans" celebrate it on New Year's Eve 1999? Consumerism and spin-doctors, that's why.

Images relayed on TV screens and in newspapers create a perception that is far greater than reality. The spin-doctoring surrounding the alleged legitimacy of the presidential claims and lawsuits on the validity of the ballots cast in Florida and their recount is a glaring example. The Republican spin-doctors conveyed a far more effective image of Gore as a loser than the Democrats did of Gore as the winner. Their placards and protestors conveyed and shaped the public's opinion that Gore is a "Sore Loserman", "Commander in Thief" and "Chad Molester". Bush conducted this campaign even though the Texas statute says a ballot should be counted where "an indentation on the chad from the stylus or other object is present and indicates a clearly ascertainable intent of the voter to vote." A 1997 amendment signed by Governor Bush favors manual counts. In Florida that could have cost him the election.

Spin-doctors are masters of the sound bite that convince us of the message they want us to believe and perceive. They are smooth and can talk at length without actually saying anything but "the message" they want you to repeatedly hear and believe.

As the reality behind a message is exposed and disseminated, people will no longer passively accept what is being disseminated. Especially by career politicians and their spin-doctors. People will seriously begin to question the purveyors of managed perception. As modern communication "highways" become accessible to the masses, facts that question images will continue to undermine misinformation and be shared faster by the community at large.

What happened to the tobacco industry is a good example. The Marlboro man is no longer glamorous. He had emphysema. Now he is dead. Tobacco companies are admitting they knew cigarettes caused cancer and withheld the information from the public. They are paying for their deliberate deceit. Hundreds of billions of dollars are settling lawsuits brought on by the victims who bought their deadly managed message. So what does Philip Morris do now? It argues that smoking is good for a government's budget because smoking caused people to die prematurely, thereby saving the government pension and health care costs!

Energy companies are also paying for their deceit. Others will, as they should, follow.

But not innocent companies like the makers of silicone breast implants. A panel of four scientists appointed by a Federal court reported that there was no evidence the implants caused disease. The lawyers and their spin-doctors had done a good job manipulating the legal system and the public.

When Kim Jong-il of North Korea launched a rocket and threatened to develop more nuclear weapons he was portrayed as a reclusive, nutty, high-heeled, pudgy, permed, playboy boozer. Lover of ladies and cognac, night and day. Once he met with the President of South Korea and reconciliation became a reality, he became a computer-literate statesman. "He appeared different from the way he was described before – jovial, forthcoming, interested, knowledgeable," Ms. Albright said. What a transformation. The Xiao Bu Shi "Little Bush" administration was not about to give in to North Korean "blackmail" and so the negative spinners of misperception were welcomed back again.

Israel is repeatedly accused of being a warring, aggressive, occupying nation. Never mind that peace (shalom in Hebrew) is the most common word in Jewish prayers. That it is endlessly repeated in synagogues, when greeting or taking leave, when getting up or going to bed. Never mind that shalom is mentioned 77 times in the Torah, and 275 times in The Old Testament. Never mind that of all the world's literature the United Nations chose to inscribe the words of Israeli Prophet Isaiah on the wall across from its building in New York. Here are these words: "And they shall beat their swords into plowshares, and their spears into pruning hooks: nation shall not lift up sword against nation, neither shall they learn war any more." Israel has always believed since early biblical days that peace is better than war. Yet Israel is still spun as a warring nation.

When Chinese students protest America's bombing of their Embassy in Yugoslavia the TV coverage covered only the trashing of the U.S. Embassy in Beijing and the burning of the American Consul's home in Chengdu. While U.S. Ambassador James Sasser was under siege in his Beijing embassy, the U.S. Consul General in Shanghai, Ray Burghardt, was out playing golf with businessmen. The TV mass coverage didn't bring this to the American public's attention. It is perhaps a back-handed compliment to the U.S. that the Chinese government still cannot believe the Americans can have been so incompetent as to bomb by mistake.

Hungry, Oppressed Terrorists?

A totemic example of state-managed hate is Osama bin-Laden. When he was in Afghanistan, being trained by the CIA to fight the Russians alongside Afghan rebels and other volunteers in the 1980s, he was portrayed as a "Freedom Fighter". Once he took on America he became a terrorist. So staged and timely were the U.S. Government's revelations about him after the embassy bombings that in much part they were suspect. Foreign governments demanded more proof. Even after September 11 and the bombing of the USS Cole, the evidence was weak and suspect until after documentary and other evidence and videos were found in Afghanistan to support and strengthen the spin.

Osama, as everyone knows, is anything but hungry and oppressed. He comes from wealth and is well-educated and well-fed. The same holds true for Mohammed Atta who led the kamikazes on September 11, and British national Ahmed Omar Saeed Sheikh who masterminded the capture and decapitation of Daniel Pearl.

A report completed in 2002 by the highly respected independent and non-profit National Bureau of Economic Research based in Cambridge, Massachusetts, concluded there is no link between terrorism and poverty. "Any connection between poverty, education and terrorism is indirect and probably weak."

Terrorism has little or no base in social circumstance based on an analysis of the background of Hezbollah and Palestinian militants. Researchers examined the jobs, educational level and family circumstances of 129 Hezbollah militants killed in operations against Israel over a 20-year period. Compared with the Lebanese population as a whole, Hezbollah personnel were less likely to come from poor families and were more likely to have completed secondary education. A similar pattern holds for Palestinian suicide bombers. The authors found a positive link between taking part in "terrorism" and educational attainment. No correlation was found between participation in violence and economic depression; instead violence seems to have increased when local economic conditions were getting better. So much for the political spin that it is the oppressed in refugee camps that become terrorists.

Terrorists Unite

The American people were led to believe they were safe and secure at home because the U.S. intelligence services could thwart any terrorist attack on American soil. They were led to believe suicide bombers exist only in the Middle East and Africa. While basking in a false sense of security, Americans watched their favorite general, Secretary of State Colin Powell, be portrayed as the invisible Secretary of State, while Dick Cheney was a very visible Vice President, and Donald Rumsfeld, the Secretary of Defense, was parodied as a later-day Dr. Strangelove for his hawkish, America-first views. That all got re-spun overnight after September 11. Fear and anxiety became synonymous with failed intelligence apparatus, Dick Cheney disappeared after the President re-appeared from his bunker, Colin Powell became very visible and Rumsfeld became a professorial spokesman. A country united in fear overnight behind a President that delayed his return to Washington because of a "credible threats" spin of attacks on the White House and Air Force One! Transformed and spun united to lead the global war on terrorism.

Polls Spin Politics

Terrorism never made the top 10 list of issues that concern Americans, according to the various polls conducted in 2000 to determine what issues politicians should address in 2001. Consequently, it never became a high priority for the career politicians who determine their political life, agenda and leadership by polls.

So what happens when career politicians are caught unprepared by a catastrophic event that their pollsters failed to register? They shut America down and regroup! America greeted the 21st century with a "closed" sign. A country hit by shock and disbelief just closed down. There was no poll showing what to do when terrorists strike

While Americans were asked to return to normalcy, work and school in defiance of the terrorist acts of September 11, all 435 members of Congress shut down the Capitol and went home out of fear of terrorism! Is this the type of inspirational leaders *We the Apathetic People* want to keep in Washington? Isn't it time *We the Maids* sweep out the career politicians who paralyzed our seat of government while urging us to go about our daily activities without panic or concern?

While career politicians were studying their polls, ignoring reports warning of terrorist attacks, terrorists on watch lists were openly slipping across America's open borders, not even bothering to disguise their identities. Those caught with forged or false passports were merely turned over to the Canadian authorities, who released them. That was the politically correct thing to do, according to the polls. Spin-doctors have spun a cocoon of patriotism around the failure of their career politicians to foresee an act of terrorism on American soil because they were misled by the polls. Anyone questioning their failures, censorship and unconstitutional behavior is unpatriotic and subjected to severe criticism because the polls also show the President has the overwhelming support of the American people. Polls have a way of coming full circle to support everything career politicians do. Especially when they are properly marketed.

The Republicans were quick to seize upon their 2002 midterm election victory and market it as justification and support for their policies. The fact that most pollsters were grossly and grievously off the mark in their projections of the outcome of the election was conveniently overlooked.

Marketing
The *souks,* bazaars and markets where I've spent endless hours in Cyprus, Israel, Greece, Turkey, China, the Philippines, Vietnam, Mongolia and still today in Hong Kong are reminders of how marketing developed locally, along the Silk Road, across the Mediterranean, and the Atlantic and Pacific, and now globally. People touch, feel and talk about goods, ideas, politics, history and religion. People interact. Just as Americans do today on the world wide web. The new local and global market where people can chat.

Globalized trade routes from Phoenicia, the Silk Road to local flea markets involve the exchange of goods and services between people for their mutual benefit and improvement.

Marketing used to be simple. It was conducted person to person. Except we then all got too busy and isolated so we came to depend on the marketers and their subtle hawkers. Celebrities endorsing and touting products without disclosing their financial interest or hefty fees leading the gullible public to believe they really believe in what they are marketing. Things have changed again with the web. People are again in direct contact with each other. Except today polls, focus groups and spin-doctors have spun themselves a multi-billion annual business.

Doc Searls and David Weinberger remind us about the awful truth about the managed misperception marketing has become in *The Cluetrain Manifesto*. "It broadcasts messages to people who don't want to listen. Every advertisement, press release, publicity shot, and giveaway engineered by a marketing department is colored by the fact that it's going to a public that doesn't ask to hear it." That hasn't changed the reality of consumerism created by spin-doctors.

Consumerism

Consumerism is now a self-defining activity. Consumerism represents an important symbol of success. Consumer confidence has become a measure of how sure a society is about itself and its prospects. "Take away the average American's credit cards and you take away a good deal of his sense of power and freedom, or even his sense of who he is," Jean Nicol, a Hong Kong-based psychologist, observes. "This may partly explain why, despite appearances, most Hong Kong people in surveys reject consumerism as an end in itself, while Westerners act as if they see it as a way to be happy and to express themselves. How they spend their money gives them a sense of fulfillment. In contrast, Hong Kong people say they regard shopping, eating out, going to the cinema and so on as a reward for hard work and as a tool for building or maintaining family ties and social relationships," Nicol concludes.

Christmas sales in the closing year of the millennium in America exceeded the $51 billion mark, with each household spending an estimated $490 on gifts. Christmas shopping and gift days such as Mother's Day, Father's Day, Easter are out-of-control commercial consumer creations that have been marketed as spiritually and family friendly. However, the way one shows one's spirituality to family and friends is by spending money on gifts. What about Christmas cards and holiday political or commercial mass mailings disguised as holiday greetings? Politicians and business people sending family pictures with seasoned greetings? Several thousand at a time to their "Dearest Friends?" At taxpayer expense!

The 20th century was "An All-Consuming Century". The fan, iron and kettle were electrified in the 1890s. Waffle irons, toasters and hot plates, vacuum cleaners, washing machines, ice boxes, cars, airplanes, telephones and radios were all developed in the first half of the last century and necessitated a proliferation of spin-doctors to convince us that we needed them all. Naturally, we needed the right size home to fit them all in. A suburban ranch house. Our whole existence has been built on the basis of over-consumption. Whether we need it or not, we have to have the latest toy and the energy and utilities that allow us to play and enjoy the toy.

Career politicians cater to consumers by trying to keep the cost of basic utilities as low as possible so that people stay at home and enjoy their toys. The fact that it may be at the expense of the rest of the world and our planet is secondary and unimportant. The depletion of the ozone layer is not as important as keeping American consumers consuming. Is this how *We the Apathetic People* want to be?

Even the tragic events of 9/11 have been commercialized. Most companies tread lightly, others are more blatant. Many claim to be part of the healing process. The Bush 2004 re-election ads included.

Most Hong Kong people wear cheap plastic or "copy watches". Most Hong Kongers don't buy or wear name brands. That is not how they judge each other. They do however compare how they are doing to other people in other places. Even the lowliest Hong Kong worker takes as much pride as the big fish with name brand items, if not more, in knowing they are swimming in a big pond. Shouldn't small fry in America as well?

Americans have to change from consumers to citizens. Become as active in the political process as they are in shopping. The pursuit of happiness is not fulfilled with consumerism. Political activism is far more satisfying. Cathartic in a constructive, cost-effective way. Short term and for the future of our children. What good are the latest gadgets our children want in a politically apathetic or repressive society? If the American consumer impulse can be transformed to a political impulse, America will regain its standing as the ideal for the 21st century. Otherwise Americans will become the perpetual slaves of a consumer culture that is repeatedly spun and sold to us as utopia. A successful consumer society can be assembled only by the breaking down of a civil one and of previous communal cultures of every sort. The election of America's 43rd President by the Supremes was just the latest example.

For the corporate world to create a consumer planet they will need the resources of several planets. Mars and the Moon are a good start. By becoming cautious, conservative, prudent consumers, we not only preserve our precious resources but also make time to become active citizens. Why can't *We the Apathetic People* binge on political activity? Why do we binge only on consumerism? If We just all went on a weekend political binge the career political aisles would empty out the way supermarket aisles and department store racks empty out after a weekend super sale.

Let's Roll 9/11 Spin

The term 9/11 has spun itself into our vocabulary because of the endless horrific pictures and events the day commemorates. It has a special meaning to everyone. The now-famous photo of President Bush's eyes popping as an aide whispers the events of September 11 into his ear seemed to represent complete surprise. However, now with all the intelligence briefings he received warning of a possible terrorist attack that picture can represent horrified confirmation. A 1999 National Intelligence Council report to the CIA predicted bin-Laden would retaliate "in a spectacular way" for the cruise missile attacks in 1998 against his al-Qaeda training camps in Afghanistan. "Suicide bombers belonging to al-Qaeda's martyrdom battalion could crash-land an aircraft...into the Pentagon, the headquarters of the CIA, or the White House," the report said. Its on-target prediction prompted new questions over how much the Government knew about potential threats, especially after the August 2001 CIA briefing Bush received on the possibility of a hijacking by al-Qaeda.

Disinformation is an old spin technique. Since 9/11 it has been used extensively. There are many examples. My favorite is the attempt to first tie Mohammad Atta to Saddam Hussein as a result of his meeting in Prague in April 2001 with Saddam's intelligence officer and then deny the meeting ever took place. Why? Did it?

Falsehoods

Everybody lies. Birds, bees, priests, lawyers, judges, career politicians and everyday ordinary people. Surprised? Don't be. Jeremy Campbell's *The Liar's Tale: A History of Falsehood* shows us that "for better or worse, lying and untruths, are not an artificial, deviant or dispensable feature of life." Falsehood is indispensable for human evolution, for we could not survive only "on a diet as thin and meager as the truth".

Darwin discovered deception and cunning in the natural world. Greek philosophers of mythology, religious prophets of old and modern-day politicians all lied. President Bill Clinton just reminded us of this human frailty. Spin-doctors perfect lies and make them sound like the truth.

President Eisenhower's State Department lied in 1960 about the Gary Powers U2 spy missions over Russia. It denied Powers was shot down deep inside Soviet territory and that there had been any deliberate attempt to violate Soviet air space. Eisenhower had to reluctantly come clean when the Russians paraded Powers in front of the media. America was shocked! President John Kennedy lied in 1961 about the CIA-backed invasion of Cuba to overthrow Castro. The Bay of Pigs fiasco again shocked America when Arthur Sylvester, Kennedy's Assistant Secretary of Defense for Public Affairs, defended the government's "right, if necessary, to lie". President Lyndon Johnson made lying a political masterpiece. The joke around Washington during the LBJ years had someone asking: "How can you tell when Lyndon is lying?" The answer: "When his lips move." Congress passed the Gulf of Tonkin resolution, authorizing Johnson to use force in Vietnam, because Johnson assured Congress and the American people that U.S. destroyers had been attacked by North Vietnamese torpedo boats. It was a lie.

Richard Nixon lied about Watergate. Ronald Reagan lied about the Iran-Contra affair and pending invasion of Grenada. Bill Clinton lied about Monica and George Dubya lied about weapons of mass destruction and his Thanksgiving trip to Baghdad. In trying to play up the secrecy and dangerous nature of the trip, Bush's aides said that a British Airways pilot spotted the president's plane, radioing, "Did I just see Air Force One?" The White House said Air Force One responded: "Gulfstream 5" – a code word to disguise the plane – and the British Airways pilot "seemed to sense he was in on a secret and replied 'Oh'."

It turned out the story was a complete fabrication, designed only to hype the story. According to Reuters, "British Airways said yesterday that none of its pilots made contact with President Bush's plane during its secret flight to Baghdad on Thanksgiving, contradicting White House reports of a midair exchange that nearly prompted Bush to call off his trip."

Cyberspace spreads lies so quickly that many are believed to be the truth because so many people have circulated the same lie so many times. Nostradamus' prediction of the September 11 bombings, the photograph of a man about to perish on top of the World Trade Center as the plane was approaching, and the Jewish plot to bomb the World Trade Center because 4,000 Jews who work there took the day off because they were tipped off, all created a global Internet craze and false information frenzy that had many believing any one or all of these falsehoods. Many in the media compounded the falsehoods by reporting them as fact.

A good 21st century example is the many accounts in British and U.S. news media in 2001 that spoke of the 15,000 child slaves on Ivory Coast's cocoa plantations, producing the chocolate we eat. The number first appeared in newspapers in Mali citing the Unicef office there. But the Mali office had never researched the issue of forced child laborers in Ivory Coast. The Unicef office in Ivory Coast, which had, concluded that it was impossible to determine the number.

Still, repeated often enough, the number was gladly accepted by some private organizations, opponents of globalization seeking a fight with Nestle and Hershey. Some reports cited the State Department's annual human rights report on Ivory Coast as the source of the 15,000 figure. In fact, the State Department report for 2000 said that according to a Unicef study, "approximately 15,000 Malian children were trafficked and sold into indentured servitude on Ivorian plantations in 1999". The report for 2001 said that "the number is difficult to estimate" because no "thorough survey has been conducted".

My personal favorite is the false report allegedly put out by the World Health Organization in 2002 that blondes are an endangered species that will become extinct in 200 years because of a recessive gene. The story was picked up by numerous mainstream publications and reported as fact until the WHO denied ever putting out such a report.

The play *Wicked* about those two powerful forces in the land of Oz, Glinda the Good Witch and the Wicked Witch of the West, is an ideal portrayal of how a nice, beautiful, self-absorbed popular blonde became the Good Witch and her nameless nemesis, an intelligent, passionate, misunderstood girl with emerald-green skin got the moniker Wicked Witch through political manipulation and corruption. It is all about false reporting courtesy of the spin-doctors and their faceless fixers – lawyers and lobbyists.

False reporting is nothing new in America. The tale of George Armstrong Custer and his heroic fight on top of Last Stand Hill on 25 June, 1876, is an early example. The site has become a holy shrine, marked by the headstones of the fallen at Custer Battlefield National Monument. The fact is Custer was a scion of American nobility with a handsome face and a somewhat sarcastic aura. Cadet Custer graduated at the bottom of his West Point class. He was reckless and brave to the point of foolhardiness, a flashy image-seeker with total disregard and disrespect for his men or their lives.

Erik Durschmied in his well researched *The Hinges of Battle* wrote a brilliant chapter on Custer entitled "The Fool Who Rode to His Death". His major error at Last Stand Hill was one of tactics. The notorious 7th Cavalry had been spotted, that much was now certain, and the element of surprise was gone. More important still, Custer didn't have the answer to the two elementary questions relevant to planning an attack: the enemy's disposition and the enemy's strength. He compounded his mistakes with his next error, perhaps the most fatal of all. The capital sin of a commander in the field is to divide his unit without detailed information about his enemy. But that is precisely what Custer did. He split his regiment up. Rushing blindly into enemy-held territory, without spare ammunition and with a regiment divided into three separate units, made each column vulnerable to annihilation by a superior force. While Custer's plan was to attack simultaneously with two battalions, the Indians could choose their time and place, pick any of the three targets and throw everything at it, before turning on the next.

The official inquiry into the Little Big Horn disaster turned into a military whitewash. Union generals would never admit that "savages" had managed to wipe out a famous U.S. Cavalry unit, one that had been victorious throughout the major battles of the American Civil War. When the verdict was announced, Chief of the Crows, Flying Hawk, put it plainly: "All the white men's accounts are guesswork for no white man knows. There was none left."

While witnesses were called and testimony taken, the court never called upon the only eyewitnesses – the Native-Americans who had taken part in the battle. The court's lame excuse was that Native-Americans were known liars.

During the McCarthy era, America was desperate to find well-known "celebrity communists" to justify its draconian measures. Charlie Chaplin, who was on a European holiday in 1952, fitted the bill perfectly. He was accused of being if not a communist then a "fellow traveler" or sympathizer. Despite the most rigorous investigations by the FBI (the reports cover more than 400 pages), no evidence could be found to show that Chaplin was other than the "nonconformist of no political party" that he claimed to be. Nevertheless, he was refused permission to return to America where he had spent 42 years of his life. In 1972, at the age of 83, he was invited back to the country he had once loved and come to deplore, to receive a standing ovation from a Lincoln Center crowd and a special Oscar for his achievement in making motion pictures "the art form of the century".

Rewriting history is not restricted to America. It is a global phenomenon engaged in by all governments and major corporations. The world's largest book publisher, Bertelsmann, had to admit in 2002 that the firm's corporate history of its resistance to Hitler and the Nazis during the World War II era, as well as its wartime activities, had been a fabricated myth widely disseminated by the media. In fact it benefited from slave labor and actively supported a number of Nazi causes.

Weapons of Mass Deception

When no weapons of mass destruction were found in Iraq, people realized that President George W. Bush and Prime Minister Tony Blair lied to justify the war. The acceptance of lies by *We the Apathetic People* from our career politicans is an unforgivable heinous crime. Weapons of mass deception are clearly the ultimate weapons of our own self mass destruction. Utterly deceived, how can America be a strong democratic republic? People's apathetic acceptance of political mass deceptions employed to foster comfortable illusions is self-destructive. When Clinton lied about Monica, impeachment proceedings were commenced against him. Aren't lies that justified a "faith-based" war and death to hundreds of American soldiers an impeachable offense?

Forged documents and a plagiarized dated graduate thesis substituted for good intelligence to manipulate and dupe *We the Apathetic People* into believing Saddam Hussein was poised and ready to unleash, within any hour of his choosing, nuclear, chemical and biological weapons of mass destruction against America and its allies. A "mushroom cloud" was imminent.

Karen Kwiatkowski is a retired Air Force lieutenant colonel who spent most of her final three years of military service in the Office of the Secretary of Defense's Under Secretariat for Policy. She shared her disgust about the political spin and weapons of mass deception used by the Bush Defense Department in an article she wrote for the *Houston Chronicle* after the Iraq War ended and no WMD were found. "What I saw was aberrant, pervasive and contrary to good order and discipline. If one is seeking the answers to why peculiar bits of 'intelligence' found sanctity in a presidential speech, or why the post-Saddam occupation has been distinguished by confusion and false steps, one need look no further than the process inside the Office of the Secretary of Defense...

"Groupthink, in this most recent case leading to the invasion and occupation of Iraq, will be found, I believe, to have caused a subversion of constitutional limits on executive power and a co-optation through deceit of a large segment of the Congress...

"Saddam is not yet sitting before a war crimes tribunal. Nor have the key decision-makers in the Pentagon been forced to account for the odd set of circumstances that placed us as a long-term occupying force in the world's nastiest rat's nest, without a nation-building plan, without significant international support and without an exit plan. Neither may ever be required to answer their accusers, thanks to this administration's military as well as publicity machine, and the disgraceful political compromises already made by most of the Congress."

The Pentagon's Defense Intelligence Agency said in September 2002 in a classified report that "there is no reliable information on whether Iraq is producing and stockpiling chemical weapons, or whether Iraq has – or will – establish its chemical warfare agent production facilities." Nevertheless, on September 18, Defense Secretary Rumsfeld told the House Armed Services Committee: "We do know that the Iraqi regime has chemical and biological weapons...His regime has amassed large clandestine stockpiles of chemical weapons – including VX, sarin, cyclosarin and mustard gas."

The "faith-based" intelligence fraud perpetrated by the Bush administration against the American people has been downplayed and minimized because of the administration's effective spin-doctors and their weapons of mass deception.

Cooking Intelligence
It is today taken as a given that the CIA and FBI failed to share crucial data that could have prevented 9/11. The Bush administration succeeded for 18 months following 9/11 to successfully prevent any public investigation into the biggest security failure in the history of the United States because it wanted to do what Bush and his oil industry cronies traditionally do. Cook the books and dupe the public.

When the evidence on his weapons of mass deception was exposed for what it is, forged and dated, CIA chief George Tenet took the heat for cooking the garbage intelligence that found its way into the president's State of the Union address to Congress.

The Bush administration's gross manipulation and over-cooking of intelligence, and then shifting the blame to the chief CIA chef after the intelligence was exposed for being over-cooked garbage per their political specifications and instructions, does not serve the best interests of America. It will merely perpetuate a culture of continuous faulty cooked intelligence. Veteran Intelligence Professionals for Sanity, a group of retired intelligence analysts, wrote President Bush to protest what it called "a policy and intelligence fiasco of monumental proportions".

"While there have been occasions in the past when intelligence has been deliberately warped for political purposes," the letter said, "never before has such warping been used in such a systematic way to mislead our elected representatives into voting to authorize launching a war.

"The glue that holds the intelligence community together is melting under the hot lights of an awakened press. If you do not act quickly, your intelligence capability will fall apart...

"There was a tendency to feed the most alarming tidbits to the president. Often it's the most ill-considered information that goes to the president," one veteran said. "So instead of giving the president the most considered, carefully examined information available, basically you give him the garbage. And then in a few days when it's clear that maybe it wasn't right, well then, you feed him some more hot garbage."

Cooking intelligence and exaggerating, actually lying, about tyrannical regimes is a well-established pattern and procedure in Washington. The Soviet threat was consciously exaggerated to justify the nuclear buildup in America. The China threat to America is also repeatedly exaggerated to justify an expensive military buildup and missile defense shield for a possible war in Asia. Cooked intelligence conditions the public to go to war without having to discuss the cost of the war and how it will be paid for.

War Costs, Beneficiaries and Beasts of Burden

Before the war on Iraq started, not a single Bushite spinner would discuss the cost of the war. It was "not knowable" and "it was too soon to say with precision how much the war will cost." Even the President refused to discuss the costs of the war. Yet five days into a war of which no-one could predict the duration and final outcome, the Bush spinners produced a precise figure – $74.7 billion to cover the war's first 30 days. If you think about it carefully, can we really believe this number was "not knowable" for weeks if not months before the war started? Will we ever know the real cost, especially if it drags out for years?

To better understand how war costs are spun to hide the real cost, real beneficiaries and real beasts of burden that are saddled with the costs, a close analysis of the 1991 Gulf War against Iraq to "Free Kuwait" is quite informative and enlightening.

The 1991 war, which lasted for six weeks, cost $40 billion. We were told that America paid only 25 percent of the cost, that is $10 billion, while the balance of $30 billion was paid by Kuwait and Saudi Arabia. Where did they get the money? The oil price before the war was approximately $15 per barrel. Once the war started it rose to $42 a barrel generating an EXTRA $60 billion. In the Arab oil-producing countries, the state keeps 50 percent of the revenues and the multinational oil companies keep the remaining 50 percent. It is known as the "fifty-fifty" law. This means Kuwait and Saudi Arabia got $30 billion and the oil companies also got $30 billion. The oil companies, Shell, Exxon, Mobil... are of course U.S.- owned. They managed to keep $9 billion and paid the U.S. government the remaining $21 billion in taxes.

The bottom line is, the U.S. government that spent $10 billion on the war made a profit of $11 billion. Kuwait and Saudi Arabia broke even, while the U.S. oil companies made a $9 billion profit! The cost to "Free Kuwait" was paid by *We the Apathetic People* who paid the extra cost per gallon every time we refilled our tanks. We believed the increased cost was because of the war to "Free Kuwait". Was it, or was it to increase the profit of the oil companies? It gets better. Let's not forget that the $40 billion spent went exclusively to pay for the equipment, ammunition, supplies and services to fight the war. The U.S. military-industrial complex.

The same analysis for the war in Afghanistan and millennium war in Iraq to "Free the Iraqi People" will come up with the same conclusions. Different numbers, but bottom line, the primary beneficiaries are the oil companies and the manufacturers of all the weaponry used. Who pays for it all? *We the Apathetic People,* our children and grandchildren! Truck drivers and all other working Bush supporters should stop and think about their blind loyal support of the Bush oiligarchy as their trucks come to a screeching halt because they can no longer afford the cost of gasoline. The oil companies are determined to pocket whatever change is left in anyone's pocket and bank account. It's time to collect what they missed in 1991 after the Gulf War.

Dr. Mathias Rath, M.D., a physician and scientist who led the breakthrough in the natural treatment of cardiovascular disease and cancer, took out a full page ad addressed to President Bush in leading newspapers a few weeks before the war with Iraq started. He argues that the main beneficiaries of the war are the pharmaceutical companies. I'm not sure I agree, but he did point out an interesting analogy between the primary beneficiary of the start of World War II and the War in Iraq. He reminds us that the main benefactor of Hitler's rise to power and World War II was IG-Farben, the largest European petro-chemical cartel seeking control of the oil and chemical industry worldwide.

In the Nuremberg War Tribunal in 1946-47 this cartel was tried for "conquest", "robbery", and "slavery" and – as a result – it was dismantled into Bayer, BASF and Hoechst. This War Tribunal established that without these corporations, World War II would not have been possible. U.S. Chief Prosecutor Telford Taylor stated: "If their guilt is not brought to the daylight, they will do even more harm in future generations."

Spin-doctors cannot change the lessons of history or the truth. They can only conceal them or re-package them. It is up to *We the Maids* to sweep away the dust hiding history and the truth.

Was 9/11 a Political Spin?

Most people in the Muslim world believe 9/11 was orchestrated, planned and executed by America and its Jewish suicide bombers. What is more disturbing is that many intelligent and credible people who love America in Europe, Germany and France in particular, are also questioning the truth about 9/11. Best sellers, documentaries, rumors and countless conspiracy theories abound about why the attacks of 9/11 were planned by America itself. A poll conducted in pro-American Germany in late 2003 by Forsa, one of Germany's leading polling organizations, found that every fifth German believes "the U.S. government ordered the attacks itself" so that it could justify going to war in Afghanistan and Iraq.

The rationale behind their logic is that if America's military and political establishment can allow the Japanese to attack Pearl Harbor to persuade Americans to enter World War II, assassinate a president to go to war in Vietnam, as many believe was the case with John F. Kennedy, why not 9/11 to go to war in Afghanistan and Iraq?

It is difficult to believe that America and its global intelligence-gathering capabilities and agencies did not know about the impending attacks of 9/11. Whether they couldn't be stopped or were allowed to happen because they would further U.S. foreign policy aims is as awesome a question as it is shocking.

Shock and Awe Urban War
The American and Iraqi public were conditioned by Pentagon spinners before the Iraqi War started that the unprecedented bombing raids on Iraq in the opening days of the war would "shock and awe" the Iraqis to surrender en masse and greet the coalition liberators with open arms, flowers and smiles. Bush spinners privately said the war might last only two or three weeks. On the opening night of the war, they took a chance on winning the war in a single night by striking at a Baghdad compound where Saddam Hussein and his sons were believed to be staying. In fact it was the Pentagon that was in shock and awed by the tough and fierce resistance the Iraqis initially put up. Marines were down to one meal a day because of guerrilla and suicide attacks that created logistical chaos and delayed the arrival of the supply convoys from the rear. Something the military planners overlooked.

Sand storms and unexpected traffic jams on the main highways made the job easier for the suicide bombers. The war required twice the number of U.S. troops than were planned for, took longer and was more costly than most Americans expected because of how we were conditioned by the war spinners and the phony rigged war games planned and played by the Pentagon. "There is a realization that we came in a little light," an officer told his troops. "It was hubris to go on Fox News and proclaim the war would be a cakewalk," a former aide to the first president Bush said. "The gods were bound to hear it."

"The enemy we're fighting is different from the one we war-gamed against," Lieutenant General William Wallace said. They were aware of the fierce loyalty of the Iraqi militia to Saddam Hussein, "but we did not know how they would fight." Why not? The CIA analysts had warned the Pentagon about the threat of the paramilitary units but the Bushies at the Pentagon decided not to fully brief the commanders in the field. Any wonder they were caught by surprise? "We misjudged their tenacity," a senior U.S. intelligence official says of Iraqi leaders. "These guys are driven by a hatred (toward the United States) that we may have underestimated." What an understatement. The Pentagon was convinced the Iraqi generals would capitulate and surrender. "Our intelligence assessments were overly optimistic," a senior U.S. military official says. "They were simply wrong."

During World War I after the British liberated the Iraqis from the Ottoman Empire, the Iraqis slaughtered tens of thousands of British soldiers who marched into Iraq expecting the same hero's welcome the coalition forces expected for liberating the country. After the way the first Bush administration let them down in 1991 when they heeded his call to rise up and overthrow Saddam that resulted in their own massacre, is it any wonder they are going to be cautious the second time around? When is America going to learn? Why not do it right the first time? Why expect people to risk their lives after they were betrayed the first time around? No spin can change this basic human survival instinct.

The urban war America got sucked into in Baghdad and other Iraqi cities was not supposed to happen, according to the Pentagon game plan. But then again, when you spin fake outcomes to war games why should we be surprised? From Stalingrad in World War II, to the U.S. Marine assault on Hue, Vietnam, in 1968 during the Tet offensive and to Mogadishu, Somalia, in 1993, when sophisticated Black Hawk helicopters were brought down by primitive shoulder-fired rocket-propelled grenades, urban warfare has always shocked and awed the superior invading army.

Central Command chief General John Abizaid, who succeeded

General Tommy Franks, said the Iraqis "are conducting what I would describe as a classical guerrilla-type campaign against us. It's low-intensity conflict in our doctrinal terms, but it's war however you describe it...The level of resistance...is getting more organized and it is learning." The general's comments contradicted Defense Secretary Donald Rumsfeld, who said five weeks earlier that it was not "anything like a guerrilla war or an organized resistance". With average daily losses of more than one U.S. soldier's life in Iraq since President Bush declared victory and an end to major hostilities on May 1, 2003, his announcement clearly rings just as empty and hollow as the flyboy suit he wore.

"Urban warfare usually benefits the defender," said Clifford Beal, the editor of *Jane's Defence Weekly,* a leading publication on military matters. Not only that, urban warfare "will negate the technological advantage of the coalition...It can bog down large number of troops. This war is being fought on a clock. And the longer it goes on, the more carnage is seen, the more difficult it is for the Bush administration to continue," Beal concluded. This was something the Bush spinners chose to downplay and avoid before the start of the war.

America has blindly established the ideal training camp for terrorists in Iraq for fundamentalist extremists to perfect their violent destructive tactics without having to risk operating in America. Vulnerable U.S. troops, military bases, power stations, oil pipelines, Red Cross and UN headquarters. The U.S. war on Iraq has created a super incubator for terrorism that is continuously attracting terrorists from the entire Muslim world. The guerrilla war veterans in Iraq are a much graver threat to America in the long run than Saddam Hussein ever was. The terror fields of Iraq are a sneak preview of what can happen in America once the sleeper cells are re-activated.

Ayatollah Muhammad Bakr al-Hakim, leader of the Supreme Assembly for the Islamic Revolution of Iraq based in Iran, a member of the main Shiite group which makes up roughly 60 per cent of the Iraqi population, repeatedly warned that he will "expel American troops from Iraq" when the war is over and Saddam's regime is removed. This was also down-played by the Bush spinners because it did not fit with their overall plan for the future of Iraq and its oil. The Ayatollah has home court urban advantage.

Saudis Real War Target

At a news conference by the Arms Control Association, a private advocacy group, Greg Thielman, who retired in September 2002 as director of the strategic, proliferation and military affairs office in the State Department's bureau of intelligence and research, said the administration misused information on Iraq. "When we began military operations, Iraq posed no imminent threat to either its neighbors or to the United States," he said. If so, why did the U.S. push so hard for a war and regime change? Amazingly, Paul Wolfowitz, Deputy Defense Secretary, has already admitted in an interview with *Vanity Fair* that Iraq's weapons of mass destruction were but a bureaucratic pretext that hid other core motives for war.

The real target of the war in Iraq was Saudi Arabia. Saudi Arabia was deeply involved in 9/11, which the U.S. Congressional investigation of events leading up to 9/11 now confirm. The first clue was the fact that 15 of the 19 hijackers involved in 9/11 were Saudi citizens.

Jeffrey Sachs reminds us that two truths have long governed U.S. energy security. The first is that Saudi Arabia is the key to world oil stability, the accommodating supplier when markets get tight. It would be a potential threat to the world economy if Saudi oil flows were disrupted. In 1973-74, with the Arab oil embargo, the Ford presidency was brought down by the disruption of the U.S. economy, a point not lost on two young senior officials at the time, Donald Rumsfeld and Richard Cheney, respectively Gerald Ford's Defense Secretary and White House Chief of Staff.

Pentagon and academic planners began making contingency plans for the military seizure of the Middle East oil fields.

Ralph Nader sums up the basic oil statistics: "The United States currently consumes 19.5 million barrels a day, or 26 percent of daily global consumption....The U.S. [has to import] 9.8 million barrels a day, or more than half the oil we consume....The surest way for the U.S. to sustain its overwhelming dependence on oil is to control the 67 percent of the world's proven oil reserves that lie below the sands of the Persian Gulf. Iraq alone has proven reserves of 112.5 billion barrels, or 11 percent of the world's remaining supply....Only Saudi Arabia has more."

The second truth in Sachs' analysis is that Saudi Arabia has been a spigot of private wealth for key U.S. figures, and for the Bush extended family in particular. The Saudi royal family lacks political legitimacy at home, so it buys U.S. protection from abroad. The Saudis purchase Washington influence through consultancy contracts, big defense outlays on U.S. military hardware, lucrative speeches for Washington insiders, and investments in U.S. businesses with influential figures. A long line of U.S. senior officials has benefited with the Ford, George H.W. Bush and George W. Bush White House and Pentagon at the front of the line. Saudi business has helped to make multi-millionaires of Henry Kissinger, Frank Carlucci, James Baker, George H.W. Bush, Mr. Cheney and dozens of other insiders.

September 11 threatened these two truths. Within hours of the attack, the White House understood that senior Saudi intelligence officials were probably involved with the 15 Saudi terrorists. They were no doubt stunned to realize that parts of the vast Saudi royal family were not only corrupt, but also deeply intertwined with anti-American terror and extremist fundamentalism. A new book by former CIA agent Robert Baer, *Sleeping with the Devil,* details how the U.S. government had systematically turned away from the growing evidence of Saudi complicity in fundamentalist terrorism, thereby frustrating the kind of investigations that might have headed off September 11.

September 11 was a dramatic confirmation that the stability of Saudi oil was in jeopardy. The regime was unstable and perhaps even a lethal threat to America. The only quantatitively significant alternative to Saudi oil was Iraqi oil, but that option was barred as long as Saddam Hussein remained in power. The long-standing contingency plans to seize Middle Eastern oil were rolled out by Rumsfeld and Cheney.

A substitute had to also be found for the U.S. military bases in Saudi Arabia. Like Saudi oil, the bases were now also under threat. Iraq would become a new base. The most important reason is that the Bush White House needed to issue a powerful threat to the Saudi leadership: one more false step and you're finished. Attacking next door neighbor Iraq was quite a persuasive diplomatic stick. A direct diplomatic attack was probably ruled out by the deep and inextricable links between the White House and the Saudi leadership. Too many lucrative contracts would be at risk. Finally, there was probably a strong hope that the persuasive media spins of weapons of mass destruction and regime change needed in Iraq would divert the public from the true roots of 9/11.

Censorship

How about HarperCollins and Moore-gate? The publisher wanted to pulp all printed copies of *Stupid White Men,* Michael Moore's satirical critique of the George W. Bush presidency after September 11. However incompetent the President appeared before September 11, because vulnerable Americans suddenly began looking to their leader for comfort, Moore's satire was transformed overnight to a scathing attack on the leader of a people at war. I can relate, because I was told the same thing by a literary agent and several publishers when they were offered this trilogy.

When Saddam Hussein gassed 6,800 Kurds in Halabja in March 1988 with the knowledge of the U.S. government, Iran was blamed for the gassing by the U.S. government spin-doctors, and the media and the public bought the spin. The U.S. government lied because at the time it was encouraging and supporting Saddam's weapons of mass destruction programs because they were critical in his defeat of Iran. In 2003 those same programs conveniently became the threat to America that justified a regime change.

Plane Spin

Isn't it an ironic media spin that the U.S. accuses China of spying when it arrested physicist Wen Ho Lee, but claims America can do so without interference when America's spy plane crash landed in China on April 1, 2001? Even when caught red-handed. It demanded the plane and crew be immediately returned. This is the same country that held a Chinese-American in jail for spying without any proof.

The spin-doctors tried to spin a story that ignores the fact that the plane was spying. The mission was a "routine signals security" flight – a military euphemism for spying. Listening to another country's military communications. To make Americans feel better, the public was assured that the crew of the U.S. spy plane had destroyed most sensitive classified information before the plane landed and America had nothing to worry about. Another timely spin. The fact is the crew did not have enough time to destroy everything and China probably got valuable intelligence secrets from the plane, according to a U.S. investigation that was made public under the Freedom of Information Act.

An analogy that really portrays the spy plane spin is a local American Beauty. A neighborhood boy peeping at his beautiful Oriental next door neighbor. He peeped every night. One day he decided to buy an expensive telescope to make sure he got a better view. He didn't think he was doing anything wrong because he was peeping from his own house. One day he got so excited at what he saw that he attracted the girl's attention. He panicked and knocked the telescope out the window into her garden and destroyed a prize collection of yellow roses. The girl came out and took the telescope and demanded he apologize for his actions and that his parents pay to replace the damaged roses. The boy refuses and instead demands the girl return the telescope. "There is a pervading view among Republicans that America carries out 'vital surveillance' to protect our interests while it is everybody else that is doing the spying," a Republican official said. "There will be little sense that we will be in the wrong."

The United States strictly enforces a 200 mile air intercept zone around America, far beyond territorial waters. What would happen if China, or any other nation for that matter, were to establish permanent intelligence facilities in Cuba, Mexico or Canada or on ships, submarines and planes off the U.S. coast to intercept U.S. military communications? They would be blasted to extinction!

When the terrorist suicide bombers blasted themselves and the U.S. image of invulnerability on September 11, China was quick to condemn the terrorist attacks and publicly support the U.S. in the struggle against terrorism. "The Chinese people stand with the American people," a Chinese government spokesman said. The fear of terrorism is a universal bond, not just a Sino-American one.

Spin-doctors are continuing to successfully create a subtle bias and hatred towards China and Chinese-Americans while trying to create an unnecessary enemy. They are re-creating an American Cold War mentality against China. Americans, by a ratio of two to one after the plane incident, view China as "unfriendly", a fifth view it as an "enemy". Half said the U.S. should regard China primarily as a military threat. This is a dramatic increase since 1998 thanks to spin-doctors. Only 47 percent at the time thought China was unfriendly.

The racist bias towards Chinese has also spread to America's former colony, the Philippines. Philippine Navy Commander Admiral Guillermo Wong, an ethnic Chinese-Filipino, was abruptly and prematurely removed from office because of fears he would yield to pressure from Beijing over the disputed Spratlys islands that both the Philippines and China claim.

Lynch Spin

The "dramatic" rescue of Private Jessica Lynch showcased to what extreme morale-boosting lies the government will resort to make Americans feel good about a war. The daring night-time operation by Delta Force troops in Black Hawk helicopters rescued a badly stabbed and shot private who fought to the death and was taken captive only after using up all her ammunition to shoot the Iraqi ambushers, according to the Pentagon. "Some brave souls put their lives on the line to make this happen," declared the Central Command spokesperson, General Vincent Brooks, "loyal to a creed that they will never leave a fallen comrade." The story was a necessary morale-booster spin at a time when the U.S.-led assault encountered stiff resistance and logistical problems.

The facts are that she was not shot or stabbed. Neither did she fight to the death as her M16 had jammed. Her multiple injuries were not sustained after she ran out of ammunition but because her Humvee rear-ended a truck. The so-called dramatic rescue was anything but dramatic. The Delta Force cruised into the hospital and encountered no resistance at all as there were no Iraqi soldiers guarding Private Lynch or the hospital. The too-good-to-be-true story was just that. A Pentagon-managed misperception.

Media Spin

The best managed misperception and hypocrisy is America lecturing

China and Hong Kong and the world on human rights. Eleanor Roosevelt was one of the prime movers behind the adoption of the Universal Declaration of Human Rights. As the *Economist* pointed out: The United States has a sorry record of shilly-shallying or plain obstruction, in the development of international law.

Instead of leading, America has ratified many human rights treaties only after most other countries have already done so. It took 40 years to ratify the Genocide Convention, 28 for the Convention Against Racial Discrimination, 26 for the International Covenant on Civil and Political Rights, the most important treaty of all. At the dawn of the 21st century, over 160 countries have ratified the convention banning discrimination against women – but not the United States. Only two in the world have not ratified the Convention on the Rights of the Child: the U.S. and Somalia, which has no effective government. And even when America has ratified treaties, it has often attached extensive reservations, making them inapplicable at home.

In the 1990s, the United States played the key role in setting up tribunals to put on trial individuals accused of war crimes and genocide in Rwanda and ex-Yugoslavia. Yet alone among its allies, it now opposes and "unsigned" the treaty that established the permanent international criminal court endorsed by 120 nations at a UN conference – primarily because it could not win an absolute exemption for its own soldiers.

The Bush administration then launched a global campaign to shield U.S. military personnel from the new court once it was established. America demanded countries sign bilateral treaties if they wanted America's support to join NATO or the EU. An obstructionist approach to public diplomacy, which can only backfire on America and reduce it to a Pacific Power. America has to lead by example not by exemption. Practice what it preaches and the values it stands for and represents to the world.

American leaders thereby gain room for maneuver. But their double standards also damage their credibility when they criticize the illegalities or human rights abuses of others, and reduce American influence over the law's development.

While seeking support of its war on terrorism, America not only opposed the establishment of the International Court, but also the International Convention on Torture, which allows an independent prisons inspection system. The Convention on Torture was passed in 1989 and has since been ratified by 130 countries.

The U.S. has also failed to back ratification on the treaty to ban land mines.

Pubic Spin

Little Bush's decision to reject the Kyoto Treaty on global warming, the Biological Weapons Convention and Anti-Ballistic Missile Treaty are 21st century examples of U.S. double standards and how it will turn its back on any global rules to suit its geopolitical agenda. The U.S., the world's largest polluter, repeatedly lectures developing countries to cut back pollution. Yet the U.S. is the biggest producer of man-made carbon dioxide emissions which many scientists say is the main greenhouse gas causing global warming.

The same applies to Bush's decision to construct a missile defense shield. He abrogated the 1972 Anti-Ballistic Missile Treaty the U.S. signed with Russia. How about the International Convention on land mines which the U.S. also refuses to sign?

"Where are you from?" asked the attractive long-haired blonde sitting at the bar in the Whisky at the Paramount Hotel on 46th Street in New York. It was the mid-1990s. I had decided to get out of the chilly arctic wind and stopped by the Whisky for a drink before my dinner meeting with some clients. It's a great place to meet and see people who go to extremes to manage their image and perception. The waitresses enhance their sexy image by wearing tight body stockings and push-up bras to expose some extra cleavage. "I'm from Hong Kong," I replied. "Wow, aren't you afraid of the communist takeover?" she asked as she leaned back to expose herself.

Here we go again, I thought. The image and perception that people have in their mind about Hong Kong is so wrong. I decided to ignore the question because I was getting sick and tired of dealing with it. "What do you do?" I asked her trying to change the subject. "I'm in public relations without the 'L' in public," she replied.

It took me a few seconds to figure it out. "That's good!" I said laughing. I hadn't heard a working girl describe her occupation that way before. *We the People* have to keep in mind that everyone in public relations has forgotten about the "L". Maybe that's why they are doing such a great job screwing people's perception of reality.

The media convey, and sometimes form and create, the managed perceptions they are fed by pubic relations firms representing the government and corporate America. Americans and Hong Kongers today distrust not just their governments and older generations but the sources of news about their governments. Near strangers constantly tell those of us in the business about their disregard for the industry. "You media people," goes the refrain, "are a bunch of arrogant, untrustworthy windbags who slant the truth and only stir up trouble."

Jessie Ventura is even more blunt. "As long as the idea of a free press has been around, reporters have gone on the warpath. But there's a major difference between the way it's done today and the way it's been done throughout history. In the past, most of the time, when the media went after people it was because they truly believed that those were in the wrong. There was passion behind their attacks; their hearts were in it. Today, the media's policy is attack now, figure out why you're attacking later." The media accept most press releases sent by pubic relations people at face value.

A few recent prominent cases that highlight the issue are worth mentioning. David Brock's apology to President Clinton for his 1993 article which started the Paula Jones sex scandal. His story alleged the Arkansas State troopers procured women for the then Governor. In his apology letter, Brock said: "The troopers were greedy and had slimy motives." He admitted being fed the story through one of Republican House Speaker Newt Gingrich's financial backers. This story started the multi-million dollar sex scandal investigation into Paula Jones. This mistake became a media feeding frenzy. The apology was downplayed by the media and most apathetic people don't know about it.

The Clinton "Gift Registry" story is another example. How the

Clintons allegedly got their friends to send them gifts for their new home after they left the White House. The entire Washington press corps discussed it, talk shows debated it, pundits pontificated as usual. The only problem was it was fiction created by spin-doctors. The gift registry never existed! Did *The New York Times* or Maureen Dowd, who said Hillary Clinton registered "like a new bride", ever bother to check their facts or apologize the same way? Of course not.

Belgian-born Italian journalist Georges Ruggiu pleaded guilty to inciting genocide in Rwanda at the infamous Radio-Television Libre del Mille Collines. "I want to confirm that it was indeed genocide and that unfortunately I participated." Shouldn't more journalists and writers admit their errors and come clean?

Journalists in Hong Kong get jailed when they are caught lying or get news tips for cash. Shouldn't their counterparts in the U.S.?

The *Boston Globe's* columnist Mike Barnicle denied knowing he had stolen George Carlin's one-liners after he was suspended by the paper claiming he had never read the comedian's book. He had the nerve to make that claim after he had held the book in question in his hand and recommended it on Boston's WCVB television. Even worse, he apparently fabricated a story about two children who had cancer. His termination by the *Boston Globe* is a long overdue step in the right direction.

The *Hollywood Reporter's* suspension of its 26-year veteran journalist George Christy for accepting favors from producers and health and pension benefits from the Screen Actors Guild Producers Pension and Health Fund is another such step.

Jack Kelley, a foreign correspondent for *USA Today,* resigned after his editors discovered he had "set in motion a plan to deceive them". He had filed false stories for over 20 years from 90 countries.

The resignation of respected *New York Times* editors Howell Raines and Gerald M. Boyd in the wake of the dozens of fabricated or plagarized Jayson Blair stories is the fallout from just the latest well-publicized example of inventive media. America's leading newspapers have all contributed to the falsehoods we are fed. *The Wall Street Journal's* columnist R. Foster Winans was convicted on 59 counts of conspiracy and fraud in 1985 for using his articles to make money in the stock market. *The Washington Post* had to return the 1981 Pulitzer Prize won by reporter Janet Cooke for her story of an eight-year-old heroin addict who turned out to be a figment of her imagination. *The New York Times* also had to acknowledge that the Pulitzer Prize it won for its one-sided coverage of the Soviet Union in the 1930s was undeserving because of its reporter's failure to report the famine that killed millions of Ukrainians.

The courts are finally coming to grips with the media's abuse of Constitutional freedoms. The Supreme Court upheld a $1 million libel judgment against the *Globe* tabloid for repeating an author's claim that a California photographer killed Robert Kennedy. The *Globe* made no effort to contact the falsely accused man, Khawar, and the publisher quickly withdrew the book.

In legal briefs, *The New York Times,* the *Los Angeles Times,* CBS, NBC and ABC argued that the tabloid was merely engaged in "neutral reporting" of a public controversy. Of course, accusing a man of a major assassination without proof also happens to be wildly irresponsible.

Alexis de Toqueville said: "It's true that the press often tells lies. But it's more important that the press acts as a watch-guard on those in power. And so I think, freedom of the press is one of the most important qualities of American society."

President John F. Kennedy defined the responsibility as well as the significance of a free press: Those "who create power make an indispensable contribution to the nation's greatness, but (those) who question power make a contribution just as indispensable... for they determine whether we use power, or power uses us."

Electronic media are not exempt from making mistakes and mismanaging perception. CNN's Peter Arnett was let go because of his narration of a disputed story on the use of Sarin gas in Laos in 1970 during the Vietnam War in an attempt to kill some U.S. deserters. When the story broke on June 7, 1998, jointly on CNN and in *Time* it featured Admiral Thomas Moorer, who had been Chairman of the Joint Chiefs of Staff in 1970, and lesser military personnel who corroborated the story. Yet the story was branded a hoax. CNN's viewership dropped dramatically as viewers perceived it to be biased and not objective. To some it became a joke. The "Clinton News Network". Even CBS got snookered twice in four months in the rush to "scoop". The media pooper scoopers are getting bigger by the year thanks to spin-doctors and pubic relations!

CNN's Christiane Amanpour made headline news when she was captured and made prisoner in Afghanistan by the Taleban who confiscated her film while doing a story on women under Taleban rule. In fact she was seated under a tree sipping a cola while the women she was interviewing explained what happened to the Taleban. It was the women she was interviewing in a hospital that called the Taleban because they were afraid that Ms. Amanpour was endangering their lives. She was. But all she wanted was a scoop at any price. Personal pubic relations.

The media's failure to fully comprehend or appreciate the public's disgust for managed perception was best illustrated during the endless coverage of Monicagate. The 1998 midterm election results finally got the media to understand people's disgust. To a lesser degree the same can be said about the media's portrayal of the Bush-Gore Florida legal challenges as a "Nation Divided" close to a "Constitutional Crisis". Why did the press downplay the fact that while Bush and his Republican commissars were opposed to the recounts in Florida, they were demanding hand recounts in New Mexico? Mickey Barnett, a lawyer for New Mexico's Republican Party, demanded hand recounts in Roosevelt County to overturn a 368-vote Gore lead. Superior Republican pubic relations.

The media played up the 2002 U.S. China Security Review Commission report that said China posed a military threat to Taiwan and other neighbors but were silent on the report's findings on Mainland Chinese media. It concluded the Chinese media are relatively balanced overall in their reporting on America. The study was done by the Institute for Global Chinese Affairs at the University of Maryland. One of the main findings was: "Chinese reporting on the U.S. appears to be relatively balanced overall. Extreme negative tones toward the U.S. are rare and appear mostly during periods of overt Sino-U.S. confrontation." Can the same be said about the U.S. media and China-bashing pubic relations firms?

Liberal Media?

Career politicians constantly blame the left-wing "liberal media" for misrepresenting the facts. Nothing could be further from the truth. Does anyone really believe that there is a left-wing liberal at the helm of GE, Disney, Viacom, Bertelsmann, AOLTimeWarner or Rupert Murdoch's Newscorp? *What Liberal Media: The Truth About Bias and the News* by Eric Alterman is a book I highly recommend to anyone who wants to find out the truth and dispel once and for all the myth of liberal media. Even arch-conservative Patrick Buchanan couldn't identify liberal media bias during his first presidential campaign. "I've gotten balanced coverage, and broad coverage – all we could have asked. For heaven's sake, we kid about the 'liberal media', but every Republican on earth does that." Even *Weekly Standard* editor William Kristol, perhaps the leading Republican publicist in America today, has come clean. "I admit it," he told a reporter. "The liberal media were never that powerful, and the whole thing was often used as an excuse by conservatives for conservative failures."

Think about it. Where on television are the liberal counterparts to such relentlessly partisan conservatives as Bill O'Reilly, George Will, John Stossell, Bob Novak, Pat Buchanan, William J. Bennett, William Kristol, Fred Barnes, John McLaughlin, Charles Krauthammer, Paul Gigot, Oliver North, Kate O'Brien, Peggy Noonan, Jonah Goldberg, Tony Blankley, Sean Hamnity, Tony Snow, Newt Gingrich, Cal Thomas, John Kasich, Michael Savage, Joe Scarborough, Brit Hume, or the ubiquitous Ann Coulter, who likes to joke about terrorists blowing up *The New York Times* and calls for the mass murder of Muslims. It's hard to come up with a TV journalist anywhere who is even remotely as far to the left as these conservatives are to the right. The same holds true for talk radio.

America Tunes Out

William J. Bennett, the author of *The Death of Outrage: Bill Clinton and the Assault on American Ideals,* was left to shake his head at how the American people had abandoned him and Washington's psycho-political babble. "For the first time in my adult life," he said, "I'm not in sync. I don't get it."

He, like most religious conservatives don't. Americans, American voters, *We the People,* the foundation of American democracy and the Constitution don't care about personal partisan political agendas! Rarely has such an unexpected popular consensus been so clear. And rarely has such a clear consensus been so unexpected. The Florida rerun confirmed America's apathetic disgust at duopolistic partisan games.

The greedy press and the Washington spin-doctors and their establishment clients have been taking a beating for getting these political dramas so totally wrong. A shocking evolution has hit the young Republic. Despite the religious gals from the Pilgrim Fathers, through the Baptists and through the Irish Catholic Cardinals, the silent majority of apathetic citizens in America has gone Expat Hong Kong. It is secular, tuned out and it doesn't give a toss! A politically correct expletive from the masters of spin.

Atlanta Braves' relief pitcher John Rocker, suspended two weeks in the regular season for uttering derogatory remarks about minorities in New York, summed up managed perception when he scolded the media. "The best thing I got out of that was that I showed you people in the media that not everyone is against me," Rocker said. "I'm well received wherever I go. But then I turn on the TV and see how horrible I am." Watching the reception he received at Shea stadium after he apologized for his earlier remarks, one can't say he is well received in New York. Especially after he pitched a perfect eighth inning.

When Rocker went to the Triple-A Richmond Braves in the minors he was welcomed with a standing ovation. "I was shocked by how the fans love him," said Richmond's third baseman Wes Helms. Spin-doctors cannot change reality. Only its managed misperception.

Just because journalism is becoming an entertainment commodity doesn't mean the truth can be re-created. Let's start dealing with reality, political, cultural and personal.

Rush To Scoop
The electronic media prematurely projected and flip-flopped Florida like a Southern pancake during the last 20th century presidential

election. From Gore to Bush. Then staying up in political spin Never Never Land. The bizarre, stranger than fiction results got Gore to concede and then withdraw his concession. The political pundits' recriminations and finger pointing further emphasized the shortcomings of the media. Their pollsters, mathematicians, statisticians and prime time talking heads. They all got it wrong. Before the second flip-flop, NBC's Tom Brokaw shared his concern. "That would be something if the networks managed to blow it twice in one night." Well guess what? Surprise. They did. CBS's Dan Rather blamed it on suspect data and said: "If you're disgusted with us, frankly, I don't blame you." How can he or anyone else in the media blame anyone but themselves?

What about Robert Philip Hanssen, the FBI agent accused of being one of America's biggest traitors in all the media? The media re-ran and repeated each other's stories about his espionage damage well before his trial. Nevertheless, the American public was convinced he was guilty before he was even tried. Why? Aren't American citizens innocent until proven guilty in a court of law or confess?

How come the media didn't give as much coverage to the story that the FBI had been warned 11 years earlier by Hanssen's brother-in-law, also an FBI agent, that he might be spying for the Russians because he "was hiding thousands of dollars in cash" in his house and "spending too much money for someone on an FBI salary"? How come this FBI blunder was downplayed?

Rocker Fred Durst, lead singer of the rap-metal band Limp Bizkit, showed the world how quick the press can jump the gun without doing even the most rudimentary homework. During his 2003 Grammy Awards speech he shared his anti-war sentiment that grated on the ears of grammarians: "I just really hope we're all in agreeance that this war should go away as soon as possible." *The Orange County Register* called him "illiterate", and other dailies had a field day mocking his grammar and the fact that agreeance is not a word. In fact agreeance is a word and all any reporter had to do is look it up in the Oxford English Dictionary.

What is the excuse for jumping the gun? The first to project? The first to scoop? This is not 1948, the year the media erroneously projected "Dewey defeats Truman". Neither is it the 1950s when every left-thinking writer was branded a communist. What is it going to take to get the media to behave responsibly in the new millennium? Boycotts, fines, jail time...

Media Overkill

The media came under severe attack when Princess "Di" died – both for their unrelenting coverage of her while she was alive and their coverage of her death and funeral.

I was in New York at the time staying with Michael Yudin, a merchant banker. I had gone to high school with his wife Michal in Israel. Mike and I "connected" right away and over the years have spent many evenings and weekends exchanging views on politics, women, kids, political systems, economics, diets, lifestyles and sex. His sister Stephanie was visiting from Florida. All the coverage and talk on every channel was the death of Diana. You would think she was the saint. Mother Teresa, who was a charitable human being, got minimal coverage on her death on the same day because Diana dominated the airwaves. The same happened with the tragic death of John F. Kennedy Jr. The death of King Mohamad Hassan of Morocco, a real King, was overshadowed by the death of America's Prince of Camelot. What stories are really important in the New World Order? Celebrities' deaths or the deaths of people who have materially contributed to the improvement of the human condition? Ideally a balance of both. Yin and Yang. Not pure commercial greed. There is a balance between public service and commercial broadcasting.

Hearing that JFK Jr.'s plane had gone missing and watching the media frenzy after it became clear he had perished in the Atlantic inevitably drew comparisons to the death and coverage of Princess Di.

The comparisons between their lives and deaths and the global emotional outpouring, from both men and women, was another millennium reminder that celebrities we admire and respect for their charitable work or emotional substitution value are a huge vicarious loss when their flashy lives are cut short by accidents caused by expensive stupidities that ordinary people couldn't even afford. The endless media coverage to increase ratings, the bottom line and viewers' appetites spin our perception and participation. Media today have as much power, and probably more, than nuclear weapons with a global fallout – although I'd prefer the *Globe* to a 40-megaton inter continental ballistic missile.

Actually, both John John and Princess Di are, both in life and death, our managed image of youth and hope for a better New World Order. They are role models for a fanciful good, volunteerism and public service thanks to their spin-doctors, pubic relations and the media.

The coverage of the Clinton-Lewinsky saga is an example of Republican spin-doctors, pubic relations, and the media overplaying their hand and role. Was it any different waiting for the outcome of the Florida recount?

What is truly remarkable about the Monica Lewinsky affair, the Florida recount and September 11 bombings, is how the American people themselves after a while say "Enough". Yet most journalists seem to come up with ever more ingenious arguments for why each event should continue to be covered!

Stuart Wolfendale, in a review of the U.S. media scene in an article he wrote for the FCC house magazine *The Correspondent,* said. "Anyone who followed the media could not deny the indiscriminate hysteria that gripped it. You could understand the 17th-century witch trials in Salem, Massachusetts, and the 'communist' paranoia of the Fifties brought by Senator Joseph McCarthy's hearings... there was the lucid anxiety over keeping up with the rest of the circus."

The decision by the U.S. House of Representatives' Judiciary Committee and their spin-doctors to release, on the Internet, every salacious detail of an investigation which in its dramatic and costly unfounded divergence from its original brief, can have no other purpose than to humiliate and ridicule a president out of office. What about the rights of Monica?

The media's decision to repeatedly replay the sexual details shows America's reckless disrespect for women. This was brought home again when news organizations repeatedly aired identifiable images of half-naked men and women in New York's Central Park after the National Puerto Rican Day when they were molested by drunk men.

The media circus continued to the bitter end of the New World Disorder. Its old tradition of overexposure continued with Elian Gonzalez, whether he was playing, drawing or wagging his finger at his father in a home-made video. Cuban protests and counter-demonstrations for the benefit of the media turned the boy into a political football. The criticism Diane Sawyer received for her interview of Elian gives us hope that maybe, just maybe, things will change.

Mythical America

John Wayne, Clint Eastwood, Shane and Fort Apache are the standouts of the many actors and movies that are at the core and foundation of America's mythology. In Fort Apache, the neo-con Wayne plays a bleeding heart liberal U.S. cavalry officer. John Wayne reminds us that infidel savages have a valid reason for fighting when the U.S. government has been starving them to death on a reservation. Director John Ford's earliest work shows how America's Manifest Destiny, backed by an army of Chinese and Irish laborers, was achieved. Gun-slinging saloon brawls only embellish, add enter-tainment value and mythology to the real blood, sweat and tears. Famously, in *The Man Who Shot Liberty Valance,* a newspaper editor puts the case for fantasy. "This is the west, sir. When the legend becomes fact, print the legend."

Ford is the supreme narrator of this legend, and also its subtlest critic. He based Fort Apache on the most miserable episode of white myth-making: the glamorization of the death of the brutal, incompetent general George Armstrong Custer and his cavalry at the battle of Little Big Horn in 1876. Ford changes names and makes the Indians Apache rather than Sioux, but his portrait of imperial folly is devastating – all the more so because he makes us like the ordinary soldiers, including a bunch of Irishmen, who, ordered by the humorless martinet Henry Fonda to destroy several barrels of whisky, do so by drinking them.

The Native-Americans fighting to hold on to what is rightfully theirs are branded "evil" savages. A spin that has been spun through 9/11, the Afghanistan and Iraq wars. Native savages being modified to Infidel Gooks and Infidel Towel Heads. Vietnam was just the 20th century instant TV documentary of America fighting the "Evil"

Commy Gooks that awakened America to the truth before the Pentagon spin-doctors and their talented career politician directors got a chance to completely rewrite the script.

The European tradition of Arthurian myths and fables was brought to America and was modified to make the New World adventurous, exciting and attractive to encourage European immigration and investment. Arthurian legends provided the popular settings for justifications for the Crusades against the Infidel Muslims. The essence of the crusading and questing themes of the Arthurian legends is the battle between good and evil, the search for purity, the vindication of civilization through force of arms, and the understanding of adversaries as demonic. The Arthurian lance and sword were replaced by the western hero with a pistol and rifle. The countless western dime novels which made their appearance in 1860 mythologized the western frontier. The western movie establishes the idea of freedom to roam and put down roots; and where the roots are set, that land becomes America. "The idea of America and the themes that would become familiar in westerns were sold through popular literature to incite and secure the creation of the settler colonies," Ziauddin Sardar and Merryl Wyn Davies astutely conclude in *Why Do People Hate America?* I and every immigrant bought into the myth and couldn't wait to come to America. Westerns were my favorite movies. That all ended when I got to America.

Travel literature, which included the efforts of what Percy Adams has called "travel liars", with their obligatory exploits, was a thriving tradition that inspired the initial settlement of America and then developed to serve the making of the nation. Radio, movies and television continue the tradition to this very day.

Native-Americans are portrayed as "Un-American". Now that's the ultimate spin! America was born out of hatred. Religiously persecuted Pilgrims who fled Europe for the New World, Paradise, Eden, the Land of Canaan. They were in total denial of the natives that welcomed them with open arms. The New World Crusaders were received by the un-Christian infidel savages who helped them survive, only to be slaughtered and hated for their un-Christian heathen ways. Violence and aggressiveness rooted in religion were the foundation stones of America – making it what it is today. A violent society.

Sardar and Davies summarize America's mythology in *Why Do People Hate America?* "In the history of America, both mythic and real, individual and communal violence created the state. Unable to provide justice and security and be an effective instrument of law, the state continued to legitimate the recourse to individual and group violence to ensure the self-preservation of the people; in this way they could make the nation state a reality. The 'manifest destiny' of the mission of America was made by violence. The western, the definitive American genre, is not merely a hymn to violence – it is a view of the essential, inescapable and enduring necessity of violence to preserve civilization. The western advances the myth that evil is intractable and can only be eradicated, that justice eventually comes down to the willingness to spill blood, that liberty resides in the right to make armed response, that the use of violence is the legitimate and only secure way to resolve a conflict. The whole world has experienced the western, and underlying its popularity is a different reaction: fear."

The fear is that the American political outlook continues to be too readily and uncritically shaped and confined by the myth of the redemptive, regenerative powers of violence. The violence is still reflected in today's popular music, movies and culture. Violence is America. Any wonder America's founding mythology permeates what *We the Apathetic Maids* accept as given without thinking of the consequences? September 11 was a grand slam home run consequence!

September 11 prompted Yankee Zoltan Grossman to publish a list of U.S. military interventions, from Wounded Knee to Afghanistan. The Congressional Records and Library of Congress Research Service provided his supporting arguments. There were 134 bloody interventions from 1890 to 2001. Domestic, regional and global. The U.S. made an average of 1.5 interventions per year until World War II; and 1.29 during the Cold War. After the fall of the Berlin Wall the interventions have increased to 2.0 per year. In other words, as politically slick oiled corporate America increases its campaign contributions to career politicians, the taxpayer-funded conflicts to protect the corporate donors, domestic and global investments and markets grow proportionately.

The failed $2 billion U.S. fax payer military installation of President Jean-Bertrand Aristide in Haiti is the latest 21st century glaring example of why America cannot instill democracy by force. Multi-billion dollar U.S. military exercises of democratic futility under the mythical guise of protecting American values must be exposed for what they are. An expensive well spun sham.

The mythical tradition that is at the heart of what is wrong with America surfaced from the deep recesses of our dumbed down subconscious and was given center stage by 9/11 and the ensuing wars in Afghanistan and Iraq. Violent wars of aggression that were conducted in our name without political debate or active citizen participation by *We the Apathetic People.* Career politicians continue to make decisions in our name without any input or participation. Decisions that affect our daily lives at home, community, country and world. How much longer can *We the Apathetic Maids* continue to accept being marginalized while ou resources, money and children are sacrificed and wrapped in the flag and buried to the rhythms of patriotic hymns?

I'm not sure whether America's guilt of its original sin is about slavery or the denial of its brutal violent behavior towards Native-Americans. The mythology created to mask these original sins is no different than the masks worn by the actors in westerns. America's mythology was planted by the Puritan European clergy whose Crusader upbringing and teachings naturally classified Native-Americans as children of the Devil. This entitled true believers to wipe out the native Infidels and appropriate their land by sword, pen or democratic vote. The Indians, having no European Christian concept of possession, were mere users of their land rather than owners. Therefore by law they could be dispossessed.

By example, in 1640, one New England assembly passed an eminently straightforward series of resolutions:

1. The earth is the Lord's and the fullness thereof. Voted

2. The Lord may give the earth or any part of it to his chosen people. Voted

3. We are his chosen people. Voted

The "Hand of Providence" myth advanced the "zealous work" of the "chosen people". It has been estimated that there were between 20 to 50 million Native-Americans when the Pilgrims first landed. By the end of the Indian Wars in the 1890s, and as a result of disease and the depredations of taming and settling the wilderness, the Native-American population was reduced to a mere 250,000. The "Hand of Providence" argument gave way in the 19th century to the nostalgic romance of the "Vanishing Indian".

John Rolfe, who was smitten by Pocahontas, not the Disney myth, but the real woman, set forth his detailed arguments in support of his marriage in a letter he wrote in 1614. The letter was a testament to the missionary zeal with which the Pilgrims settled the Promised Land. The New Testament text had strict prohibitions against marriage with unclean accursed races and therefore barred the marriage. His letter reads as a forensic dissection of the justification of empire. Since Pocahontas was willing to study the Bible and convert to Christianity, his marriage would fulfill the missionary purpose of settling the New World. Pocahontas was the first and most notable convert to Christianity in America. It is this image, the baptism of Pocahontas that is depicted in the Rotunda of the Capitol building.

Six Nations Iriquois Confederation

The U.S. Federal system of government, Constitution and Declaration of Independence are widely believed to be rooted in the ideas of individual liberties of the European Enlightenment, Magna Carta, and the unwritten "Ancient Constitution", a mythic concept that evolved over centuries in English history going back to the Anglo-Saxons. In fact, "the league of the Iriquois inspired Benjamin Franklin to copy it in planning the federation of states," President John F. Kennedy wrote in a 1960 preface to William Brandon's *American Heritage Book of Indians*. The Six Nations Iriquois Confederation was the basis and source of the Founding Fathers' concept of a federal government.

In 1744, Benjamin Franklin was printing texts of Indian treaties, including the words of Canassatego, the chief and speaker of the Iriquois confederacy. Canassatego recommended the federal system practiced by the Iriquois as a model that the English colonists should adopt and they did. It was known as the Albany Plan for colonial union presented by Benjamin Franklin in 1754.

National Brainwashing

Political romantic mythology was brought to America by the Church and the British. One of America's first masterful spins was in the Old South where slavery was portrayed as a means of "introducing benighted African savages to the blessings of Christian civilization".

The most recent 21st century spins surround the collapse of Enron and the conflicts of interest of major accounting firms and banks, which have also resulted in a modern-day enslavement of American employees and investors. People watch their life savings evaporate because of corporate fraud and greed at the highest levels of corporate America and accept it as the price one pays in a free capitalist system. Spin-doctoring at its finest. Neal Gabler points out why and how this has happened. "Class warfare has been steadily subverted over the past 20 years by defenders of the status quo: Republicans have chiefly led the fight, but so have some Democrats, captains of industry, journalists, religious leaders, radio talk show hosts and cable television babblers. They have waged this campaign on the stump, in the media and, most effectively, in the popular culture. What they have achieved amounts to a psychological revolution in which Americans not only don't think in terms of class, they don't even recognize any economic force beyond their own labor. Class warfare has been destroyed through a kind of national brainwashing."

The post 9/11 flag waving and flag lapel pins were a not so subtle form of patriotic brainwashing. Bill Moyers wrote a very astute piece expressing his disgust on how the flag had been hijacked by the government and how the public has been brainwashed to believe it is unpatriotic not to wear one or criticize the government.

> "I put the flag in my lapel tonight. First time. Until now I haven't thought it necessary to display a little metallic icon of patriotism for everyone to see. It was enough to vote, pay my taxes, perform my civic duties, speak my mind, and do my best to raise our kids to be good Americans. Sometimes I would offer a

small prayer of gratitude that I had been born in a country whose institutions sustained me, whose armed forces protected me, and whose ideals inspired me; I offered my heart's affections in return. It no more occurred to me to flaunt the flag on my chest than it did to pin my mother's picture on my lapel to prove her son's love. Mother knew where I stood; so does my country. I even tuck a valentine in my tax returns on April 15.

"So what's this flag doing here? Well, I put it on to take it back. The flag's been hijacked and turned into a logo – the trademark of a monopoly on patriotism. On those Sunday morning talk shows, official chests appear adorned with the flag as if it is the Good Housekeeping seal of approval. And during the State of the Union, did you notice Bush and Cheney wearing the flag? How come? No administration's patriotism is ever in doubt, only its policies.

"And the flag bestows no immunity from error. When I see flags sprouting on official lapels, I think of the time in China when I saw Mao's Little Red Book on every official's desk, omnipresent and unread.

"But more galling than anything are all those moralistic ideologues in Washington sporting the flag in their lapels while writing books and running Web sites and publishing magazines attacking dissenters as un-American. They are people whose ardor for war grows dispropor-tionately to the distance from the fighting. They're in the same league as those swarms of corporate lobbyists wearing flags and prowl-ing Capitol Hill for tax breaks even as they call for more spending on war.

"So I put this on as a modest riposte to men with flags in their lapels who shoot missiles from the safety of Washington think tanks, or argue that sacrifice is good as long as they don't have to make it, or approve of bribing governments to join the coalition of the willing (after they first stash the cash). I put it on to remind myself that not every patriot thinks we should do to the people of Baghdad what bin-Laden did to us. The flag belongs to the country, not the government. And it reminds me that it's not un-American to think that war except in self defense is a failure of moral imagination, political nerve, and diplomatic skill. Come to think of it, standing up to your government can mean standing up for your country.

"What do you think?"

The American dream has been a government budget surplus of $1.3 billion being given back to the wealthiest Americans instead of benefiting all Americans. New yachts and race cars are acceptable by *We the Apathetic Maids* as more important than better schools, health care.

Unlocking the Social Security "Lock Box" to pay for the War on Terror and a new budget deficit is also palatable as long as the mainstream media still repeat the death toll of the September 11 attacks was 3,000 or more when in fact the number was much lower. Isn't it time *We the Maids* sweep out these practices in the 21st century?

SARS Spin

The end of the Iraq War, according to flyboy Bush after he landed on an aircraft carrier, necessitated the media creation of another war to maintain viewership and ratings. When a war against Syria, Iran and North Korea didn't pan out, SARS became the perfect global story. A global pandemic from communist China. The war against SARS with words like "super-infector" and "corona virus" became everyday terminology as hundreds of flights were cancelled, hotels emptied out and people were subjected to quarantines and medical house arrests. Personally, I found the SARS media hype very beneficial. Air fares plummeted and free hotel rooms were included with the air fares. Lines at immigration and custom stations vanished. Taxis were plentiful and took me straight to where I wanted to go without any unnecessary detours to jack up the fare after I told them I was from Hong Kong and then started to cough.

The SARS media hype conveniently overlooked the basic facts and instead focused on and fed peoples' appetite for hysterical paranoia. Living with the Executive Director of the Hong Kong SPCA, who is a trained veterinarian who had to respond to news stories, editorials and letters to the editor hourly to correct, dispel rumors fueled by the "news stories", I realized early on how human emotions can become a feeding frenzy for the media. Mother Nature and cute little animals became the terrorists du jour. The fact that animals have been the source of most zoonotic infections – those that jump from animals to humans – since man evolved from an animal was ignored. The fact that more people died daily of the common cold, 'flu, car accidents, drug overdoses and alcoholism was ignored. The fact that not one person died of SARS in America was also ignored to focus on the daily death tallies in China.

Propaganda Spin
Making the best of a self-imposed house arrest in Hong Kong during the killer virus SARS epidemic, when schools and many businesses closed as the Iraq War got into full "Shock and Awe" mode, gave me a unique opportunity to become totally immersed and absorbed in the numerous national satellite news networks and related internet web sites covering the war ad nauseam. The same technological know-how became irritating when my engrossed TV viewing was interrupted by my mobile phone and the clients and business associates on the other end of the line who were totally impervious to either the war or the epidemic.

What a difference watching a war media spin in America and Hong Kong. In the States, most main stream media are pure patriotic Americana, with the BBC and the increasing number of Spanish and Latino channels continuously elbowing their way in to join the hundreds of ethnic and religious channels. The propaganda war to influence the public affects what we see on TV. The different angles of war presented by CNN, BBC, al-Jazeera and other Arab satellite broadcasters could easily be misinterpreted as two different wars. "Coalition forces" are "invading Americans". "Liberation" is "occupation". The differences are quite stark.

The war of words was more deadly than some of the precision high-tech super bunker busters. The Bushites' blind dialogue of the deaf missed what people were saying on the geopolitical American street. The dialogue got even more comical when one compared the Bushite press conferences to the Husseinite press conferences. Except for their collective bad taste in clothes and patriotic symbolism they do the same thing. Spin their message to their loyal supporters to pump them up, and then convince the rest of the world that the other side is lying. Liars' poker at its best. The only question is who is doing a better job and why? At least the Husseinites speak both Arabic and English. The Bushites speak cowboy rhetoric. "You dance with who brung ya," and "You're either with us or against us." Who brung us into the war?

Watching the deliberate pro-U.S. spin and perspective flood America's airwaves with the Bushites doing damage control while losing their cool is fully appreciated when sitting in Hong Kong and comparing the news coverage from America, China, UK, Spain, Russia, Germany, France, Saudi Arabia, Iraq, Qatar, Singapore, Australia, India, the Philippines and all the religious and political propaganda that each country spins. The picture looks and sounds a lot different in Hong Kong than it does in Anywhere, U.S.A.

Imran Khan, a member of Pakistan's national assembly and former cricket captain, summed it up best. "I never imagined that such a sophisticated, advanced country, one of the world's oldest democracies could have its foreign policy hijacked by powerful interest groups...The question that many are now asking is: Has September 11 been used as an excuse for the U.S. to fulfill its imperial ambitions and was the whole war against terrorism hyped to convince its public that this unjust war is justified?"

Any wonder the U.S. is becoming increasingly isolated and hated by the rest of the world? The 2003 Pew Global Attitute Project shows increasing numbers of people have negative views of America.

The Arab and Muslim world, not just the street, whether in Ankara, Baghdad, Cairo, Damascus, Islamabad, Jakarta or Kuala Lumpur echo the streets of New York, Los Angeles, London, Beijing, Tokyo, Paris, Seoul and Hong Kong. Why war? The Bush administration has chosen to ignore the street because making policy on the basis of large public protests would be like the president saying he would "decide policy based upon a focus group". Doesn't he? Bush has spent more money on polls and focus groups than any president in U.S. history.

Focus Groups

Focus groups allow politicians and corporations a glimpse into the mind of the general public so they can develop better ways to manipulate those minds to achieve their objective to determine better ways to develop their message. Representative citizens carefully selected by pollsters to test issues thought up by marketing and campaign professionals. In the words of E.J. Dionne, Jr.: "The approach to politics is not even Machiavellian; it is Pavlovian." The focus group may be the perfect symbol of what has happened to democracy in America. In so far as "the people" are consulted by political leaders these days, their reactions are of interest not as a guide to policy but simply as a way of exploring the electorate's gut feelings, to see which kind of divisive message might move them most.

The world would be a very different place without focus groups. Giving power to the people – a small, select group of people – has altered movie endings, groomed images of politicians and increased the number of products in retail stores. What they do not do is let people know where a politician stands on any particular issue. Political stands are deliberately fuzzy to confuse voters.

Ken McKenzie, the publisher of *Media* in Hong Kong, is right when he questions the advertising industry and asks: "Is anyone else out there feeling like the entire industry is being researched to death?"

It is too easy to rely on research data, to do and plan marketing strategies and campaigns in response to the findings of some new study. But where does this leave gut feel and intuition? Essentially, the human factor is under threat. We no longer trust our instincts;

we no longer believe anything that hasn't cost millions of dollars to research. Basically, if a fact lacks pages and pages of backup data – or worse, was offered as "free advice" – it is considered worthless in today's environment.

President Bush called the millions of anti-Iraq war demonstrations around the world "focus groups" he doesn't have to listen to. Why not? Everything else he and every career politician does is governed by focus groups. I guess maybe because they weren't the right conservative Christian Coalition he didn't think it necessary to tune in.

Focus groups and political pollsters who do word and message polling are the marketing tools that define how perception is to be managed! Focus groups are a vital research tool that is here to stay. If so, do the researchers and marketers that use them have to continue abusing them by creating fake politicians, fake movie endings and more of the same products that we already have too many of? Is the electorate just another marketplace to whom messages are created to make them believe it's what they want to hear because of focus groups and polls? Why does everything have to be response driven? What happened to beliefs and convictions?

The election between Gush and Bore highlighted how the candidates pre-test every issue and political sound bite. Any wonder they both sounded the same. How about addressing real issues of real concern to real people in the New World Order without the filter of focus groups? That just might ignite the interest and excitement of the people. Howard Dean proved that by speaking his mind. It might even get more to register to vote. Better yet, vote! But then again, that is not in the best interest of America's oligarchy and their focus groups.

The Web
The Internet has broken through the sterilized misperceptions and the political and corporate propaganda spin-doctors have prescribed. Their fancy packaged pill boxes, or is it bull boxes, have been pierced by the Internet which allows people to share the truth. *We The People* converse, interact and share our experiences and knowledge. The Internet has allowed people to recapture their freedom of expression as our Founding Fathers intended. The World Wide

Web has allowed people to cut through the over-spun messages of career politicians and their spin doctors' pubic relations as the first presidential election of the 21st century so vividly brought home. Howard Dean was propelled to the forefront of Democratic fund-raising by the net.

The Masters

The Church and the British have been the masters of managing perception for centuries and they did so without focus groups or opinion polls. What happened to "gut", "instinct" and "leadership"? They were alive and well with the British Empire and the Church, both Catholic and Protestant, as they exploited and colonized most of the world's surface.

Jesus was portrayed as a blond, fair skinned blue-eyed hippie. As a blond European growing up in Cyprus and Israel I knew firsthand how out of place and unlikely his blond features were. Even with a great sun tan. The people of Jesus' time in Israel and the Middle East were not much different than those of today. Dark skinned with short curly hair and trimmed beard. The climate determines one's skin color. Always has. The traditional image of the man Christians believe is the Son of God was shattered with the BBC, Discovery, and France 3 television co-production at the dawn of the 21st century.

Jesus was probably born in a cave. The Church of Nativity in Bethlehem is built over caves, not stables or an inn as Christian mythology depicts. In Jesus' time most people lived in caves, not only in Israel, but all over the world.

Caves where Jesus was probably born are similar to the caves where the Dead Sea Scrolls were found and where Osama bin-Laden feels most comfortable. The same caves where the Three Wise Men stayed, Saddam Hussein built his bunkers and the Viet Cong tunneled through to defeat America. Millions of people still live in caves around the world today. To this very day in Northwest China's Shaanxi Province, hundreds of thousands of rural residents lose their cave dwellings every time there is a heavy rainfall.

Astrologers believe Jesus was actually born in 6 B.C., six years earlier than claimed by the church. Furthermore they believe the

Three Wise Men were astrologers following the bright star of Jupiter! The bright Star of Bethlehem was the result of Jupiter being in Aries on April 17 six years before the day Jesus was supposed to have been born. Jupiter emerged as the morning star. Jupiter is the planet of kings. The Super King-Messiah. Hence the mythology created by Matthew and Luke. The myth that Jesus was the Son of God, not man. They and other students of theology agree Mary conceived out of wedlock. Therefore, it is only natural that the myth of her virginity and Immaculate Conception be spun and that Jesus became the Son of God and not man. Mary would have been stoned to death if she had a son out of wedlock in those days. Joseph married her to save her from death!

The Roman Catholics first crucified Christ, then Peter, upside down in Rome, gradually and reluctantly embraced their philosophy and beliefs and then went on to create Christian mythology, and spread Christianity and Jesus' blond image globally by brute force while blaming the Jews for his death.

The hatred of Jews was a central cornerstone of "Christian history, reaching to the core of Christian character", James Carroll reminds us. "The Blood Libel charges Jews with replaying the crucifixion of Jesus by murdering a Christian child, always a boy, and using his blood in perverse rituals that mock the Eucharist," Carroll says. After all, what kind of God shows favor to a beloved Son by requiring him to be nailed to a cross and then blames his Chosen People? Religious spin doctoring at its finest that justified repeated mass murders that led up to Hitler's genocide.

Jews prescribe washing hands before eating and washing woolens. This resulted in lower disease and death rates among Jews. It was easy for people who did not understand the value of washing to believe that if fewer Jews died it was because they had poisoned Christian wells.

Jews accounted for 10 percent of the population of the Roman Empire. By that ratio, if the Crusades, Inquisition, anti-Semitism and genocide had not intervened, there would be 200 million Jews in the world today instead of the 13 million. How we come to terms with past distortions created by spin-doctors that resulted in the deaths of millions of innocents will determine our future in the New World Order. Not just Jewish innocents, but all native indigenous innocents of the colonized Christian and Muslim worlds!

Men of the cloth in both Christian and Muslim societies were actually men of words. Wordsmiths extraordinaire. Spin-doctors who spun religious myths and their own self-importance into being accepted as the servants of God and the source of eternal salvation. With illiterate masses searching for salvation, it was easy for God's and Allah's wordsmiths to join forces with the career politicians of their day to capitalize on a mutually beneficial political pact that benefited both at the expense of the illiterate masses.

Santa Claus is another Christian myth created by religious spin-doctors. A fourth century bishop born in Patara, near Demre, Turkey, named Nicholas performed so many good deeds that he later was named a saint when he died around 343 and eventually earned worldwide renown as Father Christmas, or Noel Baba, as his predominantly Muslim countrymen call him. The current image of Father Christmas was made famous by Clement Clarke Moore in his 1822 poem, "A Visit From Saint Nicholas," and the rosy-cheeked, rotund Santa was created by Coca-Cola ads in the 1930s. Church spinners put him on a sleigh with reindeers and moved him to Lapland.

Legend has it that his love and generosity with children was boundless. These characteristics earned Nicholas his sainthood. The best story concerns three sisters who were going to sell themselves into slavery because their father could not afford dowries. Learning of their plight, Saint Nicholas threw bags of gold coins down their chimney, one of which landed in a stocking that was hung near the fire to dry. Thus began the tradition of hanging stockings on the mantel for presents.

The English are such masters of spin that they have the world believing that the English created the British Empire. In fact England was the first colony of the British Empire when James VI of Scotland became James I of England. Born to Mary, Queen of Scots, and Darnley, a Scot, his parents were beheaded by the English and he was raised in Scotland and France where he went into hiding to avoid the same fate. The deaths of his parents were brought about because of the religious wars between Catholics and Protestants.

The English did defeat the Scots, however, and James became king because of the British hereditary laws. No different than politics in America today. Hereditary political dynasties that so many died to abolish.

The Scots still run England at the dawn of the 21st century. Blair's a Scot and his cabinet is dominated by Scots.

The English also have the world believing they invented soccer. In fact several versions of cuju "kickball" were first played in China during the Han dynasty (206 B.C.-220 AD). The game was probably brought to Europe via the Silk Road.

The Scots have the world believing they invented golf. In fact chiuwan "beat ball" is very similar to golf and was played in China in the 10th century. This Chinese game was very popular with the Mongols and is believed to have been brought to Europe by Genghis Khan. Scottish golf dates from 1350. Pictures of these ancient sports in China survive on temple murals, porcelain pillows and calligraphy brush pots.

A silk scroll from the Song dynasty (960-1279) suggests an early version of baseball.

Britain's royal family changed its name from the House of Saxe-Coburg-Gotha to Windsor in 1917 amid anti-German feelings in Britain during World War I. Queen Elizabeth, the late Queen Mother, was born in Scotland and has more Scottish blood than English.

An amusing recent example of New World Disorder British-managed perception is the re-engineering, digitally of course, of Prince Edward's grim look to an oleaginous smile in his wedding day pictures. His wife Sophie, Countess of Wessex, the head of a pubic relations firm herself, spun herself and the royal family into a dark hole to a potential Arab client.

Britain did a great media spin covering up the fact that it recruited child soldiers and sent 17-year-olds to the Falklands and Bosnia while criticizing Sierra Leone and Sri Lanka for doing the same.

When the American-led war on terrorism was unleashed in Afghanistan, America and Britain set up the most ambitious wartime communications effort since World War II. Around-the-clock war news bureau was set up in Pakistan linked to a network of war communication offices in Washington, London and Islamabad to develop the "message of the day" after Washington became concerned they were losing the war for international public opinion. Washington went into high spin mode because although it was winning the military battle, the U.S. was losing the propaganda war to the Taleban and Osama bin-Laden, especially in the Muslim world. "How can a man in a cave outcommunicate the world's leading communications society?" former U.S. diplomat Richard Holbrooke asked. Spinners are not restricted to the Western world.

The Office of Global Communications was established as the new White House spin tank to get out the message that America is Muslim-friendly. A new Under Secretary of State for Public Diplomacy was also appointed and $20 million spent to get out America's new spin. A new Arabic-language pop-music station, Radio Sawa, has been launched and the spin goes on.

The Office of Global Communications was established when it became clear to the Bush White House that it was alienating not only the Muslim world but America's European allies because of its cowboy go-it-alone approach to foreign policy. An office that really can only be of limited effect as long as America doesn't change its approach and public policy in the 21st century.

When NATO had "image" and "presentation" problems regarding their bombings of Yugoslavia and Kosovo, what did they do? They got media reinforcements from Britain. The British Prime Minister's office dispatched media experts to improve and further manage NATO's media strategy.

Hong Kong Governor Christopher Patten perpetuated the British tradition of managing the world's perception of what a civilized job the Brits were doing and what a civilized place the Brits were handing over to the uncivil Chinese. The Chinese have a longer and richer history and civilization than the British but the Western world still accepted and bought the British version of how Hong Kong would be ruined by the Chinese if they did not accept the British demands and conditions prior to the handover.

I was pleasantly surprised to read the Chairman of Jardine Matheson

Henry Keswick's criticism of the former Governor's hypocrisy in his blistering criticism and review of Patten's book *East and West*. Keswick, a Catholic, also took exception to Patten's displays of religious conviction, taking a neat sideswipe at the crucifix displayed in the Governor's office "to remind the visitor of his Catholicism".

He should have left it there. Instead he remarked that the Governor did not do too much for the "200,000 Catholic Filipino maids who have no proper place for mass in their leisure time in Hong Kong".

In the late 1980s, Jardines gave over the large walk-through lobby of Jardine House for all-day masses on Sunday, celebrated by robed priests in front of temporary altars. Working your way through the throng of kneeling girls on route to the ferry pier, one would get caught up in at least two genuflections on the way. That facility no longer exists. Keswick and the British press are finally breaking down the facade of Britain's managed perception of its civilized and politically correct behavior towards institutions and politicians.

In Britain there is no sense of open government or of the public's right to know. The government has had little compunction about openly attacking the news media when it does not like the way it is being covered.

The best example was when the *Sunday Telegraph* published an article about a leaked government-sponsored report on racism and the police. Furious that his carefully laid plans to release the report in his own time had been so badly thwarted, the Home Secretary persuaded a judge to issue an injunction forcing the newspaper – which had already printed and shipped off some 290,000 early-edition copies – to remove the article from later editions.

Foot In Mouth
The British are such masters of the art that they decided to join their U.S. allies and blame the Chinese for the Foot and Mouth epidemic that blighted their farming and tourism industries at the dawn of the 21st century. They blamed Chinese restaurants for illegally importing meat that started the epidemic. They scapegoated the Chinese because they are easier to blame than admit it was a failure on the part of career politicians and their bureaucrats.

The spin-doctors conveniently blamed the Chinese. Why not? If America does, why not support an ally to create an illusory new millennium enemy?

Career politicians and their bureaucrats are responsible for the very lax border controls in Britain. Many Brits, not just the Chinese, import all kinds of illegal products into England. Smuggling in the meat – assuming that it was smuggled – was not the cause of the outbreak. It was the lax governmental controls and supervision of making pigswill from the leftover meals from restaurants. Had the making of the pigswill been done in compliance with the high government standards, any disease in the illegal meat would have been cured before it became animal feed. God forbid the British career politicians and their bureaucratic spin-doctors admit that in the interest of saving money they didn't "Buy British Beef" like they encourage every loyal citizen to do. Instead they bought the cheapest beef they could find for the British armed forces who wound up slaughtering the British sheep and cattle they should have been eating. The British government bought the meat to feed its troops from South Africa where foot and mouth was known to exist at the time. But the price was right. No different than the U.S. military buying its black berets from China and playing the purchase down while the U.S. spy plane crew were being detained not too far from the factories making their berets.

Foot 'n Mouth disease is not limited to British cattle, sheep and career politicians. Many American politicians find their feet in their mouth every morning.

Reality Check

It is in America's interest to see China play a constructive role in Asia. Particularly on the Korean peninsula, in Palestine and Kashmir. The fact that Beijing hosted the separate talks between the two Koreas and those between North Korea and the U.S. demonstrated Beijing's keen interests in reducing danger in the peninsula and the region. The Beijing conference at the end of 2003 on how to get the Palestinian peace process back on track confirmed its commitment to regional peace and stability. Beijing has also shown its sincerity in cooling down the hostilities between its southern neighbors by holding a series of bilateral talks with both India and Pakistan.

India's External Affairs Minister Jaswant Singh flew to Beijing on the heels of his counterpart from Pakistan. China maintains a balanced relationship with both its neighbors by not siding with Pakistan on the Kashmir issue.

America needs China as a partner in Asia if it wants to ensure peace and stability in the region. America cannot go it alone or with Japan. North Korea has been corraled and broken into the New World Order because its reclusive leader Kim Jong-il is being coached by the Chinese leadership who have done much in encouraging him to meet South Korean leader Kim Dae Jung in Pyongyang – a stunning new millennium move. China is America's logical and practical regional partner. Spin-doctors cannot change this reality. Only its perception.

China does not have the ability to go head-to-head with the U.S. in a military confrontation. Moreover, there is strong belief among Chinese leaders that the key to being a great power is to have a world-class economy, which requires a stable environment. China knows well that conflict could jeopardize this growth and is to be avoided. Washington also realizes that it cannot ensure a desired outcome of Asia's security problems without Beijing's co-operation.

Banking Crisis

The 1990s global economic crisis is another exemplary example of managed perception. It was repeatedly referred to as the "Asian Crisis", "Asian Flu", "Asian contagion", Asian meltdown", "started in Asia" or "triggered in Asia". Nothing could be further from the truth. It was a crisis brought upon us by banks. It was a banking crisis. It was the Savings and Loan bailout of the eighties magnified globally in the international arena. Specifically in Asia. Banks in Thailand. Banks in Indonesia. Banks in South Korea. Banks in Japan. Banks in America. Banks in Europe and the IMF bear full responsibility for what happened. The "IMF reality gap" in Russia, their consistent funding of Russia, provided a tacit endorsement for the world's private banks to party on in Moscow. Their herd mentality and greed got them over-extended in Russia and Asia, and when reality finally set in they panicked and that same herd mentality created the liquidity problems, first in Thailand, which swiftly swept through the region. The protective banking bureaucratic regulators also are to share the blame for not forcing the banks to act sooner. Especially in Japan.

I concur with Robert J. Samuelson's observation: "Led by the United States, global agencies (the World Trade Organization, the IMF) sought to persuade poorer countries to become more open to trade and global capital. These countries tried to maximize the benefits of the process while minimizing changes in their politics and commerce.

"Mutual deception flourished. Countries like South Korea and Russia pretended that they were changing more than they did. American, European and Japanese bankers, executives and government officials pretended that the claims were true, or might become true."

No different than when banks shortly thereafter went on a frenzied stampede to finance dotcoms with no business plans or realistic source of revenue with their depositors' and investors' money. The same results highlighted new economy banking practices in the 21st century. Its always OPM – "Other People's Money."

Whose money was it that was spent by the five bankers fired from Barclays for spending 44,000 pounds sterling at Petrus in London for a meal with a lot of expensive wines that they then tried to pass off as a client expense? Depositors', investors', conflicted advisory service clients' money?

The World Bank blames the U.S. and the IMF for the financial crisis in Asia. The bank put out a 200 page report that squarely blames the U.S. Treasury and the IMF for pushing Asian nations to raise their interest rates dramatically. The report says that move was a big blunder that triggered the crisis. How much coverage did this report get? Crisis spin- doctors contained the media play.

Having founded the largest initially capitalized national bank in U.S. banking history in 1981, Mercantile National Bank, and also as a lawyer who represented several banks, savings and loans, and thrift and loans, I have some insight as to how bankers' greed gets the financial hogs slaughtered while shifting the blame to careless public butchers.

Asian crony capitalism and "Asian values" were the mantras of bankers and the media at the time. When America's corporate giants started collapsing into bankruptcy court at the dawn of the 21st century, "American values" or "Western values" were not brought up once. I wonder if they will when the derivative financial time bombs of mass destruction implode.

Managed perception at its pubic best. Actually, there was one better. After the Anglo-American-led Western NATO alliance bombed the Chinese Embassy in Belgrade. The media portrayed the Chinese protesters trashing the U.S. Embassy in Beijing as being wrong. How would Americans react if China bombed a U.S. embassy anywhere? Chinatowns would be aflame.

Sino-American Propaganda

Taiwan at the dawn of the 21st century was described as a "country" by *The New York Times*. The mayor of the city from which the distinguished paper hails, Rudy Giuliani, also referred to Taiwan as a "country". Examples of expensive Taiwan spin-doctors doing their job.

The Bush Administration promised Taiwan diesel submarines. The media spun the story everywhere, endlessly thanks again to Taiwan's effective spin-doctors. The only problem is, the U.S. doesn't make diesel submarines, and countries that did didn't want the business because it could damage their relations with China! The end result is no one wants to make them.

Zhang Yimou, the Hollywood-acclaimed Chinese director, sums it up best.

The Chinese government twice prohibited his films from competing in the Cannes Film Festival. His film *Not One Less* was permitted to be entered. It is a realistic, charming story of children in the countryside struggling to stay in school, a movie that finally won authorities' consent for entry at Cannes. But during the selection process, Zhang heard, a Cannes screening committee member called the film "propaganda". Stung, the director yanked it out of competition. He also pulled another film, *The Road Home,* that he had planned to screen during the festival.

"It seems that in the West, there are always two 'political criteria' when interpreting Chinese films, either 'anti-government' or 'propaganda'," he wrote in an open letter to Cannes festival director Gilles Jacob. "This is unacceptable."

Chinese Premier Li Peng in an interview mocked what he called ignorant U.S. senators whose views of China came from old films and novels. Li also took a swipe at the Western media for faking the news, and poured scorn on U.S. boasts to have the world's greatest democracy. "In the mind of some U.S. senators we have spoken with, China is still the backward image described in old movies and novels, and they know very little about the present China, or what they have learned is a pack of completely distorted facts."

When China started arresting democracy advocates after signing the UN Human Rights Convention and after the televised debate between Jiang Zemin and Bill Clinton in 1998, American papers headlined the crackdown and prompted critics in Washington to question the White House's approach of engagement rather than confrontation. Kenneth Lieberthal, head of Asia policy at the National Security Council, is correct when he said administration critics sometimes have unrealistic expectations.

"I sometimes see criticism along the lines of, 'Gee, you said this would lead to democracy in China and it hasn't'," he said. "I don't know anyone here who said it would lead to democracy in six months or two years."

Hollywood Hype
Amusing to see the moguls behind the Hollywood facade and their managed perceptions act with the same violence towards each other that they package into their neo-imperialist productions. Jeffrey Katzenberg the K in Dream Works SKG vs. Michael Eisner the CEO of Disney. So much pique, so much ego, so much obsessing about who's where in the food chain. Hard to think of them as moguls making family entertainment, but as the eighth and ninth dwarfs, Greedy and Nasty with well-spun pubic images.

The spin Hollywood puts on itself and America creates the illusion that all that glitters is gold, and that all is well on "Gold Mountain". A spin that has people believing that America's political culture and democracy must be emulated by the whole world if they want to live the Hollywood fantasies portrayed on screen. Unfortunately, the Hollywood sets and makeup mask the truth and create a mythical facade of the American ideal. Democracy, religious tolerance, racial equality, education, equal political participation in the political process in America, like Hollywood sets, are an illusion *We the Apathetic People* have come to accept thanks to the web of Hollywood hype we have been caught up in.

Career politicians hire spin-doctors and Hollywood producers to spin us dizzy until we come to accept whatever message they want to convey.

During the Afghan war on terror, Hollywood producers were recruited en masse, as portrayed in *Wag the Dog,* to convince the public that what America was doing was right. Who better to deliver the knock-out punch than Muhammad Ali?

Feet On The Ground

Alain Peyrefitte, Minister of Justice and adviser to Charles de Gaulle, has long pondered the British Diaspora's remarkable expansion and continuing global influence. It is a question that has confounded generations of Frenchmen – as well as other Europeans – who have watched the island race and its offspring snatch the largest share of the world's riches, power and influence.

Today it is the American Diaspora of the British that constitutes the core of the developed society. "A century has passed since the apogee of the British empire, but the nations it spawned – the United States, Canada, Australia and New Zealand – still account for 13 of the world's largest companies, over half the GDP of the world's seven leading industrialized countries, and by far the largest portion of overseas foreign investment stock, more than Japan and Germany combined," Peyrefitte says.

Great Britain not only colonized the world, globalized English, capitalism and democracy, but sports as well. Soccer, tennis, golf, cricket and rugby are all British exports which went with trade and took root with the flag.

To Peyrefitte, the source of this enormous Anglo-American triumph lies not in any inherent technological or managerial genius. The

British, he notes, even at the height of empire, had chosen to place profits over strengthening the state. Both America and Hong Kong are the beneficiaries of this policy. The French and Spanish colonies are the losers for putting religion ahead of commerce.

Dom Vessigault had lived in Hong Kong for 28 years at the time of the handover. He was the head of the French Chamber of Commerce and the Perfume Association. He had very serious concerns about the Chinese "scrapping Legco (Hong Kong Legislature) and putting a Chinese flag on the building". He had a son in California and like many Hong Kongers spent most of his time on the road, in his case between Europe and the U.S. "I'm an old colonial warhorse that doesn't like to see the fodder changed in its stable," he responded to my question about how he felt about Hong Kong after the handover. We were having lunch at the FCC, exchanging views on the reality in Hong Kong, the perceptions of colonial warhorses who had made contingency plans to leave if the disaster scenarios portrayed by Governor Patten materialized. "Actually, surprisingly, things are quite good. The economic problems are because of the Asian banking and economic virus and not China's political interference. In fact I talked to the Financial Secretary, Donald Tsang, and he told me he hasn't received one phone call from Beijing," Dom continued. "He did on occasion get phone calls from London. In fact if things did get bad I was planning on going to the U.S. where things are much brighter economically. The French economy, in fact the rest of Europe, is terrible and with no prospects of improving. De Gaulle was right when he said the British and Anglo-Saxons had their feet on the ground as opposed to the French who had their head in the clouds."

The French are an amazing people with their head either in a cloud or where the sun don't shine. They question America's right to attack a country while they invade their former colony in Africa to "restore order". Jean-Marie Messier, the former French investment banker who became the CEO of Vivendi-Universal, is the model French banker and gentleman. He wiped out all shareholders' equity and almost bankrupted the company while building himself a lavish home in New York. Mr. Messier was too pre-occupied with his banker's merger and acquisition gigantic ego, the commission rush he got for just putting the deal together and his lofty Hollywood image. In a country like France with 270 cheeses and millions of Messiers, it is not only ungovernable as General Charles de Gaulle uttered, but also stinks to high heaven without that wonderful French creation – perfume.

Misrepresented American Empire
From its colonizer parent England, America inherited incredible skills in managing perception. The blatant land grab in Puerto Rico, the Caribbean and the Philippines, was packaged and sold by the media as "liberating" these territories from the Imperial Spanish Empire.

Mark Twain, one of America's most honest and perceptive writers, summed up what could have happened if America was true to itself and didn't manage its perception as liberator. "The game was in our hands. If it had been played according to the American rules, Dewey would have sailed away from Manila as soon as he had destroyed the Spanish fleet – after putting up a sign on shore guaranteeing foreign property and life against damage by the Filipinos, and warning the powers that interfere with the emancipated patriots would be regarded as an act unfriendly to the United States. The powers cannot combine, in even a bad cause, and the sign would not have been molested."

Before America entered World War II, it allegedly gave Britain naval destroyers under a charitable Lend Lease Program. What was overlooked by the press thanks to spin-doctors was that the payment for the ships was the oil under the British Saudi Arabian colonial desert.

The promotion of democracy while supporting repressive totalitarian dictatorships that suit America's economic interests, such as those in Indonesia, Saudi Arabia and other oil-producing countries, is an example of America's inherited marketing skills. Political regimes that benefit America economically or politically, no matter how repressive or undemocratic, are supported and portrayed in a favorable light. One that is palatable and acceptable to Americans.

America, with its history of ethnic cleansing of Native-Americans and seizure of territories from Mexico in the name of Manifest

Destiny, of enslavement of African-Americans and Chinese coolies in the interest of cheap labor, is now castigating and criticizing other countries for doing less. "Don't do as I do, but do what I say" applies to America in its criticism of other countries' political systems, labor and environmental laws, human rights and expansionist policies.

California Propaganda

The energy crisis in California during the infancy of the Bush Administration heard the President vow he opposed "price caps". Yet when he imposed them they became a "market-based mitigation plan". Let's not forget that while he was making these mythically spun pronouncements, Enron had his ear, his V.P.'s ear and a lot of other ears, mouths, stomachs and bank accounts in the Bush administration.

So did Democratic Governor Gray Davis in California. Since all the phony Enron maneuvers led to deregulation, which required elected officials to change the laws, which well-paid career politicians, their lobbyists and lawyers were happy to accommodate. The fact that the new legislation may not really be in the best interest of *We the People,* as the energy deregulation legislation seems to indicate, it is up to career politicians like Governor Gray Davis and acting politicians like his successor Arnold Schwarzenegger to make 21st century sense of it.

Maybe he should propose an emergency extension of daylight savings time to conserve energy. Daylight savings time was first brought in for two years in World War I as an energy-conservation measure. The practice was resumed during World War II when the government spinners called it War Time and it was made permanent in the seventies during the Arab oil embargo. In 1986 President Ronald Reagan lengthened daylight savings by about three weeks. The formal measurement of time is a human invention that can be spun to meet political and energy needs.

The so-called California economic and energy crisis that resulted in the recall of Gray Davis and the election of Arnold Schwarzenegger was another human invention spun to *We the Maids* by seasoned spin-doctors. Energy deregulation was legislated into law in California by Gray Davis' predecessor, Republican Governor Pete

Wilson. The California economy was also doing relatively well compared to the rest of the country when Davis was recalled. The energy crisis, the burst Silicon Valley bubble and budget deficit were spun to portray a state in recession when it was anything but. In fact military spending was up, housing starts and home sales prices had also been on the rise for a couple of years before the recall.

The business climate, workers' compensation and increased energy costs, new motor vehicle registration fees and mandatory health requirements on companies employing 20 or more people, increased the cost of doing business competitively in California. This was the message I got loud and clear from discussions I had with family members and friends when I spent a few days in California before and after the recall election. I sensed a real anger and frustration at the system and the grave injustices it had foisted on the hard-working tax paying people.

Free Trade?

When it comes to free trade, Americans think America is in the forefront. The global warrior against protectionism. For decades before September 11 America's mantra to the world was "leave it to the market". State governments should not intervene and subsidies are out. Nothing could be further from the truth. "The Americans had been teaching us the gospel of free markets," said Elie Cohen, a leading economist and advisor to Prime Minister Lionel Jospin of France. "But when it turns out the Americans are facing the same problems, they seem to forget the universal laws of the market." John Maynard Keynes, the British economist who advocated vigorous public spending, subsidies and deficit spending as tools to restore economic stability, is alive and well in America at the dawn of the 21st century.

On November 15, 2001, a day after U.S. Trade Representative Robert Zoellick aggressively promoted free trade at the end of the WTO meeting in Qatar, the U.S. Senate Agriculture Committee released a report on a five-year, $88 billion farm subsidy bill. This after the U.S. led the charge at the WTO meeting that Koreans reduce their subsidies to the country's rice farmers and open their rice market to foreign competition. "So we're contradicting ourselves," says

Gary Hufbauer, a senior fellow at the Institute for International Economics in Washington.

George Will in his book *Restoration* accurately highlights examples of American-managed misperception of protectionism. "Americans got an idea of how protectionist America is when, in late December, 1991, and early 1992, President Bush and an equally wimpy entourage of overpaid CEOs of underachieving corporations toured the Far East. They were a national embarrassment, representing the United States as the crybaby of the Western World.

"Their tour got off to a stumbling start in Australia. There Bush, with the representatives of America's industrial anemia in tow, was about to chant the mantra of 'fair' rather than free trade when the Aussie farmers drowned him out with complaints about huge U.S. subsidies of wheat exports. When President Lincoln founded the Department of Agriculture, it had one employee for every 227, 000 farms. In 1900 it had one employee for every 1,694 farms. Today it has one employee for every sixteen farms, and the laughter is a little less uproarious when a congressman proposes a law stipulating that there shall never be more Agriculture Department employees than farmers."

Responding to pressure from the U.S. steel industry, the Commerce Department announced several measures to reduce the import of cheap steel from Japan, Brazil, and Russia – i.e., win, place and show in the global economic dysfunction Derby.

The steel industry has very effective lobbyists. Every administration does them a favor in exchange for their campaign contributions. George Dubya was no different. The steel tariff was imposed by the Bush White House to garner votes in the 2002 mid term election to keep control of the House and regain control of the Senate by getting steel workers in the steel- producing states to vote Republican. Republicans as well as Democrats were opposed to the steel tariffs. So were members of Bush's own cabinet. Treasury Secretary Paul H. O'Neall told a foreign policy group he disagreed with the Bush administration decision because it risked the nation's interests as the world leader promoting free trade.

In principle, the U.S. government is committed to promoting free trade around the world – a policy supported by an overwhelming (and rare) consensus of economists. Yet politicians, not economists, make trade policy, and so the principle of free trade often loses out to the practice of protectionism. "When we build walls of protectionism around us, we doom ourselves to mediocrity," Richard Nixon said.

The irony in the steel debate is that U.S. policymakers in other parts of government are eager to send money to many of these countries, often via the IMF. The U.S. has an interest, they argue with some justification, in promoting world prosperity. Yet taken as a whole, U.S. policy conveys an insane schizophrenic message: We Americans should happily send our aid dollars to ailing economies, but we should object if they send us cheap goods in return. Why? Is this in the best economic interest of *We the People?*

America Propaganda & Labels

"The danger is that too many people believe the spin-doctors and policy advisors are running the government policies and spinning them rather than members of the cabinet who were elected to do the job," said Douglas Henderson, a former British foreign minister. Right on! It never ceases to amaze me how retired career politicians come clean and articulate reality that contradicts their practice while in office.

Another example is the justification for today's high tax rates. It is being falsely sold as "saving Social Security" – as if the government were squirreling away the decades of anticipated surplus for the boomers' rainy day. But that trust is always on loan to the Treasury.

The U.S. repeatedly criticizes China, Russia, France and others for their arms sales to developing nations. But it is America that is the world's leading arms dealer. It has cornered the market. At the end of the last millennium as the world's biggest arms dealer, according to a report by the Congressional Research Service on arms of the Library of Congress – U.S. contractors sold over $16 billion in weapons – nearly half of the world total.

The Americans repeatedly accuse the Chinese of "dumping" products in the U.S. Dumping is the legal term for a country selling products cheaper in foreign markets than at home. When the 2004 presidential election got under way China was again accused of dumping. The media and hype surrounding the announcement that China was found guilty by the Dubya Commerce Department of dumping color TVs were overwhelming. Yet when the U.S. was found guilty by the WTO of dumping newsprint on China, that story did not get much press play in the U.S.

Neither do any authoritative reports on the substantial status of marijuana and its medical benefits. No major newspaper in the United States mentioned the conclusion by *The Lancet,* Britain's leading medical journal, that marijuana is "less of a threat to health than alcohol or tobacco, products that in many countries are... tolerated and advertised".

Another British journal, *New Scientist,* revealed that sections of a World Health Organization report on marijuana had been suppressed at the last minute. The UN agency's report had concluded that marijuana is safer than alcohol and tobacco. American officials at the National Institute on Drug Abuse called for the removal of those passages, claiming they would encourage groups campaigning to legalize marijuana. A subsequent editorial in *New Scientist* criticized "the anti-dope propaganda that circulates in the U.S." and called for the decriminalization of marijuana. One NIDA researcher told *Scientific American* of the constant pressure to uncover pot's harmful effects. "Never has so much money been spent trying to find something wrong with a drug and produced so few results." It is almost as pig-headed as the struggle of the old "Creationists" against evolution.

The environment and pollution controls are another great example. The U.S. is the world's largest polluter which repeatedly makes hollow promises to create pollution controls, while demanding other countries contribute more to the fight against global warming. A country with nearly as many saloon cars as people – and many of those with gratuitously large engine capacities – wags a finger at Third World countries busting to develop because they tolerate two-stroke motor bikes, three-wheel taxis and low cost diesel trucks to bring goods more cheaply to market.

"Face it: a nation that maintains a 72 percent approval rating on George W. Bush is a nation with a very loose grip on reality," *Time* Magazine columnist Garrison Keillor astutely concludes. "The shamelessness of this government – leading the lynching of a few corporate scapegoats to distract the mob from your own sins – the naked hypocrisy of it! If you're not brave enough to have morals when you're 72 percent popular, what hope is there for you?" Keillor concludes.

China Trade

High poll ratings do not stop America's politicians from bashing China during an election year. The 2004 presidential election was the latest prime time example. U.S. politicians want to make sure that whatever blame is directed their way for their "voodoo economics", it is deflected and redirected at China. This happened repeatedly during the 2004 presidential and congressional campaigns. The arguments made on the campaign trails were pure political spin rather than facts. The fact is that most American manufacturers have moved their plants overseas, including to China, because of the high cost of manufacturing in America. As a result, American manufacturing and their labor unions are facing the worst crisis since the Depression era. Over 2.5 million manufacturing jobs have been lost to foreign manufacturers since Dubya was installed in the White House by the Supreme Court in 2001.

China had nothing to do with their relocation. They did so for pure bottom line business reasons. China happens to be a convenient political scapegoat. Trade imbalance, revaluation of the Chinese yuan and U.S. sanctions if China fails to comply became the rallying call of politicians trying to get the rust-belt votes. So much so that the Department of Commerce set up a political team to "take care" of China. Commerce Secretary Donald Evans led the charge in speeches across America. Washington would not tolerate a "stacked deck". "Without reciprocal market access and market access meaning a two-way street, it's very tough to sustain a growing relationship economically," Evans told the American Chamber of Commerce in Beijing. "Free trade has to be a level playing field." The guffaws and chuckles that comment generated at the FCC Main Bar echoed in every glass. Considering the billions of dollars America pumps into subsidies one has to question who is on the unlevel playing field with the "stacked deck". Former U.S. trade chief Mickey Kantor took issue with Evans saying the impact of the yuan on U.S. jobs was overstated. "A rapid revaluation of the reminbi is not in the best interests of China, or the best interests of the Asian economy or the best interests of the world economy," he said.

Leading world economists, including Robert Mundell, the "American father of the Euro" and a 1999 Nobel laureate in Economics, said there was no theory advocating balancing trade with exchange rates. Former U.S. Trade Representative Charlene Barshefsky said China's currency exchange rate is not to blame for the U.S.'s trade imbalance. Japan's former vice-finance minister Eisuke Sakakibara, known as "Mr. Yen" for his ability to influence financial markets, was against the revaluation of the yuan because "a floating yuan may lead to a disastrous result in Asia, even in the world."

To blame China for manipulating its currency and that being the cause for the trade imbalance between America and China is pure political spin. The fact is China has kept its currency pegged to the U.S. dollar since 1995. It has also taken the billions it has earned in trade and invested them in the U.S. buying U.S. federal bonds that help U.S. career politicians underwrite and increase *We the Apathetic People's* budget deficits. China is the second largest purchaser of U.S. bonds.

Instead of blaming China for America's economic woes caused by self-serving career politicians, America should lift many of the export restrictions it has imposed on goods and services that can be exported to China. That would certainly help balance trade. Let us not forget that America had a trade surplus with China for 21 straight years from 1972 until 1993. China started having a trade surplus with the U.S. only since 1993. More importantly, more than half of the Chinese exports to the United States are produced by foreign-funded enterprises in China, many from America.

China recently eclipsed Japan to become the world's third largest importer after America and Europe. Does it make sense to have export restrictions on a major importer that are purely political in nature and then complain about the trade imbalance? Military concerns are understandable. But why maintain outdated military trade restrictions when America's allies in Europe don't? China's new Import Fair initiative launched in 2003 encourages sellers to come to China in addition to the traditional buyers. *We the Apathetic Maids* have to wake up and sweep out spin-doctors that have us believing America's economic woes are China's fault. They are ours, thanks to the career politicians we allow to manipulate the process at our expense.

Trade Not Aid

Policymakers would do all taxpayers a favor if they heeded the old slogan of economic development: "trade, not aid." Direct payments to foreign governments, dispensed with or without IMF advice, sometimes do more harm than good. By contrast, an open trading system is one of the surest ways to promote growth around the world. Genuine open trade, the World Bank told us, would increase the income of Third World countries by $200 billion to $500 billion a year. Sadly, current American policy is getting things exactly backward. Managed perception however leads most taxpayers to believe otherwise.

Some foreign governments are treating U.S. companies badly, but not as badly as the U.S. government, at the behest of U.S. companies, is treating U.S. citizens.

If the Commerce Department were abolished, America's standard of living would rise.

Some Commerce Department officials candidly hope that the capriciousness of their decisions will deter foreign exporters. Were everyone candid, they would acknowledge that much of U.S. trade policy, stripped of highfalutin' rhetoric about "fair" trade, is just a jobs program. And among the jobs protected by U.S. protectionism are those of many incompetent and overpaid American executives whose companies are weak because they have been protected from bracing competition by government bureaucrats.

Pubic Campaign Reform

The great fanfare that heralded the new campaign finance reform bill signed into law by the President in 2002 was a classic spin of mismanaged perception. All the bill did was shift campaign contributions to state parties instead of national parties and in fact increased the amount of money individuals can contribute from $1,000 per person to $2,000! The buying of influence in politics continues uninterrupted in the 21st century notwithstanding all the press and media hype that the new law removed "big money" and soft money from politics. The McCain-Feingold and Shays-Meehan campaign reform bills were watered down to perpetuate corruption in the U.S. political system. The only campaign reform that will remove corruption from the system is the elimination of private individual and corporate contributions and replace the current system with one that is publicly financed by all American citizens.

Enron-Halliburton Spin

The media web Enron spun around itself, positioning the company as the darling of Wall Street that was in the forefront of the dot com "new economy", is an ideal example of managed misperception. While its executives raped their employees and shareholders of their life savings, they paid themselves lavish salaries, stock options and partied around the world in style, showering career politicians in both the Democratic and Republican parties with political contributions for unfettered access at all levels of government.

Enron had been accused in 1987 of making more than $136 million in fake oil trades. An "expensive embarrassment" Ken Lay said at the time. Yet this known convicted fraudster was allowed to become a major player in America's corporate and political games by his well-financed career politicians, bankers and accountants who all disregarded their fiduciary obligations to the public.

Enron became the political parking lot for numerous Bush political operatives and spin meisters while Dubya geared up his campaign to run for the White House. One such operative was Ralph Reed, the man that made Pat Robertson and the Christian Coalition look good before being parked at Enron by Karl Rove in 1997 with other "Bushies" where he was put on the company payroll until it filed for bankruptcy protection. Reed knew that Bush would win because "He (God) knew that George Bush had the ability to lead in this compelling way."

Enron Field in Houston was built by a Halliburton subsidiary while Dick Cheney was the company CEO and fund-raising for the Bush run for the White House. No wonder fellow Enron CEO Kenneth Lay became an early supporter of Mr. Bush's presidential campaign, signing on as a "pioneer" who raised more than $100,000 while other Enron executives donated an additional $114,000. Mr. Lay and Enron donated a further $200,000 for the inaugural parties. Any wonder Dick Cheney has been unwilling to release records regarding contacts and political payback his energy taskforce made to Enron while it was formulating the administration's energy legislation that was submitted to Congress?

The Enron collapse brought to light the web spun by Enron lobbyists, spin meisters, bankers, accountants and their well-funded career politicians at the expense of *We the Apathetic Maids*. Household institutional names Arthur Andersen, Citigroup, Merrill Lynch, JP Morgan Chase and Halliburton and numerous former executives from both Enron and Halliburton who are now on the taxpayers' payroll in the Dubya administration are Texas "white collar terrorists" that have spun an image of benevolent patriotic capitalists. Dick Cheney's well-spun success story has unraveled for the farce it really was. One *We the Apathetic Maids* bought hook line and stinker.

When Dick Cheney was the Halliburton CEO, he made a commercial for Arthur Andersen, the Halliburton auditor, accountant and consultant. "I get good advice, as you will from their people based upon how we're doing business and how we're operating – over and above just sort of the normal by-the-books auditing arrangement" are the complimentary words spoken by the Vice President in his thirty-five second spot for Arthur Andersen.

Dick Cheney was the Halliburton CEO from 1995 to 2000. During that period he transformed the company from a second-tier oil field services company to the industry leader. The Bush campaign regarded Cheney's corporate credentials as an important election year asset. Cheney cashed in stock and options worth more than $30 million when he left to join the Bush administration. Today Cheney, like all other suspect CEOs who profited at the expense of public shareholders who lost their savings and retirement nest eggs, is the only one who made a profit. Halliburton's stock has dived 76 percent since Cheney sold his shares. Why aren't *We the Apathetic People* outraged? Isn't that what happened to Dubya's oil company after he sold his shares and the company's financials were made public?

It should therefore come as no surprise that Halliburton under Dick Cheney's stewardship, like Enron under Lay's, booked over $100 million in disputed claims as income based on the recommendation of Arthur Andersen. Let us not forget that it was also a Halliburton European subsidiary that reported to Dick Cheney that was a major violator of the UN oil embargo of Iraq.

Enron and Halliburton are classic studies in financial and political manipulation that *We the Apathetic People* lap up like thirsty cute puppies instead of barking junk yard dogs keeping corrupt career politicians and their cash collectors out of our savings accounts and tax wallets. If *We the Maids* don't sweep in radical reforms to keep career politicians and their moneyed interests in check, our national and personal budgets will never be balanced.

Government Fraudulent Bookkeeping

South Carolina Senator Ernest Hollings validly asks: "How can Americans be confident in the stock market and the country when everything seems to be one grand fraud?" Washington has, like corporate America, been cooking the books because it is run by the same corporate CEOs and career politicians they used to lobby when they were in the private sector to pass laws favoring their misdeeds.

When the Bush-Cheney Enron oil executives came to Washington they wiped out overnight a 10-year $5,600 billion surplus and turned it into a $412 billion deficit *We the Apathetic People* have to pay because we let them take our surplus and give it to their cronies. Crony capitalism at its oil slickest spin that they accuse Third World banana republics of practicing.

In 1983, the Greenspan commission restored the soundness of Social Security with a graduated payroll tax, meant to take care of the baby boomers in this century. The commission's report required surpluses from Social Security to be put in an off-budget trust fund to be used for future generations. Back then Reaganomics, the policy of economic growth by cutting taxes, led to spending Social Security and other trust funds in order to say the deficit was decreasing, while it was in fact increasing.

President George H.W. Bush called Reaganomics "Voodoo". Now President Dubya is giving us "Voodoo II", to quote Senator Hollings. This Enron-oil industry system of accounting hides the truth by juggling two sets of books. It is like paying off one credit card with another. The Dubya administration continues this charade by dividing the budget into public debt and government debt. Both debts combined constitute the total national debt. But Bush talks only about the public debt, the bonds and notes America issues, of which trillions of dollars worth are held by Japan and Saudi Arabia, while hiding the government debt – Social Security and the other trust funds the government raids like the banana republics it criticizes for doing the same. Political spin at its finest. What the government has to talk about without the spin is the total national debt.

The budget committee tried to stop this charade in 1990 by passing section 13301 of the Budget Act forbidding the president and the Congress from citing a budget that spends Social Security. "But, no matter, the president, the Congress and the media – acting like Enron – violate section 13301 by spending Social Security and other trust funds and fraudulently reporting that they have not been spent," Senator Hollings reminds *We the Apathetic People*.

The financial markets see this fraud. They know the government will need to borrow money, coming into the market with its sharp elbows, crowding out business finance, stultifying the economy and causing long term interest rates to go up. Guess who they will go to to sell the debt? China! When Ronald Reagan came into office the interest cost on the national debt was $95 billion. By 2001 it was $359 billion! Guess who's paying it? *We the Apathetic People* who are the taxpayers.

Think about it for a minute. Every day the government borrows nearly $1 billion to service the national debt that *We the Apathetic People* have to pay back! "This is outrageous waste. But the bigger outrage is the president, Congress and the media crying foul at

Enron while engaging in the same type of fraud," Senator Hollings reminds anyone who will listen. The only beneficiaries of this endless debt are bankers!

The fraud being perpetrated by career politicians is not limited to Washington D.C. It goes on at the local state level as well. New Jersey stopped contributing to its state employee pension fund under the administration of Christine Whitman and then took existing funds and engaged in stock arbitrage. Now taxpayers have to make up a $22 billion loss. Alabama, Tennessee and countless other states engage in similar practices made public by *Business Week* the week Bush signed the Corporate Responsibility legislation. The various state pension fund losses involve the equivalent of at least fifty WorldComs. What's even more depressing is that the government's Office of Management & Budget is blatantly lying to the public about the severity of the situation.

Drinkers actually did better on their investment than bankers, pension fund managers and the investing public thanks to the fraudulent shenanigans of career politicians and the corporate lobbyists and lawyers. If a person had bought $1,000 worth of Enron stock a year before the company went bankrupt, he or she would have $16.50 of their original investment. With WorldCom, they would have less than five dollars left. On the other hand, if they had bought a $1,000 worth of Stella at the same time, drank all the beer, then returned the bottles for the five cent deposit, they would have made $107.

Civilized Face, Cruel Facts

Money fuelled the British moves to the Americas, India and China. Often this expansionism led to the most brutal forms of commercial exploitation. Along the China coast, British traders – including Scots such as the Jardines and Mathesons who had fled their ghetto in rocky, infertile Scotland – grew rich primarily through a massive trade in opium, in the process helping to turn nearly one of every eight Chinese nationals into a drug addict.

Growing up in Cyprus in the 1950s I had experienced firsthand British brutality inflicted on the Greek-Cypriots fighting for their independence from Britain. My mother chose not to live in any of the British bases or enclaves. Instead we moved into a mixed

Greek-Turkish neighborhood. I learned to speak Greek and actually looked forward to playing with the Greek and Turkish children after school because we had more freedom to roam and play in the orange groves, forests, swamps and beaches. All areas that were off limits to the British army brats. I never felt threatened and always felt welcome. Many of my Greek-Cypriot friends' older brothers or fathers never came back after being "detained" by the British armed forces because they were "terrorists". On occasion I was in their homes when the British forces and local constabulary entered to arrest them. Beating was routine. Human rights – forget it! Being blond and light-skinned and known to the local constabulary I was repeatedly told to "be a good boy and go home and stay away from these terrorists". Cyprus has a history of terrorist links going back to Jesus' disciples. Reading how today it is still used as a base by al-Qaeda does not surprise me.

Many of the toughest British regiments were in Cyprus and based in Karaolos, where I went to the Army Children's School, fighting EOKA and their leader George Grivas and their bid for independence from England. The movie *Braveheart* is a reminder of how ruthless the English were. Today's soccer hooligans are their descendants.

The toughness of rugby players makes American football players look like a bunch of wussies all dressed up to make sure they don't get hurt. At the Army Children's School students were assigned to groups named after the four Windsor castles in Britain. I was assigned to Balmoral. I used to enjoy playing rugby and soccer with my Balmoral team and then staying on after the game to watch the army Pipes and Drums and marching bands rehearse on the nearby football fields. Their military tunes and marching precision captivated me. Many an evening I got scolded by my mother for coming home too late because I got engrossed listening and watching the marching bands. I realized a few years later the significant political role marching bands and their music played in Britannia's global conquests along with its navy and army. The military and music still do for both America and Britain.

I ran into some of these very same soldiers in Hong Kong at the FCC. Pipers, drummers and gun-toting privates who were in Cyprus in the fifties. We reminisced, exchanged stories and their military experiences. Hell, they were in their twenties when they were in Cyprus. They were conscripts trying to make the best of a bad thing. "Yeah, I was in Cyprus. We were sent to kill those bloody wogs," Tony Nedderman, the FCC Treasurer, said during one of our incoherent early morning chats. It was not an unusual summary to hear from former members who served with the British armed forces in Cyprus. That was in the 1950s. The remark was made in Hong Kong in the 1990s.

Japan's Delusion

The Japanese have probably mastered the art of managed perception better than most Asians. They should for the money they have spent over the years on lobbyists and media consultants.

The Japanese still behave and continue to manage their perception as if everyone has no other sources of information. Japanese arrogance, chauvinism and ability to spend billions hiring former high American government officials to lobby on their behalf while prohibiting Americans to do the same in Japan have blindsided them.

David Halberstam summed up the Japanese perfectly: "An American journalist who describes America's fall from grace is regarded as highly intelligent and even courageous; if he brings that same critical eye to Japan's exclusionary trade policies, he is Japan-bashing."

The Japanese refuse to acknowledge any of their wartime atrocities. They are in total denial of their slave labor, "comfort women" – actually sex slaves – wholesale rape and slaughter of Chinese, Koreans, Filipinos and anyone else who was a nuisance or interfered with their territorial expansion. Unlike the Germans, they refuse to pay reparations, compensate comfort women or the heirs of their slave labor force. Since the end of World War II, scores of suits have been filed about prisoner abuse.

Japanese laws and the San Francisco Peace Treaty, under which Japan agreed to pay some reparation to war victims, have seemed to make it almost impossible to win a case in which the Japanese government is the defendant. The Japanese government, Mitsubishi, Mitsui and others should follow the lead of Kajima Corporation, Japan's largest general contractor, which agreed to compensate the slave laborers it used during the war. Yoshio Shinozuka, a member of the Japanese biological warfare unit, has testified that Japan clearly violated international law with its wartime experiments on Chinese prisoners. American, Chinese and Filipino ex-POWs are suing the Japanese companies that exploited them: Kawasaki Heavy Industries, the Mitsubishi International Corporation, Mitsui and Company, Nippon Steel and Showa Denko K.K. Chinese and Filipino wartime slaves, like their American counterparts, are suing Japanese companies in American courts. They are suing under a 1999 California law that allows victims who have been unable to pursue their claims elsewhere to file suit in California state courts against companies that may have benefited from slave labor years ago and now have subsidiaries in the United States. Japanese neo-nationalists are no different than Germany's neo-Nazis. The only difference is they still control government policy.

If the man in whose name Imperial Japan conducted its foreign and military war policy was not held responsible, why should ordinary Japanese dwell on such matters? "Eventually Hirohito became the prime symbol of his people's repression of their wartime past," Herbert Bix concludes in *Hirohito and the Making of Modern Japan*.

Fujiwara Akira sums it up best: "Knowledge of modern Japanese history among youngsters is limited. According to the policies of the Ministry of Education, modern Japanese history is excluded from college entrance exams...

"Japan will be isolated, despised and loathed in Asia, win no respect from its neighbors and hardly co-exist with other nations closely if it persists on distorting its history, failing to apologize for its war crimes and refusing to compensate for the war victims."

It is curious how apologies for sins at sovereign state level have become the fashion. As a form of admission and confession, it is something Japan cannot duck. No matter how much "face" it will cost. The alternative is its democratic "ass". The passage of years will not cause forgetting, not in China nor the rest of East Asia. There is only one person in whose name it was all done, from whom an apology can come: The Emperor. Saburo Sakai, a wartime Japanese hero, asked: "Whose name was on the battle orders?...Over three million people died fighting for the Emperor, but when the war was over he pretended it was not his responsibility.

What kind of man does that?" Given the bureaucracy and the aristocratic girdle around him, The Imperial Household Agency, an apology from him would indeed be a breakthrough for Japan. Something equivalent to the fall of the Berlin Wall.

Many of Japan's problems are the result of the American strategy during the occupation and MacArthur's comfortable Japanese compromises. McArthur bottled the explosive consequences of Japan's defeat which should have been allowed to blow as they did in Germany. The emperor system should have been ended by the removal and trial of Hirohito as a war criminal. The fat cats who formed Japan's long dominant Liberal Democratic Party, which proved such a cozy agent of U.S. imperialism, should have been ripped bare and imprisoned like their German counterparts. Ordinary Japanese people should have been allowed to ripen too. Everything about Japan since 1945 has been fake, including its prosperity and its society. The Liberal Democratic Party has repeatedly shown it doesn't care about financial reform or even good government. The resignation of Kuze Kimitaka, the point man for bank reform, in the closing year of the millennium because he received $2 million in advocacy fees from a bank was another example of business as usual and the people be damned.

"There should have been a point at which the Japanese people were allowed to move their bowels – but you Americans did not permit it," Stuart Wolfendale told me during one of our history debates at the FCC Main Bar.

The novelist Haruki Murakami is called the voice of a generation. The sense that something has gone seriously wrong in modern Japan is never far below the surface of his novels. In 1997, Murakami published a reportage book on a story truly stranger than fiction: the poisoning of Tokyo subway riders by the Aum Shinrikyo sect in 1995. "I interviewed those victims and those cult people at the same time, both sides, and what I wanted to know is what is reality to them, for the victims and for the cult people. Those people are confused, both of them, about what is right, what is wrong.

"Some people go to their company every morning, on a packed train, and other people go to their cult. At the cult they don't have to think about anything at all. The guru decides everything for them, it's very easy. And these other people, they go to their company and they do what they do, and that is easy for them because someone orders them what to do...People in Japan don't want to be free. They are afraid to be free."

Yasunori Okadome, publisher and editor of the monthly magazine *Uwasa no Shinso (Truth of the Rumors),* launched his magazine because he "wanted to print the kind of articles that reporters in the field were dying to write but knew would be killed by their own editors." Yasunori goes on to say that Japan's young generation of journalists "are becoming salary men, tamed and obedient, who can fit in the corporate system smoothly. You see, they often take exams for a bank, a securities firm and a publishing house. Many join the press not because they have a passion to become a journalist, but simply because they were admitted."

Japan's culture of denial and covering up was again brought to the world's attention when Prime Minister Keizo Obuchi was hospitalized with a coma-inducing stroke. His condition was not disclosed for twenty- two hours! Japan has a crisis of accountability. We were again reminded of this crisis of accountability when Mitsubishi Motors president Katsuhiko admitted that his company deliberately covered up complaints because "we were ashamed". The delayed Bridgestone/Firestone tire recall confirmed how deep-rooted this cultural refusal for accountability is. It was reconfirmed during the 2004 bird flu epidemic. A spate of ill-concealed scandals has cast a pall over the government and other institutions like the police. Such behavior comes from a bankrupt ethical culture that typically values appearance far more than the truth. A venerable Japanese expression about the attitude that governors should hold toward the governed says it all. "We should not inform the people, " the saying goes. "They must depend upon us." Commentators have begun to denounce the culture of concealment and opacity. "There is an attitude that we don't have to divulge information, " Manabu Hasegawa, a journalist and author, said. "A society that preserves the ideal of concealing information is a society that has distorted democracy." A warning America must heed.

Lingua Francas
Chinese should replace French at international conventions, sporting

events and international organizations. Like the opening ceremony of the 2002 Winter Olympics where Sting and Yo Yo Ma represented reality. Chinese and English should be the international languages of the 21st century. French, like Latin, is passe.

English and Chinese are the most numerously spoken languages in the world. Mandarin is clearly the largest language group, with over a billion native speakers. English is a distant second, with over 500 million, followed by Spanish at 330 million.

Why is it then that the lingua francas of international organizations like the UN are English and French? French should go and join Latin on the geopolitical lingua garbage heap. Shouldn't international organizations, if they are to be honest, reflective and representative of the New World Order, use Chinese instead of French as one of the two official languages? Never mind *We the Maids* sweeping the word French out of fries and toast. Go for the whole enchilada – make that dim sum! We must hoover the language out of international forums. This would have the entertaining effect of forcing all senior diplomats to learn spoken and written Chinese. Maybe then there won't be so many "misunderstandings" between English and Chinese speakers.

The misunderstandings between American and Chinese are best exemplified by what happened during the Asian crisis. A man walked into a bank in New York with two thousand Hong Kong dollars and walked out with two hundred and fifty nine American dollars. The following week he walked in with another two thousand Hong Kong dollars and was handed two hundred American dollars. He asked the teller why he got less that week than the week before. The teller said "fluctuations". The Chinese man stormed out, and just before slamming the door, turned around and shouted "Fluc you Amelicans too!"

I, like most Americans, like to occasionally use foul lingua. It is appropriate to use in a few places in the book but has been edited out. The words "shit" or "fuck" help further clarify a point. Yet we all have to be very careful not to offend anyone or be politically incorrect thanks to spin – doctors. Most people won't say shit if they had a mouthful in the "right" company. When it comes to the "f" word? Fuck it or forgeeetaaaboutit.

My favourite poster with the "s" word sums up religious spin and how career politicians and their religious spin meisters have us thinking otherwise.

Religious Views of Life

Taoism
Shit Happens

Confucianism
Confucius says shit happens
Buddhism
If shit happens it isn't really shit

Zen
What is the sound of shit happening?

Hinduism
This shit happened before

Islam
If shit happens it is the will of Allah

Protestantism
Let shit happen to someone else

Catholics
If shit happens you deserve it

Judaism
Why does this shit always happen to us?

Atheism
I don't believe this shit

Agnosticism
What is this shit?

Let's just reflect for a moment on the times in history when the "f" word was appropriate. "What the fuck was that?" – Mayor of Hiroshima. "Where did all these fucking Indians come from?" – General Custer. "Scattered fucking showers...my ass." – Noah. "Who the fuck is going to know?" – Bill Clinton.

The FCC is affectionately referred to by local politicians and journalists as the "Fucking Correspondents' Club". Discussing the "f" word with Arthur Hacker at the FCC one night gave me a whole new perception. "Lance Corporal Clutterbutt of the Royal Artillery went AWOL. The fucking fucker fucking well fucked off. Fuck him is all his company commander could say," Arthur chuckled as we almost choked on our drinks.

The chuckles got louder all around the FCC Main Bar when Arthur Andersen, Enron, WorldCom and other U.S. corporate financial irregularities were brought to light. American accounting terms took on a whole new meaning. EBITDA-Earnings Before I Tricked The Dumb Auditor; EBIT-Earnings Before Irregularities & Tampering; CEO-Chief Embezzlement Officer; CFO-Corporate Fraud Officer; NAV-Normal Andersen Valuation; and EPS-Eventual Prison Sentence.

Fake Images, False Perception
Bush's political promises of "compassionate" conservatism and bringing all extremes together to the center became anything but what he promised once he moved into the White House. The media played this down as they did his insider trading at Harken Oil that allowed him to raise the money to invest in the Texas Rangers. Clinton was hounded for years by a special prosecutor who spent $70 million of taxpayers' money on Whitewater to allegedly look into shady dealings and came up with Monica. Why is it when real questionable business dealings of a Republican Bush are brought to light both the government and media are mute when compared to their collective howls during Whitewater? A well managed pubic spin!

"No Smoking" flights are another example of a well-managed spin scam. No Smoking flights are marketed as healthier because of the adverse affects of secondary smoke. The reality is non-smoking flights are unhealthier because the airlines vent the planes less during non-smoking flights to save fuel. In fact tuberculosis and other infectious diseases are now known to have been passed on to healthy passengers on non-smoking flights. Airlines save as much as 25 percent of their fuel costs on non-smoking flights. The result is non-smoking flights are at least no healthier than smoking flights because of the germs passengers inhale. Every passenger with a cold, 'flu and God knows what else shares it with fellow high flyers. Why not make airlines vent the planes as much on non-smoking flights as smoking flights if health is the real concern?

Too many business travelers I know always come down with some virus after a long flight. The hidden viruses of non-smoking flights remind me of the computer viruses. "Melissa", "Papa", "Mad Cow", and "I Love You" did to computer programs what their invisible nameless brothers and sisters do on non-smoking flights and what the career politicians' Clinton Virus does to the public. They stick us with a six-inch hard drive with no memory.

During one of my trips to New York in the late nineties I again stayed with Michael Yudin and we decided to go to the movies and see *Rainmaker*. We had seen Devil's Advocate a few weeks earlier. After the movie Michael did not stop haranguing me about lawyers and the legal profession. "You're fucking whores. All of you. I am glad they are finally making movies that tell it like it is about your damn profession," he continued. "It's great, maybe things will finally change. Lawyers are worse than politicians when it comes to screwing up the economy and country. Hell, most politicians are lawyers. The cost of litigation, legislation and lobbyists is incestuously out of control." "You know, Michael, I think it is debatable as to who are bigger whores. Bankers or lawyers. Your profession isn't exactly a bunch of girl scouts." We laughed and decided to grab a bite to eat. "Hey, did you hear about the new Jewish-Japanese restaurant on 51st street?" I asked. "No, what's it called?" he asked. "So Sue Me!"

Jiang Zemin was the Mayor of Shanghai when Julia and I brought American sixties band, Jan and Dean, to perform there in 1986. He attended the concert and we exchanged views with him on "the future cultural and economic co-operation between China and America". Here he was now in New York in 1998 as the President of China.

The political and economic ramifications of the visit were monumental considering the meltdown of the Asian Tiger economies. "Peter, you better hope this visit comes off without any hitches or you might as well not bother going back. Your business will be history," Bill Spier, Michael's partner, told me. Bill used to be the vice chairman of Phibro/Solomon Brothers and we were going to be down on Wall Street for a meeting with some bankers the same day Jiang Zemin was going to be at the New York Stock Exchange.

"Never mind my business, if this visit is a failure everyone has a lot to lose. American business from New York, the Midwest all the way to the West Coast, American consumers, Chinese factories and democratic activists. We're all going to be screwed," I told him. Bill had lived in Japan for several years when he was with Solomon and had traveled throughout Asia extensively and had a good grasp of the political and economic issues of the day. "But what about Tibet, human rights and political prisoners? Don't you think these issues are going to come up? How is he going to handle them? This is America and they will be raised."

Damn! Here I am back in the States, the handover of Hong Kong to China is history and people now want to talk about human rights and Tibet. *Red Corner and Seven Years In Tibet,* controversial movies on China and Tibet, were released to coincide with Jiang's visit. "Bill, there is a lot that capitalist America and communist China have to offer each other and they should focus on the issues of mutual interest and benefit." Punishing China's leaders for human rights abuses by restricting and reducing our economic contacts does not serve the long-term interest of those Chinese who want more political freedom. In fact it doesn't serve Americans either. Our cost of living goes up. It may make us feel better, but if we close the door to economic reform, we will lock out all prospects for peaceful political change on foreign policy in the foreseeable future. That is too high a price to pay for a sense of moral superiority.

"You have to give this Jiang credit. He has brass balls to be going to Harvard to speak," Michael added. It's a good thing the questions there didn't give him the temper tantrum Hong Kong journalists did. He stayed cool. Just as he did with his television interviews with Mike Wallace, Jim Lehrer and Andrea Koppel and his debate with President Bill Clinton on national television in China.

Two years later, one of my visits to New York coincided with that of Chinese Premier Zhu Rongji. He came to the U.S. after President

Bill Clinton's trip to China, while the NATO war with Yugoslavia was raging over Kosovo. I was again subjected to the same senseless arguments which in my mind confirmed the disconnect between the East and the West. This time I was being questioned on why China insisted on reuniting with Taiwan. Here we go again, I thought to myself. The Premier had the best answer. He quoted from Lincoln's Gettysburg Address and invoked Lincoln's use of force to keep the Union together as an analogous example as to why China is justified in using force to reunite China.

The Chinese leader's visit to the U.S. was a marvelous, perhaps devious, but hellishly well-informed exercise in cultural inter-reaction. If Americans and Chinese understand each side's passions, blood-lettings and the reasons behind them, w're steps along harmony road.

Michael decided to visit me in Manila and Hong Kong and we decided to go on to China for a few days so that he could understand what I had been saying for years about why Americans just don't understand the real China and Asia thanks to the media's managed misrepresentations.

In Beijing we checked into the Grand Hotel off Tiananmen square. The Grand is a former Imperial palace that was converted to a hotel. Beijing, contrary to public perception, has many Western restaurants and other retail outlets. "I can't believe what I am seeing," Michael lamented as we drove to the hotel from the airport. "It seems there's a McDonalds on every other block. I've seen more here than in New York. These poor people, do they realize how the West has polluted and is about to screw up their heritage?" he asked, wondering out loud. "Do you know that the largest KFC outlet in the world is right here in Beijing?" I asked. "Guess how many chickens they sell a day?" He didn't know. "Twenty thousand!" Hard Rock to discos, and Middle Eastern to Mexican-type cuisine is available. Michael wanted "good New York cuisine! Think you can find that here?" "No problem. The Courtyard is really close to our hotel. You'll love it. The chef is from New York as is the ambience, art gallery and cigar divan." I could see from the look on Michael's face that he thought I was pulling his chain...hard.

As we walked in the door Michael's face lit up. The New York ambience had hustled up to the very edge of the Forbidden City. "I feel right at home. This place is right up there with the best of them," he chuckled as we sat at the bar and ordered a drink before we were seated. "I guess Mao jackets went out with high buttoned shoes. I didn't see one Mao jacket on any bicycle rider. They were all wearing Western clothes. You know, Americans really don't have a clue about the real Hong Kong or China," exclaimed this brand new member of "cognoscenti".

"Have you heard the one about the midget that went into the drug store and asked the pharmacist for the largest condom he had?" I asked Michael. He hadn't. "Well after the pharmacist gave him the largest triple XL rubber, the midget unwrapped it and put it over his head and rolled it out covering his whole body. He then looked up at the pharmacist and asked 'How do I look?'. 'Like a big dick', replied the pharmacist. 'Good, good, good', exclaimed the midget jumping up and down. I'm tired of being called a little prick'" Michael had a good laugh and agreed "That's managed perception." Maybe that is why the Chinese refer to President George W. Bush as "Little Bush".

Restless People

The American people are restless with the way career politicians have been treating them. Neither the Democrats nor the Republicans have their best interests at heart. That is why a majority of Americans belong to neither party. We the Apathetic majority are unrepresented. Isn't it time We the Apathetic People were? Isn't it time we stop being on the outside of the political system without even bothering to look in or speak up?

Live coverage of impeachment proceedings in the U.S. empowered *We the People* with the facts and details usually retained in the vest pocket of career politicians. Now that we have access to the facts, isn't it time we address political managed misperceptions? Including those we have of people of different ethnic groups, religions and countries, especially China? We are rather prone to senselessly dub each other the equivalent of big or little pricks. This has to change in the 21st century if our myths are no longer to be perpetuated. Let's start dealing with reality. Political, cultural and personal.

America and other enlightened countries may choose to follow

Hong Kong in the New World Order by opting for reality and balance against exaggerated excess. In the words of Sang-Woo Rhee, "progress is not quantity, but also quality. We want to create harmony in societies." Career politicians, lawyers, lobbyists, bureaucrats and their spin-doctors capitalize on *We the Maids'* apathy and create harmony among themselves and get away with distorting reality and what nirvana can be because we have surrendered our democratic rights to the republic. Truth, harmony, balance and restraint, not managed misperceptions, are what we should strive to teach our children in the new millennium.

Chapter Seven

Outlaw Self-Subsidizing Career Politicians and Lawyers

A statesman is a politician who places himself at the service of the nation. A politician is a statesman who places the nation at his service.
- Georges Pompidou

Changeover

The energy in the air during the 1997 handover of Hong Kong was very emotional and exhilarating. The pomp and ceremony was very moving. The lowering of the Union Flag with a teary Chris Patten. The raising of the Chinese red five star flag with Jiang Zemin, Prince Charles, Tony Blair, Li Peng, two generals and a dry-eyed Chris Patten. The pomp and circumstance were a continuation of the pomp of the centuries whenever a new Governor arrived. Much like an inauguration in Washington D.C., the heart of the world's foremost proselytizing democracy. The feeling is of butterflies in the stomach. The buzz of "hope" is everywhere, on the streets, in the parties, bars, receptions, inaugural balls and private balls. What a difference to the inauguration of George W. Bush. A lame duck the day he took his oath of office. The result of a presidential non-election thanks to judicial intervention. An illegitimate divided government unrepresentative of the majority of Americans. The first president since 1888 without the legitimacy of the popular vote.

The dense toxic legal and political fog that has settled on the Washington partisan swamp has resulted in America's constitutional separation of the legislative and judicial branches of government colliding. The resulting whiplash has crippled and paralyzed the American political process. It is sustaining itself on the public's apathetic life support system. An open lunch box that is supposed to be a "lock box". The Founding Fathers must be spinning in their graves.

I've had the privilege of also attending two inaugurations in Washington. Jimmy Carter's and Bill Clinton's first. During the Carter inauguration I also got admitted as a lawyer to the D.C. Bar. I've worked with and gotten to know many political lawyers and lobbyists over the years. It is a very lucrative business. An $18 billion-a-year cottage industry that thrives in Washington. An industry that looks to grow in the 21st century thanks to Bush's millennium Christmas gift to lawyers and lobbyists. In what was jokingly called President-elect George W. Bush's amazing holiday gift to the capital's law firms and lobbyists, Washington has scores of new official insiders. Four hundred and seventy-four of them to be exact. Those named to transition advisory teams to "provide input and related outreach activities". America started the 21st century the way it ended the 20th. With lawyers, lobbyists and career politicians figuring how to spend more of *We the Apathetic Peoples'* money and how to tax us for it.

Lobbyists
Lobbyists figure out ways to get legislation passed that gets money or other political benefits for their clients and career politicians. Many of the most powerful and effective registered lobbyists are lawyers.

When campaign finance reform was finally passed by Congress and signed into law by the President, lawyers and lobbyists were immediately hired to challenge it. Ken Starr was hired to lead the team challenging the legislation that has the potential to reduce the incomes of lawyers and lobbyists.

Some lawyers and lobbyists work for foreign governments. These lobbyists then become "agents" of a foreign government. They have to register and disclose what they get paid. But so what? They are wasting U.S. politicians' time and U.S. taxpayer money on issues that benefit only foreign and, in some cases, anti-American governments and the lobbyists' bank accounts. Issues of vital national importance are determined by a Congress pandering to one lobby or another, rather than by a carefully thought-out foreign policy agenda that is in the best interest of America.

"I have a message for the influence peddlers, for the polluters, the HMO's, the drug companies, big oil and all the special interests who now call the White House home: We're coming. You're going. And don't let the door hit you on the way out," Senator John Kerry said during his campaign for the 2004 Democratic Party nomination. For a career politician who has received over $50 million from special interests and whose lawyer brother represents the interests who have to make sure the door doesn't hit them on the way out is the hypocrisy-spin of the 2004 presidential campaign.

Retired army general Wesley Clark registered as a lobbyist before he registered as a Democrat. A pretty good indication of who he really represents.

The hypocrisy of representation escalates the deeper the pockets of the clients of these lawyers and lobbyists. Laws are rewritten to achieve their objectives as more political contributions are promised. Is that really right for *We the People?* What about the little guy and gal? Who's protecting and representing their rights and interests? What happened to their representation once their elected representatives are bought off?

Shouldn't elected officials spend more time representing *We the Apathetic People* instead of just corporate America and foreign governments? Shouldn't most of their time be spent on policy that benefits a majority of Americans?

Washington insiders consider Saudi Arabia's and Taiwan's lobbying efforts as two of the most formidable lobbying machines ever created by a foreign power. These "agents" include firms linked to all shades of the political spectrum. Agents who have branded Israel a "terrorist state" and China a "rogue state".

The lobby, together with giant U.S. defense manufacturers – such as Honeywell and Lockheed Martin – have helped give Saudi Arabia and Taiwan reputations for back-room influence in the U.S. second only to Israel's. Japan employs over 60 lobbying firms in Washington with less to show for its efforts and expense.

Power Glitches

Enron is a millennium American example of a company that knows how to empower and utilize lobbyists and lawyers to maximize its power and access to the detriment of U.S. taxpayers, shareholders and the public. White House documents reveal that Enron officials had more than 34 contacts with the Bush administration through meetings, phone calls or letters before the company filed for bankruptcy. More than 30 White House officials had contact with the company about issues relating to appointments to the Federal Energy Regulatory Commission and Vice President Dick Cheney's confidential strategic energy report. The document showed that White House Chief of Staff Andrew Card was told by Commerce Secretary Donald Evans that Ken Lay had contacted him for help with credit-rating companies on Enron's behalf.

The chairman of Citigroup's executive committee, former President Bill Clinton's Treasury Secretary Robert Rubin, also lobbied on behalf of the bank's client Enron. Citigroup tried to stave off Enron's bankruptcy filing to avoid having its sham loans disguised as energy trades from evaporating like the public's stock holdings. To this end Rubin made a call to Treasury Undersecretary Peter Fisher to inquire what he thought of the idea of calling credit-rating agencies to encourage them to work with Enron's bankers to avert an immediate downgrade of Enron's credit status.

While lobbying Washington and other national, local and state governments to deregulate their laws to suit Enron's needs, the company manipulated and rigged California's power system with fake trades to increase profits. Enron was a key player that triggered California's 2000-2001 energy crisis and the Great Blackout of '03.

While Californians were starved of energy, Enron, El Paso, Valley Electric Association and countless other energy traders were feasting and congratulating each other on how they had hoodwinked Governor Pete Wilson and the California legislature into "deregulating" the energy market. In fact it was a lawyer's dream because of the complex rules and regulations lobbyists got legislated. Wilson and his appointees to the Public Utilities Commission, encouraged by Congress and state lawmakers who were receiving generous campaign contributions, disassembled a functioning energy system and created a new one that was easy for the energy traders to manipulate to their financial gain. No different than what the automobile industry did at the beginning of the 20th century when they disassembled a functional Los Angeles public rail system to open the market to automobiles.

What happened in California was merely a minor circuit break compared to The Great Blackout of '03 that left an estimated 50 million people across eight states in Northeast America without power. At best it highlighted how effective the energy lobby is in deferring maintenance and upgrades because of its contributions and cozy relationships with career politicians. I remember living through the November 1965 New York City blackout after my recent arrival to America from Cyprus and wondering how this could happen in the most developed city in the world.

I was attending CCNY at the time and a classmate in my Spanish class, Gary Shapiro, who lived in New Jersey, was stranded. I invited Gary to stay in my room in a Spanish Harlem rooming house that was walking distance from the campus. Talk about karma, luck and timing. Gary lived in Los Angeles and was back on the East Coast to help out his father's floundering business for a semester and was going back to LA the following semester. Gary regaled me with stories of glamorous Los Angeles and talked me in to going there the following school year. Gary went on to become a spin-doctor for Columbia studios.

Here we are almost 40 years later and the biggest power blackout in North American history leaves 50 million people across the U.S. Northeast and Canada mystified and asking the same question. How can this happen in the most developed country in the world? The answer is simple. Effective lobbying at the expense of *We the Apathetic Maids.*

To understand and appreciate the subtlety and brilliance of Enron's lobbying efforts, a brief history of energy regulation and its deregulation can shed some light into the dark Third World of political corruption America has joined. Franklin Roosevelt imprisoned Samuel Insull, Ken Lay's idol and model, in 1933. Insull's Power Trust, like Enron, faked account books and ripped off consumers. Roosevelt created the Federal Power Commission and the Public

Utilities Holding Company Act. Their regulations "regulated" how utility companies could charge, set profit limits, and mandated strict maintenance guidelines. "Power markets" were banned and the executives of power companies that failed to keep the lights on were subject to arrest. FDR also banned all political contributions from utility companies.

In the 1980s Niagara Mohawk built a multi-billion dollar nuclear plant known as Nine-Mile Point, paid for courtesy of the New York State electricity ratepayers. The power consortium was found guilty of fraud and the jury hearing the case ordered Long Island Lighting Corporation, one of the partners in the venture and lead instructor in how to defraud the government and energy users, to pay $4.3 billion and, ultimately, put them out of business. After LILCO was hammered by the law, after government regulators slammed Niagara Mohawk and dozens of other book-cooking, document-doctoring utility companies all over America with fines and penalties totaling in the tens of billions of dollars, the industry leaders got together to swear never to break the regulations again. Their plan was not to follow the rules, but to ELIMINATE the rules. They called it "deregulation".

President George H. W. Bush facilitated their plan and changed FDR's strict regulations in 1992 just before he left the White House. He "deregulated" the wholesale price of electricity and set the stage for the energy industry to make massive campaign contributions to his son's campaign in 2000 as it ripped *We the Apathetic Maids* off. They collectively donated $16 million, with Ken Lay and Enron leading the pack. That set the stage for the kill. "Deregulation" of energy prices at the state level. California was the first target. With a Republican governor, the energy companies spent $39 million to defeat Ralph Nader's 1998 referendum to defeat deregulation. They then spent $37 million to juice the campaign coffers of politicians to deregulate energy in the state. The preamble to the deregulation promised electricity bills will be reduced by 20 percent. The reality was that California Governor Pete Wilson's city of San Diego, the first city to deregulate, saw a 300 percent increase in surcharges!

Enron and the pack it was leading held the state at energy rate ransom with their fake trades, pricing and ever increasing lobbying and campaign contributions. They controlled 100 percent of the Golden State's power. They had replicated in California what they had done in Texas while Dubya was governor. "Deregulated" states and blinded *We the Apathetic Maids* into an expensive and frustrating darkness. The same happened in New York when a Republican administration took over in Albany. The Niagara Mohawk Power Company was sold to National Grid of New England, which promptly fired 800 workers and produced a $90 million windfall for their shareholders and the New York grid maintenance be damned.

Enron only did what other U.S. "Blue Chip" companies do. Lobby the government for tax breaks, subsidies, handouts and other favors in exchange for campaign contributions. Another glaring example is Occidental Petroleum. Oxy stupidly spent over $100 million on building a pipeline in Colombia. It then paid $1 for every barrel of oil to the military to protect the pipeline. One in every four Colombian soldiers in the field is protecting the Oxy pipeline. Any wonder guerrilla rebels and narco-terrorists are having a field day? The guerrillas target the pipeline regularly. In the opening year of the millennium the pipeline was bombed 170 times. It was put out of commission for 260 days, "putting a definite downward drag on Occidental's profits", according to Arianna Huffington.

So what does Occidental want the U.S. government to do? After spending more than $9 million on lobbying and $1.5 million in campaign contributions, it wants the U.S. special forces to train the Colombians guarding the pipeline, at U.S. taxpayers' expense of course. Huffington adds: "And now, the oil-igarchy in the White House has chosen to reward this shining example of idiocy of capitalism with a no-strings-attached corporate welfare check." Testifying before Congress, Secretary of State Colin Powell summed up the administration's position: "We thought a $98 million investment in the Colombian brigades to help protect this pipeline [was] a wise one and a prudent one. What makes this pipeline unique is that it is such a major source of income." Income for whom?

While Powell was arguing the government's case, the U.S. Attorney General's office was investigating 44 senior Colombian police officers, including the President's security coordinator, over the disappearance of $2 million in U.S. aid meant for the war on drugs.

The overbearing influence of oil companies on U.S. foreign policy was hammered home in 2002 when a U.S. State Department letter that urged a judge to consider the political and economic implications in a human rights case against Exxon Mobil was made public. The suit was filed by the International Labor Rights Foundation in Washington D.C. on behalf of 11 villagers in Aceh who claim they were victims of murder, torture and rape by Indonesian soldiers guarding an Exxon Mobil gas field. Indonesia assigned 3,000 government troops to guard the site.

The State Department letter argued that regardless of the merits of the case it should be dismissed outright because the trial will adversely affect U.S. firms doing business in Indonesia. How such a position by the State Department can be reconciled with the U.S. government's aggressive push for democracy and human rights in Indonesia remains to be seen.

The State Department intervened in a similar case earlier the same year against mining giant Rio Tinto over the closure of its Bougainville copper mine in Papua New Guinea in 1998. The suits are filed under the 1789 Alien Torts Claims Act, which was passed to deal with the press-ganging of American seamen by the British navy.

Even more aggravating, while Bush was governor of Texas, Taleban leaders flew to Houston, Texas, from Afghanistan to meet with Unocal executives to discuss the building of a pipeline across Afghanistan. The feasibility study was done by Enron and one of the companies that was going to build the pipeline was Dick Cheney's Halliburton. When the Taleban were removed from power in Afghanistan, a former oil company consultant was installed as "interim leader" and a former Unocal consultant was appointed U.S. ambassador to Afghanistan. It then took only a few months for a new deal to be signed to build the pipeline across Afghanistan.

The same happened in Iraq a few weeks after the Iraq War started. Kellogg, Brown & Root, a Halliburton subsidiary, got the first contracts to work with the U.S. Army engineers to assess the condition of the oil fields and rebuild the oil industry infrastructure in Iraq without any public or competitive bidding. Meanwhile, Iraqi exiles and influential expatriates publicly backed the role of U.S. oil giants production-sharing with the post-Saddam regime. The group of

Iraqi exiles is of course working with the Pentagon and State Department as they chart Iraq's new oil policy.

A few weeks before WorldCom announced it had fraudulently cooked its books, it was lobbying the Bush White House and D.C. career politicians for a political edge in the lucrative high-speed Internet market. WorldCom gave $100,000 to the Republicans' fund-raising gala and was listed as vice-chairman of the event!

How about John Biggs, head of a large retirement fund and a long-standing advocate of honest accounting who was slated to become the chairman of the new audit oversight board created in the wake of Enron and company? He did not get the job because of the aggressive lobbying by the accounting firms he was going to oversee.

The media giants are my favorite powerful political lobby because they do things with such finesse. In Washington alone, they spend an estimated $125 million per year lobbying against ownership restrictions, especially under the Bush administrations. They also spend hundreds of millions at the State and global level. How to add up what they spend globally, only each company knows as they have creative ways of disguising bribes and lobbying fees as legal and consulting fees. A fact I know first hand. I enjoyed being part of the effort in 2000 when the media giants led the charge to open up trade with China and enable it to join the WTO. The issues of free speech, free press, and human rights, echoed on the airwaves by the media giants' right-wing talking heads, were ignored by the corporate honchos looking for new markets to sell their neo-media Hollywood myths. Any wonder they don't investigate and expose the career politicians they need legislative and regulatory favors from? That is why U.S. investigative journalism and news coverage are just another episode of Survivor. Programmed to dumb *We the Apathetic Maids* down while the career politicians and their corporate donors continue to survive!

The biggest glitch in enforcing campaign contribution laws is the Federal Election Commission set up to oversee and regulate campaign financing. It is a commission that puts protecting the interests of the Democratic and Republican parties ahead of policing election laws or guarding public confidence in the integrity of campaigns and elections. The FEC is run and staffed almost exclusively by party loyalists appointed to protect career politicians. The political appointments are made by both parties to make sure their collective political interests are preserved and enhanced. Congress effectively controls the selection of commissioners. Long-standing practice allows House and Senate leaders to pick those whom they want to represent their parties' interests on the FEC. They use that power to select commissioners who put the interests of the political parties foremost. Commission members are former congressmen, congressional aides and campaign officials. "For the most part, commissioners serve as captives and agents of the players in the political system: the parties, the incumbent office holders and the donors," says Fred Wertheimer, president of the advocacy group Democracy 21, who has campaigned for changes in the campaign money system for decades.

Army Business

The Iraq war brought into public view how effective lobbyists have been in getting military business to their clients. Lobbyists got the government to privatize just about everything in the military except for the fighting. Even security services! Private industry succeeded in lobbying the government and the Pentagon to privatize security services, the mess hall, recruiting, laundry services, programming of weapons to garbage detail. KBR, a unit of Halliburton, is one of the primary beneficiaries that provides these services thanks to its former CEO Dick Cheney and his army of DC lobbyists. In the 1990s Halliburton's KBR unit provided nearly all the food, water, laundry, mail and heavy equipment to the roughly 20,000 U.S. troops stationed in the Balkans for $3 billion, according to a study by the General Accounting Office and *Fortune Magazine.*

War is even better for their business as they then provide these services in the field. Outsourcing everything but fighting to the private sector puts billions of taxpayer dollars into the coffers of companies that have well- paid lobbyists. Even the security guards protecting the "interim" Afghan leader are contracted to the private sector.

During the 1991 Gulf War there was one contractor for every 100 soldiers. Thanks to the efforts of the lobbyists at the start of the Iraq war there were 10 contractors for every 100 soldiers.

The multi-billion dollar building programs to rebuild the Iraqi infrastructure damaged during the war were being lobbied for by the DC lobbyists on behalf of their clients Halliburton and Bechtel months before the war even started. After the war ended Halliburton secured the contracts to maintain the Iraqi oil fields for hundreds of millions of dollars more than originally disclosed under a U.S. Army Corps of Engineers contract. Amazingly, these were no-bid contracts. In other words, no competitive bids for any contract Halliburton or its subsidiaries received, according to The Washington Post. Likewise, Bechtel secured a contract for $350 million for infrastructure projects, again over 50 percent more than allocated. They wanted to make sure that the contract didn't go to the UN development agencies since the UN did not support the Iraqi regime change. They argued that America the "liberator" that brought democracy and economic prosperity to the Iraqi people is also entitled to prosper. After all before a country or international organization has the humanitarian right to rebuild Iraq it must earn the right by first being involved in its destruction.

Lawyers, Lawyers Everywhere

At Clinton's inauguration, like Carter's, most people I partied with were lawyers and lobbyists. Everyone from the President, his wife Hillary, top advisors, assistants, Senators, Congressmen and women, State legislators, councilmen and general hangers-on were lawyers. Lawyers dominate the political hierarchy and political establishment. An establishment that reflects American society. America has more lawyers per head than any other country. It is also the most litigious. Lawyers write laws that are unnecessary and cumbersome, many of which are proposed by lobbyist lawyers and then shepherded through the cumbersome process by elected representative lawyers. They then litigate the laws for further clarification. Securities and Exchange Commission chairman, lawyer Harvey Pitt, is a glaring example brought to light as corporate America's malfeasance was exposed. He got rich representing the industry he was asked to oversee. A lawyer who met his old clients regularly while his agency was investigating them. Any wonder he came to the job promising a "kinder, gentler" agency that offers "respect and cooperation" to those it regulates? Just another lawyer in a monkey suit conducting monkey business. Monkeys who see no evil, speak no evil or hear no evil. They just practice it.

If we baby boomers stop for a moment and think about all the laws lobbyists and lawyers have created in the last half of the 20th century and how they have changed how we and our children and grandchildren live, it is mind-boggling. For those of us who lived as children in the forties, fifties, sixties or even seventies, looking back it's hard to believe that we have lived as long as we have. As children, we could ride in cars with no seat belts or air bags. Our cots were covered with bright colored lead-based paint. We had no childproof lids on medicine bottles, doors or cupboards, and when we rode our bikes we had no helmets. We drank water from the garden hose and not from a bottle. Horrors. We would spend hours building go-karts out of scraps and then ride them downhill, only to find out we forgot the brakes. After running into the bushes a few times we learned to solve the problem. Isn't it time we solved the geopolitical and economic problems we've run into as adults with Bush's?

We would leave home in the morning and play all day, as long as we were back when the streetlights came on. No one was able to reach us all day. No mobile phones. Unthinkable. We got cut and broke bones and broke teeth, and there were no law suits from these accidents. They were accidents. No one was to blame, but us. Remember accidents? We had fights and punched each other and got black and blue and learned to get over it. We ate patty cakes, bread and butter, and drank cordial, but we were never overweight...we were always outside playing. We shared one drink with four friends from one bottle and no one died.

We did not have Playstations, Nintendo 64, X-Boxes, video games, 65 channels on pay TV, videotape movies, Surround Sound, personal mobile phones, personal computers, Internet chat rooms...we had friends. We went outside and found them. We rode bikes or walked to a friend's home and knocked the door, or rang the bell, or just walked in and talked to them. Imagine such a thing. Without asking a parent! By ourselves! Out there in the cold cruel world! Without a guardian – how did we do it?

We made up games with sticks and tennis balls, and ate worms, and although we were told it would happen, we did not put out very many eyes, nor did the worms live inside us forever. Footy and netball had tryouts and not everyone made the team. Those that didn't had to learn to deal with disappointment. Some students weren't as smart as others so they failed a grade and were held back to repeat the same grade. Tests were not adjusted for any reason. Our actions were our own. Consequences were expected. No one to hide behind. The idea of a parent bailing us out if we broke a law was unheard of. They actually sided with the law – imagine that! No lawyers necessary!

This generation has produced some of the best risk-takers, problem solvers and inventors, ever. The past 50-plus years have seen an explosion of innovation and new ideas. We had freedom, failure, success and responsibility, and we learned how to deal with it all. Wasn't it great growing up before lobbyists and lawyers managed to regulate how we grow up?

Lawyers also litigated the 43rd President, the first of the 21st century, into office. Legal armies in Florida and Washington D.C. waged a legal and political Armageddon that divided America over its antiquated political institutions and diverse voting methods. An electoral system last reformed by Congress in 1887 that is now in a state of disrepair that got rustier in the Florida legal and rainy deluge – thanks to lawyers.

Lawyers James Baker and Warren Christopher, two former Secretaries of State, are well experienced in working with tyrant career politicians and dynastic political families. They are well-suited to represent America's. Butterflies are not limited to ballots. They can include lawyers. The dictionary has many definitions and meanings.

The legal battles to seat America's 43rd President was a wake-up call for Americans to realize their apathy created political paralysis that almost drowned the country in the Florida swamps.

The decision of the Florida Supreme Court correctly upheld a state's right to oversee and judge local elections and results. Counts and recounts. Machine and human. Even the Rehnquist Supreme Court has aggressively supported state rights. The same court that gave Bush the presidency. The Supreme Court justices think they are and act as if they are gods. They support state rights as a means of punishing Congress. They supported Bush as a means of reminding *We the Apathetic People* who are the political gods in America.

Italian Prime Minister Giuliano Amato, said: "I hope the candidates in the United States escape from the grip of lawyers soon." *The Times* of London concluded: "The presidency as an institution should not be at the center of what has become a shameful legal circus."

Robert H. Bork, the justice Democrats refused to confirm to the Supreme Court, aptly said: "No court can save America." He went on to quote Learned Hand. "[This] much I think I do know – that a society so riven that the spirit of moderation is gone, no court can save; that a society where that spirit flourishes, no court need save; that in a society which evades its responsibility by thrusting upon the courts the nurture of that spirit, that spirit in the end will perish."

Will Rogers accurately described the Washington lifestyles of lobbyists. "You see the Lord in his justice works everything on a handicap basis. California having the best of everything else must take a slice of the calamities (earthquakes). Even my native Oklahoma (the Garden of Eden of the West) has a cyclone. Kansas, while blessed with its grasshoppers, must endure its politicians. New York with its splendors has its Wall Street, and Washington, the world's most beautiful city, has a lobbyist crawling out to attack you from every manhole....So every human and every place is equal after all."

The attacks of September 11 prompted Bush to propose on September 29 the USA Patriot Act and with the help of lobbyists and lawyers had it signed into law on October 26. An unprecedented record time! The act consisted of 342 pages and 350 subject areas. It covered 40 federal agencies and had 21 legal amendments. Yet there were no hearings on the bill, little legislative history, all of which bodes well for the lawyers that will litigate its numerous provisions. Michael Katz, a public defender, said the new law will have to be interpreted by the courts. "A bill like this will be reverberating for years to come," he said. "Provisions will be litigated as to whether they're constitutional."

Thinking about all the lawyers and career politicians that pushed through the USA Patriot Act, I couldn't resist thinking of Will Rogers and his observation: "I don't know who started the idea that a President must be a Politician instead of a Business man. A Politician can't run any other kind of business. So there is no reason why he can run the U.S. That's the biggest single business in the World." To make matters worse, at the dawn of the 21st century a politician who failed as a businessman was installed as president by the Supreme Court. America's Founding Fathers were businessmen and landowners. Not politicians. They were English-style landowners and traders who took on the Crown out of exasperation over taxes and being shown a lack of respect. They were not politicians and would challenge anyone who suggested so to a duel.

Government up to the 18th century was made up of successful warriors and great landowners who had such strong hierarchical and territorial interests to defend that they became government and, in rare cases, evolved as hereditary princes. With the development of towns, trade and manufacturing, businessmen went into politics to defend interests too. Politics was a power-play side effect of financial self-interest and social status. How and why career politicians, their lobbyists and lawyers came upon us – people who had no lands to expand, no industry to prosper, who are in it only to operate the mechanisms of power for their own sake and that of their clients – is a fascinating and puzzling history.

War Counsel
Even in war, every bombing run, every missile firing, every raid by U.S. soldiers is vetted by teams of lawyers who are experts on international rules of war. Any wonder Osama bin-Laden, Saddam Hussein and their top lieutenants have time to make their getaway? Until a legal opinion is rendered, time and the enemy slip away.

There are lawyers in the top-secret operations center, called The Tank, deep inside the Pentagon, 24 hours a day, seven days a week, signing off on the legality of raids and strikes. There are lawyers at the Combined Air Operations Center at Prince Sultan Air Base in Saudi Arabia, poring over lists of potential bombing targets. Teams of lawyers based on aircraft carriers brief Navy pilots on what they can and can't shoot before they jet off into Afghan and

Iraqi skies. Military lawyers on the ground in Kandahar and Bagram work hand in hand with U.S. commandos. When special operations forces head out on top-secret missions, a lawyer is often at their side. Who needs lawyers in military operations? Aren't there enough everywhere else?

As recently as the 1980s, the idea of putting lawyers in the war room with commanding officers was unthinkable. But with military operations increasingly constrained by a complex web of international laws, conventions, agreements, accords and treaties, lawyers have moved to the forefront of real war zones as well.

Democratic Rights

The war on terrorism has brought into sharp focus and conflict the question of when and how America's democratic principles and ideals are compromised by career politicians who are persuaded to do so by able well-paid lobbyists and lawyers of foreign clients and interests. This then forces Americans to resort to the judicial process to reclaim their constitutional democratic rights.

Dictators in Saudi Arabia, Pakistan and Malaysia are overnight publicly embraced instead of their democratic neighbors India, Indonesia and Bangladesh because of foreign policy U-turns.

American influence-peddlers repeatedly derail any federal investigation of the close links Saudi Arabia has with the various Florida and U.S. – based charities that funded al-Qaeda and Osama bin-Laden. The fact is if terrorism is to be stopped, its financiers have to be stopped just like any other criminal is. This includes Saudi Arabia.

No effort to prop up "friendly" Arab dictatorships by acquiescing to their demands is going to overcome Arab structural internal deficiencies that cause dangerous instabilities in the Middle East. The judicial process and public relations campaigns are not the solution. Only by encouraging a peaceful but hastened evolution of Arab regimes toward political democratization and economic liberalization – just as was done in Germany and Japan after World War II – can America hope to reverse the trend of Arab decline that moves Arab dictatorships in the direction of Saudi Arabia, Iraq, Syria and Libya.

Lebanon's Shiite leader, Mohammad Hussein Fadlallah – who is blamed by the United States for inciting the terrorist bombings that killed the 241 marines in Beirut – accurately summed up what is going on in the undemocratic Arab world. "Bin-Laden is not the leader of the Muslim world and does not represent Islam," he said. He continued to add that bin-Laden was merely "profiteering from oppression in the Arab world".

Fewer and fewer questions today seem to be settled by the democratic electoral process. Instead, political battles are fought out through court decisions, Congressional investigations, and revelations in the media, E.J. Dionne, Jr. observes. The result has been a less democratic politics in which voters feel increasingly powerless. "In the meantime, the sheer volume of money that flooded through the electoral process made it an increasingly technocratic pursuit. Democratic politics is supposed to be about making public arguments and persuading fellow citizens. Instead, it has become an elaborate insider industry in which those skilled at fund-raising, polling, media relations, and advertising have the upper hand," Dionne concludes.

Judicial Conflicts
The U.S. Supreme Court justices voted party loyalty, political protection, not equal protection. They voted for the person they wanted to see in the White House. Prudent judicial impartiality has been replaced with the same partisanship permeating throughout Washington. The neutrality of the Supreme Court as envisioned by our Founding Fathers has been exposed for the fallacious myth it is. When the judges' decision can be accurately predicted based on their previous rulings of conservative versus liberal, five to four, the judicial branch of government has to be pruned.

Justice Sandra Day O'Connor wanted Bush in the White House so she could retire. She didn't want to have to wait another four years. Justice Clarence Thomas did not excuse himself even though his wife was being paid by the conservative Heritage Foundation to screen resumes for political appointments in a Bush administration. Justice Antonin Scalia did not excuse himself even though he had two sons working for the law firms representing Bush in the Supreme Court. Banana Republicans!

Justice John Paul Stevens accurately summed up the legal state of affairs. The losers of the election are the American people and their Supreme Court. "The identity of the loser is perfectly clear. It is the nation's confidence in the judge as an impartial guardian of the rule of law. In the interest of finality," said Justice Stevens, "the majority effectively orders the disenfranchisement of an unknown number of voters whose ballots reveal their intent." The Florida Supreme Court, he said, merely did "what courts do" in reading a state statute. What the U.S. Supreme Court repeatedly ruled they should do except when it comes to a state statute that may put a Democrat in the White House.

Supreme Court Justice Stephen Breyer told the 2001 annual meeting of the American Bar Association that the controversial Supreme Court appointment of the current U.S. president is remarkable for "the fact that losers as well as winners will abide by the result, and so will the public." The public also accepted the Supreme Court decision to allow religious organizations to hold free events in public parks at taxpayer expense. This was something the courts had vigorously opposed and upheld as required by the constitutional separation of church and state. Naturally, it was Pat Robertson's The American Center for Law and Justice that challenged the law and had it reversed by a friendly and predictable Supreme Court.

The Republican U.S. Supreme Court decision to gut the Americans with Disabilities Act, passed in 1990 by a huge bipartisan majority, is another example of the Court's biased assault on representative democracy.

Judicial partisanship has been allowed to gradually percolate all aspects of our lives because *We The Apathetic People* have, by our inaction, encouraged it. Not just in the judiciary but all branches of government. Florida Governor Jeb Bush clearly had a conflict of interest. So did Florida Secretary of State Katherine Harris who co-chaired the Bush campaign in Florida. No different than Florida Attorney General Robert Butterworth who chaired the Gore campaign in Florida.

The recount of all votes cast in Florida conducted by a consortium consisting of *The Washington Post, The New York Times,* The Associated Press, CNN, the *Los Angeles Times, The Wall Street Journal* and four Florida papers concluded all the lawyers involved in the Bush-Gore litigation had it wrong. Wrong tactics, wrong legal motions and wrong strategies. Gore should have asked for a recount of all Florida votes and he would have won by anywhere from 60 to 493 votes depending on which dimples were counted.

The partisanship of all the branches of government at the dawn of the 21st century would not have been allowed to come into existence let alone dictate and impose the will of career politicians on the silent majority in the 1960s. It tried and was toppled by *We the People.* People Power brought it down. Brought about change. Isn't it time the silent majority got active again?

All judicial appointments today create the appearance of a problem or conflict because they are political. In a functional New World Order, judicial appointments should be made by impartial judicial panels. That's how judges are appointed to the bench in Hong Kong. Isn't this something *We the Maids* should sweep in to America?

Democratic Legal Confusion

The 1992, 1996 and 2000 presidential elections revealed some interesting statistics. Three voters in four believed that the United States was on the wrong track. Reverse the role of the parties, and their respective remarks about the 1876 election of Horatio Seymour, the Democrat who lost to Ulysses Grant, and they apply to 21st century America. "The Republicans have lost the confidence of the country and the Democrats have not gained it."

President Clinton, Ross Perot and George W. Bush ran as outsiders, denouncing the status quo. It seems everyone I can ever remember running for high office, especially in Washington, runs as an outsider. Even "favorite sons" like President Bush, his son George W. and Al Gore were forced to cast themselves as the candidates for change. What happened to "Joe and Jane six pack" and the average working person? Why aren't these real outsiders running for office as our Founding Fathers intended? Is it because they're not landed gentry as the Founding Fathers mandated? According to polls, distrust of government is at an all-time high. Only 42 percent of Americans have at least a fair amount of confidence in the federal government. By a ratio of more than three to one, most Americans believe that it creates more problems than it solves. That is not surprising, because they are right. The current political process is like a space simulator spinning out of control. People are jerked around at the whim of career politicians. They feel powerless and helpless. Especially the black, Latino, Asian poor and elderly Americans. The multi-cultural Republicans. Early closing of polling sites, incomplete registration lists, absence of language assistance for people who do not speak English, absence of assistance for the disabled, lost ballots, faulty machinery... "These voters should not be disfranchised where their intent may be ascertained with reasonable certainty," the Florida Supreme Court wrote, quoting an Illinois decision. "The will of the people is the paramount consideration." The justices stressed they had "used traditional rules of statutory construction to resolve the ambiguities...The will of the people, not a hyper technical reliance upon statutory provisions, should be our guiding principle."

The judicial appointment of America's 43rd President is merely reflective of its legal and political constipation and gridlock. The saying "if it ain't broke don't fix it" no longer applies. The political system of checks and balances is not only broken but bust and needs radical surgery. The Founding Fathers wanted a weak Federal Government. But not for the reasons that seated the minority 43rd President and a divided political Congress.

There is nothing wrong with the American political system that the return to the wisdom and intents of the Founding Fathers would not cure. "The Founding Fathers warned us about career politicians. They tried to tell us that if the people in public office were too far removed from the average citizens, they couldn't possibly do a fair job of representing them. As far as I can tell, the Founding Fathers meant for public offices to be filled by butchers, bakers, and candlestick makers, who would do their duty to their country for a few years, then go quietly back to their life's work. Our system encourages career politicians to build their nests in public offices and settle in," Governor Ventura correctly points out.

The Founding Fathers were not utopians but were practical idealists. Recognizing that man is inherently flawed and driven by self-interest, they sought to devise a system of government that took these realities into account. The Electoral College was the outcome. An indirectly elected President was the goal. Their aims were limited but lofty: to create a system able to maintain the conditions of freedom against internal and external threat, to administer the nation's laws effectively, and to encourage rational deliberation and choice on the part of a self-governing people. As James Madison put it in The Federalist, Number 51, "If men were angels, no government would be necessary. If angels were to govern men, neither external nor internal controls on government would be necessary."

Electoral College

Hong Kong and America have one peculiar constitutional institution in common, the Electoral College. It must have been some U.S.-phile Hong Kong or Chinese drafter of the Basic Law that came into effect upon the handover who copied the term. In fact the two bodies have identical motives for quite different purposes. Both bodies are little understood and viewed as faintly arcane Machiavellian institutions.

The Hong Kong Electoral College is a group of 800 worthies, elected by various defined interest groups who then sit and elect 10 members of the 60-seat Legislative Council. Even Chinese conservatives have been heard to say that when the election caboose next comes up for review the College may have to go. Isn't it time *We the People* do the same with the American college?

The American Constitution was adopted in 1789. The Second Article of the Constitution and the 12th Amendment govern the rules of the Electoral College. Each state is apportioned a number of electoral votes equal to the number of congressional districts in the states, plus one for each of the two U.S. senators. D.C. is the exception. It receives three electors. The winner takes all in all the states with the exception of Maine and Nebraska which apportion the returns.

The Electoral College inherently discounts many Americans ballots. Historically this has been tolerated because *We the Apathetic People* allowed career politicians to perpetuate and expand it at the peoples' expense. It was last reformed in 1887. It should have been abolished. Because of it, Americans for the fourth time in America's history saw the man who won the popular votes fail to secure the required electoral votes.

Wyoming with a population of 480,000 gets one electoral vote per 160,000 people. California with a population of 32.6 million people gets 54 electoral votes – one for every 603,000 people. Does this sound like democracy? The Electoral College favors smaller states and vested interests that *We the Maids* have to straighten out.

The President as originally envisioned by the Founding Fathers was to act as an independent magistrate to execute "impartially" legislation passed by Congress. Some of the Founding Fathers wanted the president elected by the people. Others had fears and suspicions that the ignorant, tyrannical, tempestuous masses would create heat, ferment and convulsions in the new Republic. Some of the Founding Fathers wanted the president to be selected by Congress. They reached a compromise. The Electoral College as a "buffer institution" between Congress and the masses.

Over the years the presidency expanded dramatically. From an impartial magistrate into executive leadership. Incumbents now not only enforce laws but also initiate many. Domestic and international. The presidency is now a dominant branch of government. Not what the Founding Fathers had in mind.

Earlier attempts to amend the Constitution to legitimize the office of the presidency failed. National conventions and primaries evolved as the unconstitutional way to legitimize the presidency. The evolved office of the president has to be closely re-examined in the New World Order by *We the Apathetic People* if we want change.

The 18th century institutional buffer the "Magnificent Seven" created to protect the New American Republic from the power of the "masses" or *We the Tempestuous People* is an outdated anachronism for the New World Order. Democracy in America in the 21st century deserves better than an 18th century political relic capitalized on by career politicians and their financial contributors. Soft money, unbridled spending loopholes as well as the hard ones, have to be treated like those American tourists at faraway beaches. They have to be plugged. The last presidential election of the last millennium cost $3 billion, the most expensive election in American history. Should American leadership and the future of our children depend on interest groups to turn out the vote? What about each individual's personal interest!

The American Electoral College is a constitutional relic of an antique world disorder. The Founding Fathers were not comfortable with the idea of the president being directly elected by the Congress – or the people. Sometimes the presidential election is described as "general". It is not. Technically it is "indirect". The president is elected state by state. In each state, on the ballot are candidate electors tied to each presidential candidate and the number of them that go to the College depends on the state's population. Dick Cheney's Wyoming has the minimum of three, California has 54. These are the numbers that dictate the importance of a state to a presidential candidate who needs 270 Electoral College votes to win. The American public believes it has elected its president on election day. The president is actually elected on the first Monday after the second Wednesday in December when the electors ballot in their respective state capitals and send the result to the president of the U.S. Senate. The ballots are counted and ratified in a joint session of Congress on January 6. The result is that in a nation with 100 million likely voters, the result of the presidential race can be decided by fewer than a million. Those are the undecided voters in swing states with lots of votes in the Electoral College. In obsessively courting undecided voters in a few places presidential candidates are neglecting issues of concern to the nation as a whole. Is this system still relevant in the New World Order? The last presidential election of the 20th century stripped naked the frailties and inequities of America's Electoral College in Florida, New Mexico, Iowa, Wyoming and numerous other states where irregularities were reported.

The Founding Fathers were right about the stupid masses. The "Floridiots" proved them right. Not just the voters but the career politicians with multiple conflicts of interest that actively pursued their personal and partisan agendas regardless of what *We the People* think. Isn't it time *We the Maids* remind them that we can sweep them out?

The Electoral College spotlighted in the last election of the millennium was also critical in four earlier elections in the 19th century. Three of the elections resulted in the winner of the popular vote not winning the electoral vote. In 1800 Jefferson won over Aaron Burr when the election was split and handed over to the House of Representatives. In 1824 John Adams won thanks to the House vote even though

Andrew Jackson won the popular vote. In 1876 Rutherford Hayes beat Samuel Tilden by one electoral vote even though he lost the popular vote. In 1888 Benjamin Harrison won the Electoral College even though Grover Cleveland won the popular vote. In the closing year of the millennium, Bush won the electoral vote, according to the U.S. Supreme Court, even though Gore won the popular vote. Can we afford to have this happen again in the future?

Can anything be done, short of replacing the Electoral College with direct election of the president – a very difficult reform that would require a constitutional amendment? Ideally the Constitution should be amended. However, it is also possible to transform presidential elections while keeping the Electoral College and without amending the Constitution. All we have to do is change the way states allocate their electoral votes.

Michael Lind correctly points out that: "Today all but two states – Nebraska, which has five electoral votes, and Maine, which has four – give all of their electoral votes to the winner of the state's popular vote. If every state were to divide its electoral votes among the candidates on the breakdown of the popular vote, presidential politics would be reinvigorated. Every state legislature has the power to switch from the winner-take-all system to a division of its electoral votes. Nebraska and Maine each give two electoral votes to the winner of the statewide popular vote, while allocating the remainder according to the winner of the popular vote within each congressional district." Should Americans decide to continue electing a president indirectly through an Electoral College, state legislatures should be made to change the winner-take-all electoral system so that in future elections Americans as a whole have a chance to elect a president of the United States, rather than a president of the swing states; president of the United States Supreme Court; president of any State Supreme Court; president of any Secretary of State; president of any Legislature; president of any Federal Court; or president of a newly elected Congress. After all, isn't the President supposed to be elected by *We the People?*

The last election of the last millennium saw America arrive to a place it has never been before. The pollster John Zogby said: "This election comes under the column 'We've never been here before'.'" Bush or Gore could have won the popular vote but not the Electoral College votes. In fact, that is precisely what happened to Gore. Worse they could have tied the Electoral College votes, leaving the final decision to the Republican-dominated House of Representatives. At no time in history has a candidate failed to reach a majority in the Electoral College. With the risk of faithless electors, dueling electors and rejected electors, is this any way for a true democracy to elect its leader in the 21st century?

If the vote goes to the House of Representatives, each state has one vote. Those states with an equal number of Republican and Democratic congressmen get no vote. If the House cannot reach a decision on the President the matter is sent to the Senate to decide the Vice President. The Senate may not want to make a decision either, in which case the Speaker of the House becomes temporary President. The Speaker may decline and ask the Senate President to take office, who in turn can call on the longest serving member, the Senate President Pro Tempore, to serve. In the case of the election of America's 43rd president that would have meant Senator Strom Thurmond. Had that happened the scenario would have gotten worse. He became incapacitated before he would have taken office and would have died in office.

Is this procedure and system something America wants to continue to live with in the new millennium? If the Electoral College is to be retained it should be revamped to allow for the selection of a Chief Executive like Hong Kong. The office of the president no longer has any credibility. Vice President Dick Cheney is already acting as America's first Chief Executive. Dubya is merely the Chairman of the Board. The President is an illusory relic of the last millennium.

It is for *We the People* to decide and another argument for a constitutional convention at the beginning of the 21st century.

Pork Barrel Subsidies

Nixon was right when he said: "Many lament the proliferation of big money and influence-peddling in Washington. This focuses on the symptom, not the cause of the problem. High-powered lobbyists go to Washington because of the vast expansion of government into every sector of society and the economy. Without significant retrenchment in the scope of government, lobbying and big money will be here to stay, simply because Washington is where the action is."

The problem with pork-barrel politics is that it makes no business or financial sense. "Another by-product of pork-barreling is that it encourages public servants to make a lifetime career out of politics. Pet projects aren't the only things that can be bought with pork. Politicians also use pork to purchase power, influence, and votes. A long career of garnering favors can make a politician very powerful – and very hard to budge," Ventura concludes. I concur.

Federal grants to faith-based charities are a clear violation of the Founding Fathers' desire to separate church from state. However, because they are subsidies that taxpayers fund to ensure the re-election of career politicians, they can get passed if *We the Apathetic People* continue to be part of the silent majority. No different than all other government subsidies.

Most government subsidies go to America's farmers. In eight states government subsidies make up 100 percent of all farm income! Direct payments to farmers have tripled since 1996. Over the last four years of the millennium, the top one percent of farmers in America – all fifteen of them – received an average of $616,000 each from the government. The top 10 percent – about 150 farmers – were paid an average of $308,000 per farmer. The pay-out in the closing year of the millennium shattered all previous records. "It has created some huge dependencies, no doubt about it," said Wiley Good, a grain farmer and businessman. "It's easy to say: All this cash is out there, now what can I do to farm the government?"

"Virtually every farmer in the country is on the dole in one form or the other," said Clark Williams-Derry, a senior analyst with the Environmental Working Group, a non-profit research organization that has studied farm subsidies. "It's social-engineering with nobody at the switch," he said. Former U.S. agriculture secretary Dan Glickman said farming has "become largely an income transfer program" with the government underwriting rural businesses and requiring nothing in return. "Essentially, the government's role in requiring the farmer to do something in return has been largely eliminated by Congress," Glickman continued.

Not only do the farmers of the Great Plains of the Midwest get a disproportionate share of the Electoral College, they also live off urban taxpayers' money. Yet *We the Apathetic People* choose to let them do so.

When America went to war after September 11, pork barrel spending reached a new offensive high. Corporate America, companies like General Electric and IBM that were already benefiting from the war effort, sought to reduce the taxes on their overseas investment income. This was happening while career politicians authorized $400 billion a year on defense spending, billions of which is pure political pork that goes to build outdated naval vessels and military equipment the military does not need. This happens annually so the politicians can score political points back home where the equipment is built or based. Shouldn't the money be spent on building new weapons systems? Isn't it time this porky triangle pigsty of military services, defense contractors and parochial narrow-minded career politicians be swept clean by *We the Maids?*

Legal Alternatives

The wholesale destruction of lawyers has been a rallying call for many for centuries. Many lawyers are also frustrated with their profession and pursue alternative careers. Lawyers are a necessary evil of a bureaucratic society. Career politicians and their lawyers are *Dementors* and *Dracos* in Harry Potter-speak. If bureaucracies are reduced lawyers will decrease proportionately. In the New World Order, the role of career politicians, political lawyers, lawyers in general and the judiciary have to be re-examined and contained.

The best and most glaring early 21st century example of why the wholesale destruction of lawyers echoes through the centuries is the memo leaked from Clifford Chance, the world's largest law firm. A memo that encouraged lawyers to "pad" their billable hours! This is nothing new in the legal world. I personally know of many fellow lawyers who routinely engage in the practice.

Lawyers in Hong Kong have already started the re-examination. Solicitors, non-trial lawyers not door-to-door salesmen, want to change the traditional system whereby only barristers can appear on behalf of a client in court. Solicitors want to share in this lucrative business. This will benefit clients and reduce their legal fees. They already have. Unfortunately, like America, this results in unnecessary litigation and appeals. Fortunately, Hong Kong judges, unlike judges in America, are doing something about it. In Hong Kong the losing party in a case, and sometimes their lawyers, are saddled with the cost of litigation. This forces people to think twice before they sue. A recent example was a lawyer representing 54 clients seeking the right of abode who may have to personally pay the legal costs because the litigation was without any "reasonable grounds". In other Court of Appeal cases, the judges repeatedly remind lawyers they are duty bound not to file frivolous appeals. Lawyers are publicly criticized for bringing such appeals. "There was, so far as we could see as a court of three, not the remotest chance of any success on any of the grounds, not the slightest chance," Mr. Justice Stuart-Moore said on one such appeal.

Paralegals and do-it-yourself guides allow people to get traditional legal services at a fraction of the cost. Most work in law offices is done by paralegals, yet clients are still charged lawyers' hourly rates.

While going to law school I worked as an associate editor at Matthew Bender, a legal publishing house in San Francisco. My job required me to research and write legal forms for *California Legal* Forms and *California Forms For Pleading and Practice.* These forms saved lawyers time in preparing contracts or pleadings. They are tools to the shortcuts in the practice of law. In theory the time saved by the lawyers was a savings passed on to the client. In practice that doesn't always happen.

Do-it-yourself legal guides are very helpful, especially those on wills, divorces and simple contracts put out by firms like Nolo Press, Parsons Technology and E-Z Legal Forms Inc. It shocks me, but does not surprise me, that some lawyers are fighting such firms on the ground that only lawyers can practice law.

Divorce is getting just as easy, almost easier than marriage. Saint Charles, Illinois, has do-it-yourself divorce courts one night a week. No lawyers. Just the couple involved. It is the first such program in America and started the first year of the new millennium. Since divorce is so common it is only natural that *We the Maids* will sweep out lawyers and the related hassle and expense and replace them with all the simple forms and procedures available. The United States Supreme Court affirmed the constitutional right of individuals to represent themselves in the 1975 case of *Faretta v. California.* Shouldn't *We the Maids* be sweeping out more lawyers in the new millennium as the pro se movement – a Latin term roughly meaning "for one's self"– advocates?

Texas challenged Nolo for publishing do-it-yourself guides. Nolo was founded by two former legal aid lawyers who got rich in the process of making it simple and cost-effective for people to do their own wills and divorces without the need of a lawyer. They got rich at the expense of other lawyers, not the people who buy their forms! Any wonder lawyers are trying to stop them? Fewer lawyers and more paralegals and do-it-yourself books and software are viable alternatives to lawyers in the 21st century.

The Texas challenge reminds me of the prehistoric California legal challenge in the early 1970s to the law prohibiting lawyers from advertising. Len Jacoby and Steve Meyers of Jacoby and Meyers fame were challenging the state and testing the issue. They were over at the house one day during the challenge. Nancy Platt was an old grammar school friend of my then wife Gail who was dating Len. They eventually got married. "You can't believe their antiquated reasoning for banning advertising," Len said. "They're trying to protect the old-time establishment lawyers and their fees," Steve added. They were right. They prevailed. Their victory benefited great numbers of people who can, as a result of their victory, do comparative shopping, get competitive prices, all at the expense of the legal establishment.

Lawyers in the U.S. aren't happy with legal fees. They also want to share accountants' fees and other non-legal services that are essential to the client under the euphemism one-stop-shopping.

Lawyers have been an object of literary humiliation since before the time of Shakespeare, and are commonly written off as morally corrupt people who have no sense of ethics. Lawyers in literature and poetry are often depicted as scoundrels who do nothing except steal money from the poor and exploit people's misfortunes. Lawyers are like high priests in a pagan religion. The legal ceremony in court, the way they dress, talk and the obfuscated language they create to justify their fees in order to "translate" to mere mortals what the law means. These characters exist in literature of both the past and the present. They also exist in Washington D.C. and throughout America.

William Shakespeare, Charles Dickens, Jonathan Swift, Samuel Johnson, Oliver Goldsmith, Lewis Carroll, Henry Fielding, Anthony Trollope and William Wordsworth chose to portray lawyers as people who were actually the lowest members of society. From Elizabethan times to the present the role of lawyers has changed dramatically. However their position in literature has remained consistent.

Theater of the Absurd

William Shakespeare is the most cited writer when it comes to condemning lawyers. Shakespeare's line, "The first thing we do, let's kill all the lawyers," appears in *Henry VI;* this quote is one of the most popular literary references to lawyers. This line seems to sum up the attitude that Shakespeare and many people throughout the last millennium held concerning lawyers.

The second year of the new millennium was greeted by gunshots from law student Peter Odighizuwa's .38-caliber pistol. He took Shakespeare literally and killed lawyers and aspiring lawyers at West Virginia's Appalachian School of Law. A 21st century reminder of Shakespeare's famous quote.

The pomp and circumstance of the opening of the Hong Kong judicial year combines the best of Shakespearean theatre and circus act. Chinese judges in white horsehair wigs posing alongside their white and other Asian colleagues all of them dressed like stuffed penguins. A reminder of Elizabethan times with Chinese characteristics. In Elizabethan times the courtroom took on the same role that a theater did: a place for spectacle and entertainment. The public would regularly gather in courtrooms in order to be entertained. The theater reappeared in electronic Shakespearean theater grandeur in Florida's canvassing boards in the counties where the recounts took place at the end of the 20th century. The dramatic charges and insults bellowed by lawyers prompted Charles Lichtman, a lawyer for the Democrats, to comment: "Great theater...No wonder people hate lawyers." David Letterman added: "Every big-shot attorney in the United States is now in Florida, so here's what happens: if we were to have a hurricane...this whole thing could still have a happy ending."

September 11 saw lawyers, lobbyists and career politicians work together to again protect government and big business at the expense of the victims of the terrorist bombings. Less than two weeks after September 11, on September 21, Congress passed the law that set up the September 11 Victim Compensation Fund. The act was passed as part of the airline bailout program and was intended to shield the airlines, airport security companies, airplane manufacturers, the owners of the World Trade Center and the government from potentially crushing liabilities for their negligence. Victims had to also offset any amount they collected from their own insurance company. That didn't stop the families of about 600 killed in the September 11 attacks from filing a $100 trillion lawsuit against Saudi banks, charities and individuals.

Rodney King best expressed how victims of unnecessary violence feel. "I feel like first I took an awful beating from the police, and now my own lawyers are beating up on me," King said more than 10 years after the Los Angeles police beating case. His lawyers made more money on his case than he did. He felt they had cheated him. "I feel like they took advantage of my lack of understanding and, you know, they muscled their educational background to deceive, mislead and rob me out of monies," he said. King sued some lawyers, some of them sued him, and some of them sued each other.

People who traditionally depend on legal aid or pro bono legal work are also taking a beating and are sore because of their lack of representation. Vera Kennedy is one of the many frustrated by the lack of free legal representation. Her apartment was among those in a San Francisco public housing development that the city wanted to demolish and rebuild. When similar buildings were torn down in the past, prominent firms stepped forward to make sure residents got adequate interim housing and were allowed to return to the area when work was finished. Local public interest lawyers have been scrambling to find a firm to do the same but have had no luck. "There are mothers with young children here," she said. "They need the protection of having a place to live."

Los Angeles skid row lawyer Nancy Mintie protects such children.

Her nemeses are the city's worst slumlords. She sees children covered with rat bites, and others who have cockroaches embedded in their ears. Mintie has won multi-million dollar awards for her clients. Some have used the money to buy homes for their families. Others have set aside funds to send their children to college. "When they go to college, they can get jobs; help their parents, brothers and sisters; and then the cycle of poverty is broken," she says.

What happened to other charitable lawyers? Several things. In 1996, Congress prohibited lawyers who get legal-services money from engaging in class-action lawsuits of any kind, or taking cases on a number of issues, including abortion, illegal immigration and welfare revision. Also since 1996, Legal Services Corp., a major source of representation for low income people in non-criminal cases, has lost a quarter of its financing from the federal government, the source of the bulk of its budget, leading to hundreds of layoffs among its legal staff nationwide. To top it off, the escalating costs of lawyers in the private sector resulted in America's top law firms cutting back on their pro bono work. The roughly 50,000 lawyers in America's 100 highest-grossing firms spent an average of eight minutes a day on pro bono cases in 1999, according to a survey by American Lawyer magazine. That comes out to about 36 hours a year, down significantly from 56 hours in 1992, when the magazine started tracking the volunteer hours. Lawyers today charge more, make more and contribute less to the community that supports them.

They're so busy trying to win big money cases that they don't care if America loses. Loses not just the political legal game governed by the antiquated constitutional rules and regulations of the current system – but the country.

Great Britain granted the colonies full independence as long as Americans were able to govern themselves. Should Americans fail to provide a democratically elected president, Great Britain reserved the right to annex the United States, as millions delightedly noted in the wake of the Florida election farce. The Internet almost crashed because of the number of messages winging their way around the globe reminding Americans of The Treaty of Yorktown and Britain's Notice of Revocation of American Independence pursuant to Article

III of the surrender at Yorktown in 1781. This would serve *We the Apathetic People* right. Can this human cultural shift be allowed to continue in the New World Order?

Legal Abuses

When Andrew Hart, a Hong Kong solicitor, stopped by New York, I gave him a quick tour of the city. As we walked on Fifth Avenue I asked him if he had heard the joke about the barrister that had become a solicitor. He hadn't. As we crossed the street at Fifth Avenue and 50th and started ascending the stairs to Saint Patrick's Cathedral I proceeded. "Well, there was this well-known English barrister who was running late to court. As she ran up the stairs in a hurry she dropped her briefs and became a solicitor." Andrew, a British solicitor, entered God's house guffawing.

California Governor Pete Wilson's veto of the California Bar's fee bill, which reduced California Bar dues from an average of $458 plus to just $75, was a step in the right direction. A pity it has been restored. The Governor was correct when he said the Bar is "bloated, arrogant, oblivious and unresponsive". The same holds true for its members, especially independent counsel.

Attorney General Janet Reno appointed as many as seven independent counsels. Smaltz vs. Espy, Barrett vs. Cisneros, Pearson vs. Brown, Von Kann vs. Segal, Bruce vs. Babbitt, Lancaster vs. Herman and Starr vs. Clinton.

Gore Vidal wrote a great piece for the *Los Angeles Times* on what career politicians and their lawyers have done to the country. In discussing the Clinton-Lewinsky media and legal circus he pointed out: "Foreigners are mystified by the whole business, while thoughtful Americans - there are several of us – are equally mystified that the ruling establishment of the country has proved to be so mindlessly vindictive that it is willing, to be blunt, to overthrow the lawful government of the United States – that is, a president elected in 1992 and re-elected in 1996 by *We the People,* that sole source of all political legitimacy, which takes precedence over the U.S. Constitution and the common law and God himself."

In the same article Vidal goes on to point out that "two-thirds of all the world's lawyers are American, and they have made a highly profitable, for them, mess of our American legal system. They could not prove in the 1950s that Alger Hiss had been a spy for the Soviets so they sent him to prison on an unconvincing perjury charge. Al Capone was never convicted of murder or extortion; he was put in jail for income tax evasion." Lawyers can, as Ken Starr has proven, be creatively abusive. Reading and hearing what he did to Hong Kong-based Jim Guy Tucker, the former Arkansas Lieutenant Governor who succeeded Clinton, in the Whitewater investigation was reprehensible. "They still re-run the old stories," Jim Guy told me during a lunch at the FCC after another derogatory article appeared in *The Asian Wall Street Journal.*

Abuses by lawyers are endless. Kenneth Starr exemplified the Bar's reputation at a cost of more than 73 million taxpayer dollars! I don't remember hiring him. Do you? Most taxpayers don't. Our elected career politicians hired him. Are they out of pocket by just $1 or just out of touch? The EPA superfund lawsuits dragging innocent local business people into court are another perversion of justice, again at taxpayers' expense. Sexual and racial discrimination, sexual harassment, workers' compensation, whiplash, breach of contract be it government, military or private sector are just as totally out of control.

The worst legal criminal culprits are the lawyers that enable corporate America and its management to enrich themselves at the expense of their employees and shareholders. Outside counsel giving legal opinions that perpetuate fraud and corporate general counsel that enrich themselves together with the corporate CEOs they are supposed to admonish and advise in the interest of their shareholders. The most despicable ones are those that sign secret agreements with the CEOs which guarantee their income will rise and fall – but usually rise – with the CEOs' – as investigators believe Tyco's Dennis Kozlowski did with his general counsel Mark Belnick. If lawyers wants to stop being company employees representing shareholders and want to become entrepreneurs, they should quit and go do that with their own money and investors'. That's what I did.

The more the press and pundits criticize career politicians the more ridiculous are the laws they seem to pass. Nixon had an explanation that I don't accept. However, it sheds light on how tricky politicians think. "Pundits frequently ridicule members of the House and Senate for failing to have the guts to vote for what is right even if they risk their seats by doing so. But expecting politicians to cast votes against their political interest is just as unreasonable as expecting reporters to turn in exposes of the business affairs of their publishers. Legislators, like journalists, are only human." This is one of many issues I take exception to and disagree with Nixon. In the credible press it is expected that journalists report on the affairs of their publishers. "In fact often they will go and pursue harder, driven by fear of playing it favorite," Luke Hunt, an FCC Board member and journalist for AFP, exclaimed in utter disbelief when I raised the question with him. This was confirmed by the role the press played in the downfall of media moguls Robert Maxwell and Conrad Black.

Is it any wonder that China, like most countries, tries to keep American law firms and their lawyers out?

Legal Rights
In 1991 Vice President Dan Quayle, addressing the American Bar Association Convention, suggested that something is wrong when America has 70 percent of the world's lawyers. It has almost 800, 000 of them, one for every 311 citizens. It is actually amazing that the power of the subject was strong enough to make the Vice President articulate enough to get it all out. Will Rogers puts the dilemma lawyers and society have in the right political prospective. "Did you read how many thousands (not hundreds) but thousands of students just graduated all over the country in law? Going to take an awful lot of crime to support that bunch."

Hong Kong, which has only a total of 4,600 solicitors and 670 barristers, is already talking about scaling back.

Responding to Quayle, a law professor said: "We have a lot of lawyers because we have a lot of rights....That's democracy. That's equality... we have environmental rights...discrimination rights... consumer rights... safety rights..." Can there be too many rights? There can, when every social problem is presented as a clash of rights, and all advocacy is couched in the language of rights. The costs of these habits are calculated in a timely book *Rights Talk:*

The Impoverishment of Political Discourse, by Mary Ann Glendon, a professor of law at Harvard University.

Until the 1950s, she notes, the focus of constitutional law was not on personal rights as the bulwark of liberty. Rather, it was on the structure of our political regime – the allocation of powers among the federal government's branches and between the federal and state governments. The strong tradition was that great controversies should be settled in representative political institutions, not in courts, unless the Constitution's text clearly indicated otherwise. But literary theories ("deconstruction" and all that) have been imported into jurisprudence to "prove that the texts are of indeterminate meaning, and political theories have stigmatized tradition as oppressive. This has emancipated the discretion of judges and has licensed social reformers to prefer litigation, with its promise of quick and sweeping victory, over the slow, incremental progress of persuasion and legislation. Thus federal judges, egged on by academic admirers, have been running schools, prisons, hospitals and other things, always in the name of an expanding menu of rights. Rights which should be protected by locally elected officials at state levels."

Not only is America exceptionally lawyer-ridden, but lawyers' roles there are exceptionally adversarial. Courtroom law talk, Glendon notes, proceeds from the premise inimical to civil discourse: that two theses pushed to extremes will enable a third party to determine the truth. Our political discourse is so saturated with rights talk that the Supreme Court has gone as far as to define citizenship as "the right to have rights".

The exaggerated absoluteness of the American dialect of rights talk implies that Americans are too childish or volatile to be trusted to respect rights that are subject to reasonable limitations. Our hard-edged rights talk slights the grammar of cooperative living and also slights the art of building coalitions by achieving compromises. The language of rights – universal, inalienable, inviolable rights – leaves no room for compromise. As Glendon says, "The winner takes all and the loser has to get out of town. The conversation is over." Rights talk, she warns, reinforces an all-too-human failing that also is encouraged by the language of psychotherapy, the tendency to place the self at the center of the moral universe. Prodigality in the bestowing of the label "right" is a tactic to give specious dignity to unbridled desires. It multiplies occasions for civic discord and leads to indignation about the inescapable limits inherent in life in society.

Despotic individual rights cost all taxpayers one way or another. Higher taxes, retail prices, insurance premiums, unnecessary medical tests to avoid litigation and our general cultural impoverishment by not being able to see our children play in sandboxes, on climbing equipment or merry-go-rounds while we eat pasteurized Brie.

A case in point is Patricia Alice McColm who has filed more than 50 lawsuits and hundreds of police complaints over the past 25 years. As of 1996 she was officially declared a "vexatious litigant" and as such is barred from filing lawsuits without the permission of a judge. She is also required, in some cases, to put up a bond to cover the legal costs of defendants should she lose. "She has an incredible ability to use the legal system and the police as a club to beat her opponents into submission," says Alex Bannon, an Oakland lawyer who defended a carpet cleaner whom McColm claimed literally pulled the rug from under her (allegedly breaking her toe) when she refused to pay his bill.

The 21st century is starting like the last one ended. More dumb lawsuits. Attorney Peter Angelos filed a class action lawsuit against cell phone manufacturers for failing to warn users of cell phones of the risks that may be inherent in using the phones. To date the American Medical Association and National Institutes of Health have found no such connection. It may be that in the future research will establish such a link. If they do that is when the suit should be filed.

My personal favorite is obese people suing fast-food restaurants. Like lawsuits are going to make them thinner?

The linguistic and conceptual deficiencies of rights talk in our law-saturated society result in the portrayal of Americans as solitary wanderers in a land of strangers, throwing out aggressive rights claims, like sharp elbows, in an endless jostling for social space.

"By neglecting the social dimension of personhood and by exalting autonomy, rights talk creates a climate of callousness toward the very young, the severely ill and disabled and the frail elderly," Glendon correctly points out.

Neglecting the dimension of personhood can get real extreme as a couple of wigs and I conjured up typical absurd legal arguments at the FCC Main Bar. The winner was the hypothetical case of two gentlemen who, one evening after leaving the FCC, were walking to the nightclub quarter of Lan Kwai Fong when they observed a rather well-dressed and attractive young lady walking ahead of them. One of them turned to the other and remarked: "I'd give $250 to spend the night with that woman." Much to their surprise, the young lady overheard the remark, turned around, and replied, "I'll take you up on that offer." She had a neat appearance and a pleasant voice, so after bidding his companion good night, the man accompanied the young lady to her apartment.

The following morning the man presented her with $125 as he prepared to leave. She demanded the rest of the money, stating, "If you don't give me the other $125 I'll sue you for it." He laughed, saying, "I'd like to see you get it on these grounds." Within a few days, he was surprised when he received a summons ordering his presence in court as a defendant in a lawsuit. He hurried to his lawyer and explained the details of the case. His lawyer said, "She can't possibly get a judgment against you on such grounds, but it will be interesting to see how her case will be presented."

After the usual preliminaries, the lady's lawyer addressed the court as follows: "Your honor, my client, this lady, is the owner of a piece of property, a garden spot, surrounded by a profuse growth of shrubbery, which property she agreed to rent to the defendant for a specified length of time for the sum of $250. The defendant took possession of the property, used it extensively for the purposes for which it was rented, but upon evacuating the premises, he paid only $125, one half of the amount agreed upon. The rent was not excessive, since it is restricted property, and we ask judgment be granted against the defendant to assure payment of the balance."

The defendant's lawyer was impressed and amused by the way his opponent had presented the case. His defense, therefore, was somewhat different from the way he originally planned to present it. "Your honor," he said, "my client agrees that the lady has a fine piece of property, that he did rent such property for a time, and a degree of pleasure was derived from the transaction. However, my client found a well on the property around which he placed his stones, sank a shaft, and erected a pump, all labor performed personally by him. We claim these improvements to the property were sufficient to offset the unpaid amount, and that the plaintiff was adequately compensated for the rental of said property. We therefore, ask the judgment not be granted."

The young lady's lawyer answered: "Your honor, my client agrees that the defendant did find a well on her property. However, had the defendant not known the well existed, he would never have rented the property. Also, upon evacuating the premises, the defendant removed the stones, pulled out the shaft, and took the pump with him. In doing so, he not only dragged the equipment through the shrubbery, but left the hole much larger than it was prior to his occupancy, making the property much less desirable to others. We, therefore, ask that judgment be granted."

In the judge's decision, he provided for two options: "Pay the $125 or have the equipment detached from its current location and provide it to the plaintiff for damages." The defendant wrote a check immediately.

I can't wait to see the rights arguments about the world wide web, space, Internet, satellites, docking stations, the Moon, Mars and the universe in general. The space and cyberspace ambulance chasers arriving at every scene of a cyber, satellite, or space ship collision looking for whiplash and wrongful death claimants are going to really push the rights envelope.

Let's just look at some of the rights arguments in the closing years of the last millennium. Stella Leibeck successfully sued McDonald's because she was burned when she spilled hot coffee on her thighs. She was a passenger in a stationary car at the time, clasping the cup of hot McDonald's coffee she had just bought between her legs. The case inspired the Stella Leibeck Awards for the most frivolous successful lawsuits in America.

The top Stella Awards for 2002 were:

Fifth place tied: Kathleen Robertson of Austin, Texas, was awarded $780,000 by a jury of her peers after breaking her ankle tripping over a toddler who was running inside a furniture store. The owners of the store were understandably surprised at the verdict, considering the misbehaving toddler was Ms. Robertson's son. Nineteen-year-old Carl Truman of Los Angeles won $74,000 and medical expenses when his neighbor ran over his hand with a Honda Accord. Mr. Truman apparently did not notice there was someone at the wheel of the car when he was trying to steal the hubcaps. Terrence Dickson of Bristol, Pennsylvania, was leaving a house he had just finished robbing by way of the garage door. He was not able to get the garage door to go up since the automatic door opener was malfunctioning. He could not re-enter the house because the door connecting the house and garage locked when he pulled it shut. The family were on vacation and Mr. Dickson found himself locked in the garage for eight days. He subsisted on a case of Pepsi he found and a large bag of dry dog food. He sued the homeowner's insurance claiming the situation caused him undue mental anguish. The jury agreed to the tune of $500,000.

Fourth Place: Jerry Williams of Little Rock, Arkansas, was awarded $14,500 and medical expenses after being bitten on the buttocks by his next door neighbor's Beagle dog. The Beagle was on a chain in its owner's fenced yard. The award was less than sought because the jury felt the dog might have been a little provoked at the time as Mr. Williams who had climbed over the fence into the yard was shooting it repeatedly with a pellet gun.

Third Place: A Philadelphia restaurant was ordered to pay Amber Carson of Lancaster, Pennsylvania, $113,500 after she slipped on a soft drink and broke her tailbone. The beverage was on the floor because Ms. Carson had thrown it at her boyfriend 30 seconds earlier during an argument.

Second Place: Kara Walton of Claymont, Delaware, sued the owner of a night club in a neighboring city when she fell from the bathroom window to the floor and knocked out two of her front teeth. This occurred whilst Ms. Walton was trying to crawl through the window in the ladies room to avoid paying the $3.50 cover charge. She was awarded $12,000 and dental expenses.

First Place: The 2002 runaway winner was Mr. Merv Grazinski of Oklahoma City, Oklahoma. Mr. Grazinski purchased a brand new Winnebago motor home. On his trip home from a football game, having driven on to the freeway, he set the cruise control at 70 mph and calmly left the driver's seat to go into the back and make himself a cup of coffee. Not surprisingly the RV left the freeway, crashed and overturned. Mr. Grazinski sued Winnebego for not advising him in the owner's manual that he could not actually do this. The jury awarded him $1,750,000 plus a new Winnebago motor home. The company actually changed their manuals on the basis of this suit just in case there were any other complete morons buying their recreation vehicles.

What Charles Dickens did with *Jarndyce v. Jarndyce* in Bleak House as an index of cultural conditions, perhaps some modern novelist will do with *Trimarco v. Colgate Palmolive et. al.*

The et al.s include some other manufacturers of toothbrushes, and the American Dental Association. All are to be hauled before the Bar of Justice by Mark Trimarco, speaking for himself and – this is a class-action suit – "all others similarly situated". The others are suffering from what Trimarco's complaint calls "a disease known as 'toothbrush abrasion'". Abrasion a disease? The plaintiff's materials also call it "an injury". And "a distinct clinical entity caused by toothbrushes of the following bristle types: firm, medium and soft both natural and synthetic".

The complaint says people suffering from this self-inflicted injury are consumers who were not "informed or warned about the danger of toothbrush abrasion". So, you brush your teeth and it hurts a bit which is why children quite understandably don't want to do it, Trimarco has just found out.

Overweight Americans suing four leading fast-food chains claiming their obesity, diabetes, high blood pressure and cholesterol are due to their addiction to the fast-food meals they eat several times a week is a millennium classic.

Or what about the personal injury case New York's Mayor Rudolph Giuliani had to sit in on as a juror, and jury foreman at that! The case involved a man's claim that water in a shower scalded his genitals so badly he was unable to have sex with his wife. What's he complaining about? A light spray of hot water on the balls, a rash or an itch area is often better than sex.

On a more relevant rights argument, let's take a look at what some of the parents whose innocent children were killed in school shootings are doing to be compensated for their losses. In Paducah, since the funeral, many locals have been more devoted to finding lawyers than finding Jesus. The lessons the town offers mourners of Colorado's catastrophe are mostly dispiriting ones: the need to assign blame eventually leads to the courtroom. "In American culture, money makes the system tick," says Michael Breen, lead lawyer for the victims' parents in several suits now pending. "You need financial damages to get accountability." But the courtroom seems to lead nowhere, except to additional grief. "Everybody sympathizes with [the parents] who lost children," says Paducah Sun editor Jim Paxton, whose editorials have criticized the lawsuits brought by the parents of the three dead girls. "But they don't have a monopoly on victimhood."

Lonely hearts are also turning to the law as the multi-million dollar dating industry fails to match up to expectations.

One woman dissatisfied by an agency's failure to introduce her to suitable partners became the first person to resort to the courts after she didn't find a soul mate despite paying for the service.

A proliferation in dating agencies in the closing years of the millennium has forced governments to regulate the industry, which at one time was little more than a cover for prostitution.

A tourist in San Francisco went into a curio shop in Chinatown. He saw a brass rat that he really liked and asked the shopkeeper how much it cost. "Twelve dolla for the rat and one thousand dolla for the stoly," was the answer. The tourist decided to just get the rat and forget about the story. As he walked out the store he noticed rats were coming out from behind buildings and following him and people were scurrying out of his way. After a few blocks there were hundreds of rats following him. He picked up his speed and after a few more blocks there were thousands of rats. He started running towards the bay. The faster he went the faster the rats multiplied and followed. When he got to the bay he threw the brass rat as hard as he could into the bay and jumped on to a bench and grabbed on to a lamp pole as all the rats followed the brass rat into the San Francisco Bay. Relieved the tourist went back to the curio store. "Ah, you come back for stoly?" the store owner asked. "No, but do you have a brass lawyer?"

I went to a Chinese court to hear a contract dispute. A judge in a military uniform presided over the case. When the lawyers tried to make their opening statements he interrupted and said: "One of the parties must be lying or you would not be here today with your lawyers. If you are honest and sincere in resolving your misunderstanding, and are unable to do so, then your lawyers must be lying." Interesting concept! The judge must have been a Will Rogers fan. Will said: "I have always noticed that any time a man can't come and settle with you without bringing his lawyer, why, look out for him."

"Since I believe the parties in their sincerity to resolve any misunderstanding, I will send the lawyers to jail for one week for wasting my time and your money," the Chinese judge continued as he looked at the parties. I was stunned. "Don't worry," a Chinese lawyer whispered to me as the bailiff led the lawyers to the local jail. "They will settle in a few moments and be back soon to go to lunch." Sure enough he was right. The case was settled within an hour of starting and the judge was on to his next case. What a concept! The judicial practices have changed dramatically in China since the early eighties.

The Difference

To fully appreciate why the Chinese dispense justice differently than in America and the West one has to understand the historical development of the concept and practice of the rule of law and of the judicial system in China. When President Clinton visited the terracotta warriors in Xian, he was paying respect to Emperor Qin Shihuang (221-207 B.C.) in whose tomb the 6,000 life-sized warriors and horses were placed to protect him. Journalist Jasper Becker explained concisely the symbolic and legal differences between China and American legal Wild West.

"The Qin emperor who created the first unified Chinese state achieved victory over five rivals thanks to ruthless implementation of a system of laws which for the first time made everyone, irrespective of rank, subject to the absolute power of the state and its ruler.

"A great question now facing China and its partners like America is whether this ancient tradition that every dynasty has perpetuated is being modified to accommodate capitalism, human rights, private property and the rule of law....

"Mr. Jiang and other Chinese leaders seem to be actively encouraging this notion. Mr. Jiang told the Asia Society in Washington that China would 'expand democracy, improve the legal system, run the country according to law and build a socialist country under the law'. And he promised Chinese citizens would enjoy 'extensive rights and freedoms under the law'.

"Yet some scholars, like California-based Fu Zhengyuan, author of *Autocratic Tradition and Chinese Politics,* believe Mr. Jiang means something different from Mr. Clinton.

"They are talking across each other. When they talk about the rule of law, they are using the same vocabulary but they are not communicating," Becker said. Fu argues that the legal system Jiang refers to is related to the 'rule of law', or Fa Jia political philosophy expounded by a rival of Confucius, Han Fei, and that Westerners are mistaken in believing Confucianism has been the most influential philosophy shaping Chinese culture.

"Legalism made the Qin dynasty a superpower," explains Beijing University philosophy Professor Dong Hongli. "Although it did not last long because of a rebellion, the rulers of the next dynasty, the Han, learned some lessons and became much smarter." While the Qin emperor burned Confucius' works and buried Confucian scholars alive, the succeding Han dynasty adopted a policy of *ru wai, nei fa,* or outwardly Confucian but inwardly legalistic. "They put on an outward show of adopting Confucianism but practiced Legalism in a hidden way," Professor Dong said. "It looks like they are in favor of Confucianism but in fact they are continuing the same dictatorship."

Another professor at Beijing University, Shang Dewen, explained:

"Confucianism was helpful because it stresses benevolence. It is ethical and stresses the importance of morality." Confucius wanted to continue the old feudal system with its privileges and powers for the aristocracy, but in 350 B.C., a reformer in the Qin state, Shang Yang, introduced a system of severe punishment to ensure everyone, except the ruler, could be punished.

Fu said: "They proposed that the political power of the state must never be restricted by law although they advised the ruler to utilize the law as a tool to control his subjects."

Legal scholar Guan Zi wrote: "The law is the means by which the ruler unifies and controls the people," and that "the law restrains the people like the mold shapes the pottery." Doesn't that sound like what is going on in America?

"The legal codes of the Qin were basically adopted by all the succeeding dynasties," Fu said. "It was a major factor for Sinofication of alien conquerors because they came to like and rely on this system of rule."

The thinking of the Legalists has such deep roots in the Chinese psyche that it helps explain why the Kuomintang failed to introduce Western legal concepts in the 1920s and 1930s and why Mao reverted to absolutism.

Marxism-Leninism and the fundamental principles of the Legalist school share many similarities, Fu believes. And he is not alone. The story of the Qin empire exerts a great fascination for contemporary Chinese writers and film-makers.

"Mao consciously modeled himself on Qin Shihuang," Mr Fu alleges. In one famous passage in 1969, Mao boasted: "We have outdone Emperor Qin Shihuang more than a hundredfold...People always condemn Emperor Qin Shihuang for burning books and burying alive Confucian scholars and list these as his greatest crimes. I think however he killed too few Confucians... All those Confucian scholars were indeed counter-revolutionaries."

After 1979, Deng Xiaoping's government began to restore the rudimentary legal system that Mao had swept aside in the early 1950s. Mao had exercised "rule by man" under which his words had the force of laws. Under Deng China began to draw up and publish laws.

Yet, under the four basic principles which Deng set out at the time, the party's authority is inviolable and above the law.

Since 1979, the party has passed no laws protecting the individual's right to question or oppose the state. The power of the state is so firmly embodied in Chinese concepts that some foresee change developing only over a very long period. Ever since the Qin dynasty the Chinese language has made no distinction between the terms "state" and "country". It is an attitude which reinforces the authority of every state official and denies legitimacy to anyone who is not.

Throughout his visit to the terracotta warriors, Beijing would like Clinton to acknowledge that China is different, a vessel formed from very different clay, and has a right to continue to be so.

The Chinese believe in resolving disputes amicably and through consensus. This usually means keeping the lawyers out of sight and solving the problems between the parties. This method of resolution of disputes is far more cost-effective.

I have been involved in many businesses in China as a lawyer, businessman, correspondent, editor and publisher. The only time I personally have been in a legal dispute that wound up in court is with an American client, partner and Chinese wife. If there is ever a dispute between any local and myself we usually work it out over tea, lunch or dinner. Granted that doesn't always work. It certainly didn't when Julia and I got divorced. When it doesn't we bring in mutually agreed-upon mediators, usually friends or associates. If that fails then litigation is the last resort.

In the early days of television distribution in China, piracy was rampant. Disney decided to sue the pirates. After spending close to a million dollars they won their case and got a judgment for a couple thousand dollars. I decided to take the pirates out to dinner and see how we could structure a working relationship in the future "since we know they enjoy seeing and selling our programs." We toasted a barter syndication deal whereby we share the revenues from the advertising we sell into the commercial spots in our programs. After the numerous toasts we said: "We thought it was only fair that we should be paid for the previously pirated programs and that we would be happy to offset a percentage of the future monthly revenues due them under our new deal until the agreed-upon price of the pirated programs was paid off." We finished several bottles of the fiery Mao Tai spirit toasting our "mutual friendship and comprehensive co-operation". The benefits and savings in time, money and lawyers in the different approaches are obvious. The lawyers are the losers. The clients the winners.

Bob Alter and I were discussing the contrast in legal systems during one of our many dinners on Martha's Vineyard. He had worked with Richard Li and his father Li Ka-shing, Hong Kong's richest businessman, at Star TV in Hong Kong and shared a conversation he had with "KS", the patriarch's nickname. "You know I asked KS how come he was pulling back from his North American ventures and going back to Hong Kong when there are so many opportunities here. You know what he said?" "Too many lawyers in America."

KS is right! He's up there with Shakespeare, Dickens and the public at large that have all had it with lawyers and the so called "rule of law".

There is an over-production and supply of lawyers which is creating a disruptive and non-productive environment for business and government.

The Political Class

In *Restoration,* George Will argues for term limits on congressmen and senators and explains why he believes career politicians and their armies of lawyers and lobbyists just keep growing. "The academic culture, which is inhospitable to term limits, is an important tone-setting portion of what Irving Kristol calls 'the new class'. It consists of people, often well-schooled and upper-middle-class, who have a keen desire for political power. They also have a firm conviction that they are especially qualified to exercise power in the national interest, which they are especially qualified to define. This class practices 'supply side politics'. Their political entrepreneurship creates a demand for the programs they supply. These people produce government services, which then generate a demand for the defense and enlargement of the services. This demand becomes incarnate in permanent interest groups. And, says Kristol, because the intervention of government in society 'involves large numbers of accomplices – sometimes whole professions or institutions – it creates a substantial political base for itself.' Lawyers, lobbyists and consultants who specialize in dealing with legislatures, regulatory agencies, bureaucracies and public opinion management are in professions that expand as government expands. So there is a symbiotic and mutually aggrandizing relationship between government and the interest groups that government's activities generate."

When the Founding Fathers established a federal system of government it was envisioned that the politicians would serve the public and do so part time while pursuing their everyday careers and professions. That vision and practice still holds true in the Hong Kong Special Administrative Region of China today. Politicians in Washington have become established career politicians that have lost touch with what everyday working folk have to endure. Hong Kong politicians convene periodically and then go back to their jobs and homes. Will Rogers' wisecrack slogan, "Be a politician; no training necessary" still holds true. Those arguing against term limits on the grounds that political experience is necessary are ignoring the underlying foundations of the Constitution. "That's par for the course for today's career politicians: they twist the truth; they don't give you the whole picture. They give you only the portion that suits their particular agenda, the same way the media do. It's far more common than the public realizes," Governor Ventura opines. If Washington was today what it was when it was established as the capital, no career congressman or senator would ever want to go back.

Washington was a dirty, rank city with a plethora of livery stables and rancid saloons. Pigs rooted in the dirt streets slanting off from Pennsylvania Avenue, and sewage marshes lay at the foot of the President's park south of the old mansion. At the northern edge of the garbage-strewn Mall ran an open drainage ditch "floating with dead cats and all kinds of putridity," said an observer, "and reeking with pestilential odors." In the early morning, a stench hung over the city. Still does. In the 19th century accepting a job in Washington involved, for many people, tolerating the discomfort of living in the cramped quarters of a boarding house. In February 1869, while President-elect Grant was cobbling together a cabinet, one lady called wishing to speak to the general. When asked what she wanted, she told an aide that she was calling to learn whom he had chosen, as she had rooms to rent. Few people were drawn to the capital by glitter, and few who came as congressmen could bring comfort with them or afford to buy it in Washington.

That is one of several reasons why relatively few members of Congress – far fewer than today – made running for re-election the great constant of their lives. Perpetual incumbency was not the normal career aspiration for members of Congress. For a long time Washington was not a place where many people who had a choice chose to linger. People came to Congress for a while, then departed, either because they had other things they wanted to do – perhaps other political offices to seek – or because they were defeated. This mitigated the tendency – a tendency in any political branch of any government – of Congress to become an insular ruling class, resented by a suspicious public.

Impeachment

Mark Twain may well have said that history doesn't repeat itself, it rhymes. Or maybe someone else did. In any event, in early 1868, while awaiting publication of *The Innocents Abroad,* the 32-year-old writer found himself witness to a curious piece of history that proves the point – the first impeachment of a president.

Twain was working that winter as a journalist, filing dispatches from Washington to newspapers around the country, when Andrew Johnson's enemies in Congress finally found ammunition they thought would remove the President from office.

A Tennessee Democrat, President Johnson had been Lincoln's running mate in 1864 on a "National Union" ticket but had run afoul of the radical Republicans since succeeding Lincoln. He fought them often over their efforts to harshly punish the South. Congress repeatedly sought to strip him of power and radical Republicans tried several times to impeach him. The climactic battle came when the President fired his Secretary of War, Edwin M. Stanton, in the face of a law designed to give Congress control over Cabinet officers' tenure.

Twain's opinion of politicians wasn't high. "The political and commercial morals of the United States are not merely food for laughter, they are an entire banquet," he once wrote. Impeachment gave him a lot to dine out on. Amazing are the similarities between the two historical impeachments. The suspicious public still resents the politicians and doesn't trust them, and President Clinton's public opinion polls soared after his impeachment to remind us that nothing has really changed since Johnson's experience except that politicians are now career politicians with an army of lawyers in tow who do not give a damn what the public, *We the People,* think.

Career Politicians

If people served in legislatures only briefly, as they did when America was founded, they would have less incentive to shovel out "pork". The primary function of "pork" is to buy the gratitude and contributions, qualities that the career legislator can translate into votes, and hence into longevity. And if legislators were not separated for too long from normal citizens and normal life in normal communities they might retain the ability to discriminate between appropriate and inappropriate functions for the federal government. "That's the problem with a politician's life. Somebody is always interrupting it with an election," Will Rogers quipped. He went on to add: "Politics is a great character builder. You have to take a referendum to see what your convictions are for the day." Is this what government for the people by the people is all about? Can we allow this to continue in the New World Order?

George Will also points out: "In the era of America's founding, the most frequent arguments for term limits were that limits would be prophylactic measures against tyranny. Thus the Massachusetts delegation to the Constitutional Convention was specifically instructed 'not to depart from the rotation established in the Articles of Confederation'. Delegate John Adams believed rotation would 'teach' representatives 'the great political virtues of humility, patience, and moderation without which every man in power becomes a ravenous beast of prey.' Adam's colleague, Elbridge Gerry, said, 'Rotation keeps the mind of man in equilibria [sic] and teaches him the feelings of the governed.' It counters 'the overbearing insolence of office'. Adams and Gerry were echoing the thinking that produced Article VIII of the Declaration of Rights in the Massachusetts Constitution of 1780, which declared that citizens have a right to expect 'public officers to return to private life ... in order to prevent those, who are vested with authority, from becoming oppressors'."

The near total disregard for the public that has become all too common with career politicians reached its zenith during Clinton's impeachment hearings in Congress. It reached its apex during the Bush-Gore legal battles until Gore conceded the presidency. Have our career politicians forgotten, or have they chosen to disregard, the will of the Founding Fathers? After all, neither the bible belt nor the beltway define or dictate what is right for *We the Apathetic People. We The People* Do. Why Aren't We?

Career politicians are not only oppressors, but because they are not businessmen, they can't even balance a check book. Not only the countrys', but their own. When the General Accounting Office released its report on the bank run for members of the House of Representatives on September 18, 1991, it became clear to the world that the career politicians were not only bouncing the country's checks and saddling future generations with the responsibility to cover them, they were bouncing their own. Any wonder the public doesn't have much faith any more?

"I wish America could get some of the political bandits that live off this country to come in and give up. Then we would know just what we were paying them to live on, instead of the present system of letting them grab what they can," Rogers said. My favorite Rogers quips are: "But a politician is just like a pickpocket; it's almost impossible to get one to reform." Or on a more serious note: "There is no way to stop this country. Just quit listening to the politicians...The Constitution will remain as is. The Russians are not going to take us." Rogers was right. Why is it then that Americans who laugh at Will Rogers' humor don't stop listening to political story telling and do something about it?

The thing about lawyers is they are very good storytellers. Look at Bill and Hillary. Lawyers are the only storytellers who can out story-tell Will Rogers. They do such a good job telling their clients stories that they even get career politicians to believe them! Legislation is their voluminous novel and short stories.

Unfortunately, the states have mirrored the political and bureaucratic models of Washington while gradually ceding their own power. This has to change and states, like the federal government, have to go back to their founding principles and start taking corrective steps to shrink their growing political and bureaucratic tumors in the 21st century.

Career politicians in totalitarian governments corrupt the system by taking what belongs to the people for themselves. In democratic systems people allow the career politicians to take and use the peoples' hard – earned money as taxes and subsidies. On both fronts in both systems the people have no one to blame but themselves.

Time magazine's 1998 Man Of The Year typifies what has happened to men and mankind. We need two men, Clinton and Starr, to make one man! Lawyer and politician to boot! What does it take to be a man today? Especially a macho man! A double-faced, two-sided lawyer fine-slicing the legal definitions of the Founding Fathers? We as a nation are the descendants of Puritan Pilgrims who fled and fought for freedom of expression and association regardless of color, religion, sex, politics or any combination thereof. Politicians were part-timers. Men were men, with strong women behind them. Somehow things got twisted around. We now have full-time career politicians with a variety of different family values, structures and relationships.

In the early years Washington D.C. was a swampland that was humid and unbearable for many months of the year. Air conditioning came along and changed everything. All of a sudden dirty, damp D.C. became bearable. Career politicians and their lobbyists and lawyers turned politics and Washington into a full-time political tumor and employment agency for themselves and bureaucrats. Maybe air conditioning should be turned off in government and lobbyist offices in Washington. That will get rid of career Washington politicians and lobbyists real fast.

We the Apathetic People take air conditioning for granted and usually don't give a second thought as to what life was like without it or how it was developed. Before the advent of air conditioning, life in America was much like it is in many parts of Africa and Asia today. People in New York and the South spent the summers sleeping on the stoops of their homes. Fire escapes and the grass in parks were crowded with people hoping to catch a cool breeze. People died by the thousands during heat waves. Even today, heat kills an average of 1,500 people a year – mostly city dwellers who don't have air conditioning.

In 1902 an engineer at the Buffalo Forge Company named Willis Carrier designed and installed an Apparatus for Treating Air in a printing plant in Brooklyn. The Sackett-Willhelms Lithographing and Publishing Company had ordered a machine to stabilize lithographs, which changed size and image with fluctuations in heat and humidity in the summer. Air conditioning was invented.

The world and its work changed forever. Cities such as Hong Kong, Houston and Washington D.C. sprang up in the humid environs of southern China, Texas and D.C. In 1917, in Chicago, the first movie theater put in Carrier equipment and hung out a banner decorated with painted icicles, saying "Air Cooled". People there went to the theater all day and didn't much care that they saw the same film over and over again. No different than much of Africa or Asia today. Parks and fire escapes at night and theatres and shopping malls during the day.

D.C. career politicians of the 21st century are spending less time in Washington than their predecessors in the 1960s and 1970s when they used to get together with lobbyists for sing-alongs. There is no reason why this trend should not snowball. With the Internet and workstation there is no reason elected officials can't spend more time in their home districts close to constituents and communicate with their fellow office-holders and committee members by video conference phones or the Internet. They can also vote electronically from their home district.

Makeover
Isn't it time to re-evaluate the foundations our Founding Fathers laid? Isn't it time for a Constitutional Convention to re-examine the working-pentagon of the Executive, Congress, Judiciary, Media and Independent Counsels?

Our Founding Fathers warned us in every way they could that if we took our eyes off our government for too long, extremists and fanatics would creep in and start bending the government to their will. Well, guess what happened? The Founding Fathers tried to warn us. Back in 1789, when Ben Franklin was asked what kind of government the Continental Congress had created for the new United States of America, he replied: "A Republic, if you can keep it." Franklin knew it would be an uphill battle. He and the other Founding Fathers were aware that everyone in the world is highly susceptible to corruption. "They knew that a government that truly served the people was extremely rare. And they believed that without the public's constant vigilance, extremists and tyrants would work their way into the system, and bend the system to their own will, so that it served their own ends instead of the people's. Well, guess what? The Founding Fathers were right," Governor Ventura points out.

If Milosevic, Shevardnadze, and five Argentinean presidents can be swept out of office and into jail by *We the Maids,* who did so under the most difficult of circumstances, why can't *We the People* do the same in America under less trying conditions? No one should spend more than one term in any elected office. That forces them to focus on the job that needs to be done for *We the People.* After the office-holder returns to the private sector they can run again for another public office or the same one they held before. That is how you get rid of career politicians, their lawyers and lobbyists and get true public servants. Why shouldn't *We the People* have the best qualified people in office to serve us? Isn't that what our Founding Fathers wanted?

Shrinking government and its Siamese twin, bureaucracy, at all levels will result in fewer career politicians, laws, regulations and the need for lawyers and lobbyists to lobby, write, prosecute and legislate them into law. Furthermore, eliminating outdated laws and subsidies that dominate our lives will result in tremendous tax savings in the 21st century. After all, *We the People* have been bearing both the cost and expense of these highly paid self-serving hired guns. Let's make sure *We the Maids* use any and all bug sprays to get rid of the millennium bugs, not the computer type but rather the career politicians and their lobbyist lawyers. Otherwise life in the New World Order will continue being an ongoing futility of "in" and "out" trays dealing with legal and political bitches. Life for Americans is a bitch because *We the Apathetic People* allow political animals to run it.

Chapter Eight

Down on Main Street
Lovesick Blues - Hank Williams

The Blues

        Listening to in-house musician Allen Youngblood play the blues while thinking and writing on the corner bar stool at the entrance to Bert's in the FCC basement is a great way to contemplate and address the sorry state of contemporary geopolitical and personal reality. Bert's is a great hideaway from the Main Bar upstairs. Its live blues tunes, periodically pierced by the nearby pool players breaking, often remind me of how I had been whacked by Julia when she filed for a divorce. Downing straight whiskies only gets me more depressed as I listened to the rhythms of my mind while I drowned my sorrows, pain and fears. The thought of not being able to see and play with Austen every day is always heart-wrenching. The fact that Julia had Shanghaied him and our money to China made me angry. Coming to Bert's straight from the Central Police Station after being released on bail after being arrested for "theft" on a phony burglary charge filed by my wife only made matters worse. Catatonic!

A poster of John Lee Hooker, the one chord desolate bluesman from the Mississippi Delta, who sang of lust and loneliness, rage and despair hangs on the column facing my favorite stool and his words of wisdom periodically echo in my ears. "No matter what anybody says, it all comes down to the same thing," he once said. "A man and a woman, a broken heart and a broken home." George Strait's All My Ex's Live In Texas took on a whole new meaning after divorce number two. It doesn't really matter where they live physically because mentally and emotionally they live in your head. Eric Clapton's *Nobody Knows You When You're Down* and Bob Seeger's *Down on Main Street* both came to mind periodically. Both tunes and lyrics intertwined and wrapped themselves in my head and would bring me back to my favorite Will Rogers saying. Rogers said in the 1920s as the Depression was descending on America: "Live your life so that whenever you lose, you are ahead." That philosophical outlook helped me get back on my feet and pull through some tough moments over the years in both the States and Hong Kong. When Pauline Taylor came up to me and took my hand and gave it a re-assuring squeeze, she brought a smile to my face and I couldn't help think of the Pinkard and Bowden country song *I Lobster but Never Flounder*.

After September 11, the new 9/11 American blues, from Neil Young's *Let's Roll* to New York City firefighter Hughie Lynch's *Tomorrow,* fused with Hooker's harsh realities. "I turn the corner, fire's out of control/ There's people dying – why I just don't know, So I reach out my hand to do all that I can so that one might live tomorrow."

Families and friends in Hong Kong are a lot more supportive. The couple of times I was down and out on Main Street, Hong Kong, during personal or business shortcomings, family and friends were always there. Pauline Taylor bailed me out of jail in Hong Kong, just like my family had in Santa Monica. My family was always there for me in the States. My so-called friends in times of need became rare. An endangered American species.

Friends in Hong Kong who knew that I was going through a difficult divorce would always come over and ask how they could help. When I was in a real down mood in Bert's or the Main Bar I not only got drinks from friends but good advice, conversation, company and moral reminders of Will Rogers' philosophy. Women were the greatest boosters because they also suggested to me I'm still in demand.

Family and Friends
Family and friends in America ain't what they used to be. If they were there wouldn't be so many homeless. Walking the streets of Hong Kong after leaving the States, not only during the recession

in America, but during the Asian banking crisis, one never experienced the numbers of homeless one saw on Main Street, Anywhere, USA.

The recession of the late 1980s and 1990s hit the U.S. and California in a major way. I received calls from friends every other week once I moved to Hong Kong announcing the dilemma or catastrophe a mutual friend or acquaintance was going through. "Peter, you were lucky you went through your hard times when you did. It is really bad now for everyone in the real estate business. Banks are foreclosing. People are just walking away from their projects," Russ Barnard informed me during one of our long-distance conversations. Russ and his brother Doug were the "Designers to the Fugitives" I engaged to design a hotel I wanted to build in Santa Monica. They also did a lot of work for Marc Rich and his partner Pincus Green. We became friends and I was trying to secure a couple of design projects for them in Palau and China. Russ sat on the Santa Monica building commission and was lamenting the state of the construction industry. I was getting ready to visit Santa Monica and had called to schedule a time to get together.

Santa Monica had adopted a very homeless-friendly city policy. They fed the homeless at City Hall every day, which resulted in hundreds, if not thousands, of homeless people inundating Santa Monica from all over Los Angeles County, California and the rest of America. The sight of troops of homeless people on Main Street, the parks and beaches begging, sleeping, arguing among themselves or talking and screaming to themselves or no one in particular was very depressing. Everywhere I walked to from my mother's apartment, which was also on Main Street, the wretched smell of musty urine from homeless campsites filled the air. The mood was also very depressing. Everyone seemed "down and out", "bummed out", or damn right suicidal. "I can't believe how depressing things are here," I told Russell during lunch. "Everywhere I've been, New York, Washington, Dallas, San Francisco and LA the mood is wrenchingly miserable," We ordered up a quick coffee and the check.

"I've never seen it so bad. I can't remember it ever being this bad," Russ shook his head with a distant glaze as he stared at the coffee. He was born in Los Angeles. He was echoing what I had been hearing everywhere I went. We paid the bill and walked back on to Main Street. We had the same conversation in 2004. America lost over two and a half million industrial jobs between 2001 and 2004 and the cost of living was rising along with the daily body counts of Americans in Iraq. People are disgusted and frustrated. I could feel the depression and anger build like a tidal wave.

I had been through some bitter battles with the local homeowners, renters, local merchants and miscellaneous kvetchers for three years in the mid-1980s trying to get the necessary approvals to build a hotel on the site where Scratch, my wife's restaurant, was housed. The delays, hearings, variances and final approval for the hotel arrived, a year too late, when the real estate market in southern California was collapsing and banks were no longer interested in financing anything. Financial institutions were going through their own problems as the Savings and Loans collapsed and debacles were hitting the market full force simultaneously. "It's all right to let Wall Street bet each others' millions of dollars every day but why make these bets effect the fellow who is plowing a field out in Claremore, Oklahoma?" Rogers asked as the Depression hit America. The same thought crossed my mind as I drove down Main Street at the beginning of the 21st century.

I had one group of investors and partners in the restaurant and another in the hotel. A few were in both. Neither set was happy. Not with the status of their investments or me. Reaganomics and the "go go" years of the early eighties, like Dubya's deficit spending tax cuts of the new millennium, came home to roost with a screech. Not only on Main Street in the Peoples' Republic of Santa Monica, but throughout California and America. The cutbacks in the defense industry, aerospace, S&L failures and the entertainment industry were all being whip-sawed by the afterglow of the "supply side economics" of the Reagan and Bush administrations.

"What are we going to do and what do we tell the investors of the restaurant to get their sympathy and support?" Michael and Gail, my soon to be ex, who was the executive chef and creator of the whole concept of Scratch, asked in unison as we prepared for a meeting with the investors at our lawyers' office. The concept of Scratch was that everything was made from scratch and we hoped to make some scratch in the process. "Are you kidding me? Us or the investors get sympathy? Look in a dictionary. It's between shit and syphilis," I answered in a frustrated and angrier tone. "We have to tell it like it is and it ain't pretty," I continued. "They are all big boys and girls. There was no guarantee we would succeed. There is no guarantee to guarantee a guarantee. Not even with Savings and Loans. So how can I guarantee these risky investments?"

"What about Ed?" Gail probed delicately. "How are you going to handle him?"

Ed Broida was not only a partner in both ventures, but a dear personal friend. Ed was a lover of red wines. He had one of the best wine collections west of the Rockies. Ed was also a lover and collector of contemporary art. He had made his money in real estate and was the "B" in R&B that developed the swinging single Oakwood apartments in the 1960s. Ed's priceless art hung on the walls of the restaurant when we weren't exhibiting a specific local artist. Local artists like Charles Arnoldi, Judy Stabile, Laddie John Dill, John Ohkulick, De Wain Valentine, Peter Alexander, Billy Al Bengston, Robert Graham and John Van Hamersfeld, who also designed the Scratch logo, would have showings. Their art would be on the wall for a couple of months at a time. Ed would then loan the restaurant his art until the next show. This had been one of the many attractions of Scratch.

Gail was right. Telling Ed the facts was not going to be easy. Especially since his son Eric, a local real estate broker, had scared away our lead financier and investor group in the hotel by telling them to deal through him rather than directly with me. They got mixed signals and didn't want to be in the middle of a lawsuit and decided to pass on the deal. "Easy, if all else fails, since he has the first mortgage on the property, he can foreclose and take the whole damn enchilada, land, licenses and three years of sweat blood and endless aggravation," I responded as I took a shot of tequila. I was feeling no pain and felt like a cornered dog.

"They picked up Nickolai again," my administrative assistant, Shelly Wax, informed me as I got off the phone with Ed, "and this time they are going to put him to sleep unless you remove him from the county," she continued. Nickolai was my black Labrador retriever and Dalmatian cross-breed who had had several public encounters with the neighbors, animal control officers, a trial and numerous visits to the pound. He was back in the pound and Shelly wanted to know what I wanted to do. Shelly had been with me for a couple of years and had adopted Nickolai as her son in the midst of all my other problems. "Get a court date and let's get him out right away," I responded as I wanted my best friend back home and was prepared to go to court and do battle again.

What the hell, it seemed like I was in court every other day anyway, either fighting off creditors, restaurant partners, or attending settlement conferences with the IRS or restaurant suppliers. What was one more court appearance on behalf of my best friend Nickolai! He was the only calming influence in the office during the endless siege. I loved bringing him to the office when I went there straight from the house.

I was also a principal in several thrift and loans and a bank that were the vogue and rage at the time thanks to de-regulation. Well, the S&L crises saw the regulators seize several of the thrifts on whose board of directors I sat. That required several emergency board meetings to decide what course of action the directors, collectively and individually, should take. I resigned and announced I had enough other personal problems to contend with and that I was prepared to forfeit any potential return on my investments in the institutions as I didn't have an extra minute to spare to deal with bureaucratic regulatory investigators and their costly destructive probes and inquiries. Ken Starr exemplifies many Federal regulators and prosecutors. They are not "independent" even though they're supposed to be. They all have an agenda and constituency to account to.

Finley, Kumble, the law firm I left a few years earlier, went into bankruptcy and there went all the fees and monies I was earning from clients I had brought to the firm. That had been a steady source of income for a few years and helped pay bills.

With my sources of income diminished, lawsuits being filed by banks, creditors and partners, and IRS liens on everything I owned it was only a matter of time before the banks would foreclose on our home. When they did, I was relieved I was able to negotiate a private sale before the foreclosure sale that generated enough money to pay off the mortgage, liens and leave enough money for a new home for Gail, Alexandra and Jonas. I was getting ready to spend more time in Hong Kong and get away from all the process servers and "court dates" they brought with them. Those were dates I did not look forward too. I enjoyed the ones in Hong Kong a lot more.

California Senator Alan Robbins, who had been "Of Counsel" to my firm before I sold it, was indicted for corruption and bribery, as were several other California legislators. The witness that turned him in was one of my partners in one of the thrifts and a bank. Rumor had it that contracts were out on him and others. A client, in an unrelated matter, had been assassinated as he came home; others were just dying off because of the pressure. Things were getting too messy and complicated. A big dark cloud was beginning to form over my head on Main Street in the People's Republic.

A Geographic
Hong Kong was a lot friendlier with a lot less hassle. Side trips to Mongolia, Palau, Thailand, Philippines and China were a delightful respite to what was going on in California. Not knowing it at the time, I was adopting the Hong Kong Chinese philosophy of "run". The great Chinese writer Shih Nai-an wrote in his classic *The Water Margin:* "Of the 365 ways of avoiding disaster, running away is best." I pulled a "geographic" as we say in the States.

Traditional Main Street, USA, as we know it, decayed and turned into a boarded-up reminder of all the things that went wrong in the waning decades of the last millennium. Main Street has moved to Wall Street, Pennsylvania Avenue, the malls and shopping centers. All it symbolized culturally, politically and economically has evaporated. It has become the repository of the homeless, needy, mentally ill and financially and spiritually bankrupt. Thousands of Main Streets in little towns across Middle America have lost their population in the last decades of the last millennium to prospering cities and states in the East, Southwest and West. Their people have also lost their life savings to investment bankers. Modern-day pioneers, who like their immigrant forebears, are searching for a better life.

The politics of the White House on Pennsylvania Avenue and the gyrations of Wall Street's Dow and Nasdaq indices have a collective impact on Main Street. The dawn of the 21st century saw more Americans than ever invested in stocks either directly or through mutual funds and retirement accounts. When *We the Apathetic People* who own these stocks are oblivious to what is going on Wall Street and Pennsylvania Avenue we get wiped out financially. Isn't it time *We the Maids* sweep Main Street clean?

Today's Main Street politics, like the rest of the Street, have to give way to the new alternative routes available to us to fulfill the vision and ideals of our Founding Fathers. Main Street has to reclaim its mainstream respectability and again become the local cornerstone of the community if America is to survive in the cyber New World Order of the 21st century.

What department stores did to Main Street, USA, the web will do to Mainstream America in the 21st century if *We the People* don't go back to basics.

The lot where Scratch stood was still vacant at the end of 2003. I'd bulldozed the restaurant and other structures on the site in 1986 to build "Hotel California." I can't help think how symbolic it is of the personal, political and economic failures Americans have all faced and lived with. Looking at the vacant lots where the glorious World Trade Center and adjoining buildings once stood at the dawn of the 21st century only magnified America's shortcomings.

We all have to deal with personal, family, communal and national adversities and issues honestly and directly if we are to survive and grow in the New World Order.

Anyone who has ridden a horse knows that occasionally you get thrown. Life, like a horse, can throw us and get us down, not just on Main Street, but Anywhere, USA. Personally, economically, socially and politically. Nevertheless We... have to get up and jump back on to the horse and continue our ride. The sore bumps and bruises buffered with experience and knowledge make the ride easier. Staying balanced in the saddle is essential for survival in the 21st century...

THE POST-GLOBAL INTERLOCAL SINO-AMERICAN CENTURY

which can be

MADE TO ORDER FROM SCRATCH.

Doctor J.,

Whisky For My Men, Beer For My Horses

-Toby Keith with Willie Nelson-

Author's Note
Waiting for a Break - Day One

The people and personal experiences discussed in the book are real. In the interest of fluidity and easier reading, several events and conversations were transposed and condensed into one. Many clients' briefs and the results of their research assignments have also been included in the book in the form of opinions or conversations. Some of the facts are exaggerated for dramatic effect. Many individuals, groups and incidents have not been mentioned. It is not my intention to slight or hurt anyone. Editorial restraints necessitate limited examples. The observations are honest notwithstanding the occasional heated, controversial debates and name-calling they may generate. God knows, I've already been called every imaginable name in more languages than I know. As a student of life absorbing and questioning its essence I've been labeled an asshole, pugnacious, revolutionary, dogmatic, radical, visionary, porter with excess baggage, user, loser and jerk to name a few of the more memorable monikers.

We the People cannot even agree when the old millennium ends and the New World Order starts in the New World Disorder. Is it 2000 or 2001? The book refers to 2000 as the last year of the last millennium and the year 2001 as the first year of the 21st century.

Many great politicians, philosophers, historians, political scientists and writers' ideas that I endorse and echo are incorporated or referenced. Rather than italicize or quote, I thought it better to write a seamless book, a written montage. After all, what is truly original today? "Immature poets imitate; mature poets steal; bad poets deface what they take, and good poets make it into something better, or at least something different," T.S. Eliot wrote in 1922.

The Wall Street Journal writer Luke Torn said it best: "Artists don't steal, they synthesize." The chapter notes give full credit to the authors and writers whose ideas have been incorporated. I encourage those who want to stop running on empty, who want to explore or learn more, to carefully read the chapter notes and relevant bibliography. The Chapter Notes and Bibliography can be downloaded from the *custommaid.net* web site at no cost. Let me know it you prefer to have the chapter notes in the book in the next volumes.

It took me over 35 years to come up with the title and reduce it to what you see. I sincerely believe we are living in an American World Disorder that is totally hypocritical, dysfunctional, dishonest, disorderly and full of dust. I hope Volume One conveys in a comprehensible way my observations, conclusions and rationale for my interpretation of the discussions with the people I have had the pleasure of meeting, reading, watching and listening to.

Scratch was a popular bar and grill my wife Gail created on Main Street, Santa Monica, in 1984. Everything served was "made from Scratch," with a different menu each week during its three-year existence. Many of the ideas articulated in this book were also created from Scratch at Scratch as a result of late-night – or more accurately, early-morning – loaded discussions with "glassmates". It was a popular watering hole that attracted worldwide politicians, celebrities, has-beens, movie stars, musicians, titans of industry, drug dealers, wanabees, ne'rdowells, movers and shakers, users, losers, financiers, real estate developers and real salt of the earth. Many were told to "kiss my glass".

Scratch also metaphorically symbolizes the numerous creative watering holes where I "gassed up" globally and exchanged many sober and incoherent frustrations and ideas over the last 35-plus years.

Issues of the day were discussed with family, friends, business associates, clients and strangers. The people, conversations and concerns are real, universal and represent personal encounters with people of all ethnic, racial, religious and sexual orientations. My memory and recollections of incidents and conversations are, thank God, still intact.

Many writers have written about peace and prosperity. Writers, politicians, philosophers and prophets have preached and advocated better understanding, co-operation and justice among *We the People*. Others have put forth many of the ideas I have proposed at different times, ways, mediums and places. I just hope this trilogy is a helpful condensed version of the relevant history, and religious, political and economic ideals necessary to improve our world in the new millennium. The tables of contents for volumes II and III, which expound upon the issues and solutions needed, can be found on the following pages. Any other ideas, amplifications, clarifications or additions that readers think should be included in the next edition are welcome.

I am not proud of some of the things I have said or done. In fact I am downright embarrassed and ashamed. Nevertheless, they must be shared if my observations and conclusions are to be honest and understood. To those I unintentionally or thoughtlessly hurt, insult or offend I sincerely apologize.

Contents Volume II

The Post-Global Interlocal Sino-American Centuty

Contents Volume III

Made To Order From Scratch

Morality comes with the sad wisdom of age, when the sense of curiosity has withered - Graham Greene-

Invitation

Dear Fellow Citizen,

Now that you have read the book, you are cordially invited to become an active citizen. If you are not already registered to vote, please register as soon as it is personally convenient.

Your participation in the political process is essential if *We the Maids* are to sweep out career politicians and re-capture our government. We the People have the authentic power and ability to bring about our desired changes. If you would like to receive the CALMaid quarterly newsletter to be kept up to date on how you can better serve your community, just complete the attached form and return it at your earliest convenience.

You are also invited to share your opinions and desires about any of the ideas articulated in this book. Your thoughts can be sent to me personally at peter@custommaid.net. I look forward to sharing your thoughts. Should you have any questions regarding how to most constructively participate in the political process, please do not hesitate to ask me. *We the People* are America's "spiritual partners". Equal soul mates who are collectively empowered to change America's political system. I hope you agree.

Warmest Regards,

Peter de Krassel

CALMaid Membership Application

Please enroll me as a member of CALMaid and send me your quarterly newsletter to:

_____

Name

_____

Address/Apt

_____

City/State/Province

_____

Country/Zip

_____

e-mail address

Return to: Peter de Krassel, GPO 7288,
Central, Hong Kong SAR, China

Hong Kong Blues
-Hoagy Carmichael-

Index